CRITICAL ACCLAIM FOR THE BERKELEY GUIDES

"[The Berkeley Guides are] brimming with useful ___ ___ ___ ___ low-budget traveler—material delivered in a fresh, ___, and often irreverent way." **—The Philadelphia Inquirer**

". . . hip, blunt and lively . . . . these Cal students boogie down and tell you where to sleep in a cowboy bunkhouse, get a tattoo and eat cheap meals cooked by aspiring chefs." **—Atlanta Journal Constitution**

". . . Harvard hasn't yet met 'On the Loose's' pledge to plant two trees in Costa Rica for every one felled to print its books—a promise that, given the true grit of these guides, might well mean a big new forest in Central America." **—Newsweek**

"[The Berkeley Guides] offer straight dirt on everything from hostels to look for and beaches to avoid to museums least likely to attract your parents . . . they're fresher than Harvard's Let's Go series." **—Seventeen**

"The books are full of often-amusing tips written in a youth-tinged conversational style." **—The Orlando Sentinel**

"So well-organized and well-written that I'm almost willing to forgive the recycled paper and soy-based ink." **—P.J. O'Rourke**

"These guys go to great lengths to point out safe attractions and routes for women traveling alone, minorities and gays. If only this kind of caution weren't necessary. But I'm glad someone finally thought of it."

—Sassy

"The very-hip Berkeley Guides look like a sure-fire hit for students and adventurous travelers of all ages. This is real budget travel stuff, with the emphasis on meeting new places head on, up close and personal . . . . this series is going to go places." **—The Hartford Courant**

"The guides make for fun and/or enlightening reading."

—The Los Angeles Times

"The new On the Loose guides are more comprehensive, informative and witty than Let's Go." **—Glamour**

the BERKELEY guides

THE BUDGET TRAVELER'S HANDBOOK

PARIS

ON THE LOOSE

1995

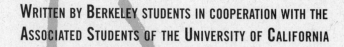

WRITTEN BY BERKELEY STUDENTS IN COOPERATION WITH THE
ASSOCIATED STUDENTS OF THE UNIVERSITY OF CALIFORNIA

PARIS ON THE LOOSE

Editors: Loretta Johnson, Virginie Pelletier
Editorial Coordinators: Laura Comay Bloch, Sharron Wood
Executive Editor: Scott McNeely
Creative Director: Fabrizio La Rocca
Cartographers: David Lindroth, Inc.; Eureka Cartography
Text Design: Tigist Getachew
Cover Design and Illustration: Rico Lins Studio (Rico Lins, Mauricio Nacif)

SPECIAL SALES

Contents

PRESENTING AN INDEPENDENT APPROACH TO TRAVEL.

If you have independent ideas about travel, we specialize in putting you exactly where you want to be. And with over 100 offices worldwide, we'll take care of you when you're there. So when it's time to plan your trip, call us at 1.800.777.0112.

New York: 212-477-7166
Washington DC: 202-887-0912
Philadelphia: 215-382-2928
Boston: 617-266-6014
Los Angeles: 213-934-8722
San Francisco: 415-391-8407

STA TRAVEL
We've been there.

What the Berkeley Guides Are All About

Three years ago, a motley bunch of U.C. Berkeley students spent the summer traveling on shoestring budgets to launch a new series of guidebooks—*The Berkeley Guides*. We wrote the books because, like thousands of travelers, we had grown tired of the outdated attitudes and information served up year after year in other guides. Most important, we thought a travel guide should be written by people who know what cheap travel is all about.

You see, it's one of life's weird truisms that the more cheaply you travel, the more you inevitably experience. You're bound to experience a lot with *The Berkeley Guides,* because we believe in doing as much as you can for as little money as possible. You won't find much in our guides about how a restaurant prepares its duck à l'orange or how a hotel blends mauve curtains with green carpeting. Instead, we tell you if a place is cheap, clean (no bugs), and worth the cash.

Coming from a community as diverse as Berkeley, we also wanted our books to be useful to everyone, so we tell you if a place is wheelchair accessible, if it provides resources for gay and lesbian travelers, and if it's safe for women traveling solo. Many of us are Californians, which means most of us like trees and mountain trails. It also means we emphasize the outdoors in every *Berkeley Guide* and include lots of info about hiking and tips on protecting the environment. To minimize our impact on the environment, we print our books on recycled paper using soy-based inks.

Most important, these guides are for travelers who want to see more than just the main sights. We find out what local people do for fun, where they go to eat, drink, or just hang out. Most guidebooks lead you down the tourist trail, ignoring important local issues, events, and culture. In *The Berkeley Guides* we give you the information you need to understand what's going on around you, whether it's the latest on a Métro strike or yet another protest for student rights in the Left Bank.

The Berkeley Guides began by covering Eastern Europe, Mexico, California, and the Pacific Northwest and Alaska. In the course of research our writers slept in whorehouses in Mexican border towns and landed bush planes above the Arctic Circle. The second year was no different: Our student writers weathered guerrilla attacks in the Guatemalan Highlands, motorcycle wrecks in Ireland, and a strange culinary concoction in Belize known as "greasy-greasy." The result was five new guidebooks, covering Central America, France, Germany, San Francisco, and Great Britain and Ireland. This year, things were even crazier. One writer got an ulcer, one lost her skirt on a moped, two crashed their motorbikes, and another spent hours digging through a dumpster to reclaim a batch of "misplaced" manuscript. Bloodied but unbowed, *The Berkeley Guides* brings you four new guidebooks, covering Europe, Italy, Paris, and London, not to mention completely revised and updated editions of our first- and second-year guides.

We've done our best to make sure the information in *The Berkeley Guides* is accurate, but time doesn't stand still: prices change, places go out of business. Call ahead when it's really important, and always remain flexible.

Thanks to You

Putting together a guidebook covering all of Paris is no easy task. From figuring out the Louvre to getting the lowdown on the bar scene in the Marais, our writers and editors relied on helpful souls along the way. We'd like to thank the following people—as well as the hundreds of others whom our writers met briefly on the streets—for their advice and encouragement.

We want to particularly thank: Robyn Aronson (Washington, D.C.); Chiara Barbieri (Venice, Italy); Austen Barron (New Orleans); Evelyn Christman (New Orleans); Dan and Muriel Coon (Paris); Gregg Drinkwater (Berkeley); Marie-Hélène Duburcq (Lille); Eddie le crêpier (Paris); Alva French (New York); Marie-Thérèse Gagneux (Montigny-sur-Loing); Harry (Paris); Paige Herren (Kansas City); Stella Mahorner (New Orleans); Julians Q. Mettler (Sweden); Manu (Paris); Robert Morimoto (Burbank); Céline Parizot-Green (Lyon); Yveline Pelletier (San Rafael); Brooke Poole (Berkeley); Caitlin Ramey (Berkeley); H. Alex Rubin (New York); Thomas Sancton (Paris); Rebecca Schwaner (Los Angeles); Grayson Taylor (New Orleans); Anne Teague, Beth, Dabney, James, and Libby Landis (New Orleans); Christelle Uras (Lyon); Serge Vejvoda (San Francisco); Stevie Yung (New Jersey).

We'd also like to thank the Random House folks who helped us with cartography, page design, and production: Bob Blake, Ellen Browne, Fionn Davenport, Denise DeGennaro, Tigist Getachew, Laura Kidder, Fabrizio La Rocca, and Linda K. Schmidt.

Berkeley Bios

Behind every restaurant blurb, write-up, lodging review, and introduction in this book lurks a student writer. You might recognize the type—perpetually short on time, money, and clean clothes. Three Berkeley students spent the summer in Paris researching and writing this book. Every two weeks they sent their manuscript back to Berkeley, where a two-woman editorial team whipped, squashed, and pummeled it into shape.

The Writers

Counting a lifetime of ordering at restaurants in her native New Orleans as adequate preparation, **Baty Landis** was ready to take some time off from school for the ultimate Francophile dream: to live in Paris. Immediately after her arrival, she compensated for the Métro's early bedtime by moving to within walking distance of her favorite bistrots and clubs of the Bastille. The museums and boulevards were nice and all, but what Baty will miss most about Paris are the exhaustive opera seasons and excellent shoe stores. In addition to writing for *The Berkeley Guide to Paris,* Baty wrote for *The Berkeley Guide to France 1995* and edited *The Berkeley Guide to France 1994* and *The Berkeley Guide to Europe 1995.* Unless she can come up with a good excuse to leave her studies again, Baty will continue to live in Berkeley while she pursues B.A.s in music and English.

Not to be put off by a lack of formal training in French, **Oliver Schwaner-Albright** spent his free time making up jokes that nobody—especially the French—understood (e.g., "Je voudrais le café, et je ne veux pas dire le boisson!"). He walked the streets of Paris trying desperately to experience its pleasures as an insider, but the memories of a few chaotic moments when he was suddenly caught in the perfume pit of Galeries Lafayette still terrifies him. In addition to working on *The Berkeley Guide to Paris,* Oliver wrote the Burgundy, Alsace, and Champagne chapters for the *The Berkeley Guide to France,* the Greece, Turkey and Bulgaria chapters for the 1995 *The Berkeley Guide to Europe,* and the Bulgaria chapter for the 2nd edition of *The Berkeley Guide to Eastern Europe.* Oliver was born in Chile and grew up in Los Angeles, but he has signed a pact with the devil (and his mother) to remain in Berkeley until he completes his B.A. in art history.

Before setting out to attack the rest of the country for *The Berkeley Guide to France 1995,* **Remy Garderet** trekked through the Ile de France, biking among the châteaux and trees. A strong believer in the budget traveler's diet of bread, cheese, and alcohol, he is delighted to have found the country with the best of all of them.

The Editors

Loretta Johnson studied philosophy and comparative literature at several colleges until 1993, after which she devoted herself to writing and studying languages. Her chapters are interpretations of the existential dilemma. Among her most celebrated info boxes is a profound analysis of the status of lesbian nightclubs and bookstores in Paris. She is moving on from *The*

Berkeley Guides to annoy anti-educationalists and occasionally enjoy a pastis (or six) with her co-editor. Long live small presses.

After juggling jobs and men, **Virginie Pelletier** finally settled down to the daily editing grind. Following a rather inauspicious birth, she joined the circus as a teen, later singing on street corners and in cabarets. She soon felt the pressure and insecurity of sho' biz and moved on to more academic pursuits, getting a B.A. in poli sci and a masters in journalism. Virginie is investigative by nature. She especially likes to check out new books, films, bars, and bands (and vocalists) and can recite lines from '30s and '40s films at will. She plans to work on a film project, then travel and write (and hopefully get paid for it).

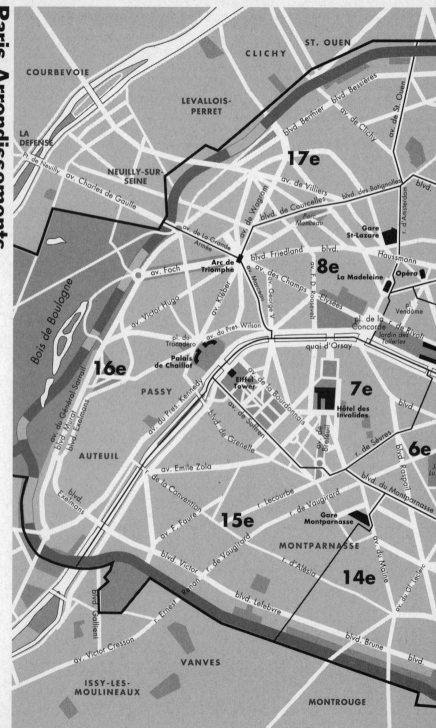

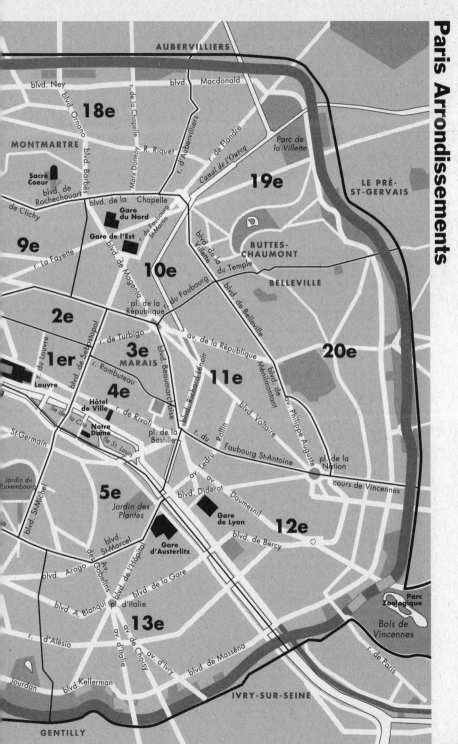

BASICS

By Baty Landis and Oliver Schwaner-Albright

If you've ever traveled with anyone before, you know the two types of people in the world: the planners and the nonplanners. You also know that travel brings out the very worst in both groups: Left to their own devices, the planners will have you goose-stepping from attraction to attraction on a cultural blitzkrieg, while the nonplanners will invariably miss the flight, the bus, and the point. This Basics chapter offers you a middle ground, providing enough information to help plan your trip without saddling you with an itinerary or invasion plan. Keep in mind that companies go out of business, prices inevitably go up, and, hey, we're only too human. Stay flexible; if you want predictability, you should stay home and watch reruns of *The Brady Bunch.*

Planning Your Trip

WHEN TO GO

Paris gets its bulk of visitors between Easter and early September. April through June are fine times to visit, but July sees an unsavory mix of crowds and heat, while August is flat out depressing—much of the city simply closes down. Cultural life awakens from its summer hibernation in September, when the weather is usually glorious. November through January—if you can stand the weather (*see* Climate, *below*)—offer ballet, theater, and opera performances in full swing.

CLIMATE Telling your friends that you are going to Paris in the springtime may sound romantic, but it can be distressingly damp if you show up before Easter. The weather tends to be pleasantly warm by June but can be sultry and dusty in July and August. September and early October are almost ideal, with lots of sun and moderate temperatures. Come November, expect a grab bag of wet-and-cold and warmish-and-sunny days, until the really grim cold sets in from December to March.

NATIONAL HOLIDAYS France is traditionally a Catholic country, and you can guess which days most everything will be closed; here's a quick list of the dates:

January 1, Easter Monday, May 1 (Labor Day), May 8 (World War II Armistice Day—a new holiday that's not observed as extensively as others), Ascension (five weeks after Easter), Whit Monday (early June), July 14 (Bastille Day), August 15 (Assumption), November 1 (All Saints Day), November 11 (World War I Armistice), and December 25 (Christmas). If a public holiday falls on a Tuesday or Thursday, many businesses *font le pont* (make the bridge) and close on that Monday or Friday, too.

FESTIVALS Paris loves to fête. Most of the following festivals are Paris-specific, although some are celebrated nationwide. Check the tourist office for details on dates and tickets.

➤ **SUMMER** • The **Fête de la Musique** is not to be missed. Held annually on June 21, the festival celebrates the summer solstice with an explosion of all types of live music, performed throughout the streets, cafés, and public spaces of Paris (and all of France). The Palais Royal, Bastille, and other areas host music until the sun comes up. The **Festival du Marais,** celebrated between mid-June and mid-July, stages music, dance, and theater in the churches and historic hotels of the Marais. Also in the classical music mode, the **Musique en l'Ile** series of concerts is held in the 17th-century Eglise St-Louis on the Ile St-Louis every July and August. The oddly named **Festival Estival de Paris** features classical music concerts throughout the city from mid-July to late September.

On Bastille Day in 1994 the Germans created a furor by marching down the Champs-Elysées during the annual parade. For some, the sight of Germans in full military regalia marching through Paris conjured up frightening memories of World War II, while others saw it as a step toward healing old wounds.

Course des Garçons de Café is a famous waiter race in which more than 500 professionals scurry through the streets of Paris carrying trays of bottles and glasses. The fastest racer who spills the least wins. The race happens at the end of June and starts and finishes at the Hôtel de Ville.

Bastille Day (July 14) celebrates the storming of the state prison during the early days of the Revolution. Most locals are so caught up in the parades and fireworks that they probably won't notice a foreigner or two joining in.

The **Tour de France,** held annually at the end of July, is the world's most famous bicycle race. Anyone who is not along the route itself is glued to the TV set, and when the race winds up on the Champs-Elysées in Paris, the whole city seems to pour into the streets to cheer on their favorites.

➤ **AUTUMN AND WINTER** • Late October brings the **Festival de Jazz de Paris,** the culmination of a summer full of jazz all over France. Subscription tickets are good for events taking place in clubs and concert halls. For more info, call 1/40–56–07–17. The **Festival d'Automne,** from mid-September to the end of December, features yet more music, as well as theater and dance, throughout Paris. **Chinese New Year** is rung in in the 13th arrondissement, between avenue d'Ivry and avenue de Choisy, in late January or early February, depending on when the New Year falls.

➤ **SPRING** • May 1 is celebrated as **May Day,** honoring workers worldwide. Trade unions organize marches through the streets of Paris, museums and shops close, and newspapers stop their presses. Street vendors sell lilies of the valley, symbolic of the labor movement.

Average Maximum and Minimum Temperature for Paris

Jan.	*43F*	*6C*	*May*	*68F*	*20C*	*Sept.*	*70F*	*21C*
	34	*1*		*49*	*10*		*53*	*12*
Feb.	*45F*	*7C*	*June*	*73F*	*23C*	*Oct.*	*60F*	*16C*
	34	*1*		*55*	*13*		*46*	*8*
Mar.	*54F*	*12C*	*July*	*76F*	*25C*	*Nov.*	*50F*	*10C*
	39	*4*		*58*	*14*		*40*	*5*
Apr.	*60F*	*16C*	*Aug.*	*75F*	*24C*	*Dec.*	*44F*	*7C*
	43	*6*		*58*	*14*		*36*	*2*

The **French Open** brings tennis greats and their fans to beautiful Roland Garros stadium (2 av. Gordon-Bennett, 16e) every year at the end of May. If you plan a year in advance and can afford a ticket, you'll be able to watch the best battle it out on the red-clay courts. Call the French Tennis Federation at 1/47–43–48–00 for info.

GOVERNMENT TOURIST OFFICES

Aside from offering the usual glossy tourist brochures, the French Government Tourist Offices, also known as the Maison de la France, can answer general questions about staying in Paris or refer you to other organizations for more information. If writing for information, be specific about your interests, be they biking, film, or food, because they may not be addressed in the generic brochures.

IN THE UNITED STATES The **French Government Tourist Offices** (610 5th Ave., New York, NY 10020, tel. 212/757–1125; 645 N. Michigan Ave., Suite 630, Chicago, IL 60611, tel. 312/337–6301; 2305 Cedar Springs Rd., Suite 205, Dallas, TX 75201, tel. 214/720–4010; 9454 Wilshire Blvd., Suite 303, Los Angeles, CA 90212, tel. 310/271–6665) can mail you a stack of shiny brochures that advertise travel packages like "Paris Aristocrat" and "Monte Carlo Magnifique." If you want to ask specific questions, you'll have to call their Information Center (tel. 900/990–0040) and pay 50¢ per minute.

IN CANADA If you want to practice your French before you go, talk to the bilingual staffers at **Maison de la France** (1981 av. McGill Collège, Suite 490, Montréal, Qué. H3A 2W9, tel. 514/288–4264) or call the Toronto regional office (30 St-Patrick St., Suite 700, Toronto, Ont. M5T 3A3, tel. 416/593–6427).

IN THE UNITED KINGDOM The British branch of the **French Government Tourist Office** (178 Piccadilly, London W1V OAL, tel. 071/629–12–72) distributes maps and brochures.

Council Travel Offices

ARIZONA: Tempe (tel. 602/966–3544). CALIFORNIA: Berkeley (tel. 510/848–8604); Davis (tel. 916/752–2285); La Jolla (tel. 619/452–0630); Long Beach (tel. 310/598–3338 or 714/527–7950); Los Angeles (tel. 310/208–3551); Palo Alto (tel. 415/325–3888); San Diego (tel. 619/270–6401); San Francisco (tel. 415/421–3473 or 415/566–6222); Santa Barbara (tel. 805/562–8080). COLORADO: Boulder (tel. 303/447–8101). CONNECTICUT: New Haven (tel. 203/562–5335). FLORIDA: Miami (tel. 305/670–9261). GEORGIA: Atlanta (tel. 404/377–9997). ILLINOIS: Chicago (tel. 312/951-0585); Evanston (tel. 708/475–5070). INDIANA: Bloomington (tel. 812/330–1600). LOUISIANA: New Orleans (tel. 504/866–1767). MASSACHUSETTS: Amherst (tel. 413/256–1261); Boston (tel. 617/266–1926 or 617/424–6665); Cambridge (tel. 617/497–1497 or 617/225–2555). MICHIGAN: Ann Arbor (tel. 313/998–0200). MINNESOTA: Minneapolis (tel. 612/379–2323). NEW YORK: New York (tel. 212/661–1450, 212/666–4177, or 212/254–2525). NORTH CAROLINA: Chapel Hill (tel. 919/942–2334). OHIO: Columbus (tel. 614/294–8696). OREGON: Portland (tel. 503/228–1900). PENNSYLVANIA: Philadelphia (tel. 215/382–0343); Pittsburgh (tel. 412/683–1881). RHODE ISLAND: Providence (tel. 401/331–5810). TEXAS: Austin (tel. 512/472-4931); Dallas (tel. 214/363–9941). UTAH: Salt Lake City (tel. 801/582–5840). WASHINGTON: Seattle (tel. 206/632–2448 or 206/329–4567). WASHINGTON, DC: (tel. 202/337–6464).

We Go Where You Go.

Photo Credit: Greg Posey

Lowest student/budget airfares anywhere

International Student ID Cards
International Youth ID Cards
Eurail and Britrail passes
issued on the spot

Hostel Cards
Work Abroad Programs
Travel Gear and Guidebooks
Expert travel advice

IN AUSTRALIA The **French Tourist Office** (Kindersley House, 33 Bligh St., Sydney, N.S.W. 2000, tel. 612/233–3277) is happy to answer any travel questions by mail or over the phone. New Zealand doesn't have its own tourist office, so Kiwis should also contact the Australian office for information.

BUDGET TRAVEL ORGANIZATIONS

Council on International Educational Exchange (CIEE) is a nonprofit U.S. organization dedicated to the pursuit of work, study, and travel abroad. Through its two subsidiaries, **Council Travel** and **Council Charter,** it offers discounted airfares, rail passes, accommodations, and guidebooks. Council Travel is an international network of travel agencies that specializes in the diverse needs of students, youths, teachers, and other budget travelers. It also issues the ISIC, IYC, ITC, and youth hostel cards (*see* Student ID Cards, *below*). Forty-one Council Travel offices serve the budget traveler in the United States, and there are about a dozen overseas (in Britain, France, Germany, and Japan). University travel centers may also carry CIEE's *Student Travels* magazine, a gold mine of travel tips (including work- and study-abroad opportunities). **Council Charter** (tel. 212/661–0311 or 800/223–7402) buys blocks of seats on commercial flights and sells them at a discount. Call for info. *205 E. 42nd St., New York, NY 10017, tel. 212/661–1414.*

Student Travel Australia (STA) has 120 offices worldwide and offers low-price airfares to destinations around the globe, as well as rail passes, car rentals . . . you name it. STA issues ISICs and its own STA Travel Cards (*see* Student ID Cards, *below*). Write or call an STA office for a slew of free pamphlets on services and rates.

Travel CUTS is a full-service travel agency that sells discounted airline tickets to Canadian students and issues the ISIC, IYC, and HI cards. Its 25 offices are on or near college campuses. Call weekdays 9–5 for information and reservations. *187 College St., Toronto, Ont. M5T 1P7, tel. 416/979–2406.*

Hostelling International (HI) is the grandmammy of hostel associations, offering dorm-style beds ("couples" rooms and family accommodations are available at certain HI hostels) and kitchen facilities for about $4–$22 per night at nearly 5,000 locations in 65 countries around the world (three in Paris, over a hundred in France). All HI-affiliated hostels bear the blue triangle with a hut and tree inside. The French division of Hostelling International is **FUAJ,** or Fédération Unie des Auberges de Jeunesse; your HI card is good at any FUAJ hostel. Membership in any national youth hostel association (*see below*) allows you to stay in any HI-affiliated

STA Offices

UNITED STATES. ARIZONA: *Scottsdale (tel. 602/596–5151 or 800/777–0112).* **CALIFORNIA:** *Berkeley (tel. 510/642–3000); Los Angeles (tel. 213/934–8722); San Francisco (tel. 415/391–8407); Santa Monica (tel. 310/394–5126); Westwood (tel. 310/824–1574).* **MASSACHUSETTS:** *Boston (tel. 617/266–6014); Cambridge (tel. 617/576–4623).* **NEW YORK:** *New York City: Columbia University (tel. 212/854–2224), East Village (tel. 212/477–7166).* **PENNSYLVANIA:** *Philadelphia (tel. 215/382–2928).* **WASHINGTON, DC:** *(tel. 202/887–0912).*

ABROAD. AUSTRALIA: *Adelaide (tel. 08/223–2426); Brisbane (tel. 07/221–9388); Cairns (tel. 070/314199); Darwin (tel. 089/412955); Melbourne (tel. 03/349–2411); Perth (tel. 09/227–7569); Sydney (tel. 02/212–1255).* **FRANCE:** *Paris (tel. 01/43–25–00–76).* **NEW ZEALAND:** *Auckland (tel. 09/309–9995); Christchurch (tel. 03/379–9098); Wellington (tel. 04/385–0561).* **UNITED KINGDOM:** *London (tel. 0171/938–4711).*

hostel at member rates. Members also have priority if the hostel is full. A one-year membership is available to travelers of all ages and runs about $25 for adults (renewal $20) and $10 for those under 18. A one-night guest membership is about $4. Family memberships are available for $35, and a lifetime membership will set you back $250. If you forgot to get your card before you left home, you can pick one up for 116F at any of the HI hostels in Paris or at one of the FUAJ offices (*see* HI Hostels, in Chapter 3). Handbooks listing all current hostels are available from the national associations; Volume 1 covers Europe and the Mediterranean, while Volume 2 covers Africa, the Americas, Asia, and Australasia ($10.95 each). *733 15th St. NW, Suite 840, Washington, DC 20005, tel. 202/783–6161.*

Hostelling International member organizations include **American Youth Hostels** (**AYH**) (733 15th St., Suite 840, Washington, DC 20005, tel. 202/783–6161), **Canadian Hostelling Association** (**CHA**) (1600 James Naismith Dr., Suite 608, Gloucester, Ont. K1B 5N4, tel. 613/748–5638), **Youth Hostel Association of England and Wales** (**YHA**) (Trevelyan House, 8 St-Stephen's Hill, St-Albans, Herts. AL1 2DY, England, tel. 01727/855215), **Australian Youth Hostels Association** (**YHA**) (Box 61, Strawberry Hills, Sydney 2012, N.S.W., tel. 02/212–1266), and **Youth Hostels Association of New Zealand** (**YHA**) (Box 436, Christchurch 1, tel. 03/799–970).

STUDENT ID CARDS

The **International Student Identity Card (ISIC)** entitles students to special fares on some forms of transportation and discounts at museums, theaters, sports events, and many other attractions. If purchased in the United States, the popular $17 ISIC card also buys you $3,000 in emergency medical coverage; limited hospital coverage; and access to a 24-hour international, toll-free hot line for assistance in medical, legal, and financial emergencies. In the United States, apply to CIEE or go to STA; in Canada, the ISIC is available for C$15 from Travel CUTS (*see* Budget Travel Organizations, *above*). In the United Kingdom, students with valid university IDs can purchase the ISIC at any student union or student-travel company. Applicants must submit a photo, as well as proof of current full-time student status, age, and nationality.

The **STA Travel Card** is available to travelers age 35 and under for $6. With it, you'll gain access to discounted student fares and *Discount Counter,* a coupon book that offers dollars-off coupons for a limited number of subscribing businesses' services. Purchase the STA card *before* departing.

The **Go 25: International Youth Travel Card (IYC),** formerly known as the FIYTO (Federation of International Youth Travel Organizations) card, is issued to travelers (students and nonstudents) under age 26 and provides services and benefits similar to those given by the ISIC card. The $16 card is available from the same organizations that sell the ISIC.

PASSPORTS AND VISAS

Although Brits need only a Visitor's Passport (a more restricted version of a passport) to enter France, everyone else needs at least a passport and possibly a visa (*see* Obtaining a Visa, *below,* to see if this applies to you). If you lose this piece of identification while you're traveling, it's going to be a pain to get another one, so make a couple of copies, leave one at home, and carry the other with you, separate from your original. Better yet, give a copy to your traveling companion.

OBTAINING A PASSPORT The wheels of bureaucracy grind slowly, so apply for a passport several weeks before your planned departure.

➢ **U.S. CITIZENS •** First-time applicants, travelers whose most recent passport was issued more than 12 years ago or before they were 16, travelers whose passports have been lost or stolen, and travelers between the ages of 13 and 17 (with a parent in tow) must apply for a passport in person. Other renewals can be taken care of by mail. Apply at one of the 13 U.S. Passport Agency offices (*see below*) a *minimum* of five weeks before your departure. For fastest processing, apply between August and December. If you blow it, you can have a slightly more

TOP 5 Ways to Save Money While Traveling

5. Ship yourself in a crate marked "Livestock." Remember to poke holes in the crate.

4. Board a train dressed as Elvis and sneer and say "The King rides for free."

3. Ask if you can walk through the Channel Tunnel.

2. Board the plane dressed as an airline pilot, nod to the flight attendants, and hide in the rest room until the plane lands.

1. Bring a balloon to the airline ticket counter, kneel, breathe in the helium, and ask for the kiddie fare.

But if you're serious about saving money while you're traveling abroad, just get an ISIC--the International Student Identity Card. Discounts for students on international airfares, hotels and motels, car rentals, international phone calls, financial services, and more.

For more information:
In the United States:

 Council on International Educational Exchange
205 East 42nd St.
New York, NY 10017
1-800-GET-AN-ID
Available at Council Travel offices
(see ad in this book)

In Canada:

Travel CUTS
243 College Street,
Toronto, Ontario M5T 2Y1
(416) 977-3703
Available at Travel CUTS offices nationwide

expensive passport issued quickly if you have your plane ticket in hand, proving you leave within five days. Local county courthouses, many state and probate courts, and some post offices also accept passport applications. Have the following items ready when you go to get your passport:

(1) A completed passport application (form DSP-11), available at courthouses, some post offices, and passport agencies. (2) Proof of citizenship (certified copy of birth certificate, naturalization papers, or previous passport issued in the past 12 years). (3) Proof of identity with your photograph and signature (for example, a valid driver's license, employee ID card, military ID, or student ID). (4) Two recent identical, two-inch-square photographs (black-and-white or color head shots). (5) A $55 application fee for a 10-year passport, $30 for those under 18 for a five-year passport. First-time applicants are also hit with a $10 surcharge. If you're paying cash, exact change is necessary; checks or money orders should be made out to Passport Services.

For more information or an application, contact the **Department of State Office of Passport Services** (tel. 202/647–0518) and dial your way through their message maze. Passport applications can be picked up at U.S. post offices, at federal or state courts, and at U.S. Passport Agency offices in Boston, Chicago, Honolulu, Houston, Los Angeles, Miami, New Orleans, New York, Philadelphia, San Francisco, Seattle, Stamford, and Washington, DC.

Those lucky enough to be able to renew their passports by mail must send a completed Form DSP-82 (available from a Passport Agency); two recent, identical passport photos; their current passport (less than 12 years old); and a check or money order for $55 ($30 if under 18). Send everything to the nearest Passport Agency. Renewals take from three to four weeks.

➤ **CANADIAN CITIZENS** • Canadians should send a completed passport application— available at any post office or passport office—to the **Bureau of Passports** (Suite 215, West Tower, Guy Favreau Complex, 200 René Lévesque Blvd. W, Montréal, Qué. H2Z 1X4, tel. 514/283–2152). Include C$35; two recent, identical passport photographs; a guarantor (as specified on the application); and proof of Canadian citizenship (original birth certificate or other official document as specified). You can also apply in person at regional passport offices in many locations, including Edmonton, Halifax, Montréal, Toronto, Vancouver, and Winnipeg. Passports have a shelf life of five years and are not renewable. Processing takes about two weeks by mail and five working days for in-person applications.

➤ **U.K. CITIZENS** • Passport applications are available through travel agencies, a main post office, or one of six regional passport offices (in London, Liverpool, and Peterborough, England; Belfast, Northern Ireland; Glasgow, Scotland; and Newport). The application must be countersigned by your bank manager or by a solicitor, barrister, doctor, clergyman, or justice of the peace who knows you personally. Send or drop off the completed form; two recent, identical passport photos; and a £15 fee to a regional passport office (address is on the form). Passports are valid for 10 years (five years for those under 18) and take about four weeks to process.

➤ **AUSTRALIAN CITIZENS** • Australians must visit a post office or passport office to complete the passport application process. A 10-year passport for those over 18 costs A$76. The under-18 crowd can get a five-year passport for A$37. For more information, call toll-free in Australia 008/02–60–22 during regular business hours.

➤ **NEW ZEALAND CITIZENS** • Passport applications can be found at any post office or consulate. Completed applications must be accompanied by proof of citizenship, two passport-size photos, and a letter from someone able to confirm the applicant's identity. The fee is NZ$50 for a 10-year passport. Processing takes about three weeks.

OBTAINING A VISA If you are an American, a Canadian, or a New Zealander, you need a visa only if you plan to stay in France longer than three months in a row or if you're enrolling in classes or working there. Brits need a visa only if enrolling in classes in France. Australians need a visa for a visit of any length. Student visas are pretty easy to get; just apply a few weeks in advance. Long-stay and work visas, on the other hand, take several months to go through the system, so plan ahead. Contact the French consulate nearest you for more information. If you didn't *plan* to stay but just can't bear to leave your hostel in the mountains or your new French sweetie, contact the French immigration officials well before your three months is up.

LOST PASSPORTS If your passport is lost or stolen while you're traveling, you should immediately notify the local police and nearest embassy or consulate (*see* Embassies and Consulates, in Staying in Paris, *below*). A consular officer should be able to wade through some red tape and issue you a new one, or at least get you back into your country of origin without one. The process will be slowed considerably if you don't have other forms of identification on you, so do carry some—a driver's license, a copy of your birth certificate, a student ID—separate from your passport, and tuck a few photocopies of the front page of your passport into your luggage and your traveling companion's pockets.

A U.S. embassy or consulate will issue a new passport only in emergencies. In nonemergency situations, the staff will affirm your affidavit swearing to U.S. citizenship, and this paper will get you back to the United States. The British embassy or consulate requires a police report, any form of identification, and three passport-size photos and will replace your passport in four working days. Canadian citizens face the same requirements as the Brits, but you must have with you a guarantor: someone who has known you for at least two years, lives within the jurisdiction of the consulate or embassy, and is a member of one of several approved professions. There is also the option of paying an officer of the consulate/embassy to be your guarantor if you don't know anyone who fits the proper categories—proving that throwing enough money at a problem usually makes it go away. A replacement passport usually takes five working days. New Zealand officials ask for two passport-size photos, while the Australians require three, but both can usually replace a passport in 24 hours.

RAIL PASSES

Obviously, if you're flying into Paris and staying put for the length of your stay (and who could blame you?), you can skip right over this section. If, however, Paris is one destination on your grand itinerary, read on. Rail passes are a great deal if you're planning to cover a lot of ground in a short period, and they certainly save you time waiting in lines to buy tickets. Before plunking down hundreds of dollars on a pass, though, you need to consider several issues. First, add up the prices of the rail trips you plan—some travel agents have a manual that lists ticket prices, or you can call **Rail Europe** (tel. 303/443–5100), **Railpass Express** (tel. 800/722–7151), or **DER Tours** (tel. 800/782–2424), three agencies that sell rail passes over the phone. If you're under 26, subtract about 20% from the prices quoted by Rail Europe or your travel agent; that's how much you can save by purchasing a **BIJ** (Billet International de Jeunesse) ticket in Europe (*see* Coming and Going By Train, *below*).

If you decide that you'll save money with a rail pass, you have three options: some sort of Eurail-Pass, InterRail pass, or France Railpass. InterRail is available only to those who have lived in a European Union country for longer than six months, Eurail only to U.S. residents who have been in France less than three months.

If you're under age 26 on your first day of travel, it's always a better deal to get a youth pass of some sort (Europass Youth, Eurail Youth Flexipass, or Eurail Youthpass)—valid only for second-class travel. If you're 26 or over on your first day of travel, you're only eligible to buy one of the (much more expensive) passes valid for first-class travel; you might well do better buying individual tickets and traveling more cheaply in second class.

Be sure to buy your rail pass before leaving the United States; though Eurail passes are available in some European discount travel shops and major train stations (including Paris's Gare du Nord and Gare de Lyon), they're more expensive there. Also, if you have firm plans to visit Europe next year, consider buying your pass *this* year: Prices for EurailPasses generally rise on January 1, and your pass is valid as long as you start traveling within six months of the purchase date (thus, a pass bought on December 30, 1995, can be activated as late as June 30, 1996). All the rail pass prices we give were accurate for 1994. Prices might increase slightly effective January 1, 1995.

TAKE THE TRIP THAT RANKS RIGHT UP THERE WITH KITTY HAWK, APOLLO 11 AND THE INAUGURAL CONCORDE FLIGHT.

Rail Europe invites you to be among the first to ride the Eurostar train through the Channel Tunnel.

Be one of the first to take the trip that will change the history of travel. Rail Europe and the high-speed, high-tech passenger train, Eurostar, can take you through the Channel

RIDE THE EUROSTAR
CALL 1-800-94-CHUNNEL

Tunnel from the center of London to the center of Paris in three short hours. All you do is relax, enjoy a drink or a meal and become part of history in the making.

For information on a variety of affordable Eurostar tickets call your travel agent or Rail Europe.

EUROPE. TO THE TRAINED EYE.

Last warnings: Don't assume that your rail pass guarantees you a seat on every train. Seat reservations are required on some trains, including all TGVs (*see* Coming and Going By Train, *below*). *Couchettes* (sleeping compartments) on overnight trains cost about 90F extra. Also note that many rail passes entitle you to free or reduced fares on some ferries (though you should still make seat reservations in advance).

FRENCH RAIL PASSES A **France Railpass** is valid for three days of travel within a one-month period. First-class passes go for $180, second-class for $125; added days (up to six allowed) cost $39 each for first class, $29 for second. Valid for travel only within France, this pass isn't available once you're there, so be sure to pick one up before you leave home. Another good deal is the **France Rail 'n Drive Pass.** For only a bit more than the plain ol' train pass, you get three days of train travel and three days of Avis car rental within one month. A second-class pass goes for $235, and you can add car days for $39 each and rail days for $29 each. You get unlimited mileage and can pick up and drop off the car anywhere in France at no extra charge (there are 520 Avis agencies), so this might not be a bad deal for seeing those out-of-the-way châteaux. Car-rental reservations must be made directly with Avis at least seven days in advance (tel. 800/331–1084), and drivers must be age 24 or older. Neither the France Rail nor the France Rail 'n Drive pass is valid for travel on Corsica.

➤ **DISCOUNT CARDS** • You can buy a **Carte Carrissimo** discount card only in France, only if you've been living there at least three months, and only if you're between the ages of 12 and 25. Passes are good for a year and cost 190F for four one-way trips, 350F for eight trips. Calendars given out with train tickets are color-coded to indicate different fare periods; with the Carrissimo, you get no discount on red days (*période rouge*), which tend to cluster around major holidays and weekends; 50% off on blue days (*période bleue*); and 20% off on white (*période blanche*). This discount card is good for small groups, since the discount applies to up to three other people traveling with you—just be sure to stamp the card, along with your tickets, one time for each person using it.

Similar to the Carte Carrissimo, the **Carte Vermeille** gives people over age 60 two discount options. The first costs 135F and gives a 50% discount on four trips; the second is 255F and gives a 30% discount on all fares for one year. Both options apply only during the blue period (*see above*). With the **Carte Kiwi** (430F), a child under 16 pays full price, but up to four accompanying people can get a 50% discount for a full year.

EURAIL The **EurailPass** is valid for unlimited first-class train travel through 17 countries: Austria, Belgium, Denmark, Finland, France, Germany, Greece, Hungary, Italy, Luxembourg, Netherlands, Norway, Portugal, Republic of Ireland, Spain, Sweden, and Switzerland. It's available for periods of 15 days ($498), 21 days ($648), one month ($798), two months ($1,098), and three months ($1,398). You really have to be covering a lot of ground to make this pass pay for itself. If you're under 26, the **Eurail Youthpass** is a much better deal: One or two months of unlimited second-class train travel cost $578 and $768, respectively, while 15 consecutive days of travel cost $398.

If you're spreading out train trips over a two-month period, consider the first-class **Eurail Flexipass.** Valid in the same 17 countries as the EurailPass, it entitles you to unlimited rail travel for five days ($348), 10 days ($560), or 15 days ($740) within two calendar months. The second-class **Eurail Youth Flexipass**—available only to those under 26 on their first day of travel— buys you five days ($255), 10 days ($398), or 15 days ($540) of travel within a two-month period.

One of the more curious rail passes is the **Eurail Saverpass,** intended for couples and small groups. A minimum of two people must buy Saverpasses and may use them only when traveling together; between April 1 and September 30 there is a three-person minimum. A pass for first-class travel costs $430 for 15 days, $550 for 21 days, and $678 for one month.

Like the Eurail Flexipass and the Eurail Youth Flexipass, the **Europass** (first class) and **Europass Youth** (second class) are good for unlimited travel over a specific number of days within a two-month period, but in this case, only in France, Germany, Italy, Spain, and Switzerland. Five days of travel in three contiguous countries costs $280 (first class) or $198 (second class), while eight days in four contiguous countries costs $394 (first class) or $282 (second class). For 11 days in all five countries you'll pay $508 (first class) or $366 (second class). You can buy up to two extra travel days with the three- and four-country passes ($38 first class, $28 second class), up to four extra days with the five-country pass.

If you have any rail pass good on French trains, show it to the station agent in the RER (the Métro that goes through Paris and out to the burbs), and he or she will hand you a free ticket. If you don't mind walking a bit, you can see Paris for free traveling by RER.

➢ **PASS VALIDATION AND INSURANCE •** The very first time you use any Eurail pass you must have it validated. Before getting on the train, go to a ticket window and have the agent fill out the necessary forms—a painless but important procedure that could save you from being asked to get off the train or being fined. With any pass that's good for a limited number of travel days within a one- or two-month period, you also have to fill in the month and day you travel. Some travelers have found that creative use of an erasable pen comes in handy with these passes. Another pitfall to avoid is having your pass stolen or lost. The only real safeguard is Eurail's "Pass Protection Plan," which costs $10 and must be arranged at the time of purchase. If your pass mysteriously disappears, file a police report within 24 hours, keep the receipts for any train tickets you purchase, and, upon your return home, send a copy of the report and receipts to Eurail. For your trouble you'll get a 100% refund on the *unused* portion of your stolen or lost pass.

INTERRAIL European citizens or anyone who has lived in the EU for at least six months can purchase an **InterRail Pass,** valid for one month's travel in over 25 countries. A one-month InterRail pass costs about 965F if you're age 26 or older, 875F if you're under 26. The pass works much like a Eurail pass, though you get only a 50% reduction on train travel in the country where it is purchased. Be prepared to prove EU citizenship or six months of continuous residency. In most cases you'll have to show your passport for proof of age, citizenship, and residency, but sometimes they'll accept a European university ID. Be forewarned that each time passes are presented, the ticket controller has the option of looking at passports and confiscating "illegitimate" passes; bring something like a phone bill with your name and European address on it. InterRail can be purchased only in Europe, at rail stations and some budget travel agencies; try the European branches of STA or Council Travel (*see* Budget Travel Organizations, *above*).

MONEY

The units of currency in France are the franc and the centime (1 franc = 100 centimes). Bills come in denominations of 20, 50, 100, 200, and 500 francs. Keep an eye out for the cool new 50F bills with images from St-Exupéry's *Little Prince* on them. Coins are worth ½, 1, 2, 5, and 10 francs and 5, 10, and 20 centimes. When you plan your budget, allow for fluctuating exchange rates; at press time, the rate was about 5.4 francs to the U.S. dollar, 8.1 to the pound sterling, and 4.3 to the Canadian dollar.

The French use two methods of listing prices that include centimes. While 5 francs is always 5F, a price of 5 francs and 40 centimes may be rendered either 5F40 or 5,40F. In all our price listings we use the first method.

HOW MUCH IT WILL COST Prices tend to reflect the standing of an area in the eyes of Parisians; posh residential arrondissements like the 7th, 16th, and 17th are far more expensive than more student-oriented or working-class areas. The side streets of the Marais, the Quartier Latin, St-Germain, Montmartre, and Montparnasse are celebrated bohemian-chic areas, but they are often pricey. Venture into Belleville, the Bastille, the Gare de Nord and Gare de l'Est area, and even Les Halles for much better deals.

➢ **LODGING •** While hostels are marginally the best deal for solo travelers, those traveling in twos or threes are better off splitting a hotel room. Parisian hostels cost a minimum of about 105F per night and charge 20F–50F for a meal. Singles in one- or no-star hotels run at least 100F, doubles 120F. Camping isn't an option in Paris. *See* Chapter 3, Where to Sleep, for more details.

➢ **FOOD** • Sitting down in a Parisian restaurant for a multicourse meal at least once is practically a moral imperative. A three-course dinner will run you at least 70F, though the same meal will cost a lot less (maybe 50F) at lunchtime. You can survive quite well on inexpensive, fresh produce, cheese, and bread bought at outdoor markets or grocery stores, and essentials like *tarte aux pommes* (apple tart) and chocolate croissants run anywhere from 6F to 15F. *See* Chapter 4, Food, for more details.

➢ **TRANSPORTATION** • Expect to pay 30F–45F for a short taxi ride, though often at night there'll be 20F or more already on the meter when you get in. Métro and bus tickets run 7F per trek, but Paris is a great city for strolling. For details on the intricacies of the Parisian transport system, *see* Getting Around, *below*.

➢ **ENTERTAINMENT** • This is where you can go broke fast. Cover charges for nightclubs range from 70F to 140F and usually include one drink. Drinks in clubs are outrageously expensive—about 80F each. A beer in a bar goes for 15F–50F. Movies are pretty expensive (about 40F), but discount tickets are often sold for around 30F. Classical music and theater tickets are reasonable, and discounted student and rush tickets are often available.

➢ **TIPPING** • At restaurants, cafés, and brasseries, service is undoubtedly included, and it's 100% normal not to leave a centime. If you love the service, though, or someone called you a cab, then leave anywhere from 2F to 5F. In the case of taxi drivers and hairdressers, tip 10%. Ushers who help opera- and theatergoers to their seats should be tipped about 5F.

TRAVELING WITH MONEY A major U.S. credit card (especially Visa) and accompanying personal identification number (PIN) is often the safest and most convenient way to pay for goods and services in Paris; many hotels, restaurants, and shops accept credit cards, and you'll find ample ATMs that will give you cash advances at favorable rates (*see* Getting Money from Home, *below*). Traveler's checks can also come in handy. While few merchants accept them, you can exchange them for cash at many banks and almost all bureaux de change. Whichever method you use, protect yourself by carrying cash in a money belt or "necklace" pouch, and by keeping records of your credit-card numbers and traveler's check serial numbers in a few safe places.

It's always cheaper to buy a country's currency in that country; you'll get a better deal buying French francs in France than at your bank in Australia or the States. Nevertheless, it's a good idea to exchange a bit of money into francs before you arrive in the country in case the exchange booth at the train station or airport at which you arrive is closed. Most major banks can exchange your money for French francs.

CHANGING MONEY The best place to exchange your cash or traveler's checks into francs varies, though generally speaking, the Banque de France has good rates. Private exchange offices occasionally will have better rates—just watch out for commissions, which can run up to 5%. For information on specific locations to change your money in Paris, *see* Bureaux de Change, in Staying in Paris, *below*.

TRAVELER'S CHECKS An increasingly outmoded form of currency in the face of ATMs, traveler's checks can be exchanged for cash at banks, some hotels, tourist offices, American Express offices, or currency-exchange offices. Some banks and credit unions will issue checks free to established customers, but most charge a 1%–2% commission. The American Automobile Association (AAA) sells members American Express traveler's checks commission-free. Hold on to your receipts after exchanging traveler's checks; once you're home, it's easier to convert foreign currency into dollars if you have the receipts. Call any of the toll-free or collect phone numbers listed below for more information about where to buy traveler's checks.

➢ **AMERICAN EXPRESS** • Card members can order traveler's checks in U.S. dollars and six other currencies by phone for a 1% commission (commission-free with a gold card). In three to five business days you'll receive your checks; up to $1,000 worth can be ordered in a seven-day period. AmEx also issues **Traveler's Cheques for Two,** checks that can be signed and used by either you or your traveling companion. If you lose your checks or are ripped off, true to Karl Malden's repeated pledges, AmEx has the resources to provide you with a speedy refund—often within 24 hours. For locations of American Express offices in Paris, *see* American Express, in Staying in Paris, *below*. Tel. 800/221-7282 in the U.S. and Canada.

➢ **THOMAS COOK** • Thomas Cook issues **MasterCard International** traveler's checks, available in U.S. dollars and several foreign currencies. If purchased through a Thomas Cook Foreign Exchange office (formerly Deak International), no extra charge is levied to get traveler's checks in French francs. There are nine Thomas Cook exchange offices/travel agencies in Paris, including one at 125 avenue des Champs-Elysées (tel. 1/47–20–25–14), and another at 8 place de l'Opéra, 9e (tel. 1/47–42–46–52). *Tel. 800/223–7373 in the U.S.; 609/987–7300 collect from outside the U.S.; in Europe, tel. 447/335–02–995 toll-free or 07/335–02–995 collect.*

➢ **INTERPAYMENT VISA** • When two giants in the traveler's check universe (BankAmerica and Barclay's) embarked on a joint venture, their baby was born as Interpayment Visa Travelers Cheques, which are actually imprinted with the name of the financial institution that sells the checks. *Tel. 800/227–6811 in the U.S. and Canada or 813/623–1709 collect from outside the U.S.*

➢ **LOST AND STOLEN CHECKS** • Unlike cash, traveler's checks, once lost or stolen, can be replaced or refunded—*if* you can produce the purchase agreement and a record of the checks' serial numbers (especially of those you've already cashed). Sign all the checks when you buy them; you endorse them a second time to exchange them for cash or make purchases. Common sense dictates that you keep the purchase agreement separate from your checks. Caution-happy travelers will even give a copy of the purchase agreement and serial numbers to someone back home. Most issuers of traveler's checks promise to refund or replace lost or stolen checks in 24 hours, but you can practically see them crossing their fingers behind their backs. In a safe place—or several safe places—record the toll-free or collect telephone number to call in case of emergencies.

CREDIT CARDS Many restaurants, cafés, bars, shops, and hotels will accept credit cards with a 100F minimum—look for the card logo on windows. Also keep in mind that any place that accepts the French card Carte Bleu also accepts Visa. Visa and MasterCard, but not always American Express, can be used at many banks and ATMs to get a cash advance (*see* Getting Money from Home, *below*).

GETTING MONEY FROM HOME

Provided there is money at home to be had, there are several ingenious ways to get it.

AMERICAN EXPRESS If you're an American Express cardholder, you can cash a **personal check** at an AmEx office for up to $1,000 ($2,500 with a gold card) every 21 days; you'll be paid in U.S. traveler's checks or, in some instances, in foreign currency. If you don't have a check on you, you can use one of theirs (though the limit drops to $500). **Express Cash** allows cardholders to withdraw cash from their personal checking accounts via ATMs (*see* Cash Machines, *below*).

➢ **MONEYGRAMS** • An American Express MoneyGram can be a dream come true if you can convince someone back home to go to an AmEx MoneyGram agent and fill out the necessary forms (for locations of agents, call 800/926–9400; from overseas, call 303/980–3340 collect or contact the nearest AmEx agent). You don't have to be an AmEx cardholder to send or receive a MoneyGram; the sender simply pays up to $1,000 with a credit card or cash (and anything over that in cash) and, as quickly as 10 minutes later, it's ready for you to pick up. Fees vary according to the amount of money sent but average about 8% to send money from the United States to Paris. You have to get the transaction reference number from the sender and show ID when picking up the money.

CREDIT-CARD CASH ADVANCES **MasterCard** and **Visa** cardholders can get cash advances from many banks in Paris and even in small towns; check with your credit-card company before you leave home to find out how much you're likely to pay in commission fees and interest for this handy service. Each bank sets its own limits on the amount of cash you can withdraw and which cards are accepted; policies may even vary from branch to branch. Typically, the daily withdrawal limit is $300. If you have a PIN number for your card, you might even be able to make the transaction with an ATM machine in Paris (*see* Cash Machines, *below*).

You can't buy beans without francs.

You'll probably find that the country that gave us the words "gourmet," "couture" and "champagne" isn't cheap. And it's très likely you might find yourself a little short on francs. Which is why there's Western Union Money Transfer.

With Western Union you can receive money from the States within minutes. Simply call 161 43 54 46 12 in Paris or 1-800-325-6000* in the United States for the locations nearest you.

And relax, we'll send your francs as far as you need, in case yours don't go far enough.

WESTERN UNION | MONEY TRANSFER
The fastest way to send money worldwide.℠

WESTERN UNION Fees for sending money by Western Union (tel. 800/325–6000) range from 4% to 10%, depending on the amount sent. If you have a MasterCard or Visa, you can have money sent up to your credit limit. If not, have someone take cash, a certified cashier's check, or a healthy MasterCard or Visa to a Western Union office. The money will reach the requested destination in minutes but may not be available for several more hours or days, depending on the whim of the local authorities.

CASH MACHINES Virtually all U.S. banks belong to a network of ATMs, which gobble up bank cards and spit out cash 24 hours a day in cities throughout the world. In Paris they are affiliated with the **Cirrus** (tel. 800/424–7787) system *only*. If the transaction cannot be completed—an annoyingly common occurrence—chances are that the computer lines are busy— try again later. Another problem is that ATMs in France accept PINs of five or fewer digits only; if your PIN is longer, ask your bank at home about changing it. If you know your PIN number as a word, learn the numerical equivalent before you leave, since some French ATM keypads show no letters, only numbers. On the positive side, you get local currency instantly at a good exchange rate, though the transaction fee can be hefty.

➤ **CREDIT-CARD ADVANCES** • A **Visa** or **MasterCard** can be used to access cash through certain ATMs (provided you have a PIN for it), but the fees for this service are usually higher than bank-card fees. Interest charges begin to accrue immediately on these "loans" until you pay the amount back in full. Check with your credit-card company for information on fees and on the daily limit for cash withdrawals.

➤ **EXPRESS CASH** • **American Express** cardholders can withdraw up to $1,000 in a 21-day period ($2,500 for gold-card holders) from their personal checking accounts via any Crédit Lyonnais bank in France. Each transaction carries a 2% fee, with a minimum charge of $2 and a maximum of $6. Apply for a PIN and set up the linking of your accounts at least two to three weeks before departure. Call 800/CASH–NOW for an application.

DEPARTMENT OF STATE TRUST FUND In extreme emergencies (arrest, hospitalization, or worse), there is one more way American citizens can receive money overseas. A friend or family member sends money to the Department of State, which then transfers the money to the U.S. Embassy in Paris. Once the trust fund is established, you can send and receive money through Western Union, bank wire, or mail, all payable to the Department of State. For information, talk to the Department of State's Citizens' Emergency Center (tel. 202/647–5225).

WHAT TO PACK

As little as possible. Besides the usual suspects—clothes, toiletries, camera, a Walkman, and a good book—bring along some sort of day pack for excursions; you can check heavy, cumbersome bags at the train or bus station (or leave it at your hotel/hostel) and just carry the essentials with you while you go out on the town or looking for lodging.

BEDDING Hostels require that you use a sleep sheet. Some include them in the price (including the three HI hostels in Paris) and some don't. If you have a backpack, consider bringing your own makeshift sleep sheet and a sleeping mat that can be rolled tightly and strapped onto the bottom of your pack.

CLOTHING Paris is a fashionable city; locals don't throw on sweats to run to the store. Though it's important to pack pragmatically (bringing comfortable, easy-to-clean clothes), you may feel uncomfortable if you're always dressing down. It's better to have one decent shirt you can wear every other day (as the Parisians do) than a whole slew of tacky T-shirts from back home. Athletic clothes are rarely worn outside the gym. If you plan an extended stay, pack for all possible climates, and, whatever you do, don't forget your comfortable walking shoes.

LAUNDRY SUPPLIES For the average person, hotel rooms are the best place (certainly the cheapest) to do laundry. A bring-your-own laundry service includes a plastic bottle of liquid detergent (powder doesn't break down as well), about six feet of clothesline, and some plastic clips (bobby pins or paper clips can substitute). Porch railings, shower curtain rods, bathtubs, and faucets can all serve as wet-laundry hangers if you forget the clothesline. If it's hot enough, your clothes will dry overnight. When faced with a plugless sink, stuff a sock or plastic bag in the drain. Be sure to bring a few extra plastic bags for damp laundry and dirty clothes. As for detergent, plain old bar soap, dishwashing liquid, or liquid soap get clothes clean in a pinch.

TOILETRIES Use containers that seal tightly and pack them in a separate, waterproof bag; the pressure on airplanes can cause lids to pop off and create instant moisturizer slicks inside your luggage. Bring all the paraphernalia you need to conduct chemical warfare on your contact lenses if you wear them. Tampons, deodorant, soap, shampoo, and toothpaste can all be bought in Paris, but you should bring any prescription drugs you might need, since hunting down the French equivalents might take some time. Condoms and birth control products are also good to bring along, especially if you don't know the French word for "dental dam" (*see* Staying Healthy, *below*).

ELECTRONIC STUFF Before tossing a blow-dryer into your bag, consider that European electrical outlets pump out 220 volts, enough to explode or implode American appliances. If you absolutely must have that electric toothbrush, you need a converter that matches your appliance's wattage and the outlet's current. In addition to taking up precious packing space, a converter costs about $15.

MISCELLANEOUS Stuff you might not think to take but will be damn glad to have: (1) a flashlight, good for reading in the dark and exploring wine cellars; (2) a pocket knife for cutting fruit, spreading cheese, removing splinters, and opening bottles; (3) a water bottle; (4) sunglasses; (5) several large zip-type plastic bags, useful for wet swimsuits, towels, leaky bottles, and rancid socks; (6) a travel alarm clock; (7) a needle and small spool of thread; (8) extra batteries; (9) a few good books.

STAYING HEALTHY

HEALTH AND ACCIDENT INSURANCE Some general health plans cover expenses incurred while traveling, so review your existing policies (or a parent's policy, if you're a dependent) before leaving home. Most university health-insurance plans stop and start with the school year, so don't count on school spirit to pull you through. Canadian travelers, lucky to have a single-payer system with universal coverage, should check with their provincial ministry of health to see if their resident health-insurance plan covers them on the road.

Organizations such as STA and CIEE (*see* Budget Travel Organizations, *above*), as well as some credit-card conglomerates, include health-and-accident coverage with the purchase of an ID or credit card. If you purchase an **ISIC** card, you're automatically insured for $100 a day for in-hospital sickness expenses, up to $3,000 for accident-related medical expenses, and up to $10,000 for emergency medical evacuation. For details, request a coverage summary from CIEE (INS Dept., 205 E. 42nd St., New York, NY 10017). Otherwise, several private companies offer coverage designed to supplement existing health insurance for travelers; for more details contact your favorite budget travel organization or one of the agencies listed below.

The SIDA INFO SERVICE (tel. 1/05–36–66–36) answers its phones 24 hours a day. For AIDS-related information and counseling in English, go to the Free Anglo-American Counseling Treatment Support (FAACTS) at the American Church (65 quai d'Orsay, 7e, tel. 1/45–50–26–49).

International SOS Assistance provides emergency evacuation services, worldwide medical referrals, and optional medical insurance. If all fails, it also covers the return of "mortal remains." Plan A (medical insurance extra) costs $50 for up to 31 days, $95 for up to four months, $120 for up to six months. *Box 11568, Philadelphia, PA 19116, tel. 215/244–1500 or 800/523–8930.*

Travel Guard offers an excellent variety of insurance plans, many of which are endorsed by the American Society of Travel Agents. Most policies include coverage for sickness, injury (or untimely death), lost baggage, and trip cancellation. *1145 Clark St., Stevens Point, WI 54481, tel. 715/345–0505 or 800/782–5151.*

MEDICAL ASSISTANCE British travelers can join **Europe Assistance Worldwide Services** (252 High St., Croyden, Surrey CRO 1NF, tel. 0181/680–1234) to gain access to a 24-hour, 365-day-a-year telephone hot line that can help in a medical emergency. The American branch of this organization is **Travel Assistance International** (1133 15th St. NW, Suite 400, Washington, DC 20005, tel. 800/821–2828), which offers emergency evacuation services and 24-hour medical referrals. An individual membership costs $62 for up to 15 days, $164 for 60 days.

International Association for Medical Assistance to Travelers (IAMAT) offers free membership (donations are much appreciated) and entitles you to a worldwide directory of qualified English-speaking physicians who are on 24-hour call and who have agreed to a fixed-fee schedule. IAMAT also distributes helpful health pamphlets, like the "World Malaria Risk Chart." *417 Center St., Lewiston, NY 14092, tel. 716/754–4883; 40 Regal Rd., Guelph, Ont. N1K 1B5, Canada, tel. 519/836–0102; Box 5049, Christchurch 5, New Zealand.*

Medic Alert offers an internationally recognized identification bracelet and necklace that indicate the bearer's medical condition, drug allergies, or current medication information. It also provides the number of Medic Alert's 24-hour hot line, through which members' medical histories are available. Lifetime membership in the United States is yours for the cost of the ID bracelet or necklace, from $35 to $75. *Medic Alert Foundation International, Box 1009, Turlock, CA 95381, tel. 800/432–5378; in Canada, tel. 416/696–0142 or 800/668–1507; in Australia, tel. 09/277–9999 or 08/274–0422; in New Zealand, tel. 05/288219; in the U.K., tel. 0171/833–3034.*

PRESCRIPTIONS Bring as much as you need of any prescription drugs (*ordonnance* in French), as well as your written prescription—packed separately. Ask your doctor to type the prescription and include the dosage, the generic name, and the manufacturer's name. To avoid problems clearing customs, diabetic travelers carrying syringes should have handy a letter from their physician confirming their need for insulin injections.

Most pharmacies close at 7 or 8 PM, but the *commissariat de police* in every city has a list of the *pharmacies de garde*, the pharmacists on call (literally, on guard) for the evening. This is an emergency-only service, and you may have to go to (as opposed to just call) the commissariat in order to get the name. Pharmacies de garde are also sometimes listed in newspapers or posted on the doors of closed pharmacies.

FIRST-AID KITS For about 97% of your trip, a first-aid kit may mean nothing to you but extra bulk. However, in an emergency you'll be glad to have even the most basic medical supplies. Prepackaged kits are available, but you can pack your own from the following list: bandages, waterproof surgical tape and gauze pads, antiseptic, cortisone cream, tweezers, a thermometer in a sturdy case, something for diarrhea (Pepto-Bismol or Immodium), and, of course, aspirin. If you're prone to motion sickness or are planning to cross the English Channel during your travels, take along some Dramamine. Remember that self-medicating should be relied on only for short-term illnesses; seek professional help if medical symptoms persist or worsen.

CONTRACEPTIVES AND SAFE SEX AIDS (in French, SIDA) and other sexually transmitted diseases do not respect national boundaries; protect yourself when you travel as you would at home. If you're planning a rendezvous and have neglected to bring condoms from home, pick up some at a French pharmacy. You won't find spermicidal nonoxynol-9 versions here, though; sales were discontinued a few years ago. However, women can add to condoms' effectiveness with *ovules* (spermicidal vaginal suppositories).

Condom—un préservatif;

STD—une MST (maladie sexuellement transmissible);

AIDS—le SIDA (syndrome immunodéficient acquis).

Condoms are available in dispensers outside many pharmacies for your late-night needs—you'll even find a dispenser in the Charles de Gaulle–Etoile Métro station. In general, though, you'll have a hard time finding contraceptives in stores other than pharmacies. Condoms go for about 1OF for two, 49F for a box of 12.

So, you're getting away from it all.

Just make sure you can get back.

Here's a travel tip that will make it easy to call back to the States. Dial the access number for the country you're visiting and connect right to AT&T. It's the quick way to get English-speaking AT&T operators and can minimize hotel telephone surcharges.

If all the countries you're visiting aren't listed above, call **1 800 241-5555** for a free wallet card with all AT&T access numbers. Easy international calling from AT&T. **TrueWorld Connections.**

AT&T

All the Best Trips Start with Fodor's

Women should bring any birth-control paraphernalia from home, because it may be difficult to find the exact equivalent in France. If you forget your prescription for the Pill (*la pillule*), a sympathetic pharmacist may forgo the formality. IUDs and diaphragms are available, but you have to see a doctor to get fitted, and it's hardly the sort of thing you'd want to do on a vacation. Pack condoms or diaphragms in a pouch or case where they will not become squashed or damaged. If all of the above fails and the *test de grossesse* (pregnancy test) from the pharmacy is positive, your options in France are limited: Given

The French legislature finally made sexual harassment a crime in 1994, but the maximum sentence is only one year.

the more conservative political climate of late, abortion services are now legally available only to women who can prove they've been living in France at least six months.

DIABETIC TRAVELERS Diabetic travelers should contact one of the following organizations for resources and medical referrals: **American Diabetes Association** (1660 Duke St., Alexandria, VA 22314, tel. 703/549–1500 or 800/232–3472), **Canadian Diabetes Association** (15 Toronto St., Suite 1001, Toronto, Ont. M5C 2E3, tel. 416/363–3373), and **International Diabetes Federation** (International Association Centre, Rue Washington 40, B-1050 Brussels, Belgium, tel. 032/2647–4414 or fax 032/2649–3269). *The Diabetic Traveler* (1596 Washington Blvd., Stamford, CT 06902, tel. 203/327–5832), published four times a year, offers travel and medical advice. Subscriptions are $18.95. Available for free is an insulin-adjustment card and an informative article entitled "Management of Diabetes During Intercontinental Travel."

CRIME AND PUNISHMENT

DRUGS AND ALCOHOL Many young Parisians are tolerant (even enthusiastic) about drug use. Heroin, LSD, amphetamines, cocaine, and marijuana are all bought and sold here. Drug possession and consumption, however, are punishable by hefty fines. Drug *selling* is the big no-no—if you're caught, you'll go to jail for sure. If you get busted for drugs (or breaking any other law), your embassy might say a few sympathetic words but cannot give you one iota of legal help. You're on your own.

PROTECTING YOUR VALUABLES You'd be wise to carry all cash, traveler's checks, credit cards, and your passport in an inaccessible place: a money belt, a front or inner pocket, or a bag that fits underneath your clothes. Hotel rooms and especially hostels are not necessarily safe places to leave your stuff—don't leave anything valuable in the room. When sleeping or leaving your room, keep what you cherish on your body or at least inside your sleep sheet (if you're in it). And it may go without saying, but *never* leave your pack unguarded or with a total stranger in train or bus stations or any other public place, not even if you're planning to be gone for only a minute—it's not worth the risk. If you're carrying a smaller bag with a strap (or a camera), sling it crosswise over your body and try to keep your arm down over the bag in front of you. Back pockets are fine for maps, but don't keep a wallet back there.

RESOURCES FOR WOMEN

Although times are changing, the idea still exists that women traveling alone are fair game for lewd comments, leering looks, and the like. Harassment is usually verbal—always annoying, but not often violent. Although *draguers* (men who persistently profess their undying love to hapless female passersby) are very vocal, especially in large cities like Paris, the threat they pose is no greater than in any big city back home.

There are precautions you can take to avoid some harassment. Dressing conservatively helps; the more scantily you're clad, the more harassment you'll have to endure. Avoiding eye contact with potential sleazeballs also helps. Finally, be aware of your surroundings and use your head; don't do things when traveling alone that you wouldn't do at home. Hitchhiking alone, for example, is not the brightest idea, nor is walking back to your hotel at night along deserted streets. If you get into an uncomfortable situation, your best bet is to move into a public area and make your fear widely known.

PUBLICATIONS Other than the lesbian-oriented *Women's Traveller* and *Are You Two . . . Together?*, one of the only major travel publication for women is ***Women Travel: Adventures, Advice, and Experience*** ($12.95), published by Prentice Hall and available at bookstores. Over 70 countries receive some sort of coverage, usually in the form of journal entries and short articles. As far as practical travel information goes, it offers few details on prices, phone numbers, and addresses. Thalia Zepatos's ***A Journey of One's Own: Uncommon Advice for the Independent Woman Traveler*** ($13), available at most bookstores, is fun to read but has little information on specific countries or regions. Still, for women it's a good resource for general travel information.

ORGANIZATIONS Headquartered in Paris are **Mouvement Français Pour le Planning Familial** (4 sq. St-Irénée, 11e, tel. 1/48–07–29–10), part of the International Planned Parenthood Federation, and **SOS Viol,** the French rape crisis center, whose hot line can be reached at 1/05–05–95–95. A working knowledge of French is needed for both of these programs. **SOS Help** (tel. 1/47–23–80–80), open daily 3–11, offers emotional and practical support for English speakers in Paris.

RESOURCES FOR GAYS AND LESBIANS

The gay scene is alive and well in Paris, especially in the bars and clubs of the Marais, but lesbian hot spots are harder to find. Fewer hate crimes are committed against gays in France than in the United States and the United Kingdom, but once you leave Paris, a less-than-warm welcome may await you in the more conservative provinces.

PUBLICATIONS *Are You Two . . . Together?* is the best known, and perhaps the most detailed, guide for gays traveling in Europe. Slightly out of date, it's anecdotal and funny but skimps on practical details. It makes an excellent read, costs $18, and is published by Random House; ask for it at your local bookstore.

A good resource for lesbians is ***Ferrari's Places for Women*** ($13 plus shipping), with worldwide listings of gay resorts, bars, and bookstores. It also features an events calendar. *Renaissance House, Box 533, New York, NY 10014–0533, tel. 212/674–0120.*

One of the better gay and lesbian travel newsletters is ***Out and About,*** with listings of gay-friendly hotels and travel agencies, plus health cautions for travelers with HIV. A 10-issue subscription costs $49; single issues cost about $7. *For subscriptions, tel. 800/929–2268.*

Spartacus bills itself as *the* guide for the gay traveler, with practical tips and reviews of hotels and agencies in over 160 countries. It's a bit expensive at $29.95, though you do get snappy color photos and listings in four languages. *Tel. 800/462–6654.*

For the most detailed information about gay life in Paris, you should obviously look for gay publications in the city itself. The ultimate source of information and places to go for gay men in Paris is ***Guide Illico*** (64 rue Rambuteau, 3e, tel. 48–04–58–00), sold monthly for 9F at newsstands throughout Paris, and available for free at many gay restaurants and bars. Unfortunately, it's all in French. Publications Illico also put out ***Double Face,*** a free monthly supplement to gay life, and ***Trixx*** (35F), a collection of enticing photos. The ***Guide Gai,*** available for 50F from the bookstore Les Mots à la Bouche (*see* Bookstores, in Chapter 6), lists restaurants, bars, cafés, and other popular gay hangouts in the city. ***Paris Scene,*** the English-language version, costs 60F. For a large selection of gay magazines and periodicals, check out Paris's **Le Kiosque des Amis** (29 blvd. des Italiens, 2e, tel. 1/42–65–00–94, Métro: Opéra).

ORGANIZATIONS In Paris, major gay associations include the **Centre Gai et Lesbien** (25 rue Michel Le Comte, 3e, tel. 1/42–77–72–77); **Gay Pride,** at the same address and phone number; and **Syndicat National des Entreprises Gaies** (**SNEG**) (37 rue de Rivoli, 4e, tel. 1/48–04–83–02). **Act Up–Paris** (112 blvd. de l'Hôpital, 13e, tel. 1/42–01–11–47) holds meetings every Tuesday at 7:30 PM. Call for the location.

International Gay Travel Association (IGTA) is a nonprofit organization with worldwide listings of travel agencies, gay-friendly hotels, gay bars, and travel services aimed at gay travelers. *Box 4974, Key West, FL 33041, tel. 800/448–8550.*

RESOURCES FOR THE DISABLED

Accessibility may soon have an international symbol if an initiative begun by the Society for the Advancement of Travel for the Handicapped (SATH) catches on. A bold, underlined capital **H** is the symbol that SATH is publicizing for hotels, restaurants, and tourist attractions to indicate that the property has some accessible facilities. While awareness of the needs of travelers with disabilities increases every year, *budget* opportunities are harder to find. Always ask if discounts are available, either for you or a companion or both, and plan your trip and make reservations far in advance.

Though over the past decade Paris has spent a lot of money rebuilding itself, only last year was a law passed requiring that new buildings be wheelchair accessible; you'll find very few buildings are barrier free. At least the government has published an excellent, free booklet (in French), *Touristes Quand Même,* that details, region by region, which transportation systems and tourist attractions are accessible to the disabled. The booklet is available from tourist offices and from the **Comité National Français de Liaison pour la Réadaptation des Handicapés** (38 blvd. Raspail, 7e, Paris, tel. 1/45–48–90–13).

ACCOMMODATIONS Whenever possible, reviews in this book will indicate if rooms are wheelchair-accessible. However, most hotels in Paris are in buildings that are hundreds of years old and unsuited to guests with impaired mobility. In general, more expensive or chain hotels are better equipped. Talk to the **Association des Paralysés de France** (17 blvd. Auguste-Blanqui, 13e, tel. 1/45–80–82–40) for a list of wheelchair-accessible hotels.

GETTING AROUND

➢ **BY PLANE** • Most major airlines are happy to help make flight arrangements, provided they are notified up to 48 hours in advance. Some airlines, such as **Air Canada** (tel. 800/776–3000 outside Canada or 800/361–8071 in Canada), **Delta** (tel. 800/221–1212, TYY 800/831–4488), and **USAir** (tel. 800/428–4322, TYY 800/245–2966), offer a discounted "companion fare" if a passenger with disabilities needs attendant help. Ask about discounts and check-in protocol when making reservations. **AIRHOP** (tel. 1/40–24–34–76) will arrange transport within Paris and to and from airports.

➢ **BY TRAIN** • The SNCF, France's rail service, has cars on some trains that are equipped for the disabled, and wheelchair-bound passengers can be escorted on and off trains. Contact local SNCF offices to request this service in advance.

➢ **BY METRO** • Most of Paris's Métro lines (like the bus system) are unfortunately inaccessible to disabled visitors, but the RER is slightly more accessible. The following Paris RER stations have elevators: **Auber** (direction Etoile only), **Châtelet, Cité Universitaire** (direction south only), **La Défense, Denfert-Rochereau, Gare de Lyon, Gare du Nord, St-Michel** (elevator on side street rue Xavier-Privas), and **Vincennes.** Some of these may require escalator use as well, and you may have to push a call button for assistance. **Etoile** has escalators only, but they'll take you all the way to the street if you use one of the Champs-Elysées exits. **Nation** has an escalator for direction Marne-la-Vallée (toward Euro Disney, where the station is accessible). **Port Royal** has escalator access for direction Gentilly and access for exits only from direction Châtelet. For more details, ask the Régie Autonome des Transports Parisiens (RATP) (pl. de la Madeleine, 8e, tel. 1/40–46–42–17) for its brochure on accessibility.

PUBLICATIONS Disabled travelers, whether in a wheelchair or faced with less serious mobility problems, should make every effort to get a copy of *Access in Paris,* by Gordon Couch and Ben Roberts. This Brit-published book has info on accommodations, transportation, entertainment, sights, shopping—you name it. Whether it's mapping out the wheelchair-accessible bathroom at Versaille or telling you how many steps there are to the upper level of Sainte Chapelle, this book has it. Write to Access Project for a copy. There's no charge, but you are asked to make a £5 contribution (in cash if you can't write a check in pounds) toward survey and publication costs. *39 Bradley Gardens, West Ealing, London W13 8HE.*

Access to the World: A Travel Guide for the Handicapped, by Louise Weiss, is highly recommended for its worldwide coverage of travel boons and busts for the disabled. It's available from Henry Holt & Co. (tel. 800/488–5233) for $12.95; the order number is 0805001417.

Twin Peaks Press specializes in books such as *Travel for the Disabled*, which offers helpful hints as well as a comprehensive list of guidebooks and facilities geared to the disabled. *Directory of Travel Agencies for the Disabled* lists more than 350 agencies throughout the world. Each is $19.95 plus $2 ($3 for both) shipping and handling. Twin Peaks also offers a "Traveling Nurse's Network," which connects disabled travelers with registered nurses to aid and accompany them on their trip; an application is $10. *Box 129, Vancouver, WA 98666, tel. 206/694–2462 or (for orders only) 800/637–2256.*

ORGANIZATIONS Mobility International USA (MIUSA) is a nonprofit organization that coordinates exchange programs for disabled people around the world. MIUSA also offers information on accommodations and organized study programs for members ($20 annually). The French affiliate is **Comité National Français de Liaison pour la Réadaptation des Handicapés** (*see above*). Nonmembers may subscribe to the newsletter for $10. *Box 3551, Eugene, OR 97403, tel. and TYY 503/343–1284.*

The **Society for the Advancement of Travel for the Handicapped** is a nonprofit educational group that works to inform and educate people about travel for the disabled. Annual membership costs $45 ($25 for students and senior citizens) and entitles you to a quarterly newsletter that details new tours and late-breaking political advances for the disabled. Members can also request information about a specific destination; send $1 and a S.A.S.E. *26 Court St., Brooklyn, NY 11242, tel. 718/858–5483.*

WORKING IN PARIS

If you're not currently a student (or recent grad), France won't grant you a work permit unless you already have a French employer who can convince immigration officials that she absolutely, positively needs you, and not a native French person, to fill the position. That said, plenty of native English speakers find work teaching their mother tongue to Francophones. Getting a decent teaching position isn't easy, but with some perseverance it's possible to find a job that will keep you in Paris. Hundreds of private language schools exist throughout the city— many congregate in the 16th arrondissement. Each school has its own guidelines and restrictions; many require a Teaching of English as a Foreign Language (TEFL) certificate, obtainable after an expensive, intensive four-week training course, and some hire only older, experienced teachers. The best place to get addresses and phone numbers is the Parisian *Pages jaunes* (yellow pages), and the best time to look is in late summer, since school generally starts sometime around the beginning of October.

PUBLICATIONS CIEE (*see* Budget Travel Organizations, *above*) publishes two excellent resource books with complete details on work/travel opportunities. The most valuable is **Work, Study, Travel Abroad: The Whole World Handbook** ($13.95), which gives the lowdown on scholarships, grants, fellowships, study-abroad programs, and work exchanges. Also worthwhile is CIEE's **Going Places: The High School Student's Guide to Study, Travel, and Adventure Abroad** ($13.95). Both books can be shipped to you book rate ($1.50) or first class ($3). World Trade Academy Press (50 E. 42nd St., No. 509, New York, NY 10017, tel. 212/697–4999) publishes **Looking for Employment in Foreign Countries** ($16.50 plus $3.50 shipping) and provides lists of American firms in France for $28. Addison Wesley (tel. 800/447–2226 to order) publishes **International Jobs: Where They Are, How to Get Them** for $12.45.

Believe it or not, the U.S. government actually publishes a very useful pamphlet about looking for jobs in a foreign country—**Employment Abroad: The Facts and Fallacies.** Send a check or money order for $8.50 and a S.A.S.E. *U.S. Department of Commerce, 1615 H St. NW, Washington, DC 20062.*

The U.K.-based Vacation Work Press publishes two first-rate guides to working abroad: **Directory of Overseas Summer Jobs** (£9) and Susan Griffith's **Work Your Way Around the World** (£12). The first lists over 45,000 jobs worldwide; the latter has fewer listings but makes a more interesting read. Look for them at bookstores, or contact the publisher directly. *9 Park East End, Oxford OX1 1HJ, England, tel. 0865/241978.*

ORGANIZATIONS Students interested in working in a foreign country should consider the **CIEE Work Abroad Program.** CIEE arranges work permits for about $100 for students or recent grads that are valid for three to six months and can help you find short-term employment in Europe, Latin America, and New Zealand. Pick up CIEE's "Work Abroad" pamphlet from any Council Travel office (*see* Budget Travel Organizations, *above*). *205 E. 42nd St., New York, NY 10017, tel. 212/661–1414, ext. 1130.*

CIEE's Work Abroad Program is open only to U.S. students; Canadians should contact **Travel CUTS,** which has similar programs for Canadian students who want to work abroad for up to six months. *SWAP, 243 College St., 5th floor, Toronto, Ont. M5T 2Y1, tel. 416/977–3703.*

Au Pair Abroad arranges boarding and lodging for people between the ages of 18 and 26 who want to work as nannies for up to four months in a foreign country. Basic language skills are required, and all applicants must go through a somewhat lengthy interview process. *1015 15th St. NW, Suite 750, Washington, DC 20005, tel. 202/408–5380.*

International Schools Services (ISS) is like an employment agency for would-be teachers. It's a nonprofit enterprise, and your $50 application fee goes toward placing you in one of ISS's 220 affiliated American or international schools worldwide. *Box 5910, 15 Roszel Rd., Princeton, NJ 08543, tel. 609/452–0990.*

IAPT (International Association of Practical Training) sends full-time students abroad to practice their engineering, mathematics, and computer skills in over 50 countries. You don't get paid much, though the program is designed to cover day-to-day expenses. Applications are due as much as six months in advance of travel, so get going. *10 Corporate Center, Suite 250, 10400 Little Patuxent Pkwy., Columbia, MD 21044, tel. 410/997–2200.*

STUDYING IN PARIS

Studying in another country is the perfect way to scope out a foreign culture, meet locals, and improve your language skills. You may choose to study through a U.S.-sponsored program, usually through an American university, or to enroll in a program sponsored by a European organization. Do your homework; programs vary greatly in expense, academic quality, exposure to language, amount of contact with locals, and living conditions. Working through your local university is the easiest way to find out about study-abroad programs in France.

The **American Institute for Foreign Study** and the **American Council of International Studies** arrange semester and year-long study-abroad programs in universities throughout the world. Applicants must be enrolled as full- or part-time students. Fees vary according to the country and length of stay. *313 E. 43rd St., New York, NY 10017, tel. 800/727–2437.*

CIEE's **University Programs Department** manages study-abroad programs at various European universities. To help guide you through the maze of programs, purchase CIEE's excellent *Work, Study, Travel Abroad* (*see* Working in Paris, *above*).

The Information Center at the **Institute of International Education (IIE)** publishes the helpful *Academic Year Abroad* ($42.95), which lists over 1,900 study-abroad programs for undergraduates and graduates. If you're more interested in summer-abroad and living-abroad programs, check out IIE's *Vacation Study Abroad* ($36.95). Order either from IIE Books (tel. 212/984–5412).

Coming and Going

CUSTOMS AND DUTIES

ARRIVING IN PARIS Going through customs in Paris is usually pretty painless. The officials will check your passport and a form you'll fill out on the plane, but probably won't touch your luggage unless you look shady or their dogs have caught a whiff of something interesting in your bags. If you bring any foreign-made equipment with you from home, such as cameras or video gear, carry the original receipt or register it with customs before leaving the United States (ask for U.S. Customs Form 4457). Otherwise, you may end up paying duty on your return. Don't even *think* about drugs. Being cited for drug possession is no joke, and embassies and consulates often can't or won't do much to persuade officials to release you if you get tossed in prison. On top of that, immigration officials have been getting tougher, conducting random searches of any traveler they think looks remotely suspicious.

RETURNING HOME

➤ **U.S. CUSTOMS** • You're unlikely to have run-ins with customs when you return home, as long as you *never* carry any illegal drugs in your luggage. When you return to the United States, you have to declare all items you bought abroad, but you won't have to pay duty unless you come home with more than $400 worth of foreign goods, including items bought in duty-free stores. For purchases between $400 and $1,000 you pay a 10% duty. A free leaflet about customs regulations and illegal souvenirs, "Know Before You Go," is available from the **U.S. Customs Service** (Box 7407, Washington, DC 20044, tel. 202/927-6724).

➤ **CANADIAN CUSTOMS** • For scintillating details about Canadian customs' requirements, request a copy of the brochure "I Declare/Je Déclare" from **Revenue Canada Customs, Excise and Taxation Department** (2265 St-Laurent Blvd. S, Ottawa, Ont. K1G 4K3, tel. 613/957-0275).

➤ **U.K. CUSTOMS** • For information or a copy of "A Guide for Travellers," which details standard customs procedures as well as what you may bring into the United Kingdom from abroad, contact **HM Customs and Excise** (Dorset House, Stamford St., London SE1 9PY, tel. 0171/928-33440).

➤ **AUSTRALIAN CUSTOMS** • For rules and regulations, request the pamphlet "Customs Information for Travellers" from a local **Collector of Customs** (GPO Box 8, Sydney, NSW 2001, tel. 02/226-5997).

➤ **NEW ZEALAND CUSTOMS** • Although greeted with a "*Haere Mai*" ("Welcome to New Zealand"), homeward-bound travelers face a number of restrictions. For details, ask a New Zealand consulate for the pamphlet "Customs Guide for Travellers."

GETTING THE BEST DEALS

When your travel plans are still in the fantasy stage, start studying the travel sections of major newspapers: Courier companies, charter flights, and fare brokers often list incredibly cheap flights. Travel agents are another obvious resource, as they have access to computer networks that show the lowest fares before they're even advertised. However, budget travelers are the bane of travel agents, whose commission is based on the ticket prices. That said, agencies on or near college campuses—try STA or Council Travel (*see* Budget Travel Organizations, *above*)—actually cater to this pariah class and can help you find cheap deals.

While a last-minute, round-trip ticket to Paris on Air France can cost $1,200 from New York and $1,600 from San Francisco, bargain-basement prices can go as low as $450. Flexibility

As a rule, the further in advance you buy the ticket, the less expensive it is. Keep in mind that "advance purchase" to an airline does not mean a week before departure.

is the key to getting a serious bargain on airfare. If you can play around with your departure date, destination, amount of luggage carried, and return date, you will probably save money. Options include charter flights, flying standby, student discounts, courier flights, and APEX (Advanced Purchase Excursion) and Super APEX fares; read on to help get through this maze. Another useful resource is George Albert Brown's *Airline Traveler's Guerrilla Handbook* (Blake Publishing Group, 320 Metropolitan Sq., 15th St. NW, Washington, DC 20005, tel. 800/752-9765; $14.95), an in-depth account of how to find cheap tickets and generally beat the system.

Hot tips when making reservations: If the reservation clerk tells you that the least expensive seats are no longer available on a certain flight, ask to be put on a waiting list. If the airline doesn't keep waiting lists for the lowest fares, call them on subsequent mornings and ask about cancellations and last-minute openings—airlines trying to fill all their seats sometimes add additional cut-rate tickets at the last moment. When setting travel dates, remember that off-season fares can be as much as 50% lower. Ask which days of the week are the cheapest to fly on—weekends are often the most expensive. If you end up biting the bullet and paying more than you'd like for a ticket, keep looking for better deals your airline may offer; some airlines will refund the difference in ticket price when they lower fares and you call them on it.

APEX TICKETS APEX tickets bought directly from the airlines or from your travel agent are the simplest way to go if you know exactly when you want to leave and it's not tomorrow (or the next day, or the next . . .). Regular APEX fares normally apply to tickets bought at least 21 days in advance; you can get Super APEX fares if you know your travel plans at least one month in advance. Here's the catch: If you cancel or change your plans, you'll pay a penalty, usually $50 to $100.

CONSOLIDATORS AND BUCKET SHOPS Consolidator companies, also known as bucket shops, buy blocks of tickets at wholesale prices from airlines trying to fill flights. Check out any consolidator's reputation with the Better Business Bureau before starting; most are reliable, but better safe than sorry. If everything works according to plan, you'll save 10%–40% on the published APEX fare.

It goes without saying that you can't be too choosy about which city you fly into. Other drawbacks: Consolidator tickets are often not refundable, and the flights to choose from often feature indirect routes, long layovers in connecting cities, and undesirable seating assignments. If your flight is delayed or canceled, you'll also have a tough time switching airlines. As with charter flights, you risk taking a huge loss if you change your travel plans. If possible, pay with a credit card, so that if your ticket never arrives you don't have to pay. Bucket shops generally advertise in newspapers—be sure to check restrictions, refund possibilities, and payment conditions. One last suggestion: Confirm your reservation with the airline both before and after you buy a consolidated ticket. This not only decreases the chance of fraud but also ensures that you won't be the first to get bumped if the airline overbooks. For more details, contact one of the following consolidators.

Airfare Busters specializes in European and Central American destinations. *5100 Westheimer Ave., Suite 550, Houston, TX 77056, tel. 713/961–5109 or 800/232–8783 in the southern U.S.*

Airhitch provides low-price, last-minute seats on airplanes bound for Western Europe. The Airhitch staff will help you work up a list of possible destinations and departure dates. The week before you leave, they will contact you and give you a list of the flights they think they can get you on. You're obligated to accept one of these flights, even if it wasn't your first choice. One-way tickets to Europe from the East Coast cost $169, from the West Coast $269, and from selected points in between, $229. *2790 Broadway, Suite 100, New York, NY 10025, tel. 212/864–2000; 1341 Ocean Ave., Suite 62, Santa Monica, CA 90401, tel. 310/458–1006.*

Globe Travel has consolidated tickets to "any place you want." The best deals are to Europe. *507 5th Ave., Suite 606, New York, NY 10017, tel. 800/969–4562.*

UniTravel offers good deals to Europe, South America, and even some destinations within the United States. *1177 N. Warson Rd., Box 12485, St. Louis, MO 63132, tel. 314/569–2501 or 800/325–2222.*

STANDBY AND THREE-DAY-ADVANCE-PURCHASE FARES Flying standby is almost a thing of the past. The idea is to purchase an open ticket and wait for the next available seat on the next available flight to your chosen destination. Most airlines have dumped standby policies in favor of three-day-advance-purchase youth fares, which are open only to people under 25 and (as the name states) can only be purchased within three days of departure. Return flights must also be booked no more than three days prior to departure. If you meet the above criteria, expect 10%–50% savings on published APEX fares.

A number of brokers specializing in discount and last-minute sales offer savings for unsold seats on commercial carriers and charter flights, as well as tour packages. If you're desperate to get to Paris by Wednesday, try **Last Minute Travel Club** (tel. 617/267–9800).

CHARTER FLIGHTS Charter flights have vastly different characteristics, depending on the company you're dealing with. Generally speaking, a charter company either buys a block of tickets on a regularly scheduled commercial flight and sells them at a discount (the prevalent form in the United States) or leases the whole plane and then offers relatively cheap fares to the public (most common in the United Kingdom). Despite a few potential drawbacks—among them, infrequent flights, restrictive return-date requirements, lickety-split payment demands, frequent bankruptcies—charter companies inevitably offer the cheapest tickets around, especially during high season, when APEX fares are most expensive. Make sure you find out a company's policy on refunds should a flight be canceled by either yourself or the airline. Summer charter flights fill up fast and should be booked a couple months in advance.

You're in much better shape when the company is offering tickets on a regular commercial flight. After you've bought the ticket from the charter folks, you generally deal with the airline directly. When a charter company has chartered the whole plane, things get a little sketchier. You can minimize risks by checking the company's reputation with the Better Business Bureau and taking out enough trip-cancellation insurance to cover the operator's potential failure.

Council Charter has the scoop on hundreds of different charter and reduced-fare flights. *Tel. 212/661–0311 or 800/800–8222.*

DER Tours is a full-service travel store, with rail passes, discounted airfares, and listings of charter flights. *Box 1606, Des Plains, IL 60017, tel. 800/782–2424.*

Tower Air specializes in domestic and international charters. On the plus side, you get to deal with the airline directly. On the downside, Tower is notorious for overbooking. Even so, they offer some amazingly cheap deals. *Tel. 800/34–TOWER.*

Travel Charter caters to students bound for Europe, though some of their charters are loaded with restrictions. *1120 E. Long Lake Rd., Troy, MI 48098, tel. 810/641–9677 or 800/521–5267.*

Travel CUTS is part of the CIEE umbrella, which means it's a reputable place for Canadian students to book their charter. *187 College St., Toronto, Ont. M5T 1P7, tel. 416/979–2406.*

STUDENT DISCOUNTS Student discounts on airline tickets are offered through **CIEE,** the **Educational Travel Center, STA Travel,** and **Travel CUTS** (*see* Budget Travel Organizations, *above*). Keep in mind that you will *not* receive frequent-flyer mileage for discounted student, youth, or teacher tickets. For discount tickets based on your status as a student, youth, or teacher, have an ID when you check in that proves it: an International Student Identity Card (ISIC), Youth Identity Card, or International Teacher Identity Card.

Campus Connection, exclusively for students under 25, searches airline computer networks for the cheapest student fares to worldwide destinations. They don't always have the best price, but because they deal with the airlines directly, you won't get stuck with a heavily restricted or fraudulent ticket. *1100 E. Marlton Pike, Cherry Hill, NJ 08032, tel. 800/428–3235.*

COURIER FLIGHTS A few restrictions and inconveniences are the price you'll pay for the colossal savings on airfares offered to air couriers—travelers who accompany letters and packages between designated points. The way it works is simple. Courier companies list whatever flights are available for the next week or so. After you book the flight, you sign a contract with the company to act as a courier (some places make you pay a deposit, to be refunded after the successful completion of your assignment, should you agree to accept it). On the day of departure, you arrive at the airport a few hours early, meet someone who hands you a ticket and customs forms, and off you go. After you land, you simply clear customs with the courier luggage, and deliver it to a waiting agent. Don't worry about what you're transporting—we're talking business documents, not drugs or weapons.

The main restrictions are (1) flights can be booked only a week or two in advance, often only a few days in advance; (2) you are allowed one piece of carryon luggage only, because the courier uses your checked-luggage allowance to transport the time-sensitive shipment; (3) you must return within one or two weeks, sometimes within 30 days; and (4) most courier companies only issue tickets to travelers over the age of 18.

Check newspaper travel sections for courier companies, check your yellow pages, or mail away for a telephone directory that lists companies by the cities to which they fly. One of the better publications is *Air Courier Bulletin* (IAATC, 8 S. J St., Box 1349, Lake Worth, FL 33460, tel. 407/582–8320), sent to IAATC members every two months once you pay the $35 annual fee. *A Simple Guide to Courier Travel* gives tips on flying as a courier (send $15.95 to Box 2394, Lake Oswego, OR 97035, tel. 800/222–3599). Another good resource is the newsletter published by **Travel Unlimited** (Box 1058, Allston, MA 02134), which costs $25 for 12 issues.

Discount Travel International has courier flights to destinations in Europe, Central America, and Asia from the hubs of Miami and New York. *169 W. 81st St., New York, NY 10024, tel. 212/362–3636; 801 Alton Rd., Suite 1, Miami Beach, FL 33139, tel. 305/538–1616.*

Now Voyager departs from New York, Newark, Miami, or Houston; destinations may be in Europe, Asia, or Mexico (City, that is). Most flights are one week in length, with round-trip fares ranging from $150 and up. A nonrefundable $50 registration fee, good for one year, is required. Call for current offerings. *74 Varick St., Suite 307, New York, NY 10013, tel. 212/431–1616.*

BY AIR

On your fateful departure day, remember that check-in time for international flights is a long two hours before the scheduled departure. Flights lasting more than six hours are smoking flights, so if fumes make you queasy, book short hops or ask for seats as far away from the smoking section as possible.

Paris's main airports lie a fair distance outside town—**Orly** is 16 kilometers (10 miles) to the south, **Charles de Gaulle** (also called Roissy) 26 kilometers (16 miles) to the northeast—but transportation to both is extensive (*see* To and From the Airports, in Getting Around Paris, *below*). If you plan to fly out of Paris, arrive at the airport a full two hours before departure time; you'll probably encounter long lines at the ticket counters and baggage check and a measure of indifference from airline employees if you're about to miss your flight. Both airports have currency exchange desks and 24-hour cash exchange machines. *Airport information: Charles de Gaulle, tel. 1/48–62–22–80 24 hours a day; Orly, tel. 1/49–75–15–15 6 AM–11:30 PM.*

If you can't get a cheap flight into Paris, look into other destinations. Flying into Brussels is convenient; the train trip to Paris costs about $35 second class and takes about three hours, and the train station connects to the airport in Brussels. Amsterdam and Frankfurt are also good bets.

MAJOR AIRLINES WITH OFFICES IN PARIS

Air Canada, tel. 1/44–50–20–20; Air France, tel. 1/44–08–24–24; American Airlines, tel. 1/42–89–05–22; British Airways, tel. 1/47–78–14–14; Continental, tel. 1/42–99–09–09; Delta, tel. 1/47–68–92–92; Northwest, tel. 1/42–66–90–00; United, tel. 1/48–97–82–82.

FROM NORTH AMERICA The flight from the East Coast to Paris takes about eight hours. Plenty of U.S. airlines, including **American** (tel. 800/433–7300), **Continental** (tel. 800/231–0856), **Delta** (tel. 800/221–1212), **TWA** (tel. 800/892–4141), and **United** (tel. 800/241–6522), fly from all over the United States to Paris. **Air France** (tel. 800/237–2747) has frequent flights to Paris and other French cities. Call around to see who is offering the best fare at the moment. If you're extremely lucky, you might find a special fare for as little as $450, but prices go all the way up to $1,200 or so. With a little advance planning and flexibility, you should be able to get a ticket for about $600 almost any time of year.

Air Canada (tel. 800/361–8620 in Québec; 800/268–7240 in Ontario) flies to Paris direct from Montréal, Toronto, and sometimes Vancouver. **Canadian Airlines** (tel. 800/426–7000) has lots of flights from Toronto, while **Canada 3000** (tel. 416/674–0257 in Toronto) flies charter planes to Europe, Asia, and North America.

FROM THE U.K. Air France (tel. 081/759–2311) and **British Airways** (tel. 081/897–4000) make the hour flight from London's Gatwick and Heathrow airports to Paris several times a day. The cost of a round-trip ticket is almost halved if you purchase it 14 days in advance and stay over a Saturday night. Both airlines also fly to Paris from London's most central airport, London City, a few times a day. **Nouvelles Frontières** (tel. 071/629–7772) in London can give you information on discounted airfares between the two countries.

FROM DOWN UNDER Qantas (tel. 02/957–0111) recently began flying to Paris from Sydney by way of Bangkok and Frankfurt. **Continental** (tel. 02/693–5266 in Sydney, 09/379–5682 in Auckland) flies from Melbourne and Sydney and from Auckland, New Zealand, to Paris by way of Los Angeles and New York. Round-trip fares go as low as A$2,000 but are often as high as A$6,000. Talk to the STA offices in Victoria or Auckland (*see* Budget Travel Organizations, *above*) for info on discount fares.

TAKING LUGGAGE ABROAD U.S. airlines allow passengers to check two pieces of luggage, neither of which can exceed 62 inches (length + width + height) or weigh more than 70 pounds. If your airline accepts excess baggage, it will probably charge you for it. Foreign-airline policies vary, so call or check with a travel agent before you show up at the airport with one bag too many.

Most airlines will ship bikes as luggage, provided they are dismantled and put into a box. Call to see if your airline sells bike boxes (around $10). International travelers can usually substitute a bike for the second piece of checked luggage at no extra charge; otherwise, it will cost $100 extra.

If you're traveling with a pack, tie all loose straps to each other or onto the pack itself, as they tend to get caught in luggage conveyer belts. Put valuables like cameras and important documents in the middle of packs, wadded inside clothing, because outside pockets are extremely vulnerable to probing fingers.

Anything you'll need during the flight (and valuables to be kept under close surveillance) should be stowed in a carryon. Foreign airlines have different policies but generally allow only one carryon in tourist class, in addition to a handbag and a bag filled with duty-free goodies. The carryon cannot exceed 45 inches (length + width + height) and must fit under the seat or in the overhead luggage compartment. Call for your airline's current policy. Passengers on U.S. airlines are limited to one carryon, plus coat, camera, and handbag. Carryons must fit under the seat in front of you; maximum dimensions are 9 x 45 x 22 inches. Hanging bags can have a maximum dimension of 4 x 23 x 45 inches; to fit in an overhead bin, bags can have a maximum dimension of 10 x 14 x 36 inches. If your bag is too porky for the compartments, be prepared for the humiliation of rejection and last-minute baggage check.

BY TRAIN

The railway system in France is fast, extensive, and efficient. All French trains have a first and second class. First class is 30% to 50% more expensive, though the difference in comfort between the two is minimal, except on the lightning-fast TGV trains on which first class is really deluxe. First-class sleeping cars are very expensive, but second-class *couchettes,* bunks that come six to a compartment, cost only 86F more (and are worth every centime). For long distances, it's best to take the TGV trains (*see box, below*), though a seat reservation (18F–36F) is required without exception on these trains.

An often overlooked option for budget travelers *without* a rail pass is the **Billet International de Jeunesse** (International Youth Ticket), usually known as a **BIJ** or **BIGE** ticket. Here's how it works: Travelers under the age of 26 can purchase a second-class ticket between two far-flung European cities at a 20% savings, then make unlimited stops along the way for up to two months. BIJ tickets are available throughout Europe at budget travel agencies; try the European offices of STA and Council Travel (*see* Budget Travel Organizations, *above*).

Joker is a price-reduction deal on second-class train travel that will work with a little advance planning. If you buy your ticket eight to 29 days before your departure, you'll get a 15%–40% discount, depending on your destination, but the ticket is not refundable. (SNCF will keep only 30% of the ticket price, though, if you cancel or change your plans at least four days before departing.) The reduction goes up to 35%–60% if you buy a ticket 30–60 days ahead of time; this ticket is good only during the blue and white (non-peak) periods, and not during the red (peak) period. You can pick up a calendar telling you which days fall under which color-coded period in any train station in France. SNCF's **"Guide des prix réduits"** is a handy guide to discount train options and includes a list of Joker ticket prices to cities throughout France.

Purchase tickets at the ticket booth before boarding the train. Don't forget to validate them (*composter le billet*) at the orange ticket punchers, usually located at the entrance to the *quais* (platforms). Train schedules for individual lines are available at all the stations the line runs through. Complete SNCF timetables are available at the information counters of large stations. It's a good idea to bring food and drink with you on long trips; the food sold on the train is usually very expensive and very bad.

BY EUROTUNNEL Since the early 1800s, visionaries have dreamed of building a tunnel between France and England, but endless obstacles have stood in the way. The channel itself wasn't a problem; the chalk on the channel floor is actually quite firm and amenable to tunneling. Still, bureaucratic fumbling and money problems delayed the opening of the tunnel considerably. At press time, Eurostar had just begun selling tickets for the train trip from London to Paris. Second-class, one-way tickets cost about $120, only $74 if you buy your ticket 14 days in advance, and the trip takes three hours. For more information, talk to the extremely friendly folks at Eurostar Enquiries (19 Worple Rd., Wimbledon, tel. 0181/784–1333) in England. Once the Eurotunnel opens, you'll be able to zip from London to Paris in about 3½ hours (though taking the ferry will probably still be cheaper).

PARIS TRAIN STATIONS Six major train stations serve Paris; all have cafés, newsstands, bureaux de change, and luggage storage. You can abandon your belongings in a locker, usually with a coded lock, for 15F–30F for 72 hours. Most train stations have tourist offices (*see* Visitor Information, in Staying in Paris, *below*), and each is connected to the rest of Paris by the Métro system. *For all train information and reservations, tel. 1/45–82–50–50.*

➤ **GARE D'AUSTERLITZ** • Trains from here serve **southwest France and Spain,** including Toulouse (7 hrs, 410F), Barcelona (10–14 hrs, 470F), and Madrid (11 hrs, 550F).

➤ **GARE DE L'EST** • This station serves **eastern France, Germany, Austria,** and **Eastern Europe,** with trains leaving

Almost all train stations in France have a computerized ticket service, which is a godsend for planning your next trip, whether or not you end up buying the ticket. Just choose the English instructions, and the screen will guide you through, from any starting location to any destination on any day. Finally, when you punch in a time, it'll list all your train options for that day, complete with necessary train changes.

Flying through France on the TGV

The TGV (Train à Grande Vitesse), or high-speed train, flies through the French countryside at an average speed of 293 kilometers per hour (182 mph). The first line opened in 1981 between Paris and Lyon; today several TGV lines link Paris to Marseilles and Nice, to the Loire Valley and Bordeaux, to Lille and Calais, to some destinations in Switzerland, and to Bourg St-Maurice in the Alps (thanks to the '92 Winter Olympics). You have to make a reservation to travel on the speedy TGV, but it's probably worth it for longer trips.

daily for Frankfurt (6 hrs, 380F), Prague (16 hrs, 775F), and Vienna (13 hrs, 905F). The station is smaller than nearby Gare du Nord and its services are more limited, but there's still a tourist office and a Thomas Cook bureau de change (open daily 7–6:45). The neighborhood is a bit scary at night.

➤ **GARE DE LYON** • Trains from here serve the **south of France, the Alps, Switzerland,** and **Italy.** Plenty of trains run to Lyon (5 hrs, 265F), Lausanne (4 hrs, 310F), Milan (7½ hrs, 400F), and Rome (14 hrs, 545F). This is one of the bigger stations, with a full range of services, including combination luggage lockers and a bureau de change (open 7 AM–11 PM).

➤ **GARE DU NORD** • Trains travel from here to **northern France** (Calais and Lille), and to **Belgium, the Netherlands,** and points in **Scandinavia.** Regular trains run to Amsterdam (6 hrs, 340F), Copenhagen, (16 hrs, 1,010F), and London (8 hrs via Dieppe, 470F). Showers cost 20F; soap and towels are extra. The neighborhood gets sketchy at night.

➤ **GARE MONTPARNASSE** • Trains travel from here to **Brittany** and **southwestern France.** Daily trains run to Bordeaux (3 hrs, 330F), Rennes (2 hrs, 260F), and Biarritz (5 hrs, 385F).

➤ **GARE ST-LAZARE** • This station serves **Normandy** and some destinations **north of France.** Regular destinations include London (8 hrs via Dieppe, 470F) and Amsterdam (6 hrs, 340F). This is the only major station without a tourist office.

BY BUS

Eurolines is the only bus company in Paris and offers international service only. If you take a bus into Paris, it will most likely drop you off at the Eurolines office. Some of its most popular routes are to London (9 hrs, 220F), Barcelona (15 hrs, 425F), and Berlin (12 hrs, 325F). The company's international buses also arrive and depart from Avignon, Bordeaux, Lille, Lyon, Toulouse, and Tours. *28 av. du Général de Gaulle, Bagnollet, tel. 1/49–72–51–51. Métro: Gallieni. Open daily 8–8.*

BY FERRY

Lots of ferry and hovercraft companies transport travelers and their cars across the Channel. With the arrival of the Eurotunnel, routes and prices are changing; Calais is becoming the Channel-crossing hub, and only **Hoverspeed** (tel. 21–30–27–26) still sends speedy Seacats between Boulogne and Folkestone (mid-April–September only). From Calais, **Sealink** (tel. 21–46–80–00) and **P & O Ferries** (tel. 21–46–04–40) make the 1½-hour ferry trip to Dover for 230F, 190F students; **Hoverspeed** (tel. 21–46–14–14) sends hovercraft over in half the time but charges 240F and offers no discount.

Getting Around Paris

If you don't get anything else straight, for God's sake learn the difference between the Rive Gauche (Left Bank) and the Rive Droite (Right Bank) before you step off that plane. The simplest directions will refer to these two sides of the Seine River, and if you have to ask which is which, you're likely to be sniffed at violently. In the most stereotypical terms, the Rive Gauche is the artistic area; the Sorbonne and the Quartier Latin are here, along with many other bustling neighborhoods full of young people. The Rive Droite, on the other hand, is traditionally more elegant and commercial, though its less central areas are actually much cooler that the Left Bank. It's home to ritzy shopping districts and most of the big-name sights like the Louvre and the Arc de Triomphe. Between the two banks you have the Ile de la Cité, where you'll find the Cathédrale Notre-Dame, and the smaller Ile St-Louis.

Once you have the left and right banks figured out, move on to the *arrondissements,* or districts, numbered one through 20. (For all addresses in this book, the arrondissement number is given, since it's the most common way to describe a location.) Arrondissements one through eight are the most central and contain most of the big tourist attractions, while the ninth through 20th gradually spiral outward toward the outskirts of the city.

For a city of over two million people, Paris is quite compact; you could walk from one end to the other in a few hours. The city is a weird combination of wide, majestic boulevards and self-contained quarters with tiny, winding streets. If you've got the time, you should explore both aspects of Paris—the expansive, majestic Paris of the monuments and cafés, and the bustling, less glamorous Paris of the family restaurants, local bars, and *boucheries à cheval* (butcher shops that sell horsemeat).

To figure out the zip code of any point in Paris, just tack the arrondissement number onto the digits 750. For example, for the fifth arrondissement, 5e (cinquième), the five-digit zip code would be 75005—turning 5 into 05.

When you've had enough walking and you just want to *get there,* the city has an excellent public transportation system consisting of the Métro (the subway system) and the municipal bus system, both operated by **RATP**. If you plan to stay in Paris for only a short time, stick to the Métro; it's efficient and easier to use than the buses. To avoid getting lost on a regular basis, buy a *Plan de Paris par Arrondissement*—a booklet of detailed maps showing all Métro stops and sights—as soon as you arrive. An index at the front alphabetically lists all streets and their arrondissement. You can also get less useful but free maps from the tourist offices (*see* Visitor Information, in Staying in Paris, *below*). For information on all public transport, call 1/43–46–14–14 from 6 AM to 9 PM, but you might find it difficult to get through.

TO AND FROM THE AIRPORTS

Both airports are served by **Air France buses** that depart for Paris every 12–15 minutes between 6 AM and 11 PM. The bus from Charles de Gaulle (48F) stops at the Air France office at Porte Maillot, not far from the Arc de Triomphe; the one from Orly (32F) runs to the Hôtel des Invalides. The trip takes about 20 minutes from Orly and 40 minutes from Charles de Gaulle, depending on traffic.

If you can afford a **taxi** from the airport, you've got more money than we do; it costs about 200F to get to the center of Paris from Charles de Gaulle and 160F from Orly. If you have a lot of stuff, you might want to take the Air France bus or public transportation into Paris and then catch a cab to wherever you're staying. For taxi information, *see* Other Options, *below*.

CHARLES DE GAULLE/ROISSY If you're trying to catch a plane out of Paris, your safest bet is to take **RER A** to the airport, since you won't have to worry about traffic, which can delay the buses for up to an hour. A free *navette* (shuttle bus) takes you between the airport gates and the RER station in both directions. Tickets cost 31F and up, depending on how far from the airport your stop is, and the ride takes around 45 minutes. Trains start running at 5:30 AM toward the airport and at 6:30 AM toward town; either way they keep going until nearly midnight.

The **Roissybus,** run by the RATP, is also easy and convenient, though traffic can render the projected 45-minute ride time laughable. It costs 35F and takes you straight from your terminal door to the Métro stop Opéra Garnier between 5:45 AM and 11 PM.

ORLY Again, the **RER** is your most reliable option. RER line C2 plus a free shuttle brings you to the airport door for around 25F (depending on which Paris stop you use) in about 30 minutes between 5:50 AM and 10:25 PM; trains in the other direction run from 5:30 AM to 11:30 PM. For 25F, the RATP-run **Orly Bus** links the terminals with Métro Denfert-Rochereau, just south of the Quartier Latin.

BY METRO AND RER

Except for the fact that it closes soon after midnight, the Métro is the epitome of convenient public transportation. Thirteen Métro lines (14 in 1996) crisscross Paris and the suburbs, and you will almost never be more than a 10-minute walk from the nearest Métro stop. Any station or tourist office can give you a map of the whole system. Métro lines are marked in the station both by line number and by the names of the stops at the end of each line. Find the number

Paris Métro

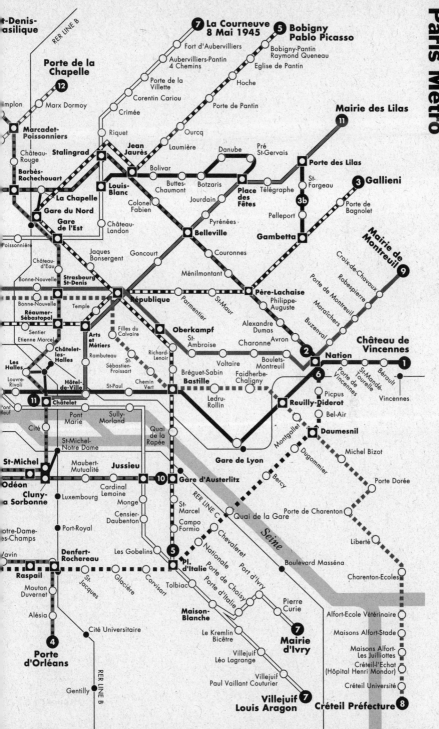

Paris Métro

of the line you want to take and the name of the terminus toward which you will be traveling, and follow the signs.

To transfer to a different line, look for orange signs saying CORRRESPONDENCE and for the new line number and terminus you need. The blue-and-white signs that say SORTIE (exit) will lead you back above ground. You can identify Métro stations by the illuminated yellow M signs, by the round red-and-white METRO signs, or by the old green art nouveau arches bearing the full name, METROPOLITAIN.

The first Métro of the day heads out at 5:30 AM, the last at 12:30 AM. Often the directional signs on the quays indicate the times at which the first and last trains pass that station. Individual tickets cost 7F, but it's much more economical to buy a *carnet* (book of 10) for 41F. You can use one ticket each time you go underground for as many transfers as you like. For extended stays consider getting a Carte Orange, for which you need a photo-booth picture of yourself. You can fill the card with a *coupon semaine* (weekly pass; 63F) or *coupon mensuel* (monthly pass; 219F). Whatever you use, hang on to your ticket until you exit the Métro in case some uniformed French dude wants to see it, a danger particularly toward the end of the month.

Several Métro stations also act as **RER** stations. The RER is a higher-speed, larger rail system that extends throughout the Parisian suburbs and is a fast way to travel between major points in the city. The four principal RER lines are also marked on the Métro maps. You can use normal Métro tickets on them within Zones 1 and 2. To venture farther into Zones 3–5, for example to Versailles, you need to buy a separate, considerably more expensive ticket.

BY BUS

Taking the bus offers the distinct advantage of letting you see where you're going, how you're getting there, and anything interesting along the way. During rush hours it offers the distinct disadvantage of getting there verrry, verrry slowly.

Métro tickets are accepted on the buses. Theoretically you need one to three tickets, depending on how far you're going, but it is highly unlikely anyone's going to check up on how many you use. In fact, even a *used* Métro ticket will fly on most buses if you're subtle and don't mind a slight risk factor. If by some quirk you're caught, you'll have to pay about an 80F fine. Stamp your ticket in the machine at the front of the bus. If you have a Carte Orange, though, don't *ever* stamp it, or it will become invalid—just flash it to the driver.

There are maps of the bus system at all bus stops; all 63 bus lines run Monday through Saturday from 6:30 AM to 8:30 PM, with limited service until 12:30 AM and all day on Sunday. A handy little service, the **Noctambus,** runs 10 lines every hour on the half hour between 1:30 AM and 5:30 AM; all lines start at Châtelet Métro, leaving from just in front of the Hôtel de Ville. Stops served by the Noctambus have a yellow-and-black owl symbol on them. A single ride technically gobbles up four tickets, though rarely does anyone pay all four; a monthly or weekly Carte Orange works on Noctambuses, too. For a map of the night-bus routes, ask for a "Grand Plan de Paris" at any Métro station; the Noctambus lines are drawn in the corner. April 15 through September, on Sundays and holidays from noon until 9, the RATP runs a bus line called the **Balabus,** which hits all major sights in the city and takes about an hour one-way. Buses start at the La Défense or Gare de Lyon Métro stations and stop at all bus stops with the sign BB-BALABUS. The full ride costs three normal tickets, though again you can probably get away with stamping just one.

The Noctambus is a good way to meet drunk people of all nationalities and possibly learn some dirty songs in French.

BY CAR

Getting around Paris by car is a very bad idea, but if you're planning to cruise the countryside, having a car gives you the ultimate travel freedom. Gas, however, is expensive in France (about 5F30 per liter for regular unleaded, 5F70 for super unleaded). Remember while driving in France that the driver on your right, even if he or she is coming from a minor road, has the right of way—and will take it. If you plan to rent a car abroad, you should probably get an **Interna-**

tional **Driver's Permit (IDP)** before leaving home. The IDP is available from the American Automobile Association (AAA) for $16, $10 if you bring two of your own passport-size photos (non-AAA members pay a few dollars more).

The French **Automobile Club National (ACN)** (5 rue Auber, 75009 Paris, tel. 1/44–51–53–99, fax 1/49–24–93–99) charges a small fee for towing (tel. 05–05–05–01) and roadside breakdown service. If you're a AAA member, you can get reimbursed for ACN charges when you get home. For more info stop by your local AAA branch and ask for the pamphlet "Offices to Serve You Abroad," or send a S.A.S.E. to the AAA's head office (1000 AAA Dr., Heathrow, FL 32746).

RENTING A CAR Although renting a car is more expensive in France than in the U.S., several agencies offer pretty reasonable rates, which are worth it if several people split the cost. The cheapest cars are very small stick-shifts that go for around 300F per day or 1,000F–1,500F a week. Some agencies include mileage in the cost, while others may charge you extra

Rues with a View: Scenic Bus Rides in Paris

There are several bus lines that you can ride from one end of Paris to the other for a good, cheap tour of the city, sans irritating commentary. Some of these lines are traveled by buses with small balconies at the rear; though the proximity to gusts of carbon monoxide is less than pleasant, it's an improvement over stuffy bus interiors. Among the best bus lines for exploring are:

- *No. 29: The interesting section of the 29 stretches from Gare St-Lazare, past Opéra Garnier and the Pompidou, and through the heart of the Marais, crossing the place des Vosges before ending up at the Bastille. This is one of the few lines that run primarily through the small streets of a neighborhood, and it has an open back.*

- *No. 69: Get on at the Champ de Mars (the park right by the Eiffel Tower) and ride through parts of the Quartier Latin, across the bridge to the Right Bank near the Louvre, by the Hôtel de Ville (City Hall), and out to the Bastille area.*

- *No. 72: River lovers will adore this line: It follows the Seine from the Hôtel de Ville east past the city limits, hitting the Louvre, the Trocadéro, and most of the big-name Right Bank sights. You'll also get good views of the Left Bank, including Invalides and the Eiffel Tower.*

- *No. 73: You can pick up this short line at the top of the Champs-Elysées or all the way out at La Défense. It travels all the way down the Champs-Elysées, through the place de la Concorde, crossing the river and ending up at the Musée d'Orsay.*

- *No. 84: Pick up the 84 at the Panthéon and take it along the Jardin du Luxembourg, through St-Germain-des-Prés, into the seventh arrondissement, across the river to the place de la Concorde, up around the Madeleine, and on through the ritzy Eighth out past Parc Monceau.*

- *Montmartrobus: If you want to see all of Montmartre without facing the hills à pied (by foot), pick up this bus at Pigalle for a winding tour of the area, including a pass under Sacré Coeur.*

once you reach a certain number of kilometers. Many agencies require that you be at least 23 years old and have a credit card.

Major car rental companies include **Auto Europe** (Box 7006, Portland, ME 04112, tel. 207/828–2525 or 800/223–5555), **Avis** (in Paris, tel. 1/45–50–32–31), **Budget Rent-a-Car** (3350 Boyington St., Carrollton, TX 75006, tel. 800/527–0700; in Paris, tel. 1/46–86–65–65) and **Renault** (tel. 800/221–1052; in Paris, tel. 1/40–40–32–32). There's also **Europe by Car** (1 Rockefeller Plaza, New York, NY 10020, tel. 800/223–1516 or 800/252–9401 in CA), **Foremost Euro-Car** (5658 Sepulveda Blvd., Suite 201, Van Nuys, CA 91411, tel. 818/786–1960 or 800/272–3299), and **Kemwel** (106 Calvert St., Harrison, NY 10528, tel. 800/678–0678). Airports and large train stations have rental agencies on site.

OTHER OPTIONS

BY MOTORBIKE OR MOPED Any two-wheeled vehicle that goes over 50 kilometers (31 miles) per hour needs to be registered and licensed at the nearest *préfecture* (local police department). This means most mopeds don't have to be registered and most motorbikes do. Renting a moped is expensive (about 150F to 300F per day) but may be worth doing to really get off the beaten track for a day or two. To buy a used moped or motorcycle, check the listings in *Argus,* a weekly publication available at most newsstands.

BY BOAT During the summer, hordes of *bateaux mouches* (literally, "fly boats") travel up and down the river, shining their lights on the already illuminated buildings at night and offering a running commentary in five languages. The lights make people living along the river mad as hell, but they do show off the city at its glitziest. Dress warmly enough to ride on the upper deck, and you might avoid the crush below. Board the boat for a 30F, 1¼-hour tour at the Pont de l'Alma. From April to September, a less touristy but more expensive alternative is the **Batobus** (tel. 1/44–11–33–44), a small boat-bus that runs between Pont de la Bourdonnais at the Eiffel Tower and the Hôtel de Ville. There are five stations along the way, and you'll pay 12F for each station you pass or 20F for the journey from Hôtel de Ville to the Eiffel Tower; 60F gets you a day pass to the whole line. The boats begin running at 10 AM every day and leave about every half-hour until 7 PM.

BY BIKE It's not uncommon to see hardy souls with baguettes in their backpacks maneuvering their way on two wheels through Paris's treacherous traffic—bicycling is one of the more efficient ways to get around the city, especially if you manage to emerge with your baguette intact. Before hopping the nearest three-speed, however, be aware of traffic patterns and the general chaos that reigns on the streets of Paris. If you feel tentative about braving the streets alone, especially during the heavy tourist season, you may want to take a guided mountain bike tour, offered spring through fall by the **Three Ducks Hostel** (*see* Hostels and Foyers, in Chapter 3). For 118F you get bike rental, insurance, and a six-hour tour of Paris in English or French—a great way to see the city. They won't go out without a minimum of three people, so get a group together or call in the morning to find out if a trip is happening. The hostel also rents bikes for 90F a day, plus a 2,500F deposit (Visa accepted).

Paris-Vélo rents bikes as well, for 90F per day, 140F for 24 hours, 160F for two days and one night, and 500F per week. Again, you have to provide a hefty 2,000F deposit. They accept Mastercard and Visa. *2 rue du Fer-à-Moulin, 5e, tel. 1/43–37–59–22. Métro: Censier-Daubenton. Open Mon.–Sat. 10–12:30 and 2–7.*

BY TAXI Getting a taxi in Paris can be frustrating as hell, especially in summer. During rush hours (7–10 AM and 4–7 PM) allow yourself a couple of hours to secure one. Trying to hail one on the street is difficult—only taxis with their signs lit are available, and these are few and far between. Your chances of picking one up are better at major hotels. In the better-traveled parts of the city people line up at makeshift taxi stations; try to find one of these, or call individual taxi companies. Rates are approximately 8F per kilometer; they may go up a *bit* after dark, but not more than 50 centimes or so per kilometer. Two good companies are **Taxis Radio 7000** (tel. 1/42–70–00–42) and **Taxis Bleus** (tel. 1/49–36–10–10).

Staying in Paris

VISITOR INFORMATION

The **Office de Tourisme de Paris,** Paris's main tourist office, has a helpful multilingual staff who will load you down with brochures, give you information on public transport and other practicalities, and tell you about current cultural events. They will also book hotel rooms for the same night only, though this is not how you'll find the cheapest place to crash. *127 av. des Champs-Elysées, 8e, tel. 1/49–52–53–54. Métro: Charles de Gaulle–Etoile. Open daily 9–8.*

Six branch offices also reserve rooms and dole out general information on the city. The one at the Eiffel Tower (7e, tel. 1/45–51–22–15) is open May through September only, from 11 to 6. Other branch offices are in the main train stations and are open from 8 to 8 most of the year and until 9 in summer (though Austerlitz closes at 3 PM): Gare d'Austerlitz (13e, tel. 1/45–84–91–70); Gare de l'Est (10e, tel. 1/46–07–17–73); Gare de Lyon (12e, tel. 1/43–43–33–24); Gare du Nord (10e, tel. 1/45–26–94–82); and Gare Montparnasse (15e, tel. 1/43–22–19–19).

The **Accueil des Jeunes en France** (Reception Center for Young People in France) or **AJF** is a useful organization that is more in tune with the backpack set. As well as booking you a room in a budget hotel or hostel, the friendly folks that staff the Accueil's four offices will sell you a student or youth discount card, help you wangle cheap train fares, and give you info on staying in Paris on a budget. Beaubourg: *119 rue St-Martin, 4e, tel. 1/42–77–87–80. Métro: Rambuteau. Open Mon.–Sat. 9–5:45. Gare du Nord: 10e, tel. 1/42–85–86–19. Métro: Gare du Nord. Open summer, daily 8 AM–10 PM. Quartier Latin: 139 blvd. St-Michel, 5e, tel. 1/43–54–95–86. Métro: Port Royal. Open Mar.–Oct., Mon.–Sat. 10–6.*

The American Church (65 quai d'Orsay, 7e, tel. 1/47–05–07–99) hosts concerts and holiday meals; lists jobs, apartments, and contacts for expatriates; and is a great place to meet other Americans staying in the city.

AMERICAN EXPRESS

At any of Paris's three American Express travel offices, cardholders can pick up mail, buy traveler's checks in several currencies, and cash personal checks (*see* Money, in Planning Your Trip, *above*). Non-cardholders can also receive mail (though it costs 5F for each pickup) and buy traveler's checks with French francs. Everyone can use the travel agencies and currency exchange offices or have money sent from loved ones via a MoneyGram (*see* Getting Money from Home, *above*). *11 rue Scribe: 9e, tel. 1/47–77–79–50. Métro: Opéra. Open weekdays 9–6:30, Sat. 9–5:30. 38 av. de Wagram: 8e, tel. 1/42–27–58–80. Métro: Ternes. Open weekdays 9–5:30. 5 rue de Chaillot: 16e, tel. 1/47–23–72–15. Métro: Iéna. Open weekdays 9–5.*

BUREAUX DE CHANGE

During business hours (9 or 10 AM to 5 or 6 PM) you can get good currency-exchange rates around the Opéra Garnier and the Champs-Elysées; just be sure you stop in at an official bank and not one of the bureaux de change, which keep longer hours but get away with worse rates. The bureaux at the train stations stay open until at least 8 PM, sometimes as late as 10 PM, and have slightly worse rates than banks. Rates are generally worse on the Left Bank than on the Right.

For late-night transactions, use one of the automatic cash exchange machines that are popping up all over. To use exchange machines you need cash—and relatively crisp cash at that—and the exchange rate is not that great, but at 3 AM, who cares? Locations of 24-hour exchange machines include **Crédit du Nord** (24 blvd. Sébastopol, 1er), **CCF** (115 av. des Champs-Elysées, 8e), and **BNP** (2 pl. de l'Opéra, 2e).

BUSINESS HOURS

Most museums are closed one day a week (usually Monday or Tuesday) and on national holidays (*see* When to Go, in Planning Your Trip, *above*). Normal opening times are from 9:30 to 5 or 6, occasionally with a long lunch break between noon and 2. Large stores stay open without a lunch break from 9 or 9:30 in the morning until 6 or 7 in the evening. Smaller shops often open an hour or so earlier and close a few hours later, with a lengthy lunch break in between. Banks are open weekdays (and sometimes Saturdays) roughly from 9:30 to 4:30. Most banks, but not all, take a one-hour or even a 90-minute lunch break.

DISCOUNT TRAVEL SHOPS

Several places offer discount plane tickets and other travel services for the cash-strapped voyager. The following agencies can get you cheaper rates than most commercial travel agencies, as well as student identification cards (ISICs): **Access Voyages:** *6 rue Pierre Lescot, 1er, tel. 1/40–13–02–02. Métro: Rambuteau. Open weekdays 9–7, Sat. 10–6.* **Council Travel:** *16 rue de Vaugirard, 6e, tel. 1/46–34–02–90. Métro: Luxembourg. Open weekdays 9:30–6:30, Sat. 10–5.* **Forum Voyages:** *140 rue du Faubourg St-Honoré, 8e, tel. 1/42–89–07–07. Métro: Franklin D. Roosevelt. Open weekdays 9:30–7, Sat. 10–1 and 2–5.* **Usit Voyages:** *6 rue Vaugirard, 6e, tel. 1/43–29–85–00. Métro: Odéon. Open weekdays 9:30–6, Sat. 1:30–5.*

Nouvelles Frontières. This is the place to go for discount airfares, including (at press time) a 1,890F round-trip ticket to New York. *Central office: 63 blvd. des Batignolles, 8e, tel. 1/43–87–99–88. Métro: Villiers. Open Mon.–Sat. 9–7, Thurs. until 8:30.*

Wasteels. This is the best-represented youth travel organization in town, with branches near most train stations. Here those under 26 can get 20% discounts on all train tickets beginning or terminating in France. *Addresses include: 113 blvd. St-Michel, 5e, tel. 43–26–25–25, Métro: Luxembourg; 5 rue de la Banque, 2e, tel. 42–61–53–21, Métro: Bourse.*

EMBASSIES AND CONSULATES

Australia. *4 rue Jean-Rey, 15e, tel. 1/40–59–33–00, 1/40–59–33–01 in emergencies. Métro: Bir-Hakeim. Open weekdays 9–5:30.*

Canada. *35 av. Montaigne, 8e, tel. 1/44–43–29–16. Métro: Franklin D. Roosevelt.*

New Zealand. *7 ter rue Léonard-de-Vinci, 16e, tel. 1/45–00–24–11. Métro: Victor Hugo. Open weekdays 9–1 and 2–5:30.*

United Kingdom. *35 rue du Faubourg St-Honoré, 8e, tel. 1/42–66–91–42. Métro: Madeleine. Open weekdays 9:30–1 and 2:30–6.*

United States. *2 rue St-Florentin, 1er, tel. 1/42–96–14–88. Métro: Concorde. Open weekdays 9–4.*

EMERGENCY NUMBERS

In an emergency, dial 17 for the **police,** 15 for an **ambulance,** and 18 for the **fire department.** For nonemergency situations, look in the phone directory for the number of the nearest *commissariat, prefecture,* or *gendarmerie,* all terms for the local police station; here you can report a theft or get the address of the local late-night pharmacies or pharmacist on call. **SOS Help** (tel. 1/47–23–80–80), open daily 3–11, is a hot line for Anglophones in Paris. The staff is friendly and provides practical information, emotional support, or help in a crisis.

ENGLISH-LANGUAGE BOOKS AND NEWSPAPERS

The Free Voice, a free monthly paper available at English-language bookstores, some restaurants, and the American Church (*see* Houses of Worship, in Resident Resources, *below*), provides an outlet for English-language comment upon Parisian life and lists upcoming events in the Anglophone community. English-language bookstores also carry the free *France-USA Contacts,* which has classified listings in English and French for apartment rentals, goods for sale, work exchange, etc. Most newsstands carry the *International Herald-Tribune,* as well as international versions of *Time* and *Newsweek.*

For 24-hour information on the week's cultural events (in English), call 1/49–52–53–56.

Pariscope (3F) has an English-language section called "Time Out" with recommendations for concerts, theater, movies, museum expositions, and even restaurant and bar picks. Their info is sometimes slow on the update, so cross-check with the French-language listings. For more information on English-language bookstores in Paris, *see* Chapter 6, Shopping.

FOREIGN TOURIST OFFICES

When long weekends leave you longing to get out of the country, foreign tourist offices can arrange visas and help plan trips. Most offices cluster around the Opéra Garnier and Madeleine and are open regular business hours. Here are a few: **Austria:** *47 av. de l'Opéra, 2e, tel. 1/47–42–78–57. Métro: Opéra.* **Belgium:** *21 blvd. des Capucines, 2e, tel. 1/47–42–41–18. Métro: Opéra.* **Finland:** *13 rue Auber, 9e, tel. 1/42–66–40–13. Métro: Auber.* **Greece:** *3 av. de l'Opéra, 1er, tel. 1/42–60–65–75. Métro: Palais Royal–Musée du Louvre.* **Italy:** *23 rue de la Paix, 2e, tel. 1/45–66–66–68. Métro: Opéra.* **Morocco:** *161 rue St-Honoré, 1er, tel. 1/42–60–63–50. Métro: Palais Royal–Musée du Louvre.* **Netherlands:** *31 av. des Champs-Elysées, 8e, tel. 1/42–25–41–25. Métro: Franklin D. Roosevelt.* **Norway:** *88 av. Charles-de-Gaulle, 92200 Neuilly-sur-Seine, tel. 1/46–41–48–00. Métro: Les Sablons.* **Poland:** *49 av. de l'Opéra, 2e, tel. 1/47–42–07–42. Métro: Opéra.* **Portugal:** *7 rue Scribe, 9e, tel. 1/47–42–55–57. Métro: Opéra.* **Spain:** *43 ter av. Pierre-1er de Serbie, 17e, tel. 1/47–20–90–54. Métro: Iéna.* **Sweden:** *146 av. des Champs-Elysées, 8e, no phone. Métro: George V.* **Switzerland:** *11 bis rue Scribe, 9e, tel. 1/47–42–45–45. Métro: Opéra.* **Turkey:** *102 av. des Champs-Elysées, 8e, tel. 1/45–62–78–68. Métro: George V.* **United Kingdom:** *19 rue des Mathurins, 9e, tel. 1/44–51–56–22. Métro: Havre Caumartin.*

LOST-AND-FOUND

The entire city shares one lost-and-found office, the **Service des Objets Trouvés.** They won't give information over the telephone; you have to trek over to see if you can find your grubby backpack among the Louis Vuitton bags. *36 rue des Morillons, 15e, tel. 1/45–31–14–80. Métro: Convention. Open weekdays 8:30–5, Tues. and Thurs. until 8.*

MAIL

Airmail letters and postcards to the United States and Canada cost 4F30 for 20 grams. Letters to the United Kingdom cost 2F80. Postcards sent to most European countries cost 2F80, 5F10 to Australia and New Zealand. Buy stamps in post offices if you really like standing in line. Otherwise, buy them at one of the ubiquitous *tabacs* (tobacco shops). Mail your postcards of the Eiffel Tower early; mail takes about seven days to make its way from France to the United States, about half that to get to Britain, and 10 days to two weeks to get to Australia.

You can identify post offices by the yellow signs with blue letters that say LA POSTE. Mailboxes are yellow, with one slot for letters to Paris and one for AUTRES DESTINATIONS (everywhere else).

The **Hôtel des Postes** (central post office) is open 24 hours for limited services—you can send packages or buy stamps any time, day or night. During extended hours the office offers mail, telephone, telegram, Minitel (*see* Phones, *below*), photocopy, and poste restante services. During regular business hours (weekdays 8–7, Saturday 8–noon) you can also use the fax machines and exchange money. All post offices in Paris accept poste restante mail, but this is where your mail will end up if it is just addressed to you, "Poste Restante, Paris." Bring your passport with you to pick it up. *52 rue du Louvre, at rue Etienne-Marcel, 1er, tel. 1/40–28–20–00. Métro: Sentier.*

The post office near the rond point des Champs-Elysées (a major intersection on the avenue) has extended hours for mail, telegram, and telephone service. *71 av. des Champs-Elysées, 8e, tel. 1/44–13–66–00. Métro: Franklin D. Roosevelt. Open Mon.–Sat. 8 AM–10 PM, Sun. 10–8.*

RECEIVING MAIL American Express (tel. 800/543–4080 for a list of foreign offices) will hold mail gratis for cardholders, about 5F per pickup for the rest of the world, at any of their Paris offices (*see above*). Local post offices also hold mail that is marked POSTE RESTANTE. Have your pen pals address your letter with your last name first, in capital letters, and make sure they include the postal code.

MEDICAL AID

HOSPITALS AND CLINICS The **Hôpital Américain** (American Hospital), about a 45-minute trip outside Paris, operates a 24-hour emergency service, and, just like American hospitals, is very expensive. A consultation with a doctor costs 500F. If you're American and lucky enough to have Blue Cross/Blue Shield (carry your card with you), they should cover the cost at the time of your visit. Otherwise, you have to pay up front and hope to be reimbursed by your insurance company when you return to the States. EU citizens also have to pay first but can be reimbursed while still in France if they have form E-111, available at some of the bigger post offices. *63 blvd. Victor-Hugo, Neuilly-sur-Seine, tel. 1/46–41–25–25. Take Métro to Pont de Neuilly, then follow blvd. du Château 15 min.*

The **Hôpital Anglais** (English Hospital) in Levallois, again about 45 minutes outside Paris, has 24-hour emergency service and two British doctors on duty. A general consultation costs 90F; a consultation with a specialist costs 140F. Here again, Americans have to pay up front and get reimbursed at home; EU citizens pay up front and can be reimbursed through form E-111. Be warned that most of the staff speaks no English. *3 rue Barbès, Levallois, tel. 1/46–39–22–22. Métro: Anatole-France.*

Centre de Soins MST (Center for Sexually Transmitted Diseases) provides free consultations on a drop-in basis, weekdays 5–7 PM. Although the staff speaks some English, flip through your dictionary before you come in to prevent hazardous misunderstandings. *At Institut A. Fournier, 25 blvd. St-Jacques, 14e, tel. 1/40–78–26–00. Métro: St-Jacques.*

EMERGENCY HOT LINES Hot lines to a dentist (**SOS Dentaire,** tel. 1/43–37–51–00), a rape crisis center (**SOS Viol,** tel. 1/05–05–95–95), and a poison center (**Centre Anti-Poison,** tel. 1/40–37–04–04) are available for emergencies. There are no doctors on call at English-speaking **SOS Help** (tel. 47–23–80–80), but from 3 PM to 11 PM they'll help you with medical referrals.

PHARMACIES Besides basic over-the-counter medication, pharmacies (identifiable by green neon crosses) provide all sorts of useful health and beauty aids. Certain *pharmacies homéopathiques* specialize in herbal (homeopathic) medicines. While regular pharmacy hours are about 9 AM to 7 or 8 PM, **Pharmacie Dhéry** (84 av. des Champs-Elysées, 8e, tel. 1/45–62–02–41) is open 24 hours, and **Drugstore Publicis** (149 blvd. St-Germain, at rue de Rennes, 6e, tel. 1/42–22–92–50) is open daily until 2 AM.

PHONES

Public phones are never far away in Paris; you will find them at post offices and often in cafés. All French phone numbers have eight digits; to call *from* Paris *to* any place in the country outside Paris, you need to dial an area code (16) before the number. When calling to Paris or the Ile de France from anywhere else, you dial 1, then the eight-digit number.

LOCAL CALLS Local calls cost a minimum of 1 franc for six minutes. Almost all French phones nowadays accept only the *télécarte,* a handy little card you can buy at tabacs, post offices, or Métro stations; it costs 40F for 50 units or 90F for 120 units. The digital display on the phone counts down your units while you're talking and tells you how many you have left when you hang up. The occasional old-fashioned phone will take 50-centime, 1F, 2F, and 5F coins but won't make change.

You can find local phone directories in all post offices; some now also have directories on the computerized service Minitel. For local and national directory assistance, dial 12 on any phone.

INTERNATIONAL CALLS To dial direct to another country, dial 19 + the country code (61 for Australia, 64 for New Zealand, 44 for the United Kingdom, and 1 for the United States and Canada) plus the area code and number. The cheapest time to call is between 10:30 PM and 6 AM (about 6F per minute to the States, 3F per minute to Britain). Middling rates apply from 6 to 8 AM and 9:30 to 10:30 PM; rates are reduced all day Sunday and holidays. Calling anywhere over 100 kilometers (60 miles) from France in the middle of a weekday will run you around 75 centimes per 19 seconds. If you're calling direct from a pay phone, *this* is where that télécarte might come in handy, although you could eat up your entire card in five minutes if you call in the middle of the day. To use an AT&T calling card or to talk to AT&T's international operators, dial 19–00–11. For MCI, dial 19–00–19; for Sprint, dial 19–00–87. Within France, you can call collect by dialing 12 for the operator and saying "*en PCV*" ("on pay say vay").

Resident Resources

ACADEMIC AND CULTURAL RESOURCES

AMERICAN CENTER After 50 years at the same spot on boulevard Raspail (where the Fondation Cartier now stands), the American Center moved in 1994 to a spiffy new Frank Ghery–designed building way out in Bercy. While the new home has added a higher profile, the center seems to be going through growing pains—it doesn't really *do* anything yet. There are several galleries, a cinema, and a theater, in addition to plans for a bookstore, a café, and a restaurant, but no library or services are in place yet. They promise things will soon change for the better. *51 rue Bercy, 12e, tel. 1/44–73–77–00. Métro: Bercy. Wheelchair access.*

AMERICAN LIBRARY Here you'll find the largest collection of English-language books in Paris, with over 80,000 volumes. Anyone can use it, as long as they're willing to pay 60F for a single day's admittance—so much for free public libraries. If you actually want to take books out, you have to sign up for the year, for 550F (440F if you're a student). A summer subscription, good June through August, costs 220F. Membership also gets you into the smaller collection at the American University in Paris. *10 rue du Général-Camou, 7e, tel. 1/45–51–46–82. Métro: Ecole Militaire. Open Tues.–Sat. 10–7; shorter hrs in Aug.*

BIBLIOTHEQUE FORNEY Housed in the beautiful Hôtel de Sens is the best collection of art and architecture materials in Paris. The *hôtel particulier* (mansion) recently received a major face-lift, and the beautiful sculpted stone and wood-paneled reading rooms were restored. The extensive collection of books and periodicals, in both French and English, are accessible to all, but to check out materials you need a picture ID and proof that you are a Paris resident of at least three months. *1 rue du Figuier, 4e, tel. 1/42–78–14–60. Métro: Pont-Marie or St-Paul. Open Tues.–Fri. 1:30–8:30, Sat. 10–8:30.*

BIBLIOTHEQUE NATIONALE DE FRANCE A seat in this megalibrary's splendid 19th-century reading room is by far the most coveted study space in all of France. The intelligentsia of the world vie for access to what is considered to be the largest library collection ever: 10 million books, 1.5 million photographs, 1.5 million music manuscripts, 1.1 million discs and videos, 650,000 maps, 350,000 manuscripts, and 350,000 periodicals—and this doesn't even count the collections in the satellite libraries and what's in storage in Versailles. The collection won't be fully on-line until the library moves across the Seine to the new Grande Bibliothèque de France (*see below*). Access is open to citizens of all nations, provided that they present a letter of accreditation from their university stating that they are either a professor or a graduate student in their third year of a Ph.D. program. Nonacademics are allowed to peek in and look around. *58 rue Richelieu, 2e, tel. 1/47–06–30–00. Métro: Bourse. Main reading room open daily 10–6.*

BIBLIOTHEQUE STE-GENEVIEVE Founded when the library of the now-demolished Eglise Ste-Geneviève was nationalized during the Revolution, the Bibliothèque Ste-Geneviève sports a collection spanning all disciplines, with an emphasis on 19th- and 20th-century documents. The library is a popular studying place for students from the neighboring universities and is open to students from any university (even non-French); for a library card, bring a passport-size photo, a student ID, and a phone bill or other proof that you're a Paris resident of at least three months. If you're lacking any of these items, a day pass can provide you with limited access. Both cards only gain admittance to the study hall—there is no borrowing. *10 pl. du Panthéon, 5e, tel. 1/43–29–61–00. Métro: Maubert-Mutualité. Open Mon.–Sat. 10–10; closed Aug. 1–15.*

CENTRE DE DOCUMENTATION JUIVE CONTEMPORAINE Above the Memorial du Martyr Juif Inconnu, this center is far and away the best resource for Jewish studies in town. The small but dense library has Jewish history and philosophy works in any language you could possibly want, with the bulk in French, English, and Hebrew. They also have a spectacular back collection of periodicals, and the staff is wonderful about helping you find articles or books on any subject. Technically, there's a 30F fee per day or 150F (80F students) annual membership, but if you just want to use it for a short time they're usually pretty lax about collecting. *17 rue Geoffroy-l'Asnier, 4e, tel. 1/42–77–44–72. Métro: Pont-Marie or St-Paul. Open Mon.–Thurs. 2–5:30.*

CENTRE GEORGES POMPIDOU The Pompidou is like a kingdom of city-states warring amicably: In addition to housing the **Musée National d'Art Moderne (MNAM)** (*see* Major Museums, in Chapter 2), the Centre hosts services that fall under the control of the **Centre des Créations Industriel (CCI),** a contemporary architecture, urban planning, and design institute; the **Bibliothèque Publique d'Informations (BPI),** a very popular library; and the **Institut de Recherche et Coordination de l'Acoustique et la Musique (IRCAM),** sponsoring musical programs. All of these organizations are devoted to the President Pompidou–stated goal of allowing people to experience tons of art and culture all within a single building.

The CCI has domain over two galleries on the mezzanine, both of which have rapidly changing temporary exhibits, usually free of charge. The CCI also sponsors speeches and discussions, usually in association with the IRCAM.

The BPI, on the ground, first, second, and third floors, is about as exciting as a library can be: several huge open floors filled to capacity with books and quiet people doing mind-expanding stuff. It's open to the public; no identification is needed to access the 3,000 periodicals (including foreign presses), 14,000 records and CDs (with listening stations), 2,000 films on video (with monitors), and 400,000 books (many in English). The BPI has an extensive CD-ROM library, with over 150,000 images catalogued to date, all of which must be used on the premises. Over 13,000 people use the place daily (it was designed to handle 1,500), and

Reading, Writing, and a Royal Library

The Bibliothèque Nationale de France traces its start to 1368, when Charles V first founded a library in the Louvre. François I expanded the collection in 1537 when he decreed that all publishers must send him a copy of every book they published—this not only brought in more books, but it allowed the king to keep a close eye on what was being written. When the library of the cloisters at St-Germain-des-Prés was nationalized during the Revolution, its books became part of the same massive collection. The block-long complex of buildings now housing it all has a soaring iron-and-glass, nine-domed main reading room designed by Henri Labrouste in 1863 and draws as many architectural admirers as scholars.

there's often a line to get in. The worst part about the library is the policy of no staff reshelving during the day, so if you come in the evening you could have a hell of a time finding what you need. *Tel. 1/44–78–44–83.*

The first floor of the BPI holds the **Salle Jorge Luis Borges,** a room named after the famous Argentine writer and designed especially for use by the visually impaired. The room is staffed by volunteers and open only by appointment; call Monday, Tuesday, Thursday, or Friday to set something up. *Tel. 1/44–78–44–83 or 1/44–78–60–98.*

You're most likely to encounter the **IRCAM** through performances at its multipurpose performance hall, located under the adjacent place Igor Stravinsky. This hall hosts all kinds of performance art events (*see* Performing Arts, in Chapter 5), as well as lectures, philosophy seminars, and debates. The organization also operates its own tiny performance-art–related library. *31 rue St-Merri, on pl. Igor Stravinsky, 4e, tel. 1/42–17–12–33. Open Mon.–Thurs. 9:30–1 and 2–6, Fri. 9:30–1 and 2–5; library open Mon. and Wed.–Fri. 2–6. Tickets for events at the ticket counter on the ground floor of the Centre.*

GRANDE BIBLIOTHÈQUE DE FRANCE Set to open in March 1995 as the new home to the Bibliothèque Nationale's world-renowned collection, this 5.2-billion-franc monument to Mitterrand, Le Corbusier's urban ideals, and (hopefully) learning is the latest installment of Paris's *grands projets.* The massive library—its 395 kilometers (245 miles) of shelves are supposed to make it the largest in the world—is a tribute to urban renewal. Four buildings designed to look like huge books standing open will enclose a vast rectangular park. All administrative and circulation activities will take place in quarters under the park, while the books will be stored in the towers. The buildings were constructed almost entirely of clear glass until architect Dominique Perrault realized that the sun would damage the books; the windows were being tinted at press time. *Quai de la Gare, 13e. Métro: Quai de la Gare.*

INSTITUT DU MONDE ARABE This institute has quickly become the center of Arabic studies in all of France. Its library has 50,000 volumes and 1,000 periodicals in Arabic, French, and English. The stacks and reading room are open to the public, but only a small number of volumes can be checked out, and a library card costs 250F (students 150F) for one year. The audiovisual center has a collection of 15,000 images. More than anything, the institute acts as a meeting place for those interested in Arabic studies; the café and terrace on the ninth floor are the main gathering spots. There's also a museum of Arabic artifacts that organizes blockbuster temporary exhibits (*see* Not-So-Major Museums, in Chapter 2). *1 rue Fossés-St-Bernard, 5e, tel. 1/40–51–38–38. Métro: Jussieu or Cardinal Lemoine. Open Tues.–Sat. 1–8. Wheelchair access.*

INSTITUT FRANCAIS D'ARCHITECTURE The small library of this institute has a decrepit reading room with a decent number of books and periodicals on architecture, urban planning, and design, including a section in English. *6 rue de Tournon, 6e, tel. 1/46–33–90–36. Métro: Odéon. Open weekdays 1:15–5:15.*

PAVILLON DE L'ARSENAL The library of the Centre d'Urbanisme et d'Architecture de la Ville de Paris (*see* Not-So-Major Museums, in Chapter 2) has a fine collection of French- and English-language books and periodicals, but its collection of 70,000 photographs and images of Paris is truly spectacular. The modern steel-and-exposed-conduit renovation of the old arsenal makes for a nice study space. *21 blvd. Morland, 4e, tel. 1/42–76–33–97. Métro: Sully-Morland. Open Tues.–Sat. 2–6.*

MEDIA

NEWSPAPERS AND MAGAZINES The French press has taken a beating in the last several years, with newspapers and magazines going out of business at an alarming rate. The following are a few of the more popular choices.

Le Monde is an eminently respectable centrist daily with good arts and books supplements. Famous philosophers often write difficult articles—sometimes stridently nationalist—for the front page. The Paris daily *Le Figaro* has been around since 1866. It leans to the right a little more than the others, and its business section is very reputable. Jean-Paul Sartre was the first editor of *Libération,* a witty, slangy weekly paper that is one of the best and most accessible. The slant is to the left but is becoming less so. Looking for something a little further to the left? Affiliated with the French Communist Party, *L'Humanité* is still running, though with a little ideological confusion. You have to be *very* up on your French slang to understand the satirical weekly *Le Canard Enchaîné,* which has funny cartoons and investigates the latest political scandals with biting humor.

Weekly magazines include the extremely popular *Le Nouvel Observateur,* with middle-of-the-road articles on politics à la *Time* or *Newsweek. L'Evenement de Jeudi* also tackles politics but specializes in random amusing articles on topics like "The Ten Smallest Countries in the World." *L'Express* is less fun and more businesslike and conservative, and *Le Point* tends to lean even a little more to the right than *L'Express.* For those dying for celebrity gossip and scandal, check out *Paris-Match,* where you can read more stories about various royal families than you thought possible. *L'Equipe* is a comprehensive magazine for sports buffs.

RADIO France has an enormous array of stations. Some to check out are **Fréquance Gaie** (94.4), aimed at the gay community; **Fréquence Juive** (94.8), for Jewish listeners; and **France Maghreb** (94.2), targeting Paris's North African community.

Africa No. 1: 107.5. This station is generally upbeat, playing mostly West and Saharan African tunes with few interruptions. *Tel. 1/45–74–83–83.*

FIP: 105.1. Not for those who cling to stability, this station spins an arbitrary mix of classical, contemporary French favorites, and jazz. They're short on commentary but will usually tell you what you're listening to. *Tel. 1/42–20–12–34.*

France Musique: 91.7 and 92.1. This classical station usually oscillates between Rossini melodies and Schoenberg dissonance but also gives air time to non-Western classical music. Artists performing in Paris often come by for a chat and an occasional studio performance. *Tel. 1/42–30–18–18.*

M40: 105.9. In the wee hours of the morning (around 4:30), this mainstream station actually counts down *Billboard's* weekly Top 40. *Tel. 1/40–39–09–09.*

Radio Nova: 101.5. A cool mix of traditional and contemporary jazz makes this the favorite of many a Parisian jazz buff. *Tel. 1/43–46–88–80.*

HOUSES OF WORSHIP

English speakers profit from the incredible number of Anglophone residents and services in Paris. It may be a Catholic country, but nearly all major religions can find English-language services.

American Cathedral of the Holy Trinity. Episcopalian-Anglican. *23 av. George V, 8e, tel. 1/47–20–17–92. Métro: George V or Alma-Marceau. Holy Eucharist Sun. at 9 and 11, weekdays at noon.*

American Church in Paris. Interdenominational Protestant. *65 quai d'Orsay, 7e, tel. 1/47–05–07–99. Métro: Invalides or Alma-Marceau. Sun. adult church school at 10, worship service at 11.*

Christian Science Church. *36 blvd. St-Jacques, 14e, tel. 1/47–07–26–60. Métro: St-Jacques.*

Church of Jesus-Christ of Latter-Day Saints. Call to find out about meetings, which take place in chapels at Porte des Lilas, Clichy, and Malakoff. *23 rue du Onze Novembre, 78110 Le Vessinet, tel. 1/39–76–55–88.*

Great Synagogue. Synagogue and offices of the Consistoire Israëlite de Paris, where you can get information on the Jewish community in Paris. Services in Hebrew. *44 rue de la Victoire, 9e, tel. 1/45–26–90–15. Métro: Le Peletier.*

International Baptist Fellowship. *123 av. du Maine, 14e, tel. 1/47–49–15–29. Métro: Gaîté.*

Liberal Synagogue. Services in Hebrew. *24 rue Copernic, 16e, tel. 1/47–04–37–27. Métro: Victor Hugo.*

Quaker Society of Friends. *114 bis rue de Vaugirard, 6e, tel. 1/45–48–74–23. Métro: Montparnasse or St-Placide. Sun. Bible sharing 10 AM, worship 11 AM, noon lunch.*

St. Joseph's Church. Roman Catholic. *50 av. Hoche, 8e, tel. 1/42–27–28–56. Métro: Charles de Gaulle–Etoile. Eucharist weekdays 8:30 AM; Sat. 11 AM and 6:30 PM; Sun. 10, noon, and 6:30.*

The Scots Kirk. Church of Scotland–Presbyterian. *17 rue Bayard, 8e, tel. 1/48–78–47–94. Métro: Franklin D. Roosevelt. Morning service Sun. 10:30.*

Unitarian Universalist Fellowship of Paris. *1 rue de l'Oratoire, 1er, tel. 1/42–78–82–58. Métro: Louvre-Rivoli.*

EXPLORING PARIS 2

By Baty Landis and Oliver Schwaner-Albright

Home to a huge number of the paintings and sculptures you studied in art history, and former home to half the authors you read in Western Civ class, Paris could take you two lifetimes to explore from top to bottom—and that's not counting the Louvre. If you have only a few days or weeks in the city, strategy is key. The Métro system is extremely efficient and will aid those of you engaged in the see-and-flee mode of sightseeing, though moving around on the bus or, better yet, your feet is much better if you want to get a real feel for the city. The center of town is quite walkable, and Parisian street life—its glamour, its leisurely pace, its little piles of doggie doo—is an important element of any visit. The following are some efficient walks in the center of Paris:

• Along the Seine between the Eiffel Tower and Cathédrale Notre-Dame. You'll see the Trocadéro, the Louvre, the Musée d'Orsay, the Ile de la Cité, and the Ile St-Louis. Travel time: one hour, double that at night when you have someone sexy on your arm.

• The Louvre to the Arc de Triomphe. Majestic with a capital *M,* this walk hits many vestiges of aristocratic Paris, including the Jardin des Tuileries, the place de la Concorde, and the Champs-Elysées.

• The Louvre to the Panthéon. Cross Pont Neuf, walk through place Dauphine toward Notre-Dame, cross the bridge at the west of place Parvis, and follow rue St-Jacques and you'll see the Ile de la Cité and some of the crowded little streets of the Latin Quarter.

With luck you'll have time for a little aimless wandering as well; the Marais, Montmartre, the Bastille, Belleville, the Quartier Latin, and St-Germain (*see* Neighborhoods, *below*) will all treat you well if you get lost in their streets. Another priceless experience is to take walks late at night or early in the morning. Afterwards you'll probably become one of those people who raves about how nothing compares to the beauty of Paris—as if we didn't know.

Paris's many sights are arranged according to category in the following pages, so you'll find Notre-Dame under Houses of Worship, Père Lachaise under Dead Folk, the Institut du Monde Arabe under World Cultures in the Not-So-Major Museums section, the Jardin du Luxembourg under Parks and Gardens, etc. Maps of individual neighborhoods appear in the neighborhoods section at the end of the chapter.

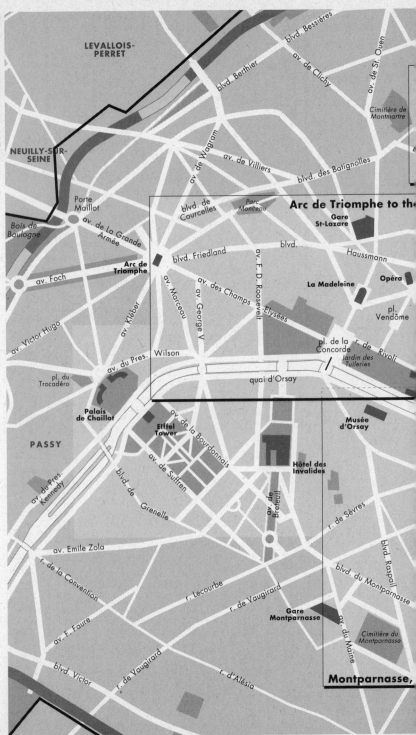

LEVALLOIS-
PERRET

blvd. Bessières

av. de St. Ouen

av. de Clichy

blvd. Berthier

Cimitière de
Montmartre

NEUILLY-SUR-
SEINE

av. de Wagram

av. de Villiers

blvd. des Batignolles

Porte
Maillot

Bois de
Boulogne

av. de La Grande
Armée

blvd. de
Courcelles

Parc
Monceau

Arc de Triomphe to the

Gare
St-Lazare

blvd. Friedland

blvd.

Haussmann

av. F. D. Roosevelt

Arc de
Triomphe

av. Foch

La Madeleine

Opéra

av. Marceau

av. des Champs

pl.
Vendôme

av. Kléber

av. George V

-Elysées

av. Victor Hugo

pl. de la
Concorde

r. de Rivoli

Jardin des
Tuileries

av. du Pres.

Wilson

pl. du
Trocadéro

quai d'Orsay

Palais
de Chaillot

av. de la Bourdonnais

Musée
d'Orsay

Eiffel
Tower

PASSY

av. de Suffren

Hôtel des
Invalides

av. du Pres.
Kennedy

blvd. de
Grenelle

av. de
Breteuil

r. de Sèvres

av. Emile Zola

r. de la Convention

r. Lecourbe

r. de Vaugirard

blvd. du Montparnasse

blvd. Raspail

av. F. Faure

Gare
Montparnasse

av. du Maine

Cimitière du
Montparnasse

blvd. Victor

r. de Vaugirard

r. d'Alésia

Montparnasse,

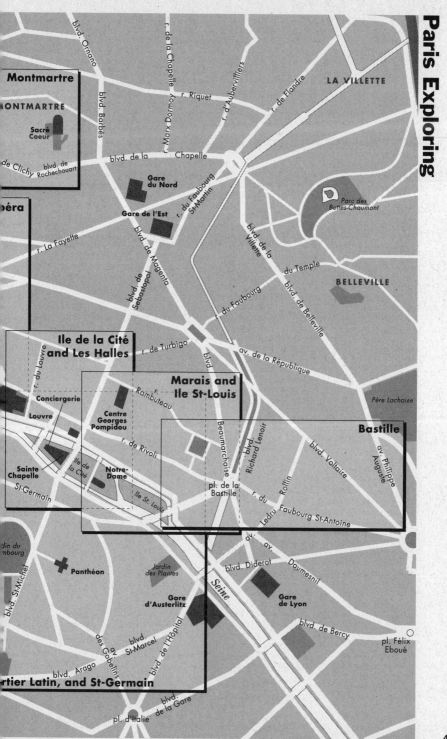

Montmartre

MONTMARTRE

Sacré
Coeur

blvd. Ornano

r. de la Chapelle

r. Riquet

r. Max Dormoy

r. d'Aubervilliers

r. de Flandre

LA VILLETTE

blvd. Barbès

de Clichy

blvd. de
Rochechouart

blvd. de la   Chapelle

Gare
du Nord

r. du Faubourg St-Martin

Parc des
Buttes-Chaumont

péra

r. La Fayette

Gare de l'Est

blvd. de Magenta

blvd. de
la Villette

du Temple

BELLEVILLE

blvd. de
Sebastopol

du Faubourg

blvd. de Belleville

**Ile de la Cité
and Les Halles**

r. de Turbigo

av. de la République

r. du Louvre

r. Rambuteau

**Marais and
Ile St-Louis**

Père Lachaise

Conciergerie

Centre
Georges
Pompidou

r. de Rivoli

Beaumarchaise

blvd. Richard Lenoir

blvd. Voltaire

Bastille

av. Philippe Auguste

Louvre

Sainte
Chapelle

Ile de
la Cité

Notre-
Dame

Ile St. Louis

pl. de la
Bastille

r. du

Rollin

Ledru

Faubourg St-Antoine

St-Germain

din du
nbourg

blvd. St-Michel

Panthéon

Jardin
des Plantes

blvd. Diderot

Daumesnil

av.

av.

Seine

Gare
d'Austerlitz

Gare
de Lyon

des Gobelins

blvd.
St-Marcel

blvd. de l'Hôpital

blvd. de Bercy

pl. Félix
Eboué

blvd. Arago

rtier Latin, and St-Germain

blvd.
de la Gare

pl. d'Italie

Monuments

ARC DE TRIOMPHE

Never one renowned for subtlety or modesty, Napoléon I, celebrating his successful battles of 1805–1806, commissioned the architect Jean-François Chalgrin to design a permanent monument to his military prowess. Definite plans weren't accepted until 1809, and when Marie-Louise of Austria arrived in 1810 to marry the little man, only the foundation had been completed. No problem—he simply had a full-size wooden mock arch set up, disguised by trompe-l'oeil canvas. In 1815, when Napoléon met his Waterloo, the Arc de Triomphe was still only half finished, but Louis-Philippe completed it in 1836. Although the plaque on it now calls the arch simply a "tribute to the French military," the names of Napoléon's 128 victorious battles and 660 generals are inscribed on the inner faces.

Joseph Sigisbert Hugo was apparently the only one of Napoléon's generals left off the list of names etched into the Arc de Triomphe; son Victor avenged the omission by writing poetry that attacked the arch and immortalized his father's name.

Napoléon's coffin was rolled under the Arc de Triomphe in 1840, inaugurating the arch as a site for public ceremonies. Victor Hugo's remains rested underneath for a night before being moved to the Panthéon. In 1919, the triumphal parade marking the end of the war passed below, and in 1920, the Unknown Soldier was buried here; an eternal flame, relit each evening, has watched over him ever since. Hitler strode through the arch in 1940 to encounter a largely deserted Paris; four years later Charles de Gaulle victoriously followed the same route, this time met by thousands of jubilant Parisians.

The Arc de Triomphe remains the largest triumphal arch in the world and is an impressive example of the era's classicism. The sculpture surrounding it includes François Rude's famous *La Marseillaise,* depicting the uprising of 1792. Climb the 50-meter (164-foot) arch for one of the better views of Paris, highlighting the city's unmistakable design. Radiating out from the arch are 12 avenues (increased from the original five by city planner extraordinaire Baron Haussmann—*see box, below*); gaze along the precise lines to La Défense, down the Champs-Elysées to place de la Concorde and on to the Louvre. And you're in the middle of it all. *Pl. Charles de Gaulle–Etoile, intersection of 8e, 16e, and 17e, tel. 1/43–80–31–31. Métro: Charles de Gaulle–Etoile. Admission: 31F, 20F students. Open Apr.–Sept., daily 9:30–6, Fri. until 10; Oct.–Mar., daily 10–5:30.*

EIFFEL TOWER

The first time you surface from the Métro in Paris, you may wonder, "So where is it?" You kind of expect it to greet you no matter where you are in the city, a constant reminder of everything Parisian—grandeur and artifice, a perfect combination of steel and air arching to an impossible height. But you don't see it from the airport, you don't see it from the train station, and you don't even see it from the center of the city (if you see it from your hotel, you've bought the wrong guidebook), and maybe you begin to wonder if your idea of Paris is based on a mirage or a myth . . .

In fact, your idea of Paris is based on an antenna. In 1885, the city held a contest to design a 300-meter (984-foot) tower for the 1889 World Exposition. Competing with proposals for a monster sprinkler and a giant commemorative guillotine, Gustave Eiffel, already well known for his iron works, won the contest with his seemingly functionless tower, which was slated for the junkyard even as it was being built. Somewhere along the way, however, people realized it might actually have a practical use or two, and it was saved; it has gone on to help decipher German radio codes during World War I, capture Mata Hari, measure atmospheric pressure, and act as the chosen place of suicide for over 350 people. To top it all off, artists and sensitive hearts have had a ball painting, singing about, writing to, and philosophizing about the tower that has come to symbolize Paris.

The close-up view of the tower—a 10,000-ton dark metal structure that somehow remains graceful and unthreatening—is considerably more striking than that from across town. When you venture a glance down from the top and your stomach drops, remember that this was the world's tallest building until New York's Chrysler Building took over that title in 1930. Nowadays, it's simply a source of wonder for legions of visitors, especially at night when it's entirely lit up. The hour-long lines to ascend the tower in summer are decidedly less wonderful; to avoid them, try visiting early in the morning or late at night, though the best view is on a clear day an hour before sunset, when visibility from the top extends 90 kilometers (56 miles). To save money and get some exercise, walk up to the second level and take the elevator from there to the top. *Champ de Mars, 7e, tel. 1/45–55–91–11. Métro: Bir-Hakeim. RER: Champ-de-Mars. Admission (elevator): 20F to 1st level, 36F to 2nd level, 53F to top. Admission (stairs): 12F to 2nd level. Open 9 AM–11 PM.*

Just across the Pont d'Iéna bridge from the Eiffel Tower is the **Trocadéro** plaza, home to gardens, spectacular fountains, and the Palais de Chaillot museum complex. The view of the Eiffel Tower from here is unsurpassed, especially when the fountains are shooting up and framing it. During the day and into the evening in summer, performers, vendors, skateboarders, and tourists all gather around the plaza and do their thing. Some even visit the museums.

HOTEL DES INVALIDES

Built by the warmongering Louis XIV in 1674 to house soldiers wounded during his various military campaigns, the Hôtel des Invalides now houses more recently wounded soldiers, as well as a huge military museum and a pair of churches. The free digs must have come as a mixed blessing to the 4,000 veterans who lived here under Louis: Although they had what was essentially a small town within the elaborate and admittedly beautiful complex, their lives were still run by the military, and they were watched over by captains who supervised daily work in artisanal studios.

City Planner Baron Haussmann Put Paris Before the People

When Napoléon III wasn't out waging war with Bismarck, he was turning Paris inside out. An Anglophile, he had visited London and fallen in love with its orderly parks and wide boulevards. Wanting to create a capital city for which he would be remembered and revered, Napoléon set out to turn Paris's narrow, winding medieval streets into grand boulevards—with a bit of help from Baron George-Eugène Haussmann, his formidable city planner, who shared his love of imperial order.

From 1853 to 1870, Paris was one huge construction site. Haussmann created a system of "places rayonnantes" (roundabouts) from which a total of 36 wide boulevards radiated. The roundabouts aided traffic circulation, and the boulevards aided the police in the suppression of worker revolts. New buildings lined the boulevards in a monotonous, imperious style (good examples are on avenue de l'Opéra); English-style parks were created; and Paris's urban space was forever transformed into what you see today.

Unfortunately, it wasn't all spacious avenues and gardens. Most of the working-class people who had lived in the city center were forced to move to the outskirts—in large part because the city's new ethic of efficiency and grandeur didn't have a lot of space, literally or figuratively, for the people who worked there.

The **Musée de l'Armée** studies the evolution of weaponry and warfare, though the collection of fancy canons in the (free) central courtyard may be enough. A temporary exhibit celebrating the 50th anniversary of the liberation of Paris, on display until mid-1995, focuses on the "flame of the French underground movement" rather than the folks who actually did the liberating. Admission to the museum also buys a visit to the tomb of Napoléon Bonaparte, housed in the **Eglise du Dôme.** Here the little megalomaniac lies ensconced in five coffins, one inside the next, to keep him nice and cozy. The church backs up to its twin, the **Soldiers' Church,** where mass is still held for current Invalides residents. *Esplanade des Invalides, 7e, tel. 1/44–42–37–67. Métro: Latour-Maubourg or Varenne. RER: Invalides. Admission (valid for 2 days): 34F, 24F students under 30. Open Apr.–Sept., daily 10–6; Oct.–Mar., daily 10–5.*

Houses of Worship

BASILIQUE DU SACRE-COEUR

Since 1885, someone has been continually on duty praying for the sins of the citizens participating in the Paris Commune of 1871 (*see Paris Commune box, below*), and they've been doing it in this horrific white concoction dreamt up by overzealous Catholics specifically to "expiate the sins" of the Communards. The structure, built between 1875 and 1914, is Romanesque-Byzantine in style and is so white because the stones (taken from Château-Landon, southeast of Paris) secrete calcite when wet: The more it rains, the more Sacré-Coeur gleams. The architectural plans of Paul Abadie met with criticism even before construction, and Montmartrois continue to bemoan the basilica's design and placement at the top of the hill, though tourists have for some reason made it the most popular postcard subject in Paris. The interior is uninspired at best and gaudy at worst, though the red-toned stained glass can give off a fiery glow in the evening. The 15F view from the 112-meter (370-foot) bell tower gives a good view of the city, but you can get the same view for free from the front of the basilica. *35 rue du Chevalier-de-la-Barre, tel. 1/42–51–17–02. Métro: Anvers. Basilica open daily 6:45 AM–11 PM. Tower open summer, daily 9–7; winter, daily 9–6.*

CATHEDRALE DE NOTRE-DAME

For centuries Notre-Dame has watched Paris go through all sorts of phases, riding out periods of neglect and hostility like a patient parent. Such patience is not without its payoffs, and today Notre-Dame is one of the best-known houses of worship in the world. Unfortunately, its current condition gives us barely an idea of its previous states: During the Gothic era, the fashion was to cover everything in bright paint, so the statuary on the facade was colorful and highlighted by a gilded background. The now-colorless portals are still fantastic, depicting (from left to right) the Virgin (to whose glory the cathedral is dedicated), the Last Judgment, and Ste-Anne, Mary's mother. Above is a row of 28 kings of Judah and Israel, all of whom lost their heads during the Revolution, when the cathedral became the Temple of Reason. Once all the fuss had died down, the great architect Viollet-le-Duc rolled up his sleeves and took on serious restoration, including replacing the kings' heads. Turns out, some Royalist had stashed the originals away in his basement; they were discovered a couple decades ago and are on display in the Musée de Cluny (*see* Art and More Art, in Not-So-Major Museums, *below*).

The interior of Notre-Dame is vast and hollow; again, we are missing out on the original idea. Before the Revolution, rich tapestries and paintings adorned the interior, diminishing the tomblike aura of today. Even the stained-glass windows have changed: In the 18th century, the originals were removed to let in more light! The gray windows that replaced them were then replaced this century by abstract patterns created with medieval colors and techniques. Luckily, three spectacular rose windows were left intact.

Throughout the centuries, kings, lords, generals, and other churches have sent gifts of everything from statues to war banners; in the 13th century, the side chapels had to be added to hold all the gifts. Notice the statues flanking the altar: They represent Louis XIII, who, after years of trying unsuccessfully for a child, promised to repay the Virgin if she would grant him a son; and Louis XIV, who carried out his father's vow with these gifts to the cathedral.

Climb the cathedral's towers (around to the left as you face the building) for a gape at tons (literally) of bells and eerie statues of monsters, views of Paris, and close proximity to gargoyles. Come on a Sunday for free concerts on the enormous organ. *Pl. du Parvis Notre-Dame, tel. 1/43–26–07–39. Métro: Cité. Admission to tower: 31F, 20F students. Open daily 7:45–7, Sun. until 8.*

LA MOSQUEE

Behind the Jardin des Plantes, the city's main mosque is both the religious and the intellectual center of the Parisian Muslim community. Built in the 1920s as a memorial to North African Muslims who died fighting for France in World War I, the walled complex unveils its most modest face to the street. Around the intricately tiled courtyards lie the prayer room, *hammam* (baths), and tearoom (*see* Cafés, in Chapter 4, Food), all designed in the tradition of North African secular architecture. Upstairs from the peaceful public gardens are institutes devoted to the study of Islam and Arab cultures. The price of admission to the whole complex is 15F, students 10F, but you can wander around the garden for free.

Since the prayer room is used continually throughout the day (daily prayer times are posted inside), you should be aware of some basic customs before entering. Cover all skin above the elbow and above the calf and remove your shoes; the more traditional insist that you also cleanse your face, neck, ears, arms, and hands with water. The carved wooden altar indicates the direction of Mecca; if you sit, point your feet away. Non-Muslims are never allowed in during daily calls to prayer, and at other times, depending on the orthodoxy of the person nearest the door, women, non-Muslims, or both may be asked to view the prayer room only from the courtyard. *Pl. du Puits-de-l'Ermite, 5e, tel. 1/45–35–97–33. Métro: Monge. Open for tours Sat.–Thurs. 10–noon and 2–5:30; in winter, until 6:30.*

SAINTE-CHAPELLE

Sainte-Chapelle is a simple building made sublime by an abundance of stained glass. Ascending to the upper chapel is like climbing into a jewel-box: Brilliantly colored windows fill the interior with light—you get the overwhelming feeling that the building has walls of glass. The less-grand lower chapel, once reserved for the king's servants, is paved with the faceless, worn tombstones of clerics and forgotten knights.

The chapel remains a fine example of the extremes to which men will go when they get hold of a holy relic or two. In the mid-13th century, Louis IX bought the alleged crown of thorns and a part of *the* Cross from Constantinople. In order to adequately house these treasures, as well as a portion of John the Baptist's skull and Mary's milk and blood, he ordered the building of

Steam Baths Are a Turkish Delight

For a decadent experience, spend an afternoon at the hammam (39 rue Geoffroy-St-Hilaire, 5e, tel. 1/43–31–18–14), the Turkish baths in the Mosquée. Hang out in one of the steam rooms or in the bathing area, or lie around naked, listening to Arabic music and drinking mint tea (10F). All-out hedonists can get a rub down for 50F. To maximize your sensual pleasure, bring some clay or something else to slather all over your body, a loofah or sponge, and some water and fruit so you don't get dehydrated. Women are admitted Monday, Wednesday, Thursday, and Saturday; men on Friday and Sunday. Admission is 63F, towel rental 10F.

Sainte-Chapelle. The elegant result was completely unlike massive contemporaries Chartres and Notre-Dame; rather than impressing with scale, Sainte-Chapelle turns its efforts to piously luxuriant details. Louis's influence is everywhere in the cathedral. As the first staunchly Catholic French king, he was understandably enthusiastic about the then-new royal symbol of purity—the fleur de lis—so he had painters slather the thing all over along with the symbol of his mother, a golden church. She had ruled on his behalf until she finally deemed him worthy to take over at age 28, all the while raising him with the strictest of Catholic morals. *Inside Palais de Justice, 4 blvd. du Palais, 1er, tel. 1/43–54–30–09. Métro: Cité. Admission: 25F, 17F students and senior citizens, 40F joint ticket with the Conciergerie. Open Oct.–Mar., daily 10–5; Apr.–Sept., daily 10–6.*

NOT-SO-MAJOR HOUSES OF WORSHIP

BASILIQUE DE ST-DENIS The first major Gothic building built anywhere in the world, the Basilique de St-Denis sits in the square of a villagelike suburb to the north of Paris. The place achieved Christian sanctity somewhere between the 3rd and 6th centuries, when the just-decapitated St-Denis wandered head-in-hand from Montmartre with a choir of angels before keeling over on the hill. In the 12th century, Abbot Suger decided to build a church on the site according to his notion that God equaled light, and that daring expanses of glass allowing light into a cathedral would bring worshipers closer to the divine. The resulting cathedral, with loads of stained glass, high-pointed arches, and a rose window with the signs of the zodiac, would set the style for French cathedrals for the next four centuries.

The real excitement of a trip to the cathedral involves the distinguished (though dead) company you will keep. The 26F (students 17F) price of admission to the choir, ambulatory, and crypt allows access to 15 centuries of French royalty, including peeks at their mismatched bones and a delightful cabinet of embalmed hearts—including one former pumper encased in a glass bulb. All of your favorites are here, including Catherine de Médicis (depicted in one statue as conspicuously young, dead, and naked), Marie Antoinette (gently grazing her right nipple for all eternity), and Louis XIV (buried under a modest black stone). While taking a look at the corpses, notice the foundations of previous crypts; the site has been used as a necropolis since Roman times. *Tel. 1/48–20–02–47. Métro: St-Denis-Basilique. Crypt open Mon.–Sat. 10–6:30, Sun. noon–4:30. Sun. mass at 7:30, 8:30, and 10 AM.*

EGLISE DE LA MADELEINE Under sporadic construction for 80 years, the Eglise de la Madeleine finally opened its huge bronze doors in 1842, becoming one of the largest French neoclassical buildings. The church stands alone in the center of a busy thoroughfare as a proudly inflated, though unfaithful, version of the classic Greek temple. The loose interpretation was intentional: The overproportioned porticoes, the interior barrel vaults-cum-domes, and the opulent versions of the Ionic and Corinthian orders were meant to be Parisian one-uppings of anything Athens had to offer. Changing political moods continued to alter the building's purpose—a Greek basilica one day, a temple to Napoléon's glory another, a National Assembly hall the next. The building suffered from all these vacillations, as designers razed foundations and eliminated details; much of the church's gloominess resulted from one architect filling in the stained-glass windows of another. Nowadays the opulent interior witnesses lots of concerts (many of them expensive, but there are occasional afternoon freebies), as well as daily masses. And if sitting in the cool interior of a Catholic church is not enough to make you reflect upon your sins, try viewing the huge fresco of the Last Judgment above you.

A world away from the scale and politics of the church proper is the **crypt,** in whose intimate chapel weekday masses (7:30 and 8 AM) are held. The crypt is accessible from either the nave of the church or the northwest side of place de la Madeleine. *Pl. de la Madeleine, 8e, tel. 1/42–65–52–17. Métro: Madeleine. Sun. mass at 8, 9, 10 (choral mass), and 11 AM and 12:30 and 6 PM.*

EGLISE ST-EUSTACHE The Eglise St-Eustache, right next door to the ultramodern shopping structure Les Halles, presents a ponderous reminder that it wasn't always all glitz and neon on the Right Bank: The site was once the city's main marketplace and happenin' spot, which Emile Zola called "the belly of Paris." Through the years St-Eustache has seen lots of famous people at important moments in their lives: The composer Rameau was buried here; little Louis XIV took his first communion here; and both Richelieu and Molière were baptized here. Lesser notables have also left their mark: Much of the chapel and artwork were donated by the food guilds and merchants of the old Les Halles.

The structure was built over nearly a hundred years (1537–1632), at the tail end of the Gothic era, but it was during the 19th century, when Liszt directed his *Messe de Gran* here and Les Halles was still a real market, that the cathedral was at its height. These days, however, the bland reconstructed facade and gloomy interior aren't worth going out of your way to see. The presence of a Rubens painting in one of the side chapels potentially salvages the church's appeal, except that no one is quite able to prove *which* Rubens did it. Do look for *The Departure of the Fruits and Vegetables from the Heart of Paris* (1968), Raymond Mason's animated and very unchurchlike interpretation of the closing of Les Halles marketplace. *Pl. René Cassin, 1er, tel. 1/42–36–31–05. Métro: Les Halles. Sun. mass at 8:30, 9:30, and 11 AM and 6 PM.*

EGLISE ST-GERMAIN-DES-PRES The oldest church in Paris, St-Germain-des-Prés traces its roots to the 6th century, when then-archbishop Germanus (now known as St-Germain) built an altar to St-Symphorien on land left to the Benedictine monks by Childebert I. Though most of the present church dates from the 12th and 13th centuries, the purported remains of the original altar still stand near the south side of the entrance. The abbey became one of the great centers of learning in France, with its complex of buildings stretching from the Seine well into the present-day Quartier Latin. Here the Benedictines busied themselves completing the first French translation of the Bible in 1530 and amassing a library that would be appropriated during the Revolution to found the Bibliothèque Nationale (*see* Resident Resources, in Chapter 1). Almost all of the abbey buildings were torn down in the years after the Revolution, while a renovation in the 1950s removed the paint on the ceiling ribbing. Some of the remains of René Descartes have found peace in the seventh chapel. *Pl. St-Germain-des-Prés, 6e, tel. 1/43–25–41–71. Métro: St-Germain-des-Prés. Sun. mass at 9, 10, and 11:15 AM and 5 (in Spanish) and 7 PM.*

EGLISE ST-SEVERIN This ivy-covered Gothic isle of calm amid the craziness of the St-Michel area dates from the 11th century, though most of what you see comes from 16th-century construction efforts and 18th- and 19th-century renovations. The double aisle of the ambulatory has a subterranean feel, with the ribbing of the vaults looking more as if it were holding up the earth than soaring toward the heavens, while the column behind the altar is twisted like a contorted tree trunk. The church is at its best at night, when the only lighting comes from the base of the columns and from behind the altar. Daylight, however, is necessary to fully appreciate the stained-glass windows (1966–1970) depicting the Seven Facets of the Sacrament. *Cnr rues St-Jacques and St-Séverin, 5e, tel. 1/43–25–96–63. Métro: St-Michel. Sun. mass at 10 AM, noon, and 6 PM.*

EGLISE ST-SULPICE Facing a tranquil place just off bustling boulevard St-Germain, St-Sulpice is an unusual departure from most Parisian churches: The double-story loggia with free-standing columns was the first example of French neoclassicism on a monumental scale. The facade was designed in 1736 (after most of the church had already been constructed) by painter Jean Nicolas Servandoni, who conceived the scheme with little regard for stodgy architectural tradition. Free organ concerts are often held in the church. *Pl. St-Sulpice, 6e, tel. 1/46–33–21–78. Métro: St-Sulpice. Sun. mass at 7, 9, and 10:30 AM, noon, and 6:45 PM.*

ST-ETIENNE-DU-MONT Tucked away behind the grandiose Panthéon, the chapel of St-Etienne, begun in the 13th century, is home to the remains of Ste-Geneviève, the patron saint of Paris. The interior features subtly creative interpretations of various forms of the Gothic style: Arches blend into the nave's columns without capitals, and a double-spiral staircase ascends the only remaining rood screen in Paris. Recent restorations have left the place clean, luminous, and one of the best churches to visit in Paris. A stroll behind the altar will reveal plaques marking the remains of Ste-Geneviève, Pascal, Racine, Mirabeau, Clovis, and Marat. A faded red engraving at the portal end of the nave indicates where Monseigneur Sibour, a 19th-century archbishop of Paris, was stabbed to death by a mad priest. It must have been a bad era to be taking vows: Three Parisian archbishops were assassinated within 70 years. *1 rue St-Eti-*

enne du Mont, 5e, tel. 1/43–54–11–79. Métro: Cardinal Lemoine. Sun. mass at 9 and 11 AM and 6:45 PM.

Major Museums

Paris's museums range from the ostentatiously grand to the delightfully obscure—the French seem hell-bent on documenting everything any of its citizens have ever done. In addition to the three biggies—the Louvre, the Musée d'Orsay, and the Pompidou—we've listed all sorts of smaller spaces that may fit your various moods, including science and history museums, individual-artist museums, and photography exhibits. The city also has many galleries that have no permanent collections but host traveling shows; check *Pariscope* (see English-Language Books and Newspapers, in Chapter 1) and posted flyers to find out what's in town.

Paris museums are not cheap, and youth/student discounts are iffy—sometimes they're given only to those 25 and under, sometimes only to students, sometimes only to students 25 years and under. Other discounts are available to the elderly, children, and the unemployed (though you must be a citizen of a European Union nation to get this one); in national museums, visitors in wheelchairs and their attendants also receive discounts. All kinds of other special stipulations exist, but no matter what the rules, a reduction may depend largely on the mood of the person in the ticket booth—bring all kinds of ID and hope for the best.

If you want to pop into a museum just before closing, keep in mind that ticket offices close 15 to 45 minutes before the posted closing time of the galleries.

The association InterMusée spends a large sum of money advertising its *Carte Musées et Monuments,* valid for entry to most of Paris's museums. The pass—valid for either one day (60F), three days (120F), or five days (170F) and sold at participating museums and most major Métro stations—is only a deal if you both (a) don't qualify for any discount admissions; and (b) have the stamina of a marathon runner. Remember that at the Louvre 40F gets you 6,000 years of art; if you plan to go to the d'Orsay (40F) and then pay your respects to the Parisian dead at the Catacombs (25F) all in the same day, this pass might be for you.

MUSEE DU LOUVRE

This may very well be the grandest museum in the world—and not only because recent renovations have made it the largest, nor because it is the oldest and most visited. The Louvre is the queen of museums because it displays the most stunning artwork in the most elegant of settings. But you don't need to buy into the grandeur thing: The Louvre possesses an overwhelmingly comprehensive collection of art and artifacts from almost all ages, cultures, and regions. It doesn't have everything, but it comes closer than anybody else. *1le, tel. 1/40–20–53–17. Métro: Palais Royal–Musée du Louvre or Louvre–Rivoli. Admission: 40F, 20F under age 26, 20F daily after 3 PM and all day Sun. Open Wed. 9 AM–10 PM, Thurs.–Mon. 9–6 (Richelieu open until 10 PM Mon.); galleries start emptying 30 min before closing time. Cafés and stores in Carrousel du Louvre open daily 9 AM–10 PM.*

Unless you enjoy standing in line, the Grande Pyramide is not the quickest way into the Louvre. Try the staircases by the Arc du Carrousel (called the Porte Jaujard) or the passageway from the Palais Royal–Musée du Louvre Métro stop, both of which put you directly inside the underground mall, the Carrousel du Louvre.

PRACTICALITIES Getting into the place requires an explanation in itself. In the worst-case scenario, you may have to wait in two long lines: one outside the Pyramide and another downstairs at the ticket booths. Unless you come during the midday tourist rush, the first line shouldn't be a problem. If you're buying a full-price ticket, the second one isn't either, because you can get it at a vending machine in the downstairs lobby; for discounts, you'll have to go to a real live cashier. Your ticket will get you into any and all of the wings as many times as you like during one day.

Before you skip down that escalator and turn into the first wing you see, remember that the Louvre is *big*. We've outlined a simple guide in the following pages that is broken up by location (wing, floor, collection, and room number), rather than planning out a tour for you. If you want more comprehensive stuff, the museum kindly offers—in addition to the free, very general maps at the information desk—books and leaflets outlining four different prepackaged strategies, all available in the bookstore. The simplest is a pamphlet called *Guide for the Visitor in a Hurry* (15F), and it directs you to the biggies with room numbers and illustrations. The *Visitor's Guide* (60F) ups the number of covered works but cuts the directions—it's an abridged catalogue. The weighty *Louvre: The Collections* (120F) covers even more (though not all) of the museum's works; it's too cumbersome to be a good visitor's guide but not complete enough to be a true catalogue. Finally, you've got the cool cellular-phone–style recorded tours (28F), which lead you through the galleries and explain the highlights. The Louvre is a great place to wander mapless to just happen upon fantastic bits of art, but don't get frustrated when you don't stumble past the *Mona Lisa* after hoofing it for five hours. And, although works in the Louvre tend to stay put, various galleries are still under renovation, and some art may be moved around.

Disabled visitors have about as easy a time as could be expected getting around a Renaissance palace; you can get to everything, and in some sections you can breeze through with almost no trouble at all. Ironically, the newest wing is sometimes the most problematic: In Richelieu there are often a few steps leading from one room to another, forcing you to have to use a series of lifts and out-of-the-way elevators. Wheelchair-accessible rest rooms are in the lobby under the Pyramid.

HISTORY OF THE LOUVRE The Louvre spent its first 600 years alternately as a fortress and a palace. The original Louvre was a fortification built by Philippe Auguste in the late 12th century. A young, nervous Charles V expanded the building in the mid-14th century to distance himself from the potentially revolutionary masses on the Ile de la Cité, creating a Cinderella-like castle of moats and round towers. In the mid-16th century, François I demolished the old castle and started the Vieux Louvre, now encompassed within the Sully wing, and he initiated a cycle of major building projects that have continued more or less nonstop to this day. As construction lagged through the reign of Henri II, Catherine de Médicis started to build her Palais des Tuileries (named for the tileworks that stood close by) to the west of the Vieux Louvre. Catherine connected the two buildings with a hallway along the banks of the Seine, which eventually became the Gallerie Médicis of the Denon wing.

Contrary to popular belief, Napoléon did not take La Gioconda (a.k.a. the Mona Lisa) out of Italy during his military exploits. The painting was acquired by François I, a friend and patron of Leonardo da Vinci.

The wings were expanded and refined over the next 100 years, but it was the construction of the east facade, begun in 1668, that marked the beginning of the Louvre as we see it today. When a competition for architects to design the facade was held, a young draftsman named Claude Perrault worked with the seasoned illustrator and painter Charles Le Brun to come up with the winning proposal. Though his facade helped define French neoclassicism, Perrault didn't have the best timing—Louis XIV left the Louvre for Versailles in 1682, thus abandoning Perrault's elegant style for Versailles's frilly French baroque design.

The Louvre remained virtually untouched by royalty for the next century. The palace's apartments were rented out and very poorly kept; some even considered tearing it down in the mid-18th century. Then, in 1793, during the Revolution, the National Assembly voted to turn part of the Louvre into a public museum. The galleries were stocked with nationalized art taken from the churches, the king, and other members of the French nobility, but the greatest boon to the collection came when a tiny corporal from Corsica measured his power by how much Great Art he could take away from the rest of the world.

Napoléon Bonaparte moved into the Louvre in 1800 as his armies (always accompanied by a team of art historians and archaeologists) were marching across Europe and the Mediterranean. They stole for him the world's most famous treasures, including entire fresco-covered walls and ancient temples, which were all brought to the Louvre, then called the Musée Napoléon. Although the Louvre had always been home to royalty, the emperor's residency in the complex marked the beginning of its role as France's premier palace. With Napoléon's removal (twice) from power, the museum was forced in 1815 to return many of its works to the original owners. However, not everything found its way back home—most notably, many Spanish and Italian paintings.

During the reign of Napoléon III (1852–71), the Louvre saw its most intensive period of construction ever: The Denon and Richelieu wings were finished, the Jardin du Carrousel was landscaped, and the façades of the Cour Napoléon and on rue de Rivoli were completed in the baroque/Renaissance/neoclassical mixture that came to be known as Second Empire. During the uprisings that followed the end of the Franco-Prussian War, the royal apartments were stormed and the Tuileries were burned to the ground during the Commune, leaving the Cour Napoléon without a west side. Napoléon III was forced out of power, and little was done to improve the collection for many years. During World War II, the invading Germans looted the Louvre and used parts of the museum as office space; a classical-art buff, Hitler had the *Victory of Samothrace* installed in his office. Most of the stolen pieces were recovered after the Liberation, but no large-scale changes or innovations were made until Mitterrand was elected. In his first year in office, 1981, the president announced a plan to commence a 20-year, three-phase, 7-billion-franc ($1.3-billion) renovation and expansion.

THE LOUVRE TODAY Mitterrand declared that the remaking of the Louvre was to be the central element of his Grands Travaux, or Great Works, which makes it, according to the French, the most important building project in the world. Mitterrand, who always participates in choosing architects for Parisian projects, offered the commission to I. M. Pei, a New York–based Chinese-American architect who made his reputation designing modernist megastructures. The French were not pleased with the selection, the cost, or the proposal—namely, the relocation of all central services to an excavated Cour Napoléon, which would then be topped by a two-story glass pyramid. Pei explained that by moving the ticket windows and stores underground, the Louvre could have a single entrance that would be capable of handling the massive crowds of visitors (a projected 8 million people in 1995). At the same time, he argued that the stark style of his design for the Pyramide, lobby, and gallery space was intentionally modern so as to contrast with the older parts of the Louvre, rather than coming up with new designs that would mimic the frilly columns and statuary. Pei's proposal was pushed through, and in 1988 the Pyramide was inaugurated to a chorus of mixed reviews. The public and critics eventually warmed up to the new entrance, and when it came time to decide on an architect for the 2.7-billion-franc ($500 million) phase-two renovations, Pei was again chosen.

While the first phase of construction altered the face of the courtyard and defined the interior circulation of the museum, the second phase called for an extensive renovation of the actual galleries, as well as an expansion of the underground spaces under the Cour Napoléon. The first step was to get the Ministry of Finance out of the Richelieu wing into new digs in the 12th arrondissement, a move reluctantly made in 1989. The most controversial part of recent renovations was the expansion of the underground Carrousel du Louvre mall, a series of upscale boutiques selling clothing, records, and other decidedly non-Louvre-related merchandise. There is even a massive fast-food court—now you can get a 30F Quick burger and check out David's *Coronation of Napoleon and Josephine* all in the same building.

The most important part of the second phase has been the renovation of the old galleries, including 39 new rooms in the Sully wing dedicated to French paintings. While some critics dislike the conspicuous reds, browns, blues, and yellows used to paint the new galleries, nobody can argue about the benefit of displaying more works of art. By annexing the Richelieu wing—which added 21,500 square meters (235,000 square feet) of exhibition space to the museum's existing 30,000 square meters (325,000 square feet)—the Louvre also acquired three courtyards, which have been turned into stunning sculpture galleries. Just as the Pyramide became the symbol of the first phase of construction, these courtyards have become the postcard image of phase two (and not the inverted pyramid in the Carrousel du Louvre, as had been expected). The 76-year-old Pei was honored with a higher position in the Légion d'Honneur when the newest Louvre was inaugurated on November 18, 1993, exactly 200 years after the first Musée du Louvre was opened to the public.

RICHELIEU WING Twelve thousand works are on display in the Richelieu wing, a third of which had previously been in storage (the rest were transferred from other parts of the museum).

➢ **BELOW GROUND AND GROUND FLOOR** • Entering the Richelieu wing from the Pyramide, on the left and up a flight of stairs is a gallery that displays temporary exhibits of **French sculpture.** Straight ahead is **Salle 20,** filled with more French sculpture, including frilly busts of members of the court of Louis XIV, but most people pass through this room to get to the dramatic Cour Marly to the west or Cour Puget to the east. The **Cour Marly** is filled with sculptures taken from a garden commissioned by Louis XIV in the early 18th century. The sculptures were intended to be lighthearted additions to ultrapompous Versailles; you can just imagine all these Greco-Roman gods set into the bushes of the Sun King's garden, their clothes falling away from their perfect bodies for all eternity. The **Cour Puget** is named for the artist who created the sculpture at the Place des Victoires, now mostly reassembled in the lower court. Sculptures that once dotted the estates of nobility fill the rest of the courtyard, while the upper level has some busts of characters from the Revolution and the 1830 uprising—it's difficult to distinguish between the Parisian heroes and the gods downstairs.

Back to the southeast corner of Cour Marly: Here you will find **Salle 1** of French sculpture. The first truly French sculpture—that is, not Gallo-Roman—dates to the 11th century, when the carved column heads produced by regional artisans began to display figures or beasts instead of Corinthian capitals. In **Salle 2** are fragments of Romanesque chapels from Cluny, the powerful abbey in Burgundy that dominated French Catholicism in the 11th century. In **Salles 4–6** you can see the refinement of sculpture encouraged by the wealthy communities in the Ile de France. The **funerary art** of **Salles 7–10** can seem silly or spooky. The late-15th-century tomb

Mitterrand's Messy Past

Until recently, little had been written about François Mitterrand's life between 1934 and 1947. With the publication of Pierre Péan's work "Une Jeunesse Française" in September 1994, it became clear why Mitterrand had been so reticent to talk about these years. The book reveals the extent of Mitterrand's involvement with the Nazi-cooperative Vichy regime, and the story is not pretty.

Péan's new book reveals that Mitterrand was an enthusiastic adherent of the Vichy government's ideals—so enthusiastic, in fact, that at age 26 he received its highest honor, the Francisque, from Vichy chief Philippe Pétain. He was close friends with Pétain (the cover of the book features a photo of Pétain and Mitterrand together) and continued to lay commemorative wreaths on his grave until protests finally became too loud. And although he joined the Resistance in 1943 (when the tide was turning in Allied favor, Péan points out), he had joined the Fighter's Legion, which would become the militia that hunted Jews and Resistance fighters, only three years earlier.

Now that the skeletons are out of the closet and Mitterrand's presidency is drawing to a close (Paris Mayor Jacques Chirac and Prime Minister Edouard Balladur will be vying for the presidency in May 1995), the president has been relatively forthcoming (and unapologetic) about his past. After the book's publication Mitterrand said, "In troubled times, especially when one is young, it is hard to make choices. I think I came out of it pretty well."

of Philippe Pot in **Salle 10** is definitely eerie: You see Philippe stretched out in eternal prayer and held aloft by eight black-robed pallbearers.

Walking through **Salles 11–19,** you can see how the piety and stiffness of medieval French sculpture began to give way to the more natural style of the Italian Renaissance. Many local artists were traveling to Italy during the 16th and 17th centuries, while the French nobility were importing noted Italian sculptors. Bronze, out of favor since Roman times, was being cast again, and the subject matter, which had rarely strayed from Madonnas or saints, could now be mythological, allegorical, or classical.

To the north of the Cour Puget are **Salles 25–33,** filled with the products of the Académie Royale, *the* art school of 18th-century France. The smaller works in **Salle 25** are all admission pieces to the Académie—once admitted into the school based on previous works, the student was asked to produce a sculpture as proof of continuing worth. Mythology was a popular subject, as in Jean Thierry's 1717 *Leda and the Swan,* which depicts the unorthodox seduction scene between the queen of Sparta and Zeus in the form of a large bird. While beautiful art did emerge during the 18th century, the individual artists are of questionable creative merit: The Académie became a sort of aesthetics factory, turning out thousands of decorative marble statues depicting yet another stock Apollo figure.

To the east of the Cour Puget is the start of the Louvre's **Oriental Antiquities** collection. Within the glass case of **Salle 1** are many ancient Mesopotamian carvings, including a 5.4-centimeter (2-inch) Neolithic figure dating to the 6th millennium BC—one of the oldest statues known to humanity. Facing the case are the pieced-together fragments of the 3rd millennium BC "Stela of the Vultures," containing the oldest written history known to humanity (do you start to see a pattern?): On one side, King Eannatum catches his enemies in a net and thanks the disembodied head of his patron goddess, while on the other side vultures eat the corpses of the enemy and the king leads the infantry and chariots over more bodies as a sacrifice is offered for the victory.

Farther along, **Salle 1b** has countless examples of the wide-eyed alabaster statues produced by the Sumerians during the 3rd millennium BC. **Salle 2** is filled with statues and fragments of Gueda, a prince who supported a neo-Sumerian artistic culture in his 23rd-century BC kingdom of Lagash. Gueda commemorated his achievements through countless self-portraits he had carved from diorite, the hardest stone on Earth; notice the one headless statue depicting Gueda presiding over the architectural plans for a temple.

The centerpiece of **Salle 3** is the "Codex of Hammurabi," an 18th-century BC diorite stela that contains the oldest written laws known to humanity; near the top of the text you can see Hammurabi, king of the first Babylonian dynasty, meeting a seated Shamash, the god of justice. On the east side of Salle 3 is a lion glazed onto a piece of a terra-cotta-tile wall—just one of hundreds of similar beasts that decorated the multistory 6th-century BC "Gates of Babylon"; the rest of the Gates have been re-erected in the Pergamon Museum in Berlin.

Best Cup of Java at the Louvre: Café Richelieu, first floor of the Richelieu wing. A 10F café gets you a terrace view overlooking the Pyramide. For the swankiest cup of coffee, check out Café Marly, also in the Richelieu wing (see Cafés, in Chapter 4).

Salle 4 is the Cour Khorsabad, a re-creation of the temple erected by the Assyrian king Sargon II in the 8th century BC at the palace of Dur-Sharrukin. Walking among the temple's five massive winged bulls, known as *lamassu,* or benign demigods, is one of the most spectacular experiences in the Louvre, even though only three of the bulls and almost none of the re-erected reliefs are authentic. The originals were lost on a sunken frigate.

➤ **FIRST FLOOR** • Restored rooms from the **royal apartments** of Napoléon III fill the southwestern portion of the first floor of the Richelieu wing. **Salle 79** is the most spectacular of the lot; the corner reception room, decorated for Napoléon III's secretary of state, gives you a good idea of the audacious luxury of the Second Empire. The **gallery** running between the Cour Marly and the Cour Puget is filled with **French medieval artifacts** saved from the Revolution's zeal to destroy all things Christian and Roman. It also contains **Byzantine objects** taken as booty from non–Roman Catholic churches in Constantinople during the Crusades.

➤ **SECOND FLOOR** • Just to the east of the escalators is Salle 1, which begins the section devoted to **French and Northern School paintings.** At the entrance to this room is a single 14th-century gold-backed painting of John the Good—the oldest known individual portrait from north of Italy. In **Salle 4** is the *Madonna and Chancellor Rolin,* by the 15th-century Dutch master Jan van Eyck. The first artist to extensively use oil paints, van Eyck defined what became known as the "northern style," characterized by a light source illuminating one area on an otherwise dark background. One of the first self-portraits ever painted—a bizarre and disheveled offering by Albrecht Dürer (1471–1528)—hangs in **Salle 8.** Walking through **Salles 9–17,** you can see how the Dutch developed a fluid and comfortable representation of the body while playing with the shiny, dark palette of oil paints. In **Salle 12** you can see the 1514 *Banker and His Wife,* where Quentin Metsys (1456–1530) deftly depicts the effect of light on glass, gold, and mirrors.

The most dramatic gallery in this section is **Salle 18,** where a cycle of epic Pierre-Paul Rubens (1577–1640) canvases recounts the journey Marie de Médicis made from Florence to Paris, in what is an overbearing immortalization of a relatively cushy trip. The swirling baroque paintings were commissioned by Marie herself and originally hung in the Palais du Luxembourg. The riveting *Disembarkation of Marie de Médicis at the Port of Marseilles* depicts an artificially slimmed-down Marie about to step over the roly-poly daughters of Poseidon as a personified France beckons her to shore.

Though the still life genre may seem boring today, it was loaded with meaning for the Dutch. Ambriosius Bosschaert's (1573–1621), 1620 *Bouquet of Flowers in an Arch* in **Salle 27** is meant to represent the power of the colonially minded Dutch merchants: The flowers brought together in the vase in this painting couldn't have been gathered at any one moment in real life because of their diverse and exotic origins. In **Salle 31** are several paintings by Rembrandt van Rijn (1606–69), including a late self-portrait in which he goes nuts with the chiaroscuro. In his 1648 *Supper at Emmaüs,* he challenges many painting conventions, such as centering the subject and delineating objects with bold brush strokes. The masterpiece of the Dutch collection is the *Lacemaker,* by Jan Vermeer (1632–75), in **Salle 38.** Obsessed with optical accuracy, Vermeer painted the red thread in the foreground as a slightly blurred jumble, just as one would actually see it if focusing on the girl.

The French philosopher/writer Roland Barthes noted that only the Dutch painters allowed patricians and cows to look out and make eye contact with the viewer—glance around Salle 34 of the second floor of Richelieu and see if you agree.

SULLY WING The entrance into the Sully wing from the Pyramide is the coolest—you get to walk around and through the foundations and moat of the castle built by Philippe Auguste in the 12th century and expanded by Charles V in the 14th.

➤ **BELOW GROUND** • The foundations of Phillipe August's castle were accidentally discovered during renovations of the building in 1988. You may notice that many of the stones have squares, circles, or hearts cut roughly into them: These were used by the illiterate masons to identify the parts. The base of the circular keep you walk around was once 32 meters (105 feet) tall. Take a look at the model in the side room to get an idea of what the place used to look like.

➤ **GROUND FLOOR** • The northern galleries of the Sully are a continuation of the ancient **Iranian collection** started on the ground floor of the Richelieu wing. Conflicting styles emerged as the Greco-Roman art exported by the Roman and Byzantine empires influenced the work of indigenous artisans.

At press time, the **Crypt of Osiris** and **Galerie Henri IV,** connecting the Iranian and the **Egyptian collections,** were under renovation. These galleries normally hold early Pharaonic statues from the 3rd and 2nd millennia BC, including several likenesses of pharaohs and gods. The ancient Egyptians consider these statues to be more than images of the deceased or immortal: They were treated as the physical vessels for the soul, or *ka,* of the thing depicted. In **Salle 5** you should still be able to see the 24th-century BC *Seated Scribe,* a painted-limestone likeness of an unknown secretary. The statue is unusual because it is not an idealized interpretation of its subject—you can see his chest sag in a surprisingly human manner above his paunchy tummy.

Adjacent to the Egyptian galleries is **Salle 13,** housing the **Greek, Etruscan,** and **Roman collections** and the famous 2nd-century BC *Venus de Milo.* The armless statue, one of the most reproduced and recognizable works of art in the world, is actually as beautiful as they say—it is worth your trouble to push past the lecturing curators and tourist groups to get a close look at the incredible skill with which the Greeks turned cold marble into something vibrant and graceful. **Salles 13–17** are filled with all kinds of statuary: funerary stelae, body fragments, architectural detailings. One important form for Greek figurative statues was the kouros, an idealized youth standing staring straight ahead, an "archaic smile" (the lips are pulled back to resemble a grin, but the mouth isn't actually smiling) on his face, his shoulders squared with his hands at his sides, and one foot slightly in front of the other: You can see in these galleries how over the centuries sculptors relaxed and naturalized the stance. The statues in **Salle 17,** known as the Caryatid Room (named for the 16th-century female figures standing as columns at either end of the hall), are Roman copies of original Greek works.

➤ **FIRST FLOOR** • The northern galleries of the first floor continue with the *objets d'art* **collection** started in the Richelieu wing, picking up at the 17th century and continuing through the Revolution to the Restoration. Running alongside the remaining **Egyptian galleries** to the south are works from the early period of the **Greek collection**—a smattering of coins, pottery, and other everyday objects from the 7th to 3rd centuries BC.

➤ **SECOND FLOOR** • Sully picks up **French painting** where the Richelieu wing leaves off, somewhere around the 16th century. At this point, a conscious battle was under way in French art between the northern style, centered on the work of the Dutch, and the southern one, coming from Florence, Venice, and Rome. The result was a blending of northern style and technology (darkly painted interiors and oil paints) with southern subjects and technique (ruins-filled landscapes and one-point perspective). Charles Le Brun (1619–90), Louis XIV's principal adviser on the arts, painted massive "History Paintings," jam-packed with excruciating details depicting biblical, historical, or mythological stories. Displayed in **Salle 32** are the four canvases of his late-17th-century *Story of Alexander,* with a powerful view of the trials of the emperor (and no small reference to Louis XIV).

An academic painter of a different genre was Jean-Antoine Watteau (1684–1721). In scenes such as his 1717 *Pilgrimage to the Island of Cythera* in **Salle 36,** he depicted in wispy pastel brush strokes the bucolic and often frivolous lifestyle of the baroque-age court set. In the same room is Watteau's enigmatic 1718 *Pierrot* (also called *Gilles*), a well-known portrait of a boyish-looking actor whose costume and surroundings reflect the popularity of Italian commedia dell'arte at the time. Maurice Quentin de La Tour (1704–88) was another favorite court painter; his 1755 *Marquise de Pompadour* in **Salle 45** captures the frivolous pomp of Louis XV's court. Madame de Pompadour, mistress to the king, is shown with everything a good courtesan should have: books, music manuscripts, engravings, fine clothing, and of course, pale skin.

One Revolution and two Republics after the court painters of the 17th and 18th centuries, the Académie continued to define what Good Taste was. In **Salle 55** you can see the paintings of Jean-Auguste-Dominique Ingres (1780–1867), which depict the exotic themes popular in the Age of Empires. His 1862 *Turkish Bath* portrays an orgy of steamy women who look anything but Turkish. You can see more of his work in Salle 77 of the Denon wing and across the Seine at the Musée d'Orsay.

DENON WING

➤ **BELOW GROUND** • To the south and east from the Pyramide entrance are newly renovated galleries displaying **Italian sculpture** from the early Renaissance, including a 15th-century *Madonna and Child* by the Florentine Donatello (1386–1466).

➤ **GROUND LEVEL** • In **Salle 9** you can see the 1513–15 *Slaves* of Michelangelo (1475–1564). Carefully selecting his slab of marble, Michelangelo would then spend days envisioning the form of the sculpture within the uncut stone, without ever picking up his chisel. The sculptures that finally emerged openly eroticized the male body. The fact that many were left "unfinished" (i.e., parts of the marble were left rough, making it look as if the sculptures were trying to free themselves from the stone blocks) was controversial at first, but the style went on to inspire Rodin and other modern artists. In **Salle 10** is the 1793 *Eros and Psyche* by the great Italian neoclassicist Antonio Canova (1757–1822), whose delicate and precise touch made him the darling of European royalty.

To the east of the Italian sculpture collection are the galleries containing the sculptures of the **Greek, Etruscan,** and **Roman** periods. In **Salle 18** is the 6th-century BC Etruscan *Sarcophagus from Cerveteri*. This sarcophagus, pieced together from thousands of clay fragments, depicts a friendly couple who seem as though they would invite you to chat over a good meal.

➢ **FIRST FLOOR** • Stretching out from a tiny entry next to the Sully wing is the **Galerie d'Apollon,** a 17th-century hall decorated by the painter Charles Le Brun (who immortalized himself in one of the portraits on the wall), which now holds what remains of France's **Crown Jewels.** Around the corner from the jewels, the *Victory of Samothrace* stands regally, if headless, at the top landing of the staircase leading down to the ground floor. The spectacular 2nd-century BC statue, found on a tiny Greek island in the northern Aegean, was probably a monument to a victorious battle at sea. The goddess stood at what looks to be the bow of a ship, her thin garment clinging to her body as she plows through the spray-filled air.

The **Italian painting** collection begins at the western end of the Denon wing. The paintings in Salle 6 are large-scale canvases from the 16th-century Venetian School. Dominating the room is the massive 1562 *Feast at Cana* by Veronese (1528–88), a sumptuous scene centered on Jesus turning water into wine. Spread across the canvas are hundreds of still lifes and portraits, all little masterpieces within this huge painting. It is said that the great painters of the Venetian School—Titian, Bassano, Tintoretto, and even Veronese—are depicted as the musicians. In the same room is the 1525 *Entombment* by the quintessential Venetian painter, Titian (1488–1576). Titian used the translucent shine of the oil paints characteristic of Venetian art while contrasting dark colors against extreme whites to create a sense of light. The last great artist from the Venetian School was Tintoretto (1518–94), whose latter works look almost impressionistic, since he rejected a brush in favor of smearing the paint onto the canvas with his fingers.

And now for **Salle 7,** home to the Most Famous Painting in the World, the *Mona Lisa.* Somewhere behind the legion of video-taping tourists (think about it: videotaping *paintings*) and layers of bullet-proof glass is the painting that has inspired so much awe, emulation, and disbelief—you too may find yourself asking "*Is this it?*" when you are faced with this 70-by-50-centimeter (2½-by-1¾-foot) painting of a woman with yellowing skin and an annoyingly smug smile. But if you can somehow move to the front of the crowd to squint through the glare of the protective coating, you'll have a close look at a truly beautiful painting.

Only 15 paintings by Leonardo da Vinci are known to exist. Five of them are in the Louvre.

The 1458 *Calvary* in **Salle 8,** painted by Andrea Mantegna (1431–1506), a follower of the Florentine architect Brunelleschi's treatises on perspective, is one of the first paintings ever with a vanishing point. While the angling of the roads and people may seem severe, he opened the door for exploration of the concepts of background and foreground. Though more accomplished as an anatomist and inventor, Leonardo da Vinci (1452–1519) was originally trained as a painter. His 1483 *Virgin of the Rocks* has a pretty cool sense of spatial relationships—the four figures create the four points of a three-dimensional pyramid, while their glances and gestures keep all activity contained within this form. On the way from Salle 8 to the landing where the *Victory of Samothrace* is standing, you'll pass by Sandro Botticelli's (1445–1510) *Venus and the Graces,* a fresco chipped out of its villa in Tuscany. The painting is full of the sidelong glances and lengthy fingers associated with the Mannerist movement.

Behind the *Feast at Cana* are two passages leading to **Salles 75–77,** home of the great epic-scale canvases produced in Paris during the 19th century. When official court painter Louis David (1748–1825) produced the 1806 *Coronation of Emperor Napoléon I, 2 December*

1804, now hanging in **Salle 75,** he wisely decided *not* to capture the moment when Napoléon snatched the crown from the hands of Pope Pius VII to place it upon his own head—choosing instead to paint the new emperor turning to crown Josephine. In the same room is the 1805 painting *Empress Josephine* by Pierre-Paul Prud'hon (1758–1823), depicting the wife of Napoléon one year after her crowning and four years before she was abandoned because she could not produce a royal heir.

In **Salle 75** hang the two most famous works in the history of **French painting:** the 1819 *Raft of the Medusa* by Théodore Géricault (1791–1824) and the 1830 *Liberty Leading the People* by Eugène Delacroix (1798–1863). The *Medusa,* painted when Géricault was only 27 years old, was inspired by the real-life story of the wreck of a French merchant ship: The captain lost control, the ship was without lifeboats or supplies, and ultimately the survivors resorted to cannibalism. The painting caused a stir with the government, which took offense at the stab made at the inefficiency of authority. The Académie was aghast for formal reasons: The painting had no central subject, no hero, no *resolution.* The survivors are a mess of living and dead bodies jumbled in and out of ominous shadows.

Even though Delacroix wasn't directly involved in the "Trois Glorieuses," a three-day revolution in 1830 that ousted Charles X's autocracy and brought in a parliamentary monarchy with Louis-Philippe as king, he was compelled to paint *Liberty* to commemorate the Parisians who attempted to restore the Republic. Once again it is an unorthodox subject for a painting: Half-armed *bourgeois* and pugnacious street urchins step over the dead bodies of comrades and kill other French folk in the name of an ultimately short-lived government. The allegorical figure of Liberty is quite a character: She is shown walking barefoot over barricades, her peasant dress falling away from two nippleless breasts, the Tricolor held aloft with one well-muscled limb while the other grips a rifle. The painting was immediately bought by an appreciative Louis-Philippe, who hid it to keep from inciting his enemies.

SPECIAL EXHIBITIONS AND EVENTS Temporary exhibits are usually put up in the basement galleries of the Richelieu wing, the second-floor galleries of the Denon wing, or the showrooms of the Carrousel du Louvre. Films and lectures take place in the Carrousel's auditorium. There is often a separate price for temporary exhibitions, films, and lectures; you can check prices and events on the banners in the Pyramide lobby, and you can see what's happening that day on the TV monitors behind the main information desk.

MUSEE D'ORSAY

The Musée d'Orsay has a spectacular collection, encompassing art produced between 1848 (where the Louvre drops off) and about 1904 (where the Pompidou picks up). Of course, most of the stuff created during this time of any worth, at least according to Parisians, was French, and most was painted by the impressionists, working from the 1870s to the turn of the century. The Orsay is not just an impressionism museum, though; much more was happening during this period than blueish hues and soft brush strokes. This artistically tumultuous time saw the rise and fall of the art and literary salons and the creation of the concept of the avant-garde. The Orsay explores all of these aspects of early modern art, including, yes, an exhaustive collection of impressionist paintings.

PRACTICALITIES When you first step out into the nave of this old train station, you may be overcome by the weighty postmodern architecture, sculptures, and hordes of people furiously milling around. Take a deep breath before diving into it all. The museum shop offers *Guide for Visitors in a Hurry* (15F), an efficient if abbreviated outline of the most important works of the collection, and *Guide to the Orsay* (110F), a more comprehensive look at the collection with better pictures. The free maps available at the information desk are physically accurate, but you *will* get lost at one point or another, no matter how true your compass is.

Even though the Orsay is wheelchair accessible, it is far from barrier-free. Elevators take you to all three levels of the museum, but individual galleries may be five or more steps up or down from each other, forcing you to circumnavigate to get where you're going. Check with the information desk to find out how to operate the elevators.

HISTORY The Musée d'Orsay is a baby of a museum—it's been around in its present form only since 1986. The building has a far lengthier history, dating back to 1898, when the Gare d'Orsay was built to handle the onslaught of trains expected for the 1900 World's Fair. Architect Victor Laloux, a professor at the nearby Ecole des Beaux-Arts, designed all kinds of ornamental frippery appropriate to the dawning of the modern age. The platforms of the station were soon too short for modern trains, and the building was mostly abandoned only a few years after it opened. There were a few tenants now and then—at one point Orson Welles shot the film *Kafka* in the station, and a circus later set up shop—but it was slated for demolition as a part of the urban renewal schemes of the early 1970s. Parisians couldn't stand the thought of this beloved, unused, oversized neo-rococo dinosaur being torn down, so they successfully petitioned President Pompidou to designate it a national monument in 1973. Four years later, a competition was announced for a design to turn the old station into a museum, and the project was awarded to Italian architect Gae Aulenti.

When François Mitterrand assumed the presidency in 1981, the renovation of the Orsay had completely stalled. With a deft stroke of his pen, Mitterrand tripled the reconstruction budget; five years later the Musée d'Orsay was inaugurated, now displaying the combined collections of the Musée Jeu de Paume and the 19th-century galleries of the Louvre. Aulenti's renovation design has met with some criticism, but the crowds love the new Orsay. While preserving a single grand statue-lined promenade along the length of the building, Aulenti broke up the spacious shell of the old train station by dividing and subdividing the galleries into smaller rooms. The paintings on the ground floor, grouped one above another on the walls, reinforce this more intimate feeling. But while Aulenti successfully turned the old antiseptic, white-walled, picture-in-splendid-isolation cliché of museums on its head, she also created tight little doors and stairways that get easily clogged in the rush of tourists.

THE COLLECTION Paintings constitute the bulk of the Orsay's collection and are complemented by sculpture, furniture, decorative arts, and architecture-related exhibits. Earlier paintings and sculptures are displayed on the ground level, later sculpture and architectural design on the middle level, and the heart of the impressionist collection on the upper level.

➤ **GROUND FLOOR** • Walking up the grande promenade, the first gallery on the right contains the works of **Jean-Auguste-Dominique Ingres** (1780–1867), a sensualist (some say a dirty little man who couldn't get enough of naked girls and water) whose erotic style was called Classic by the other sensualists who ran the Académie Francaise. The next gallery along the promenade has the works of **Eugène Delacroix** (1798–1863), who managed to remain in favor with the French government for all of his career; Delacroix did a fair bit of business repainting canvases and frescoes in churches desecrated during the Revolution. Like many painters, as he got older he became more liberal with color and technique, becoming an unintentional innovator.

Salons

Up until the late 19th century, making it big in the art world in Paris meant making it into the Salon, an institution established by the French Academy of Painting. The Salon's professed goals were to review, reward, and control painters seeking official recognition and to put on a huge show of the art they deemed worthy. In reality, it served largely to encourage mediocrity and stifle individual expression. In 1863, under pressure to recognize diverse types of paintings, they came up with the spin-off Salon des Refusés for weirdos like the pre-impressionists. Not surprisingly, artists were not thrilled about being categorized as "refusé," so early impressionists formed their own salon in 1874. This brave new salon served as a model for many more alternative salons to come and helped abolish the Academy's monopoly on accepted art.

Back across the promenade, the first gallery has some figurines by the satirical illustrator **Honoré Daumier** (1808–79). Working at the beginning of the popular-press age, Daumier spent his energies mocking various members of the government and intelligentsia with biting little etchings. These caricatures included wicked likenesses of members of the National Assembly—you can see some of his paintings on the upper level. In the next gallery are works by **Jean-Baptiste-Camille Corot** (1796–1875). His uncentered landscapes are associated with the Barbizon school, an approach to painting inspired by the writings of Rousseau and the invention of a groovy new gadget, the camera.

In the first room on the left in the next bank of galleries on the promenade is the notorious *Olympia* (1863) by **Edouard Manet** (1832–83). When it was unveiled at the Salon des Refusés (*see box, above*), it drew scathing remarks. The image of the nude youngish courtesan with unfinished hands (they were described as monkey paws) stretched out next to a black cat (a symbol of female sexual prowess) with a bouquet of flowers *sketched* in paint on the bedside was far too much. Every review of the painting (save two) was negative. Next door is the work of a young **Claude Monet** (1840–1926).

A modest Gustave Courbet said, "I have no teacher, my teacher is myself. There is not, and has not been, any painter other than myself."

Between the banks of galleries running along the Seine side of the Orsay is a large, open room containing the works of **Gustave Courbet** (1819–77), considered by current scholars to be the first modernist. Courbet's highly gestural brush strokes were abhorred by the Académie Française; no matter—the painter hated the Académie just as much. Courbet's subjects—muddy country roads, poor farmers, rural dogs—embodied everything that the sophisticated Parisian art scene was not, making the artist a hero to future generations of realists. For more Courbet, check out the Petit Palais (*see* Not-So-Major Museums, *below*).

Standing under the twin battlements at the end of the promenade is the Salle Garnier, a spiffy cluster of rooms devoted to the architect **Charles Garnier** (1825–98) and his crowning achievement, the Opéra de Paris. Here you can look at models and sketches examining the Opéra's structure, but the best part is the scale model of the Opéra and surrounding neighborhood that is set into the floor under see-through tiles.

Trailing up along the staircase in the northeast corner of the museum is a montage of Parisian facades, starting from the Restoration and moving chronologically through the July Monarchy, Second Republic, Second Empire, and Third Republic.

➤ **MIDDLE FLOOR** • On the terrace overlooking the promenade are early 20th-century sculptures, including works by **Auguste Rodin** (1840–1917) and **Camille Claudel** (1864–1903). Rodin, arguably the greatest sculptor of his era, spent the last 37 years of his career working on figures for his never-finished bronze *Gate of Hell*, a plaster version of which stands between the two battlements. The *Gate* was originally supposed to depict the *Divine Comedy* of Dante, but an obsessed Rodin overreached the concept of visual narration by packing the doors with scores of figures caught in moments of agony and ecstasy. For more on the *Gate* and on Rodin and Claudel, *see* Musée Rodin, in Not-So-Major Museums, *below*.

The galleries on either sides of the battlements are filled with architecture and furniture design from the turn of the century. To the north are several rooms filled with art nouveau, including a completely reconstructed dining room by **Alexandre Charpentier** (1856–1909). Across the terrace are rooms dedicated to non-French designers of the same period, including the American "Prairie School" architect **Frank Lloyd Wright** (1867–1959) and the Scot **Charles Rennie Mackintosh** (1868–1928), an early modernist.

➤ **UPPER FLOOR** • Entering the first gallery from the northeastern stairs or elevator, you'll finally hit the impressionist stuff you've been waiting for. The impressionists challenged the status quo with their highly detailed theories about the effects of light, movement, and color, finding a slew of new subjects to paint with the advent of the Haussmann boulevards, cafés, and department stores just beginning to dominate Parisian culture in the late 19th century. A growing middle class was out having a great time in the parks and dance halls while the Second Empire was out collecting the spoils of a colonized world. In the middle of this new era, **Manet** did his controversial *Déjeuner sur l'herbe*. The subject, naked ladies and clothed men in a bucolic setting, wasn't new to the French public in 1863; everybody was familiar with similar scenes from the Italian Renaissance and French baroque paintings hanging in the Louvre. But there was something about the modern dress of the men, the discarded clothes of the women, and the way two of the figures look out at the viewer with a slightly confrontational glance, that upset the critics.

In the next gallery is the famous portrait of the mother of **James McNeill Whistler** (1834–1903), embodying all the spartan puritanism associated with the rural United States and the late-19th-century American aesthetic. In the next gallery, the work of **Claude Monet** (1840–1926) shows how the painter replaced hard delineation with soft brush strokes and colors from a muted palette. His *Fête du 30 juin 1878* tries to capture the shimmering vitality of a Paris street celebration. In the same gallery is the work of **Auguste Renoir** (1841–1919), who used to spend long hours in Paris parks catching the newly idle petite bourgeoisie at play.

The last gallery in this series is devoted to **Paul Cézanne** (1839–95), who challenged the salons of Paris by entirely ignoring them. Though he had contact with other painters like Degas and Manet, and a few young artists came to study with him in his Aix-en-Provence studio, he painted almost entirely for himself. And he painted and painted, continually playing with color and spatial relationships while selling only a few works to a wealthy doctor. Despite this isolation, Cézanne is considered one of the most influential artists of the 19th century and was hailed as a god by Matisse and Picasso.

Around the corner, past the Café des Hauteurs, is a room filled with the work of **Vincent van Gogh** (1835–90), the slightly insane Dutch painter who spent most of his years working in France. Van Gogh was doomed to a bizarre life from the outset—he was named for a dead brother who'd had the same birthday. Sure, there's the ear story, and the problems he had with prostitutes and his brother Theo, but the contribution he made to painting cannot be underestimated. Van Gogh painted a stone bridge yellow and a wheat field red because that's the way he painted them—a simple idea for later generations of artists to figure out.

Best Cup of Java at the Orsay: Café des Hauteurs, upper level. For the price of a 12F café you get a bustling crowd and a view of the sun illuminating the station's monumental clockface.

Turning the corner, you have the work of **Henri Rousseau** (1844–1910), whose cool and flattened touch delineated fairy-tale-like jungle scenes complete with exotic animals hidden in the dense underbrush. This jungle motif was popular with the style-conscious French, who were eager to get images of what they imagined to be Edenic colonies in Africa, East Asia, and the Caribbean. The symbolist **Paul Gauguin** (1848–1903) titillated an audience back in Paris with the primitivist paintings he produced while living in Tahiti; the lightheartedness of his earlier stuff is naïve compared with the fatalistically mortal imagery that came later.

Farther along are works by **Georges Seurat** (1859–91), whose use of dots of color became known as pointillism (though he found the term "divisionism" much more appropriate). At the end of the hallway are early works by **Henri Matisse** (1869–1954), whose 1904 *Luxe, Calme, et Volupté* helped him earn the label fauvist, an uncomplimentary term coined by the critics, who thought his bright colors were *comme un fauve* (like a beast). Matisse was much more than just a colorist, but his early works mark the official end (at least according to French museums) of post-impressionism and the beginning of modern art—for more Matisse, go to the Pompidou. For another big batch of impressionists and post-impressionists in a smaller setting, make time for the Musée de l'Orangerie, and Monet fans can't miss the Musée Marmottan (for both, *see* Not-So-Major Museums, *below*). *62 rue de Lille, 7e, tel. 1/40–49–48–14. Métro: Solférino. RER: Musée d'Orsay. Admission: 36F, 24F ages 18–25, under 18 free; separate admission for temporary exhibits. Open Tues., Wed., Fri., and Sat. 10–6; Thurs. 10–9; Sun. 9–6. Wheelchair access.*

MUSEE NATIONAL D'ART
MODERNE–CENTRE GEORGES POMPIDOU

Completing the chronological triumvirate of national museums is the Musée National d'Art Moderne, usually referred to as the Pompidou for its home, the Centre Georges Pompidou. The Centre itself, sometimes called the Beauborg, is one of Paris's biggest tourist attractions: Fire-eaters, jugglers, caricaturists, and rice-scribes (boasting the unusual ability to write your name on a grain of rice) cover the large plaza out front, while inside a museum, a library, a theater, and a cinema act as the "laboratory" envisioned when the Centre was first conceived in the early 1970s. Somewhere along the line, the Pompidou declared itself the fulcrum of contemporary thought; looking at the digital clock in front of the building counting down the seconds left in the millennium, you almost believe that the year 2000 will start right here.

PRACTICALITIES Stepping in through the doors of the Centre Pompidou can be either exhilarating or frustrating. The lobby is a huge tangle of signs, televised images, numbers, chairs, art, exposed pipes, escalators, and people. In addition to the museum, there is a library, a theater, a cinema, and countless conference rooms (for more on the Centre's other resources, *see* Resident Resources, in Chapter 1).

There are two breeds of art exhibits here: Those that cost money and those that don't. The free ones are scattered throughout the temporary galleries on the ground floor and in the library halls; these are usually related to the blockbuster temporary exhibit housed in the fifth-floor Grande Galerie. For everything else you need to buy a ticket from the cashier, which can be an ordeal. The signs posted above the ticket booths have several different prices, each for a different combination of exhibits. You could pay to see just the permanent collection, a specific temporary exhibition, the Grande Galerie exhibit, the children's hands-on display in the Atelier des Enfants, or a combination of any or all of the above. The permanent collection is more than enough for one day, as is the Grande Galerie, though the ambitious will pace themselves and get an all-gallery pass. Once you've announced your choice to the cashier, you will be issued something that looks like a train ticket, which you pop into a machine, Métro-style, at the entrance to your galleries.

The information desks have a smorgasbord of semi-helpful literature, the most useful of which is a bimonthly program of events printed in English. Here you have a full listing of gallery events, prices, and the wheres and whens of guided tours in your mother tongue.

Being a big, flat, practical building, the Centre is one of the best places in Paris for those with physical disabilities to move around. There are no steps that can't be avoided by a lift, and elevators are all over the place.

HISTORY It's difficult to remember today, but the '70s was a time of funky idealism, the era of *Spacelab* and electric cars. Georges Pompidou, the staid, conservative French president from 1969 to 1974, seems an unlikely cultural hero, but he was hell-bent on creating a multimedia cultural center before such a concept was ever a general topic of discussion. The fact that the project involved a favorite government pastime—urban renewal—didn't hurt either. The decrepit Beaubourg district, in decline since the late 17th century, had an estimated five million rats when Pompidou declared in December of 1969 that a new contemporary art museum and intellectual center would be placed in the decaying heart of Paris. This new center, he promised, would be more than a building; it would be a statement.

" . . . you have been trapped by this glass serpent which brings alive, with its flow of humanity, the facade of this big body. The joke is on you! You are a spectator on view!"—a reference to the Centre's glass-encased escalators, from its Practical Guide.

In 1977, after six years of demolition and construction, the riot of steel cross braces and snaky escalators designed by Italians Renzo Piano and Gianfranco Franchini and Britain's Richard Rodger was inaugurated before an astonished city—the Centre looks like God turned it inside out and then went to town on it with a box of crayons. The exposed pipeworks in bright primary colors (green for water, blue for air, yellow for electricity, red for communications) may be the most memorable part of the building, but it is with the interior structure that the architects were truly innovative. To eliminate the need for columns to hold the building up, steel beams were cross-strutted and hinged over its length and width, connecting to the exterior skeleton. Water fills the large steel tubes, stabilizing the outward push made on the structure from the pressure of the floors. This never-before-tried system was supposed to give the Centre an unheard-of flexibility—walls could be taken down or put up anywhere at will.

While the building itself became a working model for architecture classes everywhere, the Centre's two major tenants, the museum and the Centre des Créations Industriel (CCI), soon defined its role in Parisian life. The CCI, the interactive part of the center, is composed of two parts: the BPI, or Bibliothèque Publique d'Information (*see* Resident Resources, in Chapter 1), and the IRCAM, or Institut de Recherche et Coordination de l'Acoustique et de la Musique (*see* Performing Arts, in Chapter 5). The BPI, with its massive open stacks and technological resources (microfiche back then, CD-ROM today), was supposed to revolutionize the traditional library, while the IRCAM offered a venue for contemporary dance, music, and theater performances. Supported by these various divisions are all the provocative colloquia and films you'd expect of a place that prides itself on intellectual overstimulation.

THE COLLECTION The Pompidou is justly proud of its permanent collection (which picks up around 1904, where the Orsay leaves off): Encompassing over 40,000 works, it is the largest single gathering of modern art in the world. Only 850 works can be displayed at any one time, though, and even then the museum galleries on the third and fourth floors are crammed with major pieces. The fourth floor houses the historical part of the collection, while the third has later pieces. The historical part starts off with Matisse, then takes off through the cubists, futurists, suprematists, surrealists, Bauhaus, European abstractionists, abstract expressionists, pop artists, minimalists . . . don't worry, the Centre has thoughtfully placed quartets of chairs throughout the galleries for you to flop down in and prepare yourself for the next artistic movement.

Because the museum got into the collecting business rather late compared with New York's Museum of Modern Art or Guggenheim Museum, there aren't as many postcard-famous works here as you'd expect. Of course, there are some stunners: **Alexander Calder's** (1898–1976) *Josephine Baker* was one of the sculptor's earliest and most graceful versions of the mobile—a form he invented. Until **Constantin Brancusi's** workshop (in the plaza in front of the Centre) is renovated, the works bequeathed by the sculptor to the city in 1957 are on display in their own gallery on the fourth floor. Also here is **Marcel Duchamp's** (1887–1968) *Valise,* a collection of miniature reproductions of his most famous Dada sculptures and drawings conveniently displayed in their own ironic carrying case. One of the last works by the piously abstract **Piet Mondrian** (1872–1944), *New York* marks one of the few breaks with the style of the *Compositions* he had been painting for the previous 25 years. The Russian **Kazimir Malevich** (1878–1935) declared that his *Black Square* was the point from which painting left behind the frivolity of illusionism in favor of abstraction. The museum displays his work where Male-

But Is It Art?

Rumor has it that sculptor Constantin Brancusi (1876–1957) walked from his native Romania to Paris to work for Rodin, only to be disgusted by what he saw as a factory workshop. Brancusi set up his own studio in Montparnasse, defining the modern aesthetic with his highly polished bronze, simple forms, and pure curving lines. What looks mass-produced was not: The artist crafted each sculpture himself. He made history when his Bird in Space was called an "industrial machine" by the U.S. Customs House in New York, which assigned a value to it as pure metal rather than artwork. Brancusi sued, and his victory both changed restrictions on art importation and redefined the meaning of the word art.

vich intended—hanging above eye level, as Eastern Orthodox Church icons were placed in pre-Revolution Russian homes. Also here is *Out of the Deep*, **Jackson Pollock's** (1912–1956) attempt a year before his death to return to the abstraction of his earlier drip paintings, though alcoholism and fame were suffocating his career.

Accessible only from an escalator within the fourth-floor galleries is the third floor, home to more recent works from the permanent collection. While the fourth floor has the unspoken need to spell out a history of early modern art, the third floor is far more playful.

Best Cup of Java at the Pompidou: Bring a thermos and drink your own brew in the escalators while looking down on the street below—the café in the Centre isn't worth it. If you can wait and are feeling stylish, go to Café Beaubourg across the plaza (see Cafés, in Chapter 4).

SPECIAL EXHIBITIONS Temporary shows play an important role in the life of the Pompidou; nine or so galleries are set up to serve that purpose, not to mention the countless partitions that pop up in the lobbies and other public spaces. The Grande Galerie on the fifth floor holds the big exhibitions, for which the Pompidou plasters the city with advertisements. Exhibition admission is separate (*see* Practicalities, *above*). Next door to the Grande Galerie is Studio 5, a cinema that screens films and videos related to the exhibition. Smaller displays relating to the main exhibition are scattered around the building; some are free, and the ones that charge admission are available in a package deal with the Grande Galerie. The Galerie Nord and Galerie Sud on the mezzanine level offer shows not connected to the big ones upstairs; shows usually focus on the work of a single artist.

FUTURE POMPIDOU The Pompidou may seem like an unmanageable mess, but the building's inside-out architecture is only partially to blame—there are simply too many people using the place. A victim of its own success, the Centre currently attracts daily crowds of 26,000 when it was intended to handle only 8,000. Overuse has taken its physical toll, a fact painfully obvious when you look at the threadbare carpets and scratched Plexiglas escalator tube. The influx of people means the Centre can't fulfill its function as a cultural shell that is as flexible as it is grand.

A multimillion-dollar renovation project was announced in the spring of 1994, despite the fact that the center is just 14 years old. The financially strapped national government has avoided making definite plans for a new Pompidou, but rumor has it that it will close for 18 months starting sometime in late 1995 or early 1996. The Pompidou's president François Barré hopes that the renovation will better organize wasted space like the lobby, relocate late-night public areas like the cinema to more accessible ground levels, clean up the worn exterior and interior, landscape the plaza in front, and make the glass-and-steel hulk more environmentally friendly. In announcing the proposed renovation, Barré admitted that the collection could no longer attempt to be a growing contemporary art museum—there is simply too little space to acquire anything other than works of historical importance. To see more up-and-coming contemporary artists, head to the Musée d'Art Moderne de la Ville de Paris (*see* Are and More Art, in Not-So-Major Museums, *below*). *4e, tel. 1/44–78–12–33 or 1/42–77–11–12. Métro: Rambuteau. Admission: permanent collection 30F, 20F ages 18–25, under 18 free, Sun. 10–2 free for everyone; Grande Galerie 40F, 30F under age 26; Galeries Nord and Sud 25F; all galleries and permanent collection 57F, 40F ages 13–25, under 13 free. Open Wed.–Mon. 10–6, Fri. until 10. Wheelchair access/barrier free.*

Not-so-Major Museums

Paris has so many museums you could spend your entire time in the city indoors. The following museums are arranged by type so you can pick and choose ones that sound enticing.

ART AND MORE ART

FONDATION CARTIER The Fondation Cartier has a reputation as one of the corporate world's greatest patrons of contemporary art; its new exhibition space highlights its commitment. Designed by Jean Nouvel (*see box, below*), the building is one of Paris's most stunning, a mélange of vast glass panes, complicated steel structures, and exposed mechanical work, all done so damn elegantly you can't accuse the building of being some cheesy high-tech cliché. While the watch-and-jewelry empire executives work upstairs in the Cartier headquarters, the basement and ground floor of this ultramodernist building hold galleries. Exhibitions are always changing and rarely controversial (the foundation makes a point of hosting only tasteful exhibits—it *is* Cartier, after all). The best way to experience both the art and Nouvel's building is to come on Thursday nights when the series "L'Esprit du Nomade" (The Spirit of the Nomad) offers dance, performance art, or live music around and about the art. *261 blvd. Raspail, 14e, tel. 1/42–18–56–50 or 1/42–18–56–51. Métro: Denfert-Rochereau. Admission: 30F, 20F under age 26; "L'Esprit du Nomade" included in admission. Open Tues.–Sun. noon–8, Thurs. until 10. Wheelchair access/barrier free.*

GRAND PALAIS AND PETIT PALAIS Intended as temporary additions to the Parisian landscape for the 1900 Exposition Universelle, these domed extravaganzas dodged the wrecking ball to become full-time tourist attractions. The **Grand Palais** became a salon space and the site of ballooning exhibitions, at which well-hatted ladies and gentlemen would gather under the glass-domed ceilings, heads tilted toward the puffed-up names of Michelin and Goodyear, and marvel at the future of travel. In more recent years big-time art exhibitions have been filling the modest halls of the building's wings. *3 av. du Général Eisenhower, 8e, tel. 1/44–13–17–17. Métro: Champs-Elysées–Clemenceau. Admission varies according to exhibit. Open Thurs.–Mon. 10–8, Wed. 10–10. Wheelchair access—entrance to left of main entrance; no accessible rest rooms.*

The **Petit Palais,** across the street, displays works in rich, vaulted halls that ironically are grander than those of the Grand Palais. In addition to temporary exhibits, there's a permanent collection featuring 17th-century Flemish works and particularly strong coverage of 19th-century French painters, including large and plentiful works by Courbet (his risqué 1866 *Le Sommeil,* of two naked women napping together, is especially popular) and a healthy handful of impressionist-era pieces, such as Cézanne's *Les Baigneuses* (1880). There are also large cases of turn-of-the-century jewelry, including many art nouveau pieces. *Av. Winston-Churchill, 8e, tel. 1/42–65–12–73. Métro: Champs-Elysées–Clemenceau. Admission: 26F, 14F students; temporary exhibits about 20F extra. Open Tues.–Sun. 10–5:40.*

JEU DE PAUME Named for the indoor tennis court that once stood in the royal Jardin des Tuileries, the Jeu de Paume held much of the national impressionist collection until the Musée d'Orsay laid claim to all things 19th century. The building stood neglected until a recent renovation created one of Paris's most inviting spaces. Exhibitions feature modern and contemporary masters, while the theater shows related documentaries—your ticket to the gallery also admits you to the screening room. There's a small café and a bookstore with a strong collection of French- and English-language art criticism and art catalogues. Admission prices and hours vary with exhibits. *Pl. de la Concorde, 1er, tel. 1/47–60–69–69. Métro: Concorde. Admission: 35F, 25F students. Open Tues. noon–9:30, Wed.–Fri. noon–7, weekends 10–7. Wheelchair access.*

MUSEE D'ART MODERNE DE LA VILLE DE PARIS Even though it was founded at the turn of the century, this museum has had a difficult time convincing the world that there is another major venue for modern art in Paris other than the Pompidou (*see* Major Museums, *above*). Much of this has to do with the lack of high-profile pieces: The permanent collection was built largely upon works donated by artists such as Henri Matisse and Robert Motherwell, and even though major artists gave, they rarely gave major works. Wisely deciding not to compete with the Goliath across town, the museum focuses on the contemporary works of more controversial artists.

The building was constructed for the Exposition Universelle in 1937; the museum moved into the east wing in 1967. The columned modern terrace offers a great view of the Eiffel Tower and is popular with skate rats, whose careening racket echoes off the walls of the empty Palais de Tokyo. On the way to the top floor it is impossible not to notice Raoul Dufy's (1877–1953) *Fée Electricité,* in which 600 square meters (720 square yards) of bright colors fervently depict the harnassing of electricity by humanity. Off the terrace on the ground floor are a café and a bookstore that stocks a curiously diverse selection of academic books and journals in English and

French. *11 av. du Président-Wilson, 16e, tel. 1/47–23–61–27. Métro: léna. Admission: permanent collection 15F; temporary exhibitions 30F–55F, 20F–45F under age 26. Open Tues.–Fri. 10–5:30, weekends 10–7.*

MUSEE DE CLUNY This museum began in 1832 as the private—most people thought quirky—medieval art collection of Alexandre du Sommerand in an *hôtel particulier* (mansion) built over and around the ruins of some Roman baths. The state purchased the hôtel and collection soon after and turned the place into a full-time museum. Today the collection features medieval stained glass, furniture, jewelry, carvings, music manuscripts, and some exquisite tapestries. One of the finest tapestry series—found half-eaten by rats before being brought here—is *The Lady and the Unicorn,* comprising six panels in which a refined lady demonstrates the five senses to a unicorn. The museum recently acquired a set of sculpted heads of the kings of Judea that once looked out from the facade of the Cathédrale de Notre-Dame; thought to have been lost during the Revolution, they were rediscovered in a bank vault in 1977. *6 pl. du Paul-Painlevé, 5e, tel. 1/43–25–62–00. Métro: Cluny–La Sorbonne. Admission: 27F, 18F students and Sun. Open Wed.–Mon. 9:15–5:45.*

MUSEE DE L'ORANGERIE This small but rewarding collection of impressionist and post-impressionist paintings sits peacefully near the Jardin des Tuileries. The museum is especially nice if you're in the mood for some turn-of-the-century art but can't deal with the enormity of the Musée d'Orsay. Below generous rooms of Renoirs and thorough displays of Cézanne, Manet, and Modigliani lies the museum's most popular room: a magical, watery oval space lined completely with Monet's huge water-lily paintings. Inspired by Monet's home at Giverny (*see* Chapter 7), the *Nymphéas* are perhaps the best-known of his "series" works—repeated studies of the effects of different lighting upon the same subject. (Other of his series subjects include the Gare St-Lazare and the cathedral at Rouen.) After the 1918 armistice, Monet donated the *Nymphéas* to the state, though he requested they not be displayed until after his death. A 20-minute rest in the center of the room may do wonders for your stress level. *Pl. de la Concorde, 1er, tel. 1/42–97–48–16. Métro: Concorde. Admission: 27F, 18F under age 26 and Sun. Open Wed.–Mon. 9:45–5:15.*

MUSEE DES ARTS DECORATIFS You may finally realize just how big the Louvre palace is when you consider that this major collection of decorative arts occupies only a portion of one of its wings. Spread confusingly over the museum's four floors are chairs, vases, sword cases, and other necessities of life from the Middle Ages to the present. There are also many rooms that have been meticulously redecorated with furniture and other appropriate items: The game room has a backgammon board, the bathroom a soap dish, the salon an ostentatious number of chairs. The art nouveau era is best represented. *107 rue de Rivoli, 1er, tel. 1/44–55–57–50. Métro: Palais Royal–Musée du Louvre. Admission: 25F, 16F under age 26. Open Wed.–Sat. 12:30–6, Sun. noon–6.*

MUSEE MARMOTTAN A couple of years ago this museum tacked "Claude Monet" onto its official name—and justly so, as this may be the best collection of the artist's works anywhere. A sampling of works by fellow impressionists and portraitists like Louis Léopold Boilly fill out the areas of this airy hôtel particulier not claimed by Claude. Small displays include letters exchanged by impressionist painters Berthe Morisot and Mary Cassatt. Some of the rooms make you feel as if you're at an actual salon, with comfortable couches and grand windows overlooking the Jardin de Ranelagh on one side, the hôtel's private yard on the other.

While Claude shares the wall space of the bright upstairs rooms, his real display is down in the basement, where walls full of his luminous *Nymphéas* more than make up for the lack of windows. Among such well-known works as the series *Cathédrale à Rouen* and *Parlement à Londres,* you'll find *Impressions: Soleil Levant* (1873), now recognized as the first impressionist painting. The critics were not being complimentary: They saw the painting as simplistic and mocked Monet's title with such comments as "Oh, isn't it *impressive;* oh, I'm so *impressed.*" Throughout the building, notice portraits of Monet and his family, including two by Renoir—one of Monet and one of his wife—displayed in the basement. *2 rue Louis-Boilly, 16e, tel. 1/42–24–07–02. Métro: La Muette. Admission: 35F, 15F students under age 25. Open Tues.–Sun. 10–5:30.*

INDIVIDUAL ARTISTS

Although the Rodin and Picasso museums are big draws, there are a host of smaller museums dedicated to the lives and works of individual artists. The **Musée Bourdelle** (16 rue Antoine Bourdelle, 14e, tel. 1/45–48–67–27) is in the former home studio of the early 20th-century sculptor who made busts of Rodin and Beethoven.

ESPACE MONTMARTRE–DALI This compact museum boasts over 300 works by the wacked master of surrealism, Salvador Dalí (1904–89). Fans of his dream landscapes and psychedelic sculptures should enjoy what the museum has to offer, but be warned: Most of the works in the collection are lithographs and castings produced in the winter of the artist's life, when a sick and senile Dalí was signing his name to prints and sculptures that were mainly reproductions of his earlier works. *11 rue Poulbot, 18e, tel. 1/42–64–40–10. Métro: Pigalle, Anvers, or Abbesses. Admission: 35F. Open July–Aug., daily 10–7; Sept.–June, daily 10–6.*

MUSEE GUSTAVE MOREAU Symbolist painter Gustave Moreau (1826–98), the mentor of an entire generation of young symbolists and teacher of subsequent celebrities Matisse and Rouault, spent the final years of his life forming a little collection in his apartment. At his death, the collection became a public museum. Other than a few small works by Rembrandt and Poussin, the museum is devoted to the works of Moreau himself. *14 rue de la Rochefoucauld, 9e, tel. 1/48–74–38–50. Métro: Trinité. Admission: 17F, 11F students and Sun. Open Thurs.–Sun. 10–12:45 and 2–5:15, Mon. and Wed. 11–5:15.*

MUSEE NATIONAL EUGENE DELACROIX This modest museum is housed in the last apartment Delacroix occupied before his death, in 1863. Bits of Delacroix paraphernalia and furniture—a paint box here, a divan there—decorate the tiny complex of rooms, and prints and paintings cover the walls. Knowing that he painted in this space is, however, more exciting than the artwork itself. Through the back is his high-ceilinged, generously windowed studio, overlooking a quiet courtyard. *6 pl. de Furstenberg, 6e, tel. 1/43–54–04–87. Métro: St-Germain-des-Prés. Admission: 12F, 8F under age 26. Open Wed.–Mon. 9:45–5:15.*

MUSEE PICASSO Because Spaniard Pablo Picasso's family couldn't come up with enough cash to settle the taxes on his estate, they instead donated a large number of his works to the French government. The government then created a museum for them, in the beautiful 17th-century Hôtel Salé in the heart of the Marais district. The Musée Picasso is one of the most popular museums in Paris, largely because the place is so pleasant: A tailored garden out back; a stately driveway out front; a covered sculpture garden in between; and art all over the basement, the attic, and the two stories of the hôtel make this a great place to visit. Rooms in the museum are arranged chronologically, and information in each (in English) tells about major events in the artist's life. Picasso was known not only as the greatest artist of his generation, but also as somewhat of a jerk. He was rude and misogynistic; he seduced other artists' wives; and when his contemporaries (including Georges Braque and Guillaume Apollinaire) were shipped off to World War I, he stayed safely in Paris with his Spanish passport. His loutish behavior, however, could not detract from his artistic contributions. Taking their cues from the field of physics, Picasso, Braque, and Juan Gris reformulated the way three-dimensional space was represented on canvas. Though best known as a painter, Picasso was also an innovative sculptor, constructing cubist guitars and using a toy Renault for the snout of a bronze baboon. The collection here represents a sampling of every stage of Picasso's work, but there are no blue-chip pieces to be found here—those are all in New York. *5 rue Thorigny, 3e, tel. 1/42–71–25–21. Métro: Chemin-Vert or St-Paul. Admission: 26F, 17F ages 17–25 and Wed. Open Wed.–Mon. 9:30–6.*

Between drinking bouts at the local cafés, Georges Braque and Pablo Picasso were messing around in their Montmartre studio, developing a new style that came to be known as cubism. They pasted newspapers onto canvases, mixed sand into their paint, and found a thousand different ways to represent a bottle of rum. It may seem tame now, but this was sexy stuff in 1912.

MUSEE RODIN The Musée Rodin is possibly the most beautiful museum in all of Paris. The undisputed master of 19th-century French sculpture (some say of 19th-century French art) left his house, the early 18th-century Hôtel Biron, and all the works in it to the state when he died. The mansion, with the second-largest garden in the neighborhood (after the prime minister's), is as much a part of the museum as the art. In addition to the garden (which you can visit without the museum for a reduced fee) and the pavilion exhibiting temporary shows, you can see Rodin's personal collection of impressionist and post-impressionist paintings.

Auguste Rodin was simultaneously loathed and praised by the French, who both appreciated his genius and despised his vision. His career took off in 1876 with *L'Age d'Airain* (The Age of Bronze), a sculpture—in bronze, of course—inspired by a pilgrimage to Italy and the sculptures of Michelangelo. Because the work was so realistic, some critics accused Rodin of having stuck a live boy in plaster, while others blasted him for what was seen as a sloppy sculpting and casting technique. His messiness was quite intentional and became one of the defining characteristics of Rodin's style. Rather than follow the prescribed practice of smoothing over rough edges in the plaster, filling in air holes, and filing down imperfections after the bronze had been cast, Rodin created works that read like statements about the sculpting process. Fingerprints, fabric patterns (damp rags were set on the clay so it wouldn't dry out), and tool grooves were all left intact on the original models, as were all the marks made during the casting process. His marble works were also left in "half-finished" states in homage to Michelangelo (see his *Slaves* in the Louvre), though most of Rodin's works in stone were carved by apprentices.

Four years after *L'Age d'Airain,* Rodin was commissioned to create the doors for the newly proposed Musée des Arts Décoratifs. He set out to sculpt a pair of monumental bronze doors in the tradition of Italian Renaissance churches, calling his proposal the *Gate of Hell* (*La Porte de l'Enfer*). The *Gate,* a visual representation of stories from Dante's *Divine Comedy,* became his obsession: He spent the last 37 years of his life working on it, and almost all works inside his museum—the naked men and women, faces taut with pain and ecstasy while locked in impossible positions—are used somehow in the doors. As the sculptures became increasingly fantastic and erotic, the narrative of the *Gate* became more and more syncopated: Instead of each door panel representing a specific story, Rodin ignored the panels altogether, saturating the doors with chaotic figures repeated in different positions. The *Gate* was never completed, and no casts of the masterpiece were made during Rodin's life—the museum's bronze out in the garden is posthumous.

Though the *Gate* may have been the project of a lifetime, Rodin continued to work on other projects (though many were later incorporated into the doors). He often did portrait work, but pieces done in monumental scale were his greatest love, and he actively pursued public commissions for such projects. *Les Bourgeois de Calais* (The Burghers of Calais, 1884–86), in the garden, is a grouping of statues commemorating six town fathers who were ordered by England's Edward III in 1347 to exchange their lives for the safety of the city. Instead of portraying stately, virile leaders marching off bravely to face death, Rodin sculpted a group of anguished old men weighed down by chains. The town at first refused to accept the statue; later it relented but placed the sculpture on a high pedestal instead of at eye level as Rodin had planned.

Possibly Rodin's most celebrated work is *Le Penseur* (1880), the muscular manly man caught in a moment of deep thought and flex. The version here in the garden is the original—the city of Paris, its intended owner, refused to accept it. Before installing the permanent bronze statue on the steps of the Panthéon, Rodin set up a full-scale plaster cast. Its physicality horrified the public; crowds gathered around the statue, debates ensued, and Rodin was ridiculed in the press. A man who was later tried and found criminally insane hacked away at some of the plaster cast with a hatchet, giving the city a convenient excuse to refuse the statue.

It is difficult to believe that the artist so revered today could have been so controversial during his career. Though the critics may have complained and the public may have taken offense, Rodin loved the attention—he even retained a clipping service to keep up with the jabs being made at him in the press. When the sculptor died, at the height of World War I, his wake drew the largest nonmilitary crowd (26,000) of the time.

Rodin may have hogged the limelight, but his museum allows some space to works by Camille Claudel. Rodin's mistress, Claudel was a remarkable sculptor in her own right. (Look at her

L'*Age Mûr,* done in 1900, for the dynamics: The young girl is Claudel, the man Rodin, and the old woman his wife.) Shunning the monumental except for her *Persus et la Medusa* (Medusa's face was a self-portrait), Claudel experimented with smaller figures in well-defined, almost architectural settings. Her torturous relationship with Rodin drove her out of his studio—as though life weren't difficult enough for female sculptors doing nonconventional work in the late 19th century. In 1913 her family committed her to an asylum on the Ile de la Cité (*see* Neighborhoods, *below*), where she remained, barred from any artistic activities, until her death in 1943. Had Claudel's talent not been straitjacketed, today we might be seeing her sculptures at the Musée Claudel rather than squished in among Rodin's. *77 rue de Varenne, 7e, tel. 1/47–05–01–34. Métro: Varenne. Admission: 27F, 18F students under age 26, gardens only 5F. Open Wed.–Mon. 9:30–5:15.*

MUSEE ZADKINE The former studio of Ukrainian-born Ossip Zadkine (1890–1967) has become, in the 14 years since his widow bequeathed it to Paris, one of the nicest museums to visit in the city—regardless of what you think of Zadkine's work. Dozens of sculptures from his Parisian career (he moved to the city in 1909) pack the few small but bright rooms; feeling the sculptures is particularly tempting, since Zadkine worked with natural and treated woods, brass, and stone, giving the materials varying levels of shine. Only the sight-impaired can touch, though. No great innovator, Zadkine was instead a skilled imitator of the styles that passed through Paris during the early to mid 20th century—cubism, futurism, primitivism, etc.—so looking at his works is, at worst, a good art history lesson. Check out the free sculpture garden in front for a peaceful reading break. *100 bis rue d'Assas, 6e, tel. 1/43–26–91–90. Métro: Vavin. Admission: 17F50, 9F students under 26. Open Tues.–Sun. 10–5:30.*

WRITERS

Honoré de Balzac once lived in the **Maison de Balzac** (47 rue Raynouard, 16e, tel. 1/42–24–56–38), leaving behind a bunch of letters and original manuscripts. This museum is better if you read French. See the memorabilia of woman writer, bohemian, and cross-dresser George Sand at the **Musée de la Vie Romantique** (16 rue Chaptal, 9e, tel. 1/48–74–95–38), in the onetime studio of painter Ary Scheffer, where Chopin, Delacroix, Liszt, and other greats would gather in the evenings to swap artistic views and perform for one another. Both museums are open Tuesday–Sunday 10–5:40.

MAISON DE VICTOR HUGO The former home of France's literary hero has become a two-story museum in his honor, though it displays none of the manuscripts for which he was so adored. What is interesting here is the re-created rooms on the second floor (where Hugo's apartment was) and the artwork on the first, including some rather bizarre watercolors by Hugo and illustrations for his writings by other painters; Bayard's Cosette of *Les Misérables* T-shirt fame is here. The rooms upstairs represent Hugo's living style in several of his many homes; the central room of the floor, for instance, is decorated with Chinese-theme panels and woodworks he created for his mistress's home outside town. The rather intricate wooden table in the smallest room is the "Table with Four Inkwells," carved by Hugo himself and sold for charity. *6 pl. des Vosges, 4e, tel. 1/42–72–10–16. Métro: Chemin Vert or St-Paul. Admission: 18F, 9F under age 25. Open Tues.–Sun. 10–5:40.*

HISTORY

The **Musée de Montmartre** (12 rue Cortot, 18e, tel. 1/46–06–61–11) is a fascinating little collection of photos and changing exhibits on life in Montmartre, including displays about famous former inhabitants, drawings by Toulouse-Lautrec, and minor works by Modigliani, Vlaminck, Utrillo, and others. Admission is 25F, students 20F, and it's open Tuesday through Sunday 11–6. The **Musée des Collections Historiques de la Préfecture de Police** (1 bis rue des Carmes, 5e, tel. 1/43–29–21–57) will tell you all you ever wanted to know about the life and times of cops in Paris, for free, weekdays 9–5.

LA CONCIERGERIE This complex of towers and halls served as the royal palace until 1358, when a young Charles V sought to place a safe distance between himself and his assassination-prone subjects by building the Louvre across the Seine. Since the 14th century, the Conciergerie (named after the official who administered the castle) has served as a tribunal hall and prison, but its most macabre period came in the 18th century when the Revolutionary court mercilessly issued death proclamations—2,780 to be exact—from its halls. While much of the nobility passed through these cells, the most famous resident was Marie Antoinette, who spent her final days here before being hauled off on a garbage cart to be guillotined. The court disbanded after the execution of Robespierre, who became the victim of the Terror he had himself initiated. Now the Conciergerie is merely the basement of the Palais de Justice, though a motley collection of empty halls and dusty approximations of cells brings in tourists. *1 quai de l'Horloge, 1er, tel. 1/43–54–30–06. Métro: Pont-Neuf or Cité. Admission: 26F, 17F under age 26. Open Apr.–Sept., daily 9:30–6:30; Oct.–Mar., daily 10–5.*

MUSEE CARNAVALET It takes two hôtels particuliers in the Marais—the Carnavalet and Le Peletier de St-Fargeau—to house this worthwhile collection paying homage to Parisian history. Basically, the Carnavalet (through which you enter) covers ancient Paris through the reign of Louis XVI; the Peletier, the Revolution through the 20th century, though you could go crazy trying to move through the poorly marked rooms chronologically.

In the courtyard off rue de Sévigné stands the last remaining bronze statue of a Louis: Louis XIV, whose representation by Coysevox was saved from Revolutionary meltdown only by oversight—the people simply didn't notice it in the too-obvious Hôtel de Ville. Back inside, other treasures include Jean-Jacques Rousseau's inkwell and blackened blotting sponge, keys to the Bastille, and Napoléon I's death mask. Most entertaining, however, are the re-created rooms, particularly Marcel Proust's bedroom, the turn-of-the-century Fouquet jewelry shop, and a room from the Art Nouveau Café de Paris. *23 rue de Sévigné, 3e, tel. 1/42–72–21–13. Métro: St-Paul. Admission: 26F, 14F students. Open Tues.–Sun. 10–5:40.*

MUSEE DES MONUMENTS FRANCAIS This collection originally came together in 1882 to show visitors models of all of Paris's great monuments in one small space. The museum later took up permanent residence at the Trocadéro, where today it continues to house faithful monument copies, many of which are full-scale, out in the open and unprotected from your scrutinizing eyes and greasy fingers. Hundreds of reproductions of portals, statues, and other pieces represent all the blockbuster structures in France, from Chartres to Mont-St-Michel. *1 pl. du Trocadéro, 16e, tel. 1/44–05–39–10. Métro: Trocadéro. Admission: 21F, 14F under age 26. Open Wed.–Mon. 10–6. Wheelchair access.*

PAVILLON DE L'ARSENAL Home to the Centre d'Urbanisme et d'Architecture de la Ville de Paris, this spacious late-19th-century arsenal is devoted entirely to documenting and exploring the buildings of Paris. Dominating the ground floor is the *Grande Modèle*, a 40-meter- (432-foot-) square model of Paris complete with interactive video screens—you can direct a CD-ROM terminal to display any of 30,000 images of the city and its buildings. Temporary exhibits take up the ground floor and upper loft, and a library (*see* Resident Resources, in Chapter 1) provides art and architecture periodicals and books, plus 70,000 photographs of Paris. *21 blvd. Morland, 4e, tel. 1/42–76–33–97. Métro: Sully-Morland. Admission free. Open Tues.–Sat. 10:30–6:30, Sun. 11–7.*

WORLD CULTURES

INSTITUT DU MONDE ARABE More than a museum, this is a monstrous multimedia cultural center. Built with funds from the French and most Arab governments, the institute is attempting to become a "cultural bridge" between Europe and the Arab world. In addition to its huge library and audiovisual center, the institute has two exhibition spaces, one for the permanent collection and the other for traveling exhibitions. The permanent collection (admission 25F, 20F under age 26) is a combination of the institute's and some of the Louvre's Arab artifacts, with works dating from the pre-Islamic era to the present. The traveling exhibitions are usually blockbuster events, well-publicized by a large banner on the facade facing rue des Fossés-St-Bernard.

The bookstore on the ground floor sells compact discs and jewelry, along with the usual museum prints. Films are shown in the cinema on Saturday and Sunday, all in their original language with French subtitles (22F, 18F students and senior citizens). A café and a restaurant reside on the ninth floor, though the former makes you pay dearly for the view (one of the best in Paris) and the latter serves surprisingly bland food.

The building itself is a source of pride to Parisians, Arabs, and French-Arabs, all of whom consider the graceful glass institute one of Paris's finest modern structures. Designed by Jean Nouvel (*see box, below*), it is famous for the way it manipulates light. Behind the glass south wall are 240 mechanized metal plates that act like the aperture on a camera—a contemporary interpretation of the *moucharabieh* (traditional Arab light-filtering latticework). Photo cells in the wall respond to the intensity of light outside, opening and closing the spiraling plates so that the interior of the institute is never too bright or too dim. This filtering system attracts hordes of visitors each day, though the complex mechanics have been known to break down. The interior courtyard plays with light in a less flashy manner: Small squares of thinly cut white marble in the walls are carefully held in place by metal pins, allowing the sunlight to pass through the stone's patterns and illuminate the interior of the building with a soft glow. On top of this it's hard to get over the view—the spectacular panorama from the ninth-floor terrace encompasses Paris in all her glory. *1 rue des Fossés-St-Bernard, 5e, tel. 1/40–51–38–38. Métro: Jussieu or Cardinal Lemoine. Open Tues.–Sun. 10–6. Wheelchair access/barrier free.*

MUSEE DES ARTS AFRICAINS ET OCEANIENS This building, one of the first made with reinforced concrete, was designed for the 1931 Exposition Coloniale, held in the Bois de Vincennes. The museum's collection, first named Museum of the Colonies, was updated and renamed Museum of France Overseas after World War II—the "Virtues of French Colonization" display, however, still held a prominent position. Finally, in 1960, the museum settled upon its current name under the advice of France's Ministry of Cultural Affairs.

The excellent collection on display is divided by region and well-explained, *if* you read French. The ground floor houses displays on **South Pacific cultures**—including a generous selection from New Guinea—and temporary exhibits, usually featuring contemporary African artists. The first floor turns to **central African cultures,** looking at great kingdoms in the Congo and Benin. The importance of funerary rites in this region, particularly among the Ashanti, is evidenced in the death masks and other funerary objects on display. The top floor is dedicated to the heavily colonized countries of the **Maghreb** (Algeria, Tunisia, and Morocco); items from this area include some impressive Algerian jewelry, which will instill new respect in you for your mostly intact earlobes and neck. Finally, in the basement lurk crocodiles of the Nile, in a ditch that curators have tried their damnedest to transform into a natural habitat. The calm **aquarium** surrounding the crocs is home to a second ditch (filled with turtles) and some fairly beautiful sea creatures brought from the regions represented upstairs. A small **library,** open weekdays 10–6, is on the east side of the building. *293 av. Daumesnil, 12e, tel. 1/44–74–84–80. Métro: Porte Dorée. Admission: 27F, 18F under age 26. Open Mon. and Wed.–Fri. 10–5:30, weekends 10–6.*

Jean Nouvel

Jean Nouvel, an emerging visionary of Parisian architecture, has designed two of the city's most intensely scrutinized buildings: the Institut du Monde Arabe and the Fondation Cartier. His philosophical obsession with "transparency" inspired the light-manipulating wall at the institute and the mobile 8-by-3-meter (26-by-10-foot) glass panels at Cartier. Critics have termed his style "façadism," but Nouvel is quick to differentiate between his innovative use of glass—panes that fog, LCD (liquid crystal display, as found on digital watches) tinted panels, thermal plates—and run-of-the-mill corporate architecture. His latest project is the proposed Tour Sans Fin, a 400-meter (1,312-foot) cylindrical tower at La Défense, to be enclosed entirely by, of course, glass.

MUSEE NATIONAL DES ARTS ASIATIQUES–GUIMET This enormous collection of religious and secular artwork from China, Japan, India, Indochina, Indonesia, and Central Asia spans over 3,000 years of history. As specified in the late 19th century by founder Emile Guimet, the collection is divided by country; info centers in each area explain individual histories and religious developments, but only in French. Highlights include seductive statues of Hindu gods and goddesses and stunning finds from the Chinese Silk Route, including painted silk banners. Don't miss the annex at 19 avenue d'léna (same ticket), which thoroughly explores the Buddha in images from China and Japan. A comfortable **library** upstairs in the main building houses over 10,000 works on Asian arts and religions and is open to the public Monday and Wednesday–Friday from 10 to 5. *6 pl. d'léna, 16e, tel. 1/47–23–61–65. Métro: léna. Admission: 27F, 18F under age 26. Open Wed.–Sun. 9:45–5:45.*

PHOTOGRAPHY

CENTRE NATIONAL DE LA PHOTOGRAPHIE Photographs previously housed in the Palais de Tokyo have been relocated to the ground floor of the sprawling Hôtel Salomon de Rothschild. Big-name shows focusing on a single genre or artist dominate the main gallery, though peripheral rooms may display works from the permanent collection. Institutes related to photography are on the upper floors. The sizable grounds are well-tended but off-limits, affording a strictly visual appreciation of nature. Balzac died in 1850 in a house that once stood in the west garden. *11 rue Berryer, 8e, tel. 1/53–76–12–31. Métro: George V. Admission: 30F, 15F students under 27 (may vary by exhibition). Open Wed.–Mon. noon–7. Closed Aug.*

ESPACE PHOTO DE PARIS Somehow this tiny gallery is able to stage consistently great photography exhibits, thanks to an association with the cultural muscle of the Mairie de Paris. If the space feels mall-like, that's because it *is* in a mall: You can take turns contemplating the prints and looking through the plate-glass windows at happy teens shopping their way down to Fnac. *4–8 Grande Galerie des Halles, 1er, tel. 1/40–26–87–12. Métro: Les Halles. Admission: 10F. Open Tues.–Fri. 1–6, weekends 1–7.*

TECHNOLOGY AND SCIENCE

CITE DES SCIENCES ET DE L'INDUSTRIE This museum is a mammoth orgy of everything industrial and scientific, inviting you to play with, test out, or simply marvel at its many exhibits. Give yourself at least half a day to see everything. The structure is indeed the size of a small city—it's three times the size of the Pompidou—and was built in 1986 on land that once housed Paris's slaughterhouses. Now the area is all glass and stainless steel, bridges and suspended walkways.

The permanent exhibit is dedicated to scientific exploration, with explanations in English, French, German, Spanish, and Italian. Hands-on experiments include futuristic musical instruments, environmental manipulation, a simulated space voyage, and cutting-edge photography. The second-floor **planetarium** is well worth a stop. The magnificent steel sphere in front of the exhibit building is the **Géode cinema** (tel. 1/40–05–80–00), with the largest projection screen in existence; tickets for films (usually nature flicks) are sold separately for 55F, 40F for those under 26. The Cité backs up to the equally playful Parc de la Villette (*see* Parks and Gardens, *below*). *Parc de la Villette, 30 av. Corentin-Cariou, 19e, tel. 1/40–05–70–00. Métro: Porte de la Villette. Admission: 45F, 35F under age 26. Open Tues.–Sun. 10–6. Wheelchair access.*

PALAIS DE LA DECOUVERTE The worst thing about this museum, in a back wing of the Grand Palais, is the preponderance of grammar school student groups. The best thing is quality displays on all branches of science, from the solar system to the human brain. The exhibits are rarely hands-on, but they are informative and eye-catching. Sign up as soon as you arrive for one of the planetarium shows (15F extra, 10F students). *Av. Franklin D. Roosevelt, 8e, tel. 1/40–74–80–00. Admission: 45F, 27F students. Open Tues.–Sat. 9:30–6, Sun. 10–7.*

ANTHROPOLOGY AND NATURAL HISTORY

MUSEE DE L'HOMME Visiting this anthropology museum in the Palais de Chaillot is like taking a trip around the world and through about 3 million years of history. Permanent exhibits show clothing, musical instruments, and other artifacts of the major cultures of the world (African, Asian, Middle Eastern, European, Native North and South American, indigenous Australian, South Pacific, Arctic) and fossil displays from prehistory to the present. Don't miss Descartes's skull, the solution to the mind-body problem preserved forever in a little glass case. Excellent temporary exhibits highlight topics like prehistoric funeral rites. *Pl. du Trocadéro, 16e, tel. 1/44–05–72–72. Métro: Trocadéro. Admission: 25F, 15F students. Open Wed.–Mon. 9:45–5:15.*

MUSEE NATIONAL D'HISTOIRE NATURELLE This natural history museum recently reopened after being closed for over two decades. The gorgeous grand interior hall is filled with big animals—bears, tigers, elephants, whales, otters, and on and on—all stuffed for your viewing pleasure. The fourth floor affords the most horrifying view of all: You can peer down over the iron railing into an eerie layout of hundreds and hundreds of dead animals. TV screens in front of comfortable leather chairs document the fascinating art of taxidermy. So far the place is a big hit, particularly with kids. *Jardin des Plantes, 36 rue Geoffroy St-Hilaire, 5e, tel. 1/40–79–39–39. Métro: Gare d'Austerlitz or Censier-Daubenton. Admission: 40F, 30F under age 26. Open Wed.–Mon. 10–6, Thurs. until 10. Wheelchair access/barrier free.*

I Don't Think We're at the Louvre Anymore . . .

Paris is home to several museums that, for some reason, just don't pull in the tourist hordes. Here are a few:

- Musée de Cire Grévin: A wax museum covering all the big names from French history and American pop culture (including Barbie). Not exactly Madame Tussaud's, and expensive, too. 10 blvd. Montmartre, 9e, tel. 1/42–46–13–26. Métro: Rue Montmartre. Admission: 48F. Open daily 1–7.

- Musée de la Holographie: Welcome to the '90s. Niveau 1, Forum des Halles, 1er, tel. 1/40–39–96–83. Métro: Les Halles. Admission: 32F, 26F students. Open Mon.–Sat. 10–6:30, Sun. 1–7.

- Musée de la Poste: A whole museum dedicated to stamps and the history of written communication, including the balloon used to get mail out of Paris during the 1870 Prussian siege. 34 blvd. de Vaugirard, 15e, tel. 1/42–79–23–45. Métro: Montparnasse. Admission: 25F, 12F50 students. Open Mon.–Sat. 10–6.

- Musée du Parfum: Five thousand years of perfume history in one room. 39 blvd. des Capucines, 1er, tel. 1/42–60–37–14. Métro: Opéra. Admission free. Open Mon.–Sat. 9–6.

- Musée Edith Piaf: A small museum with Piaf's letters, clothes, recordings, and some photographs. Call for an appointment. 5 rue Crespin-du-Gast, 11e, tel. 1/43–55–52–72. Métro: Ménilmontant or St-Maur. Open Mon.–Thurs. 1–6.

NOT-SO-MAJOR MUSEUMS

79

MISCELLANY

MUSEE DE LA CONTREFACON Counterfeits account for 5%–9% of world trade—nine out of 10 "Levi's 501" T-shirts sold in France are fake. The Paris Manufacturers Union, egged on by such powerful companies as Cartier, opened this museum to document the problem. The resulting tiny exhibition hall lets you compare fake perfume bottles, liquor labels, and designer shirts with the real thing. *15 rue de la Faisanderie, 16e, tel. 1/45–01–51–11. Métro: Porte Dauphine. Admission free. Open Mon. and Wed. 2–4:30, Fri. 9:30–noon.*

MUSEE DE LA CURIOSITE This is in the running for Paris's most outrageously priced museum, but in certain moods it can be irresistible. Also called the Museum of Magic, the small underground gallery is crammed with optical illusions, funky mirrors, discourses on the history of sorcery, and variations on the magic wand. An in-house musician performs card tricks between more formal shows, given every half-hour or so. *11 rue St-Paul, 4e, tel. 1/42–72–13–26. Métro: St-Paul. Admission: 45F, 30F children. Open Wed. and weekends 2–7.*

MUSEE DE LA MODE ET DU COSTUME In the 1920s Paris decided it needed a fashion museum, and after a couple of trial runs at World Expos, this is where it wound up. Most of the collection has been donated; sometimes dozens of pieces are left to the museum in a single will. The strictly temporary exhibits, usually centering on fashionable aspects of Paris's past, feature hundreds of items of clothing and accessories. Admission varies according to exhibits but hovers between 35F and 40F, with a reduction for anyone under 26. *10 av. Pierre-1er-de-Serbie, 16e, tel. 1/47–20–85–23. Métro: Iéna. Open Tues.–Sun. 10–5:40.*

Dead Folk

Paris has an ever-growing population of the dearly departed, and thanks to well-labeled cemeteries, ossuaries, and reliquaries, you can pay homage to most of them. Paris's cemeteries are not just the eternal hangout of generations of famous dead folk, though; they can also be quite pleasant places for a picnic or quiet stroll. The Catacombes are another matter—eerie, dank passages filled with stacks of bones. That's not to say that all dead folk in Paris are easily accessible: Napoléon probably would find it fitting that while you could touch the tombstones of Frédéric Chopin, Gertrude Stein, and Oscar Wilde all in a short (free) visit to Père Lachaise, you have to pay around 30F to get within eyeshot of the outer layer of the erstwhile emperor's five caskets (*see* Hôtel des Invalides, in Monuments, *above*). *Hours for all city cemeteries: Mar. 16–Nov. 5, weekdays 8–6, Sat. 8:30–6, Sun. 9–6; Nov. 6–Mar. 15, weekdays 8–5:30, Sat. 8:30–5:30, Sun. 9–5:30.*

LES CATACOMBES

"Arrête! C'est ici l'Empire de la Mort." (Stop! Here is the Empire of Death.) Such is your welcome after a winding descent through dark, clammy passages to Paris's principal ossuary and most disturbing collection of human remains. The notorious Cimetière des Innocents, a stinky, overcrowded plot of common trenches, was the first to be unloaded here—leading to the consecration of the catacombs as a burial spot in 1786, when the decomposing bodies under what is now place des Innocents started invading neighboring cellars, bringing swarms of ravenous rats with them. Other churchyard cemeteries, if not quite so desperate to dispose of their residents, were nonetheless happy to dump legions of bones in the catacombs, separating them not by owner but by type—witness the piles of skulls, rows of tibias, and stacks of spinal disks. The only distinction among parts occurs in the bizarre attempts at bone art, like skulls arranged in the shape of hearts. It's all very nightmarish and unsavory and makes you feel quite . . . mortal. Among the bones in here are those of **Mirabeau,** the Revolution leader who found an early resting place in the Panthéon (*see below*) but was transferred when his ideas became unfashionable; keeping him company are the remains of fellow rebels,

The catacombs' scrawled warning to get away from the "Empire of the Dead" was enough to convince World War II German troops to leave promptly. They never guessed that Resistance fighters used the creepy tunnels as a base.

many of them brought fresh from the guillotine. Sixteenth-century satirist and writer **Rabelais** was brought from the former cemetery at the Eglise St-Paul St-Louis, and famous courtesan **Madame de Pompadour** is mixed in with the rabble after a lifetime spent as the mistress of Louis XV. Be prepared to walk long distances when you come here—the tunnels stretch for kilometers. *1 pl. Denfert-Rochereau, 14e, tel. 1/43–22–47–63. Métro: Denfert-Rochereau. Admission: 25F, 15F students. Open Tues.–Fri. 2–4, weekends 9–11 and 2–4.*

CIMETIERE DE MONTMARTRE

The Montmartre neighborhood was once home to a lively art scene, but today the dead artists in the area draw more attention than the ones still breathing. Among the former is **François Truffaut** (1932–84), who turned from critic to filmmaker with *Les 400 Coups* (1959), the flick that kicked off the French Nu Wave. Born in Cologne, Germany, the composer **Jacques Offenbach** (1819–80) linked himself to Paris forever when he standardized the cancan and became the host of great soirées. Dancer **Vaslav Nijinsky** (1890–1950) enjoyed a brilliant career in the Russian Ballet Company under the loving care of Sergei Diaghilev. But when Nijinsky suddenly married, jealous Sergei kicked him out of the troupe, inadvertently kicking him off his rocker at the same time: Nijinsky spent the last 37 years of his life as a schizophrenic.

Other colorful residents include painters **Edgar Degas** (1834–1917) and **Jean-Honoré Fragonard** (1732–1806); writers **Stendhal** (1783–1842) and **Alexandre Dumas,** *fils* (1824–95); composer **Hector Berlioz** (1803–69); social philosopher **Charles Fourier** (1772–1832); physicist **Jean Bernard Foucault** (1819–68); and poet **Heinrich Heine** (1797–1856). *18e. Métro: Place Clichy.*

CIMETIERE DE PASSY

This high-walled, intimate cemetery divides the diplomats of Passy from the skateboarders of Trocadéro. In summer the calm benches provide a welcome escape from the tourist scene across the square. Several celebrities found the place comfortable enough to stay a while. **Edouard Manet** (1832–83), shunned by the French Academy's Salon because he chose to paint nude women the way nude women actually look, spent most of his life trying to change Salon standards, finally succeeding for the benefit of artists after him. Along with Manet are buried his wife, his brother, and his brother's wife, **Berthe Morisot** (1841–95), who settled for Eugène Manet only because Edouard was taken. Morisot had a successful career herself as an impressionist and, in fact, had more luck at the Salon than her brother-in-law. **Claude Debussy** (1862–1918) helped usher in contemporary music with his unresolved dissonances and dreamy melodies. Nearby is a musical peer, **Gabriel Fauré** (1845–1924), remembered primarily for his *Requiem*. *Pl. du Trocadéro, 16e; entrance rue du Commandant Schloesing. Métro: Trocadéro.*

CIMETIERE DU MONTPARNASSE

The Cimetière du Montparnasse is an appropriate spot for the resting places of **Jean-Paul Sartre** (1905–80) and **Charles Baudelaire** (1821–67) since students throughout the quarter can still be found poring over their works. The existentialist Sartre, who frightened thousands with his portrayal of hell in *Huis Clos* (1944), is buried with his longtime companion **Simone de Beauvoir** (1908–86). Baudelaire is memorialized, but not actually buried, here, with a striking sculpture of the poet deep in thought atop a column. American actress **Jean Seberg** (1938–79) became France's sweetheart when she relocated to Paris and started adding her girlish accent to French films like Jean-Luc Godard's *Breathless*. Sculptor **Constantin Brancusi** (1876–1957) makes two appearances in the cemetery: once in his simple grave, the other in the form of his famous sculpture *The Kiss*, which portrays two lovers pressed together for an innocent smooch—or maybe more, depending on what you think's going on between those ambiguously close bodies. The couple hovers over **Tanosa Gassevskaia** (1888–1910), who killed herself over unrequited love. Company for these resting greats includes anarchist **Pierre-Joseph Proudhon** (1809–65), author **Guy de Maupassant** (1850–93), carmaker **André Citroën** (1879–1935), and **Alfred Dreyfus** (1859–1935), the Jewish military captain falsely convicted of spying for the Germans. *14e. Métro: Gaîté.*

PANTHEON

The final resting place for the officially great citizens of France is a sort of one-stop tomb and history lesson. Such was not the Panthéon's original purpose. Louis XV ordered the building of a church to replace nearby St-Etienne-du-Mont (*see* Houses of Worship, *above*) as home to the relics of Ste-Geneviève, the patron saint of Paris. Construction began in 1755, with architect Jacques-Germain Soufflot proffering a design for a soaring masterpiece of technical achievement and visual harmony. Soufflot called for a Greek cross to support a dome on a scale never before seen. Though his vision wasn't that bad, his engineering sucked, and his perfect building has spent every moment since its debut trying desperately to fall apart. The original windows had to be filled in, interior columns braced, the dome restructured; in 1985, falling stones closed the interior indefinitely. In 1790, 10 years after the death of the architect (who amazingly had the street in front of the Panthéon named after him), the structure was finished just in time for . . . the Revolution. Thereafter, the building alternated as a church and a nondenominational burial ground until the funeral procession of Victor Hugo came rolling up into the crypt, cementing its role as the Panthéon.

The family of Marie Curie was petitioned in 1994 to allow the remains of the scientist to be moved into the Panthéon, thereby making her the second woman to rest among France's great dead citizens and the first to be buried here on her own merit (Marcelin Berthelot shares the tomb of her husband). At press time the family had not yet responded.

Victor Hugo (1802–85), the prolific author and chronicler of his generation, wasn't the first resident of the Panthéon; he was joining philosopher **Jean-Jacques Rousseau** (1712–78) and Rousseau's philosophical opposite, **Voltaire** (1694–1778). The heart of **Léon Gambetta** (1838–82), a leader of the Paris Commune (*see box, below*) and eponym for countless future streets, sits quietly in its little vase. The writer **Emile Zola** (1840–1902) was a populist intellectual and a supporter of labor movements. His condemnation of anti-Semitism during the Dreyfus Affair brought out as many supporters as protesters to his funeral. When **Louis Braille** (1809–52) was born, the blind received almost no support from the public sector. Blind himself, Braille taught himself to read through feeling embossed Roman letters, eventually devising the system of raised dots we know today. Resistance leader and Nazi victim **Jean Moulin** has found an eternal place in the basement of the Panthéon. *Pl. du Panthéon, 5e, tel. 1/43-54-34-51. Métro: Maubert-Mutualité. RER: Luxembourg. Admission: 26F, 17F ages 13–25. Open daily 9:30–6:30.*

PERE LACHAISE

The world's most celebrated necropolis, Père Lachaise is the final stop for more illustrious people than you could ever meet in a lifetime. The former farm of Louis IV's confessor, Father Lachaise, has since been transformed into *the* mini-city of death and remembrance. Plots in the 118-acre cemetery are prime real estate, and now only the outrageously wealthy can afford to be laid to rest with the famous. Despite the tourists madly pointing to some little box or another and the minicam-toting hordes following the tattooed and leather-clad to the eternal party raging in Division 6, a gothic aura of contemplation pervades the place.

The oldest residents are the celebrated lovers **Abélard** (1079–1142) and **Héloïse** (1101–64), whose lives have come to define the whole medieval boy-meets-girl, boy-and-girl-fall-in-love, boy-and-girl-secretly-marry-to-avoid-wrath-of-girl's-father, girl's-uncle-gets-boy-castrated, girl-takes-vows-and-gives-birth-to-child-in-convent, boy-and-girl-comment-on-life-in-extended-correspondence thing (read the book). A likeness of the painter **Théodore Géricault** (1791–1824) gazes out over a bronze relief of his well-known painting *Raft of the Medusa*. The precocious composer **Georges Bizet** (1838–75) finally found success with his opera *Carmen* before his pitiful death at the hand of the bath (the water was too cold for his weak heart). Entombed with the negligent family he immortalized in over 3,000 pages of artful diatribes, **Marcel Proust** (1871–1922) now has the undivided attention of his mother. The dramatic death by strangulation (her long scarf got tangled up in a wheel of her convertible) of **Isadora Duncan** (1878–1927) wasn't the only freak accident in the family; 14 years earlier her children Deirdre and Patrick were swallowed by the Seine when their limousine fell into it. The body of **Oscar**

Wilde (1854–1900) was moved here nine years after his death—the quicklime that was supposed to have decomposed him actually preserved the corpse, shocking the poor guys who had to dig him up. Wilde's tombstone, by Sir Jacob Epstein, not only is known as one of the first departures toward art moderne in sculpture but is also famous for its fantastic penis, originally covered up by the order of the cemetery, only to be later lopped off by an adoring fan. In a similar vein, the family jewels of **Victor Noir** (1848–70) are in danger of being completely rubbed off. The journalist/gigolo, killed in a duel, is depicted in bronze at the moment of death, unbuttoned trousers and all; ever since the statue's, um, erection, young lovers have been petting his pride and joy for fortune and fertility. Irreverent fans pick at the face of the sculpted angel watching over **Frédéric Chopin** (1810–49) and have even gone so far as to tear off her fingers. The timid Chopin performed in public only 33 times, and then very quietly, but his intricate preludes and nocturnes inspired generations of piano virtuosos.

Even in death, there are those who are greater among equals. Here they include city planner **Baron Haussmann** (1809–91); writers **Colette** (1873–1954), **Honoré de Balzac** (1799–1850), **Gertrude Stein** (1874–1946) and (in the same grave) **Alice B. Toklas** (1877–1967), and 1967 Nobel Prize winner **Miguel Angel Asturias** (1899–1974); poet and critic **Guillaume Apollinaire** (1880–1918); playwrights **Jean-Baptiste Molière** (1622–1673) and **Pierre-Augustin Beaumarchais** (1732–99); fabulist **Jean de La Fontaine** (1621–95); painters **Camille Pissarro**

The Paris Commune

While musicians and writers make a beeline for the graves of cultural icons like Jim Morrison and Oscar Wilde, others make a pilgrimage to the Mûr des Fédérés at the southwest corner of Père Lachaise. Since 1880, when socialists first staged a demonstration at "the Wall," socialists, anarchists, and other free thinkers have come to this place where the last 147 people to die during the Paris Commune of 1871 are buried.

The Commune began when fiercely patriotic Parisians, intent on helping Napoléon III trounce the Prussians, formed political clubs. After Paris capitulated on June 28, 1871, newly elected conservative Prime Minister Adolphe Thiers signed the Treaty of Frankfurt, granting the Prussians Alsace, Lorraine, five billion francs, and the right to a victory parade through a vanquished Paris. This dishonorable peace, along with the conservative Assembly's declaration that the château of Versailles—symbol of the old absolute order—would now serve as their headquarters, was too much to bear. Angry Parisians elected a radical municipal government, and Paris's National Guard soon joined the angry citizens, giving them the firepower they needed to form an independent government and resist the onslaught of troops faithful to the national government in Versailles.

The Communards used their newly seized power to pass social legislation intended to shorten the workday, improve education, and empower the working classes. Parisians held outdoor concerts and parties during what Lenin later described as a "festival of the oppressed" and what Marx considered to be a precursor of the greater socialist revolution to come. The Communards' main goal was to organize the country into a system of politically autonomous, democratic enclaves, a vision of government radically opposed to the concept of centralized nation-state. Government troops entered Paris only 72 days after the start of the Commune, killing over 3,000 Parisians fighting from barricades and summarily massacring over 25,000 others.

(1830–1903), **Jean Auguste Ingres** (1780–1867), **Eugène Delacroix** (1798–1863), **Louis David** (1748–1825), **Amedeo Modigliani** (1884–1920), **Georges Seurat** (1859–91), and **Max Ernst** (1891–1976); illustrator **Honoré Daumier** (1808–79); philosopher **Auguste Comte** (1798–1857); doctor and revolutionary **François Raspail** (1794–1878); actress **Sarah Bernhardt** (1845–1923); singer **Edith Piaf** (1915–1963); Dominican dictator **Rafael Molina Trujillo** (1891–1961); and lizard king and drug abuser **James Douglas Morrison** (1943–71). All of these graves (and oh-so-many more) are located on free photocopied maps available at the cemetery office, or you can buy a 10F detailed map from surrounding florists. *20e, tel. 1/43–70–70–33. Métro: Père Lachaise or Gambetta.*

Parks and Gardens

Over 350 spots of green dot the city, from the two large *bois* (woods) on the western and eastern edges of the city to dozens of tiny, manicured lawns with maybe a tree and a wizened old man with a beret and a cane. Not only do Parisian parks offer a place to sit, read, and have a picnic, but they can also liven up your day with bizarre little dog-walking scenes or encounters with old ladies who know all the pigeons personally.

BOIS DE BOULOGNE

This is not the largest park in Paris, but only because the park is not officially *in* Paris. The Bois de Boulogne—"Le Bois"—has played an important role in Parisian life for the past 100 years

Pick a Park

- **Arènes de Lutèce.** *This small park just east of rue Monge sits on the foundation of an amphitheater used between the 1st and 3rd centuries. Today, a later amphitheater holds 10,000 people. 5e. Métro: Jussieu or Monge.*

- **Bassin de l'Arsenal.** *This small canal-side park south of place Bastille is complete with a restaurant that becomes a café between mealtimes. Napoléon created the canal to increase water movement through the city, and Jacques Chirac commissioned the park in the '80s. 12e. Métro: Bastille.*

- **Jardin de Navarre.** *University folk from nearby academic buildings flock to this small, hidden garden off rue Descartes. A few leafy trees provide shade over the large lawn. 5e. Métro: Cardinal Lemoine. Open Mon.–Sat. 8:30 AM–9 PM, Sun. 9–9.*

- **Parc André Citroën.** *Named for the automobile magnate, this park has all the French basics—only with modern twists. Greenhouses and shallow waterways share the park with carpet-like lawns (you can play on them), fine-tuned shrubbery, and trees arranged like an army regiment. 15e. Métro: Balard.*

- **Parc de Monceau.** *This pleasant garden in the refined eighth arrondissement, just south of boulevard de Courcelles, features meandering paths, a waterfall, Greek columns and sculptures, and the Musée Cernuschi, a small Chinese art museum featuring ancient paintings, funeral figures, pottery, and ceramics. 8e. Métro: Monceau. Park open Nov.–Mar., daily 7 AM–8 PM; Apr.–Oct., daily 7 AM–10 PM. Museum open Tues.–Sun. 10–5:40.*

and owes its position to Louis XI, who protected the park's game with his personal guards. Napoléon III shaped it into its present form, modeling the previously unlandscaped grounds after England's Hyde Park.

The late-19th-century Bois became one of Paris's great social hot spots, a place to ride disdainfully on horseback or in carriages down winding paths while watching everybody watching everybody else. It was the playground of the wealthy, with polo fields, a racetrack, tennis lawns, and the court that eventually became the Stade Roland Garros of French Open fame (*see* Festivals, in Planning Your Trip, in Chapter 1). The poorer but no less idle would simply walk around, and the impressionists and post-impressionists would paint them—there's a reason why the sculpted trees and banks surrounding **Lac Inférieur** remind you so vividly of Seurat's *Dimanche Aprés-Midi à la Grande Jatte* (1886). Boating on the lake is still an integral part of many a Parisian Sunday; you can rent a boat here for 43F per hour (400F deposit). Otherwise, to get out to the island, you must take the ferry, well worth the 6F round-trip ticket. The café out there serves expensive snacks and 17F cafés; you may want to bring a picnic.

The Bois is such a convenient and pleasant place to go to get away from the urbanity of Paris that only the Eiffel Tower has more annual visitors. You are allowed to sit on (most of) the lawns, climb the trees, and do all those other park-type things you'd never thought you'd miss until you visited the Jardin du Luxembourg (*see below*). Other attractions include the **Jardin d'Acclimatation,** a hands-on kiddie park/zoo/playground at the north end of the park, and the **Musée de la Contrefaçon,** a museum devoted entirely to counterfeits (*see* Miscellany, in Not-So-Major Museums, *above*).

While families and nice folks may use the Bois during the day, a sleazier element dominates it at night. The Bois has always been the city's prostitution center; it is estimated that over five million francs—about $1 million—changes hands here every night. Unless you yearn for the company of a Brazilian transvestite, her/his pimp, and the police officer dogging you all, avoid the park at night.

The park is huge and can be difficult to get around. The Métro stops at the perimeter, but buses (like Bus 52 or 241 from Porte d'Auteuil or 244 from Porte Maillot) cross the Bois. You can also rent bikes (20F per half-hour, 30F per hour) from the stand northwest of Lac Inférieur. *Métro: Porte Maillot, Porte Dauphine, Avenue Foch, or Porte d'Auteuil. Open dawn–dusk.*

BOIS DE VINCENNES

Southeast of the city is another huge, relatively unmanicured, wooded area. You can rent a rowboat on either of two major lakes, **Lac des Minimes** or **Lac Daumesnil,** by which you can also rent bikes. Also by Lac Daumesnil are the **Musée des Arts Africains et Océaniens** (*see* World Cultures, in Not-So-Major Museums, *above*), a **zoo** (Métro: Porte Dorée), and a **Buddhist center,** including a Tibetan Buddhist temple where you can meditate on Saturday and Sunday at 5 PM. The **Château de Vincennes** (Métro: Château de Vincennes) was yet another country home of François I, eventually deserted but becoming a fortified bastion under Emperor Napoléon I—his falling empire's last stronghold against the invading Western European powers. The proud general on guard, Daumesnil, refused to capitulate to the Russians, British, Austrians, and Prussians, waiting until he could surrender to a Frenchman. The château is now a museum, displaying a copy of Sainte-Chapelle, among other items. The **Parc Floral,** near the château, features diverse floral displays of aquatic and land-bound varieties, as well as a Four Seasons Garden. The **arboretum,** in the southeast corner of the park, has over 80 varieties of labeled plants. *16e. Métro: Château de Vincennes, Porte Dorée, Porte de Charenton, or Liberté. RER: Vincennes.*

JARDIN DE BELLEVILLE

The urban renewal of Belleville may not be to everyone's liking, but even residents have to admit that this park has added to the neighborhood. The park runs down the side of an exceptionally steep section of Belleville, the perfect setting for winding, tree-covered paths and comfortable lounging lawns—yes, you really can lounge. Generous benches let you hide in the shade of the trees or sit out in the sun watching the flowers grow in almost natural patterns. Best of all, fountains trickle down the middle of the park, creating numerous wading pools along the way that are taken full advantage of by kids and grown-ups.

The newest addition to the park is the **Maison de l'Air,** a breezy, one-room museum devoted to air and its circulation. Mobiles and displays highlight such air-related phenomena as pollen diffusion. Though very well done, it's only a small exhibit, barely worth the 22F admission, but its air-conditioned hall can be tempting on a hot summer day. *20e, tel. 1/43–28–47–63. Métro: Couronnes. Open weekdays 8:30 AM–9:30 PM, weekends 9 AM–9:30 PM.*

JARDIN DES PLANTES

Louis XIII conceived of this park in 1626, intending it to become "The King's Garden of Medicinal Herbs." The Jardin des Plantes is today the city's official botanical garden and houses over 10,000 varieties of plants (all tidily arranged in little rows and labeled, of course), a **zoo,** an **aquarium,** the **Musée National d'Histoire Naturelle** (*see* Technology and Science, in Not-So-Major Museums, *above*), huge **collections of rocks and insects,** and lots of students playing hooky from the nearby university. With the Gare d'Austerlitz along its southern edge, this park is a great discovery if you have a long wait for your train. It's also a prime spot from which to view the onset of springtime in Paris; after watching 10,000 varieties of plants bloom, you'll be ready to go out and do some cross-pollinating yourself. *5e. Métro: Jussieu, Monge, or Gare d'Austerlitz. Admission to museums: 12F–30F. Open daily dawn–dusk.*

The Open Air Sculpture Garden, on the edge of the Jardin des Plantes near the Pont d'Austerlitz, is a handy place to hang out among modern sculptures. The amphitheater steps that lead down to the river also make an ideal spot for kicking back and contemplating the murky depths of the Seine.

JARDIN DES TUILERIES

It may not be Paris's most pleasant park—scalding and dusty in summer, barren in winter—but the stately Tuileries at least offers a good lesson in the development of royal gardens. A palace by the same name had been around for centuries when Catherine de Médicis arrived in the mid-16th century, bringing Renaissance influences from Tuscany and tapping Philibert de l'Orme to design a private park; the result was the first classical French garden in the structured, manicured style we know today. A century later, André "Versailles" Le Nôtre gave the place a face-lift before it was opened to the public; it instantly became the fashionable center for strolling and showing off. The palace burned down during the Commune of 1871, but the gardens stuck it out and went on to form a nice piece of Haussmann's Paris: In one direction you can see straight down the Champs-Elysées all the way to the Arc de Triomphe; in the other, you see a long, orderly expanse of garden between you and the Louvre.

Besides small lawns you can't sit on and an occasional pick-up scene for gay men, today's Tuileries offer a series of thick-limbed women sculpted by Aristide Malliol (1861–1944) as well as a place to rest your weary feet after the trek down the Champs-Elysées. The park is a part of the big Louvre renovations, so it could come out a bit nicer in a couple years, though meanwhile you have to deal with lots of construction. If the summer heat gets to you, take refuge in one of two museums at the west end: the **Orangerie** and the **Jeu de Paume** (*see* More Art, in Not-So-Major Museums, *above*). *1er. Métro: Tuileries or Concorde. Open daily dawn–dusk.*

JARDIN DU LUXEMBOURG

The Jardin du Luxembourg possesses all that is unique and befuddling about Parisian parks: swarms of pigeons, cookie-cutter trees, ironed-and-pressed dirt walkways, and perfectly green lawns meant for admiring, not touching. The tree- and bench-lined paths offer a necessary reprieve from the incessant bustle of the Quartier Latin, and the garden offers some of Paris's best opportunities for rediscovering the breed of adorably fashionable toddlers, dotty old women, and smooching university students who once found their way into Doisneau photographs. But the park is not exactly a mellow hangout. The northern boundary is dominated by the imposing Palais du Luxembourg, which is surrounded by an equally imposing handful of well-armed guards. They are there to protect the senators who have been deliberating in the palace since 1958, and terrorist bombings in the mid-1980s have made the guards the humorless creatures they are today. The rest of the park is patrolled by a softer breed of cop, who whistle and gesture at anyone who dares to venture onto the garden's inviting lawns. You *are* allowed to sit in one of the millions of chairs scattered around the central fountain and read or enjoy a cup of coffee from the little café-kiosks.

One of the great attractions of the park is the **Théâtre des Marionnettes,** where on Saturday, Sunday, and Wednesday at 3 and 4 PM you can catch one of the classic *guignols* (marionette shows) for 2OF. The wide-mouthed kiddies are the main attraction, though; their expressions of utter surprise, despair, or glee have fascinated the likes of Henri Cartier-Bresson and François Truffaut.

While the garden may seem purely French in its curious treatment of greenery and promenading, the original 17th-century planting took its inspiration from Italy. When Marie de Médicis acquired the estate of the recently deceased Duke of Luxembourg in 1612, she decided to turn its hôtel into a version of the Florentine Médicis home, the Palazzo Pitti. She ended up with something more Franco-Italian than anything strictly Florentine: a château with vagabond Tuscan columns. The land behind the palace was also loosely modeled on that behind the Palazzo Pitti, the Boboli Gardens. The landscapers, like the architects, didn't install a true version of the Florentine garden, opting for the emerging style of a heavy-handed human manipulation of nature—more straight vistas, box-trimmed trees, and color-coordinated flowerbeds—thereby further defining the "French" garden. A tiny corner of the park still possesses the nature-on-the-brink-of-overcoming-civilization look that was the trademark of the Renaissance Italian garden—namely, the intentionally overgrown cluster of trees and bushes lining the 1624 Fontaine de Médicis. The rest of the very French park has found a place in the hearts of the Parisians since the park became public after the Revolution; thousands turned out in the mid-1800s to prevent a Haussmann-directed boulevard from being built through its middle. *6e. RER: Luxembourg. Open daily dawn–dusk.*

JARDIN DU PALAIS ROYAL

It's odd that the "Royal Palace" of Paris is about the only place in the city where a monarch never stayed. It was Cardinal Richelieu who laid claim to the land, buying up property until he found himself with a palace. When he died in 1642 he left the digs to the crown. Anne of Austria promptly took advantage of the gift, moving in 1643 to escape the stuffy Louvre. When La Fronde, a series of outbreaks between nobility and royalty, broke out, she fled Paris, and the Orléans family took her place, sticking around until the Revolution. The last Orléans, Philippe, expanded the complex in a clever attempt to make some francs by selling lots and building town houses. Things worked out exactly as planned; the town houses quickly became fashionable new places to live, and the ground floors filled with cafés and bordellos. The gardens that took over the remaining spaces became a public forum for voicing complaints against the government. Ultimately, the garden witnessed many of the key meetings leading up to the Revolution; people gathered here on July 14, 1789, before stomping off to the Bastille.

The Jardin du Palais Royal as we know it today is devoid of bordellos, and little old men who talk to sparrows have replaced the dissenters. Although work was done on the gardens and surrounding buildings after the Revolution, the setup has remained the same, and you can still order a cup of coffee from one of the cafés overlooking the grounds. The park itself is the picture of Parisian romance, with lines of trees, a dramatic central fountain, and benches for snuggling lovers. The modern layout of the park's south end is the only bad point: The gray-and-white stubby poles designed by sculptor Daniel Buren in 1986 have not been well received, though the lines of blue lights set into the pavement could be useful to an airplane needing an emergency runway. *1er. Métro: Palais Royal–Musée du Louvre.*

PARC DE LA VILLETTE

What was Paris's largest complex of slaughterhouses and stockyards is now a nice big green park with tons of high-tech buildings and toys to run around in and play with. The sheep that were once driven through this neighborhood on their way to becoming mutton left in the mid-1970s; you can check out photos documenting the days of meat-making at the **Maison de la Villette** (tel. 1/40–03–75–10), closed Monday. Most people come here to enjoy the gigantic lawns (which you can play on), nifty megaplaygrounds, and bike paths. The largest park in Paris proper, it's also the city's most fun. You've got things like Claes Oldenberg's oversize *Buried Bicycle* to ogle, monstrous dragon slides to go down, catwalks, and no less than 11 special theme gardens, like the meditative **Jardin des Bambous** (Bamboo Garden) or the steamy **Jardin des Brouillards** (Fog Garden). Park architect Bernard Tschumi divided the area into a 5-by 9-unit grid and put a big red steel contraption called a *folie* at each grid point, each with some sort of artistic or other purpose—like the *folie vidéo,* the *folie arts plastique,* or the Quick folly, which sells nasty fast food.

Most commonly known as the site of several of Paris's main attractions, the park is bordered by the **canal St-Denis** to the west and is split by the **canal de l'Ourcq** through the middle. The **information folly** (tel. 1/40–03–75–03), near the confluence of the canals, dispenses maps and general park info. To the north of the canal de l'Ourcq is the **Cité des Sciences et de l'Industrie** museum and the attached **Géode** (for both, *see* Technology and Science, in Not-So-Major Museums, *above*); and the semiburied **Argonaute,** a 1950s nuclear submarine. To the south of the canal de l'Ourcq is the **Cité de la Musique,** an assortment of theaters and recital rooms, including the slaughterhouse-turned-concert-venue **grande halle,** which hosts jazz festivals and other big events; the **Théâtre Paris–Villette** (tel. 1/42–02–02–68), a satellite stage for the larger Théâtre de la Ville at Châtelet; and the campus of the **Conservatoire National Supérieur de Musique et de Danse** (*see* Performing Arts, in Chapter 5). *19e. Métro: Porte de la Villette or Porte de Pantin.*

PARC DES BUTTES-CHAUMONT

While at the Parc des Buttes-Chaumont, take a small side trip west down avenue Simón Bolívar; when you see a tiny, steep staircase leading up to the north, follow it up. At the top you'll find a small, villagelike community with peaceful homes and views out over the north of Paris.

One of the best simulations of natural beauty in all of Paris, this park near Belleville has a hill made of cement and rock, a small waterway running through, and lots of kids playing soccer. Still, it remains one of the most comfortable places to collapse in the city; the hill and the small lake are a welcome relief after you've seen one too many stodgy French gardens whose trees all grow in a row. This park has gorgeous views of the city below, ducks to feed, and, just so you don't feel like you've completely escaped civilization, a small neoclassical temple at the top of the hill. This little oasis is brought to you by Napoléon III and Baron Haussmann, who wanted to give the working folk a green spot where they could take their families. *Bordered by rues de Crimée, Manin, and Botzaris, 19e. Métro: Buttes-Chaumont. Open daily dawn–dusk.*

PARC MONTSOURIS
AND CITE UNIVERSITAIRE

Another Haussmann project for Paris, Parc Montsouris almost succeeds in convincing you that you have somehow found yourself in an arcadian paradise. The hilly park (its name means mouse mountain) is filled with sloping fields, clusters of stately trees, and a pond. But abandoned railway tracks cross it in one direction, active RER lines in another, and the auto traffic that moves swiftly around its perimeter is never far enough away to let you have the quiet appropriate for an idyllic picnic.

Across boulevard Jourdan from the park is the Cité Universitaire, a collection of residences built by foreign countries to house their nationals while they study at Parisian universities.

John D. Rockefeller funded the development of the large swath of land in the 1920s. Each of the 35 buildings was designed independently with a world's-fair-like attitude toward national identity and architectural design. Le Corbusier designed two houses, the **Fondation Suisse** and **Fondation Franco-Brasil,** and both continue to attract architectural pilgrims. Walking around the buildings and across the lawns, you almost believe that Paris has something close to an American university-style campus, only the students here seem too serious to turn their speakers out the window, yell at one another from their rooms, and kick back in the sun. Still, the Cité itself is a good complement to the Parc Montsouris across the street, where you can run around, throw a Frisbee, or climb a tree without being pestered by the park police. *14e. Métro/RER: Cité Universitaire. Both open daily dawn–dusk.*

Neighborhoods

BASTILLE

Nowadays, all you see around the **place de la Bastille** is swarms of Parisian drivers circling a pole with an angel on top of it—the **July Column,** erected in memory of those who died during the "Trois Glorieuses" revolution of 1830. But the plaza has witnessed more than speeding Renaults. On July 14, 1789, thousands of French citizens, frustrated with Louis XVI's monarchical rule, used the prison at the Bastille to express their fury. A rather pitiful prison with only seven or so prisoners, the Bastille contained, more importantly, an arsenal. The Parisians tore it apart in an act that was more symbolic than substantive, considering that all they did was liberate a few petty criminals (including the Marquis de Sade, convicted for contributing to the deliquency of a minor and general perverseness). There turned out to be as few guns as prisoners, but the Revolution managed to go along quite bloodily without them.

That was over 200 years ago. Today the area around the former prison area is undergoing a revolution of a different sort: gentrification. Galleries, shops, theaters, cafés, restaurants, and bars have taken over formerly decrepit buildings and alleys, bringing a hip and artsy crowd to mingle with blue-collar locals. Unfortunately, everyone's been quick to point out just how cool the Bastille has become—even *The New York Times* got into the act with a 1994 article touting the place—so the parts of the 11th arrondissement nearest the place de la Bastille are already on every tourist's itinerary.

Happily, though, getting away from the crowds is easy. Walk a couple blocks east or north of the plaza and start checking out those run-down, overgrown alleys and the courtyards they open onto. Duck down one of the lonelier ones and you may be surprised to find that an art supply store has moved into the garagelike structure on the right, a well-frequented café into the old artisan workshop on the left. Especially good streets for exploration are **rue du Faubourg St-Antoine** and **rue de Charonne.** Both lead you into areas largely inhabited by African and Arab Parisians who run all kinds of shops, restaurants, and take-out joints.

The furniture stores along rue du Faubourg St-Antoine represent no recent economic phenomena; this has been Paris's furniture strip for hundreds of years.

Nocturnal activities are the Bastille's specialty, and Parisians from the farthest corners of the city make the trip to hit their favorites among the amazing variety of bars here. **Rue de Lappe** and **rue de la Roquette** are packed with bars, restaurants, and people who look just a little too self-consciously stylish. Try **rue de Charonne** to discover the places with funkier crowds.

BELLEVILLE

Belleville is one of Paris's most fascinating and, unhappily, quickly changing neighborhoods. Subject to the city's urban renewal frenzy, the area is undergoing dramatic transformations. When the powers that be suggested virtually demolishing Belleville's oldest, most typical corner (the western corner, crossed by rue de Belleville and boulevard de Belleville), neighbors

Bastille

united to fight the plan, forming a group known as the "Bellevilleuse"; they've had mixed success in gaining promises to *restore* rather than *redo* some areas. If all goes well, there will still be enough of the original Belleville left between this westernmost corner and Père Lachaise cemetery to warrant some rambling.

One of the first things you may notice while peering at a map and trying to figure out where you are among Belleville's climbing streets is the conspicuous lack of generals, presidents, and politicians among the street names. Instead, there are a lot of trees (rue des Amandiers, rue des Pruniers), farming jargon (rue des Bruyères), and country talk (rue des Prairies). You can probably guess the reason: The area began as farmland and vineyards, a country village, which, right up to the Revolution, had less than 1,000 inhabitants. The late 18th century saw the beginning of a long, slow migration into Belleville; the village was incorporated into Paris in the mid-19th century.

Part of the area's current character stems from the fact that it never charmed the bourgeoisie; it was the laboring class, pushed out of central Paris by Haussmann's huge boulevards, who lived and worked here. The arrival of waves of immigrants in the 20th century, most fleeing per-

The French Revolution

In the late 18th century, the French aristocracy was frantically trying to hold on to its traditional privileges, the middle class was frustrated by its lack of power, and the peasants were ticked off about being taxed into oblivion. Something had to happen, and that something was the French Revolution. The bourgeois members of the government kicked things off on June 17, 1789, by proclaiming themselves a new legislative body called the National Assembly and vowing to write a new constitution. A month later, Parisians of every political stripe joined the fray, storming the Bastille in search of arms for the citizen militia. During the next two years, aristocrats fled the country in droves— their property was being forcibly taken away, and they figured their heads would be next. The Parisians forced Louis XVI to leave his royal pleasure palace in Versailles and slum it at the Tuileries palace, where they could keep an eye on him. He and his wife, Marie "Let them eat cake" Antoinette, later tried to flee France but were recognized in Varennes and dragged back to the capital.

In September 1791, the National Assembly adopted a new constitution, all but shutting Louis out of the political proceedings. Unfortunately for him, that wasn't enough for the radical antimonarchists, called the Jacobins, who eventually gained control. They tried and executed the king in January 1793 on place de la Révolution. Throughout the following year, the newly appointed Committee of Public Safety manned the guillotines, eliminating thousands of "enemies of the Revolution" during a period known as "the Terror." Revolutionary ideals seemed to fall by the wayside as more and more heroes of the Revolution were tried on unlikely treason charges. In 1794 the frenzy had reached such a pitch that Jacobin leader Maximilien Robespierre lost his own head to the guillotine. With Robespierre out of the way, the quasi-tyrannical Directory of Five took control of the country until Napoléon Bonaparte worked his way up from General of the Interior to "Emperor of the French," an ironic end to one of the most important revolutions ever.

secution in their homelands, has contributed to Belleville's international esprit: Polish, Russian, and German Jews; Armenians; Greeks; Spanish Republicans; Sephardic Jews; Africans; Eastern Europeans; Chinese . . . all have brought their specialties to shops, markets, and restaurants throughout the district. If you find the picture-book Paris of grand boulevards and Coco Chanel boutiques distressing, this is the neighborhood for you.

The hill in the center of Belleville is covered with inviting alleyways, crumbling houses, winding streets, narrow stairways, and incredible views of Paris; at the base you'll find bars and cheap ethnic restaurants and shops. The most lively part of Belleville lies in the area bordered by **rue de Ménilmontant, rue des Pyrénées, rue de Belleville,** and **boulevard de Belleville.** The oldest, most recently menaced section of Belleville is around **rues Dénoyez** and **Ramponeau**—hurry before it starts to look like those suburbs you pass through on the RER. The '60s and '70s already claimed a goodly chunk of the quarter, especially near the **Jardin de Belleville** (*see* Parks and Gardens, *above*). If you arrive only to find a far too new and sterile layout, console yourself by finding a space in the park, opening up a book of Atget's early-20th-century Paris photos, and imagining what it all used to look like.

CHAMPS-ELYSEES

What was once an aristocratic pleasure park is now a commercial mess living off its reputation. The Champs-Elysées may be glorious from a distance, but get up close and you'll find car dealerships, mainstream movie theaters, and restaurant chains. The city is trying to rectify the situation by eliminating parking lanes to widen the new white-granite sidewalks and planting lots of trees, but so far it still feels like the world's grandest outdoor shopping mall: lots of French kids and tourists cruising around, scoping each other out, and taking breaks at Burger King. The only exclusive thing left in the area is the private nightclubs.

Originally an expanse of green popular primarily with cattle, the Champs was built for Louis XIV by Le Nôtre to extend the line of the Tuileries. Though place de la Concorde, at the eastern end, saw plenty of activity—including a few hundred heads rolling around during the Revolution—the extending strip stayed rural, except for a few wealthy folks' homes. In the mid-1800s, the Champs became a popular Sunday strolling ground, encouraging more and more ice cream stands, pavilions, and parties as the century went on. The decline of World Expos in the mid-20th century saw a parallel decline in the Champs-Elysées, which had been the stomping grounds of many a fair goer. A few designer names still hang around, but the avenue has lost its novelty. For a detailed map of the Champs, *see* map Arc de Triomphe to the Opéra, *below*.

LA DEFENSE

About 2 kilometers (1¼ miles) outside Paris proper, La Défense does not exactly fit the traditional idea of a "neighborhood." The 35,000 residents who live in the high-rise housing projects are easily eclipsed by the over 110,000 people who work in the complex of business towers and shops. This huge commercial conglomeration of hypermodern architecture and sculpture was built in 1958 on what had been the site of the ultimately ill-fated Parisian defense (hence the name) against the invading Prussians. By the time the developers came to the area, La Défense was just a large traffic circle with a statue in the middle commemorating the battle—the statue

Belleville Address Book

- **6 rue de Palestine: Ukrainian Orthodox Church (chanted mass on Sundays at 10 AM)**

- **Boulevard de Belleville: morning street market**

- **5 rue de Belleville: The Chinese bookstore Les Herbes Sauvages**

- **72 rue de Belleville: Edith Piaf's birth spot—on the street outside.**

still stands today, oddly isolated on an elevated island of grass. The developers sought to create an American-style business park, and they succeeded in building one of Europe's most prestigious and largest planned commercial neighborhoods.

La Défense is designed to continue the longest urban axis in the world: A straight line starts at the Louvre, passes through the Jardin des Tuileries, the place de la Concorde, and the Arc de Triomphe, and terminates at the **Grande Arche de la Défense** (next to the Métro station of the same name), an enormous arch that hides within its walls an office building. A 40F elevator ride will whisk you up through the belly of the building for a view of Paris. The Grande Arche, along with La Défense's first building, the poured-concrete, curvaceous CNIT (Centre National des Industries et des Techniques), are the sights that draw the thousands of tourists who come here daily. The axis is also lined with large, big-name corporate art.

La Défense has no intention of stopping yet. Development contracts have been added past the original 1988 time line, and construction crews are extending Métro lines and unearthing bothersome cemeteries to the west of the Grande Arche. New proposals include the Tour Sans Fin designed by Jean Nouvel (*see box, above*), which will be the tallest building in Europe and the fifth tallest in the world. Though it may not jibe with your sense of aesthetics, La Défense is too enormous, popular, and spectacular to ignore. Visit the information center by the Grande Arche to pick up a map outlining all the sculptures and architectural details, including information about the history of La Défense. *Métro: Grande Arche de la Défense or pl. de la Défense.*

GARES DE L'EST ET DU NORD

Tourists breeze through this quarter daily on their way from the center up to Montmartre; those who stop get a more satisfying taste of Paris than you could soak up from 38 portrait sittings on place du Tertre. This is a working neighborhood filled with authentic working people who shop at functional stores and eat at reasonably priced restaurants. Many of Paris's old *passages* (*see box* Parisian Passages in Chapter 6) are here, but unlike the spruced-up ones in the center, these passages are old and crumbling, housing Indian restaurants or used-book vendors. A few of the grand old cafés still call the area home, but their facades practically disappear amid the worn aspect of the streets and stores around them.

Come to the ninth and 10th arrondissements to ramble, hit some of Paris's hottest clubs, and eat. A large Jewish population sustains kosher restaurants and bakeries, especially in the area above Métro Rue Montmartre, and Indian and Eastern European joints crowd the 10th. Unfortunately, it isn't a good idea to come here alone at night, particularly if you're female or if you don't know exactly where you're going; it's one of Paris's worst areas for theft.

LES HALLES—BEAUBOURG

Many Parisians believe that the day Les Halles marketplace left Beaubourg in 1968 was the day that Paris irrevocably shuffled its priorities; tourism and consumerism were allowed to permanently supplant centuries of local tradition in a move that some call "McDonaldization." The Paris market had been here for nearly 800 years—ever since Philippe Auguste divided up the space, with central buildings for shops and surrounding open spaces for the fresh food market. The market became and remained the central Paris meeting, drinking, and entertainment spot. Napoléon I was the next leader to look at the market. Complaining that it was disorganized, he drew plans to create a covered market with umbrellas supported by an iron frame, a design that became the model for markets all over Europe.

When the demolition of the market was settled upon in 1962, Parisians showed surprisingly little resistance; in 1969 the merchants were driven out of business or dispersed to the far

Between 1968 and the opening of the Forum des Halles shopping mall in 1979, Les Halles experienced some serious growing pains. The low point came when the city abandoned its plan to build a huge world trade center here after they had already dug the foundation. While politicians haggled over the fate of the site, the wasteland came to be known as the "Largest Urban Hole in Europe."

Map labels:

17e
18e — Niel, Wagram, av. MacMahon, pl. des Ternes, r. Beaujon, av. Hoche
blvd. de Courcelles
Parc Monceau — 2
pl. de Rio de Janeiro
r. de Courcelles, Monceau, av. de Messine, r. de Miromesnil
Salle Pleyel — 1
Arc de Triomphe
pl. Charles de Gaulle
av. d'Iéna, av. Marceau
pl. G. Guillaumin
blvd. Haussmann, av. Myron T. Herrick, r. du Faubourg
av. de Friedland, r. Balzac, r. Washington, r. d'Artois, r. La Boétie, r. de Penthièvre
8e
St-Honoré
r. de Berri, r. de Ponthieu
av. des Champs-Elysées
av. George-V, av. Franklin D. Roosevelt, av. Matignon, r. du
16e
r. Galilée, r. Pierre Charron, r. Marbeuf, r. de Marignan, av. Montaigne
r. Françoisler, r. Cl. Marot, r. de Boccador
Rond-Point des Champs-Elysées — 9
av. W. Churchill — 6 7 8
4
3
r. Jean-Goujon
av. du Président Wilson
av. de New York
pl. de l'Alma
cours Albert 1er
cours la Reine
Pt. de l'Alma, Pt. des Invalides, Pt. Alexandre III
Seine
Palais Bourbon
quai d'Orsay
5
7e
pl. de la Résistance

440 yards
400 meters

r. d. Rome
r. du Rocher
Foy
Bienfaisance
r. des Londres
r. d'Amsterdam
av. de Clichy
r. Pigalle
r. de la Rochefoucauld
r. d'Aumale
N.D. de Lorette
r. des Martyrs
13
r. St-Lazare
Gare St-Lazare
r. de Châteaudun
9e
r. St-Lazare
pl. St-Augustin
r. de la Pépinière
blvd. Haussmann
r. de Provence
r. Taitbout
r. La Fayette
r. Laffitte
blvd. Malesherbes
r. Pasquier
r. Tronchet
r. Auber
r. de Caumartin
r. Scribe
pl. de l'Opéra
blvd. des Italiens
15 r. Favart
bourg. St-Honoré
r. d'Aguesseau
r. Boissy d'Anglas
12
pl. de la Madeleine
blvd. de la Madeleine
blvd. des Capucines
r. des Capucines
r. de la Paix
r. du Quatre Septembre
r. St-Augustin
Ste-Anne
2e
16 r. Vivienne
r. Royale
pl. Vendôme
r. de Castiglione
r. St-Honoré
av. de l'Opéra
r. des Petits Champs
r. de Richelieu
17
pl. de la Concorde
11
r. de Rivoli
1er
10
Pl. de la Concorde
Jardin des Tuileries
19 **18**
quai des Tuileries
Jardin du Carrousel
pl. du Palais Royal
Louvre

14

corners of the city, the 19th-century market hall was torn down and replaced with a gaping hole, and the shopping mall developers moved in. The multilevel, soulless structure you see today, the Forum des Halles, is the best they could come up with, and it may be the only piece of central Paris that has never heard a word of unqualified praise.

Though the mall below ground is an unequivocal mess, the streets of Les Halles have at least been spared from the property boom and hawkish economic developers. The Forum des Halles complex sitting on top of the underground shopping monstrosity is a ghastly collection of fast-food stalls and tourist trinket shops, but many old-time bistrots have held on in the narrow surrounding streets. The area gets going at about 5 AM, when the butchers and fish merchants arrive to set up shop, and the cafés are filled soon after with folks getting a coffee before the workday begins. Through the rest of the day, the streets fill up with students and street musicians, beer-drinking punk rockers and their dogs, wide-eyed tourists, and patrons of the porno video parlors. **Rue St-Denis** is both one of the sleaziest and one of the most inviting streets around, its bustling restaurants sharing centuries-old building space with equally busy sex shops.

Northern Les Halles has evolved into one of the hotter hot spots; a city project to redo the streets has apparently succeeded, and hip cafés surround **rue Montorgueil,** lined with food markets and restaurants. In the other direction, to the south of the Forum, you have **place des Innocents,** for ages the site of a market-side common-trench cemetery, which was emptied into the Catacombes (*see* Dead Folk, *below*) after the overabundance of bodies pushed themselves above street level and the smell became unbearable. Now it's a public square popular with pouty Parisian youth, errant musicians, and the tourist admirers of both.

Farther south are more small streets filled with jazz clubs and trendy shops until you hit **place du Châtelet** and its facing theaters. The square takes its name from a notoriously harsh prison that sat on the present site of Théâtre du Châtelet until its destruction in the 19th century. That random tower just off the place is the **Tour St-Jacques,** built as an addition to a church that was torn down during the Revolution. The tower has since served as Pasteur's lab for experiments on gravity, as a quarry, and currently as a meteorological observatory.

A couple blocks northeast from Châtelet is, despite its youth, the best-known landmark of the neighborhood: the **Centre Georges Pompidou** (*see* Major Museums, *above*). Tons of street musicians and performers gather on the sloping desert of a plaza in front of the Centre. Around the corner from the Pompidou is Charles Tingueley's wild and fanciful **fountain** at place Igor-Stravinsky. A pair of big red lips, a rotund woman, a treble clef, and other wacked sculptures turn and gurgle in the spitting streams of water, in stark contrast to the sternly Gothic Eglise St-Merri nearby.

ILE DE LA CITE

The strategic location of this island first drew a Gaul tribe, the Parisii, to the place they dubbed Lutetia in about 300 BC. Settling mainly on the island itself, they built wood bridges to the mainland. Caesar's rapid expansion plan hit Paris around 50 BC, moving the hub to the Left Bank, but as of the 4th century, the Roman governors still slept in a palace on the island. Frankish kings took over that palace—now known as the **Conciergerie**—a couple centuries later, and it remained a royal residence until the 1300s; the Capetians alone lived here for 800 years.

Grab a bottle of wine and the one you love and head out over the Seine on the pedestrian Pont des Arts, where musicians, artists, and other young experiencers of life flock to watch the sun go down behind the Eiffel Tower and come up over Notre-Dame.

Beyond its appeal as the city's ancient heart, the Ile de la Cité is home to two of the finest Gothic buildings anywhere: Sainte-Chapelle and Notre-Dame (*see* Houses of Worship, *above*). A perceived necessity to showcase the latter altered the soul of the island in the late 19th century: The tiny winding streets, churches, stalls, and houses crouching below it, along with an orphanage and invalids' hospital, were bulldozed to make way for the Haussmann aesthetic. The **Crypte Archéologique** (tel. 1/43–29–83–51), in the place du Parvis in front of

N

rue Réaumur

r. des Petits Champs

r. du Mail

rue d'Aboukir

2e

r. Greneta

pl. des Victoires

Montmartre

Montorgueil

r. St-Denis

r. de Turbigo

r. J.J. Rousseau

r. Etienne Marcel

r. Tiquetonne

blvd. de Sébastopol

r. St-Martin

r. Beaubourg

pl. du Palais Royal

r. Croix des Petits-Champs

r. du Louvre

1er

pl. R. Cassin

Pierre Lescot

r. St-Denis

3e

r. de Rivoli

r. St-Honoré

r. Bailleul

pl. R. Cassin

r. Berger

r. Rambuteau

Centre Pompidou

2

r. de l'Arbre Sec

r. des Bourdonnais

pl. M de Navarre

sq. des Innocents

r. de la Ferronerie

r. Quincampoix

r. St-Martin

pl. Igor Stravinsky

10

4e

r. au Pont Neuf

r. des Halles

r. des Lombards

r. de la Verrerie

r. du Renard

quai du Louvre

r. des Lavandières

av. Victoria

r. de Rivoli

9

Seine

quai de la Megisserie

4

8

pl. du Châtelet

pl. de l'Hôtel de Ville

15

Institut de France

Pont des Arts

Pont Neuf

pl. Dauphine

Pont au Change

Pont Notre Dame

quai de Conti

5 6

7

pl. Lépine

Pont d'Arcole

Hôtel des Monnaies

quai des Grands Augustins

blvd. du Palais

r. de Lutèce

r. de la Cité Notre Dame

Ile de la Cité

r. Chanoinesse

13

Pont Louis Philippe

r. Dauphine

r. Mazarine

pl. St-Michel

blvd. St-Michel

pl. du Parvis

11

r. du Cloître Notre Dame

12

Pont au Double

Pont St-Louis

Ile St-Louis

rue St-André des Arts

rue Danton

6e

r. de la Harpe

quai de Montebello

14

Pont de l'Archevêché

r. de Seine

blvd. St-Germain

blvd. St-Michel

r. St-Jacques

5e

0   220 yards
0   200 meters

Cathédrale
Notre-Dame, **12**

Conciergerie, **6**

Crypte
Archéologique, **11**

Eglise
St-Eustache, **1**

Eglise St-Merri, **10**

Forum des Halles, **3**

Hôtel de Ville, **15**

Louvre, **2**

Mémorial de la
Déportation, **14**

Musée
Notre-Dame, **13**

Palais de Justice, **5**

Sainte-Chapelle, **7**

Théâtre du
Chatelet, **4**

Théâtre de
la Ville, **8**

Tour St-Jacques, **9**

the cathedral, became a museum after ruins were discovered in 1965. Among the excavated details are parts of the 3rd-century wall of Lutetia, Notre-Dame's Merovingian cathedral predecessor, and bits of Roman and medieval houses. Plenty of diagrams, pictures, and photographs go along with the ruins, detailing the history of the isle. Admission to the crypt is 26F, 17F for students under 26. It's open daily 10–6, shorter hours off-season.

For the most tranquil moment you are likely to have on the Ile de la Cité, head to the island's western tip for a view out over the Seine, or picnic in the shady park of place Dauphine. The small garden behind Notre-Dame is another peaceful spot, where you can gaze at flying buttresses all day long. Also in back of Notre-Dame, near the garden, is the **Mémorial de la Déportation,** a striking tribute to the 200,000 French sent to death camps by the Vichy government—200,000 crystals inside pay tribute to the victims. The walls are lined with moving quotations by famous French poets, philosophers, and writers, scrawled in angular red letters.

ILE ST-LOUIS

If it weren't sitting directly behind Notre-Dame, attached by a bridge, most tourists probably would never think of going to Ile St-Louis. But it is, and they do, and there is an entire street of restaurants and shops waiting to greet them. Actually, the **rue de St-Louis en l'Ile** may be the most charming tourist street in Paris, and because of that plenty of locals join visitors here on warm days and clear evenings. You'll find most of them standing in line at the island's best-known feature: **Berthillon** (31 rue St-Louis-en-l'Ile, tel. 1/43–54–31–61), hands-down Paris's best ice creamery. If you've had the misfortune of tasting French ice cream, this may not sound like much of a recommendation, but Berthillon's stuff is rich and very flavorful; the apricot sorbet tastes like you're eating the actual fruit. A single scoop costs 8F, a triple 18F, and the place closes in August, though plenty of other island shops sell Berthillon ice cream year-round.

For a while a canal divided the current Ile St-Louis in two; the halves were dubbed the Ile Notre-Dame and Ile aux Vaches, the latter given over to milk cows and their attendants. And so it remained until the 17th century, when some land speculators joined the two islands, connecting them by bridges to the Ile de la Cité and the Left and Right Banks and selling plots to town house developers. After a while in the spotlight, the posh residences somehow lost their charm among the bourgeoisie, and artists, writers, and intellectuals like Cézanne and Baudelaire came to the island. As you wander around, keep an eye out for the building plaques describing who lived here when, and why it's important. An especially somber reminder adorns 19 quai de Bourbon: "Here lived Camille Claudel, sculptor, from 1899 to 1913. Then ended her brave career as an artist and began her long night of internment." Claudel's family committed her to an insane asylum where she was forbidden to practice her art until her death. Some of her works are displayed in the Musée Rodin (*see* Individual Artists, in Not-so-Major Museums, *above*).

LOUVRE TO OPERA

Yes, it's terribly expensive, snobbish, and packed with tourists. But any neighborhood that can boast the centers of the Western art, theater, and music worlds all within a 15-minute walk can't be all bad. The **Louvre** (*see* Major Museums, *above*) is the biggie here, displaying thousands of works in what was designed as a showcase for kings. Just a block above it is the **Comédie Française** (*see* Performing Arts, in Chapter 5), tacked onto another royal residence, the **Palais Royal** (*see* Jardin du Palais Royal, in Parks and Gardens, *above*), and pointing the way up one of Haussmann's favorite boulevards, **avenue de l'Opéra.** On the avenue, notice the monotony of the structures and how closely the teeny balconies cling to the buildings; Haussmann wanted to ensure that you'd be struck by the grandeur of the street as a whole, with no one well-designed building stealing the show and no protruding terraces breaking the line straight down the street. At the end of this promenade is, of course, the **Opéra Garnier** (*see* Performing Arts, in Chapter 5).

You will probably encounter this district in pragmatic situations as well—it is home to all of the major airlines, travel agencies, and tourist bureaus. Off the avenue de l'Opéra, however, are the famous restaurants, age-old bistrots, upscale shops, and *passages* (*see box* Parisian Passages, in Chapter 6) that form the opulent heart of the quarter. Lately, a sizable Japanese population has moved in, bringing restaurants, bookstores, and specialty shops with them. North of the **Palais-Royal garden** is **rue des Petits-Champs,** whose bounty of passages makes it one of the neighborhood's best spots for roaming. The street ends at the **place des Victoires,** whose matching facades were designed by Versailles architect Hardouin-Mansart in 1685. The original square was more intimate—no rue des Petits-Champs ran through it, in fact—and Louis XIV was so pleased with the results that he had Hardouin-Mansart do another, the **place Vendôme,** on the other side of avenue de l'Opéra. Snobbish and self-important, place Vendôme is also unarguably gorgeous; property laws have kept away cafés and other such banal establishments, leaving the plaza stately and refined, the perfect home for the Ritz and Cartier. Chopin lived and died at No. 12. The stick in the center was, at one point, an equestrian statue of the Sun King, but the Revolution saw to the melting down of that. Who but Napoléon could have replaced it with one of himself, on top of an exact copy of Trajan's Column in Rome?

MADELEINE

West of the Louvre and Opéra is the tiny Madeleine district, centered around the church and square of the same name. This is the area's only residential pocket, a place where the rich French do their shopping and where most tourists don't venture for fear they'll break something. A great flower market sets up on the square Tuesday–Sunday. Marcel Proust spent his childhood at 9 boulevard Malesherbes, cultivating his delicate sensibilities and pining away for Albertine. Just south of place de la Madeleine is the chic and well-policed **rue du Faubourg St-Honoré,** the Rodeo Drive of Paris, where you can gaze at the likes of Hermès, Lagerfield, and Lacroix through their windows. Don't forget to give your regards to the president at the **Palais de l'Elysée** on place Beauvau (look for all the cops hanging around), official residence of the head of state since 1873.

Next to the Eglise de la Madeleine you'll find the most beautiful pay toilets in all of Paris—a stunning display of art deco and porcelain. The cost for this luxury is a mere 2F.

LE MARAIS

Literally, *le marais* means "the swamp," indicating the condition in which the Seine formerly kept this area. Between its original existence as a swamp and its current one as a fashionable district inhabited by wealthy Parisians, the Marais has seen royalty move in (Henri IV installed his court here in the 17th century) and out (when Versailles was built) and waves of Jewish immigrants put down stakes. Philippe Auguste forced the Jews living near Notre-Dame in the heart of Paris to move outside the city walls. The Revolution granted Jews religious freedom, and in the late 1800s Jews fleeing persecution in Poland and Russia came to Paris, living in squalid conditions in the Marais ghetto and working mainly as peddlars and merchants. During World War II, the French police arrested thousands of Jews living in the Marais; the Vél d'Hiv roundup of July 16, 1942, when over 12,000 Jews were arrested in one day, marks the low point of French collaboration.

After the decimation of World War II, the Marais remained an old, decaying quarter until a 1962 law established a restoration program and developers started buying up property, fixing the facades of historic buildings, installing boutiques and galleries, and jacking up property values. Jewish immigrants from North Africa have brought new life to the neighborhood, and today you'll see a mixture of falafel stands, kosher butchers, and bookstores with books in Hebrew, French, and Arabic. The Marais covers the fourth and some of the third arrondissements, and though the narrow streets become crowded with tourists in summer, this is one of Paris's best neighborhoods for eating, drinking, singing, walking, and just generally being.

One of the few areas in central Paris left untouched by Baron Haussmann, the Marais has retained tiny, labyrinthine streets that hold all kinds of surprises, from medieval alleys to restored *boulangeries* (bakeries) and brasseries. The **Jewish quarter,** centered on rue des

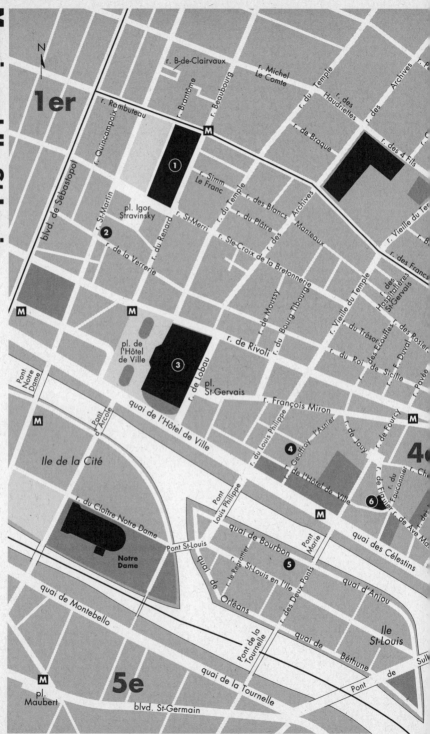

N

1er

r. B-de-Clairvaux

r. Michel Le Comte

r. du Temple

r. des Haudriettes

r. Brantôme

r. Beaubourg

Archives

r. des

r. Rambuteau

r. de Braque

r. des 4 Fils

M

r. Quincampoix

①

blvd. de Sébastopol

r. Simm Le Franc

r. St-Martin

pl. Igor Stravinsky

②

r. St-Merri

r. du Renard

r. du Temple

r. des Blancs Manteaux

r. du Plâtre

Archives

r. des

r. Vieille du Te

r. B

r. de la Verrerie

r. Ste-Croix de la Bretonnerie

r. des Francs

M

M

pl. de l'Hôtel de Ville

③

r. de Rivoli

r. de Moussy

r. du Bourg Tibourg

r. Vieille du Temple

des Hospitalières St-Gervais

r. des Rosier

r. du Trésor

des Écouffes

F. Duval

Pont Notre Dame

r. de Lobau

pl. St-Gervais

r. François Miron

r. du Roi de Sicilie

r. Pavée

quai de l'Hôtel de Ville

M

Pont d'Arcole

r. du Louis Philippe

Geoffroy l'Asnier

r. de Jouy

r. de Foucy

M

4e

r. Ch

Ile de la Cité

r. de l'Hôtel de Ville

④

r. du Fauconnier

⑥

r. de Ave Ma

Pont Louis Philippe

M

r. du Cloître Notre Dame

Pont St-Louis

quai de Bourbon

Pont Marie

quai des Célestins

Notre Dame

r. le Regrattier

St-Louis en l'Ile

⑤

r. des Deux Ponts

Pont de la Tournelle

quai d'Anjou

quai de Montebello

quai de Orléans

quai de

Béthune

Ile St-Louis

de

Sull

M

5e

pl. Maubert

quai de la Tournelle

Pont

blvd. St-Germain

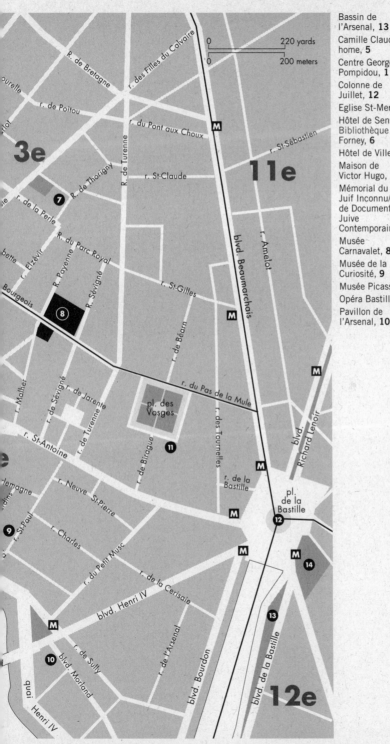

Marais and Ile St-Louis

Rosiers and rue des Ecouffes, adds to the Marais's bustling character. Though interior visits are discouraged (most effectively by the locked gate), at least walk past the **1913 synagogue** (10 rue Pavée) designed by art nouveau great Hector Guimard. The **Mémorial du Martyr Juif Inconnu** (Memorial of the Unknown Jewish Martyr) and the **Centre de Documentation Juive Contemporaine** (17 rue Geoffroy l'Asnier, 4e, tel. 1/42–77–44–72) share the same building. The memorial houses temporary art and history expositions, as well as the ashes of concentration camp victims; the center is a great resource for Jewish studies (*see* Resident Resources, in Chapter 1).

People don't come to the Marais just 'cause it's old, though—it's also happening. **Rue Ste-Croix-de-la-Brétonnerie** and **rue Vieille-du-Temple** are the center of gay life in Paris, offering a variety of gay bars, bookstores, and businesses. These streets and surrounding ones constitute one of the most stylish areas in town—you'll wonder how these guys can afford to buy Armani jackets when they're lounging around drinking cocktails at 3 PM. **Rue des Francs-Bourgeois** is another great street, full of sleek cafés and homey restaurants; north of it are a couple of the city's best museums: the **Musée Picasso** and **Musée Carnavalet** (*see* Not-So-Major Museums, *above*). And at the end of rue des Francs-Bourgeois is the serene **place des Vosges** (*see box, below*).

Between the Seine and the rue de Rivoli lies the calmer part of the Marais, beautifully packed with old hôtels and green patches. Look for the tiny garden behind the **Hôtel de Sens,** a mansion transformed into the Bibliothèque Forney, an art-history library (*see* Resident Resources, in Chapter 1). Wander along **rue St-Paul** for cool shops and antiques.

MONTMARTRE

Rising above the city on the highest hill in Paris is Montmartre, site of the **Basilique du Sacré-Coeur** (*see* Houses of Worship, *above*) and home to a once-thriving artistic community. Even now, after many of the artists have headed for cheaper quarters and tour buses deliver hordes of tourists to its minuscule streets, Montmartre remains first and foremost a village where a special breed of Parisian lives and drinks. A trip through the streets of this neighborhood will reward you with panoramic views, glimpses of gardens, small cafés filled with locals, and perhaps the sound of a practicing violinist.

Place des Vosges

Back in the old days, this rectangular square bordered by fancy residences was all the rage. In 1605, Henri IV initiated work to transform the square into the place Royale, though the poor guy died before he could move in. The king's and queen's residences, with the largest facades, faced each other from across the plaza. Between them lay what pugnacious Parisians used as jousting grounds, and so they remained until finally becoming a park later in the century.

The park itself is done in an English style and is one of the nicest spots in Paris to spend a sunny afternoon. Bring that falafel you just picked up on rue des Rosiers and stroll amid the prim, screaming darlings of the Marais's wealthy moms and dads. Besides Issey Miyake's principal boutique and a number of outrageously expensive restaurants, the surrounding colonnades harbor the open gardens of the Hôtel de Sully (see box Hôtels Particuliers, below) and the Maison de Victor Hugo (see Writers, in Not-so-Major Museums, above). Try to come on a weekend afternoon, when sporadic free classical music concerts add to the already stately atmosphere. 4e. Métro: St-Paul or Chemin Vert.

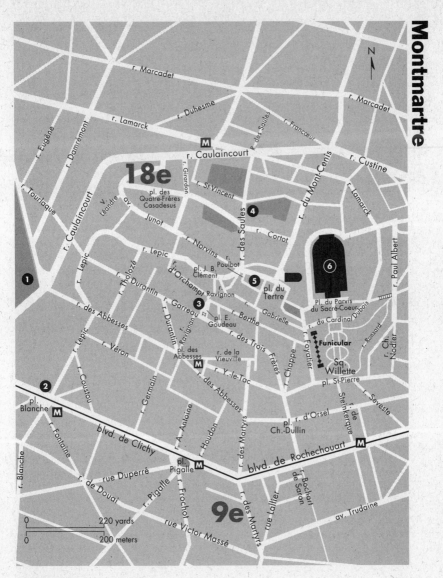

N

r. Marcadet

r. Duhesme

r. Lamarck

r. Marcadet

r. Eugène

r. Damrémont

r. Tourlaque

r. Caulaincourt

M r. Caulaincourt

18e

r. Girardon

V. Léandre

av. Junot

pl. des Quatre-Frères Casadesus

r. St-Vincent

r. des Saules

r. Francœur

r. Custine

r. du Mont-Cenis

r. Lamarck

r. Paul Albert

r. Cortot

r. Norvins

r. Poulbot

4

r. Lepic

r. Tholozé

r. Durantin

r. Garreau

d'Orchampt

pl. J. B. Clément

Ravignon

5

pl. du Terre

6

Pl. du Parvis du Sacré-Cœur

r. Ch. Nodier

r. du Cardinal Dubois

r. Ronsard

1

r. des Abbesses

r. Durantin

Ravignan

3

r. E. Goudeau

r. Berthe

Gabrielle

r. des Trois Frères

r. du Cardinal Dubois

Funicular

r. Lepic

r. Véron

pl. des Abbesses

M

r. de la Vieuville

r. des Abbesses

r. Y.-le-Tac

r. Chappe

r. Foyatier

Sq. Willette

pl. St-Pierre

2

pl. Blanche **M**

r. Coustou

Germain

r. A. Antoine

r. Houdon

r. des Martyrs

pl. r. d'Orsel

Ch.-Dullin

r. de Steinkerque

r. Seveste

M

r. Blanche

r. Fontaine

rue Duperré

r. de Douai

pl. Pigalle

M

r. Pigalle

r. Frochot

blvd. de Clichy

blvd. de Rochechouart

9e

rue Victor Massé

r. des Martyrs

rue Lallier

r. Bochart de Saron

av. Trudaine

| 0 | | 220 yards |
| 0 | | 200 meters |

Basilique de
Sacré-Cœur, **6**

Bateau-Lavoir, **3**

Cimetière de
Montmartre, **1**

Espace Montmartre–
Dali, **5**

Moulin Rouge, **2**

Vineyard, **4**

In the 19th century, vineyards and over 40 windmills covered Montmartre, which was at that time a country village. After Haussmann razed most of the working-class homes in the city center, this area saw a population boom. Among the newcomers were artists, drawn by cheap rents and the bohemian atmosphere. Picasso, Renoir, Dalí, Braque, and writer/poets like Apollinaire and Baudelaire all lived and worked here. **Bateau Lavoir** (13 pl. Emile-Goudeau; Métro: Abbesses) was an artists' colony where Picasso, Braque, Gris, and others had studios. Picasso painted the cubist classic *Les Demoiselles d'Avignon* here; supposedly a pack of prostitutes from Barcelona posed for the painting. Head south one block to the **place des Abbesses,** a tranquil old plaza with one of the two remaining art nouveau Métro entrances designed by Guimard. For more on the history and illustrious personalities of Montmartre, visit the **Musée de Montmartre** (*see* History, in Not-So-Major Museums, *above*), in the building where Renoir once had his studio.

Montmartre became famous between 1880 and 1914, from the time when the first cabarets opened to the start of World War I. The cabarets, at the bottom of the hill near **place Pigalle** and **place de Clichy,** provided new excitement for the area's bohemians, as well as for students and bourgeois couples who came to the neighborhood for a show. The **Moulin Rouge** (pl.

Hôtels Particuliers

Hôtels particuliers (aristocratic residences, usually with fancy facades and hidden courtyards) gained prominence as an architectural genre in the early 17th century. Such signs of wealth sprung up to accommodate the nobility and their hangers-on after Henri IV moved Blueblood Central to the Marais. Many hôtels turned into literary and artistic salons in the 18th century.

- *Hôtel Carnavalet: Now a museum of Parisian history (see History, in Not-so-Major Museums, above), this grand hôtel at 23 rue de Sévigné housed the most brilliant late-17th-century literary salon, that of Madame Sévigné. Her many surviving letters detail the neurasthenic vacillations of 17th-century high society.*

- *Hôtel de Clisson: This hôtel (58 rue des Archives), with its twin towers, got started early on; the entrance dates from 1380. Housing the Duke of Bedford in the mid-15th century, it later turned into another salon.*

- *Hôtel de Montmor: Behind the doors at 79 rue du Temple flowered a salon that hosted the likes of Molière and Descartes.*

- *Hôtel de Sens: Originally right on the Seine (the river has since shifted away), this hôtel at 1 rue du Figuier was built in the 15th century as a home away from home for the visiting archbishops of Sens, who once controlled the church of Paris. It's in remarkable condition, thanks to a thorough renovation by the city earlier this century, and now houses an art-history library.*

- *Hôtel de Sully: Renovations have brought this old hôtel at 62 rue St-Antoine back to its shape when Monsieur Sully, Henri IV's minister, lived here. Today the Renaissance edifice houses the headquarters of Historic Monuments and Sites in France. Though the interior is mostly inaccessible private offices, you can see the courtyard and the garden near the place des Vosges.*

Blanche), immortalized in Toulouse-Lautrec's posters and paintings, still cashes in on Paris's reputation as a city of sex and sin (*see* Cabaret, in Chapter 5). The cabaret culture and the artistic community fed off each other: The artists provided the cabarets with patronage and publicity, and the cabarets provided the artists with the intrigue and alcohol they needed to stay "inspired."

Where artists go, rich folk soon follow, and the area gradually filled with galleries, boutiques, tourist shops, and you. Today, the aggressive third-rate painters clustered around place du Tertre, one of the most tourist-attacked spots in the entire city, are the unfortunate reminders of Montmartre's artistic heritage. Real artists live behind the hill, often in million-dollar homes on **avenue Junot**. Nearby, on **rue des Saules**, is the last remaining **vineyard** in Paris, producing 125 gallons of wine per year. To the west, off **place des Quatre-Frères-Casadesus**, is a small park where old men gather every day to play pétanque. The guy holding his head in his hands in the statue here is St-Denis, Paris's first bishop. Legend has it that the Romans beheaded him here in AD 250; he then picked up his head and carried it for 6 kilometers (4 miles) before calling it a day.

The little alley at 25 avenue Junot, villa Léandre, is one of the most picturesque in Paris.

In eastern Montmartre, demarcated by rue Myrha to the north and boulevard de la Chapelle to the south, is the **Goutte d'Or** (Drop of Gold), named after the white wine its vineyards used to produce. A bastion of the Algerian independence party (the FLN) during the Algerian–French war, the area has absorbed constant waves of immigrants, most recently from the Antilles and Africa. Today, Muslim markets sit next to African textile manufacturers, wholesale grocers, and old horse butchers in this multiethnic working-class quarter. Huge crowds of people move through the streets doing their shopping while groups of men debate on corners; lone women may feel uncomfortable with the unwanted attention from men and the lack of other women on the streets. Sunday is when the neighborhood gets most festive; streets are often blocked off for daylong street markets, and most shops—most notably the enormous Tati (*see* Vintage Clothing, in Chapter 6), where you can wade through bins of dirt-cheap clothes—stay open late.

MONTPARNASSE

The name Montparnasse is burdened with images of all kinds of brilliant expatriates doing silly drunken things in the years surrounding World War I. Acting as an intellectual counterweight to all of the artistry going on up in Montmartre, a quartet of cafés on the corner of **boulevards Montparnasse** and **Raspail**—La Coupole, Le Dôme, Le Sélect, and La Rotonde—became the center for American writers who couldn't get over how much their dollars were worth here. They came, drank, slept with one another, never learned French, and changed cafés like neckties— on one eventful night the owner of Le Dôme fired his manager, threatened his waiters, and insulted his customers, only to find all three regrouped a few weeks later at La Coupole, newly opened by the ex-manager. Americans liked to think that they held court on these corners, pointing to the presence of Ernest Hemingway, Gertrude Stein, Alice B. Toklas, Paul Bowles, Zelda and F. Scott Fitzgerald, Henry Miller, and Peggy Guggenheim in their midst. But they weren't the only people around—Pablo Picasso, Georges Braque, Juan Gris, Piet Mondrian, Leon Trotsky, Jean-Paul Sartre, Simone de Beauvoir, Lawrence Durrell, Anaïs Nin, Jean Arp, Meret Oppenheim, Yves Tanguy, and Marcel Duchamp completed the picture, while an exiled Vladimir Lenin spent most of his time here shunning chitchat and honing his chess game.

The four cafés are still there, though only Le Sélect still has a stylish crowd. The rest of the neighborhood, on the surface anyway, looks like the same mixture of old buildings, manicured parks, and out-of-place new buildings that you see in the rest of Paris. The huge commercial center finished in 1973 detracts substantially from the neighborhood's charm, as does the **Tour Montparnasse**, the tallest structure (at 210 meters/690 feet) in the city; you can take an elevator up the sinister-looking tower to the rooftop bar, where an overpriced drink will get you a spectacular view. Stretching out from the tower and the Gare Montparnasse train station are several new commercial and residential developments that are about as uninspired as Paris gets. The **place du 18 juin 1940**, just north of the tower, commemorates the speech de Gaulle gave in exile in London urging the French to resist the German invaders. The huge student population in Montparnasse, having fled the expensive fifth and sixth arrondissements, ushers in the latest, but not necessarily greatest, developments in nightlife, most of them American offshoots.

A few old sights are still worth visiting. The **Parc Montsouris** and **Cité Universitaire** area (*see* Parks and Gardens, *above*) is a great place to meet other foreigners in Paris. The **Cimetière Montparnasse** has been packing them in for years, and the entrance to the network of catacombs is at place Denfert-Rochereau (*see* Dead Folk, *above*).

Montparnasse has scores of tiny streets and cul-de-sacs lined with ivy-covered houses that look more like they belong in a country village than in Paris. **Villa Adrienne,** off avenue Général Leclerc, and **villa Hallé,** off avenue Réné Coty, are both especially picturesque. Each house on villa Adrienne bears the name of a famous artist or philosopher instead of a numerical address. **Villa Seurat,** off rue de la Tombe-Issoire, saw the many comings and goings of Anaïs Nin, Henry Miller, and Lawrence Durrell. Three or four little streets lead away from Parc Montsouris off rue Nansouty. Of these, the **square de Montsouris** is most likely to make you want to become a wealthy, settled homeowner.

QUARTIER LATIN

The center of French intellectual life for over 700 years, the Quartier Latin has drawn the metaphysically restless, the politically discontent, the artistically inspired, and those who

Rodin and Balzac

It made perfect sense that the greatest French writer of his time should be sculpted by the greatest French artist of his time, and so Société des Gens de Lettres president Emile Zola awarded to Auguste Rodin the commission to immortalize Honoré de Balzac. Despite the objections of society members, who saw the artist as out-of-touch and incompetent, Rodin accepted the proposal to erect a sculpture at the small place Guillaumin, near the intersection of rue Balzac and avenue de Friedland. Though his health was failing, Rodin traveled to the town where Balzac was born and sketched local peasants as models for the long-dead writer. Several nudes—many of which are at the Musée Rodin—were rejected by the society, including one where Balzac's groin seems to extend into the earth.

The final version of the sculpture, unveiled in 1898, was a towering image of the writer with a backward-arching body, shoulders draped by a formless dressing gown and hands clutched conspicuously at the waist. Rodin insisted that the work be mounted on a tall pedestal, forcing viewers to gaze up at the sculpture. The similarity between the work and a phallus is hardly accidental—both Rodin and Balzac were notorious for their high opinions of their own virility. The pedestal, dressing-gown, quality of bronze casting, and everything else they could think of was declared unacceptable by the members of the society, who refused the work and gave the commission to A. Jolguiere. This forgotten sculptor obediently produced a larger-than-life image of Balzac sitting fully clothed in an armchair, his feet surrounded by trite symbols of intelligence and artistry. This work was installed in the place in 1900 and has been largely neglected ever since. The original Rodin Balzac has since been placed on a traffic island on boulevard Montparnasse at boulevard Raspail.

like to hang out with them to the neighborhood's universities, cafés, garrets, and alleys. In the year 1099, Peter Abélard came to the area to study with a local monk. He became a master of dialectics, or the discovery of truth through debate, and students from all over Europe came to study with him. In 1215, the Parisian crown and Roman papacy officially recognized the teachings going on in the area, though the growing school wasn't baptized until 1257, when it took on the name of Louis IX's chaplain Robert de Sorbon's neighboring boarding house. Early alums included Thomas Aquinas, Roger Bacon, and Albertus Magnus. The students in the quarter spoke Latin, even outside the classroom, hence the neighborhood's name.

The conservative Sorbonne had strong ties to the church, forcing some disgruntled students and professors to establish just next door to it, in 1530, the College of France, where the classics were taught in—gasp!—Greek instead of Latin. Intellectual life plodded along for the next 250 years, until the Revolution turned all the abbeys and cloisters of the universities into quarries. The curriculum fell under the direction of the government until 1808, when the University of Paris took over the Sorbonne. It took the 1968 student uprisings against conservative faculty and obsolete teaching methods to bring the Sorbonne into the 20th century and to "encourage" the formation of the 13 specialized schools of the University of Paris.

The presence of several institutions of higher learning keeps the quarter youthful, creative, and relatively liberal. Cafés, bookstores, bars, and cheap restaurants proliferate, and even the presence of millions of tourists doesn't break the mood, though it can seriously dampen it in summer. **Rue de la Huchette** and the surrounding streets stemming from the Seine are a real nightmare, though you might visit them for street music and a late-night crêpe. Napoléon Bonaparte settled at 10 rue de la Huchette. Just to the west, **place St-Michel** and its fountain act as a meeting/pickup spot for tourists year-round.

An especially rewarding jaunt is through the labyrinthine streets between **place Maubert** and the Seine end of boulevard St-Michel; these streets manage to retain their medieval feel despite the presence of fast-food stops and expensive residences (Mitterrand's private home is at 22 rue de Bièvre). The **square René-Viviani,** just east of the Huchette madness, is an eminently pleasant little park with the oldest tree in Paris, sprouted in 1601. **Shakespeare and Co.,** a required stop for literary Anglophones visiting Paris, is next door (see English-Language Bookstores, in Chapter 6). The area around the Sorbonne and behind the **Panthéon** (see Dead Folk, *above*) merits serious exploration as well. **Rue de la Montagne-Ste-Geneviève,** winding between the Panthéon and place Maubert, is one of the oldest streets in Paris, with a number of buildings dating from the Middle Ages.

ST-GERMAIN-DES-PRES

It has happened and is still happening all over Paris, but perhaps never so drastically as in St-Germain: This onetime haven for the intellectual, the beat, and the bohemian has relinquished its spirit to the hands of the mainstream, the upscale, and the comfortable. Where there used to be swinging jazz bars, bistrots, and bookstores, there are now clean, well-packaged, and rather sterile versions of the same; though plenty of students still roam the streets, they are wearing sport coats and Hermès scarves—few berets, very few berets. Centered around **Eglise St-Germain,** the oldest church in Paris, and running through the sixth arrondissement from about the Seine to the Jardin du Luxembourg, the quarter harbors some of Paris's best memories.

A short walking tour: Start at Eglise St-Germain, where monks who set up camp here infused the area with its initial intellectual flair, bringing international art and culture to the city. Rousseau and Voltaire, unable to get support elsewhere, were published in the St-Germain abbey. Literati have continued to haunt the neighborhood, particularly the tables of **Les Deux Magots** and **Le Flore,** two overpriced neighboring cafés on boulevard St-Germain. Deux Magots was the favorite of Verlaine and Mallarmé, Le Flore of Jean-Paul and Simone, Camus, and Picasso. From the Eglise St-Germain, take **rue Bonaparte** toward the river and you'll soon reach the once-great **Ecole Nationale Supérieure des Beaux-Arts,** which trained the likes of architect Julia Morgan. Take a detour to your right down **rue Visconti:** At No. 17 a young Balzac founded

Seine
Pont Royal
quai Anatole France
quai du Louvre
Louvre

M blvd. St-Germain
r. de Solférino
r. de Lille
quai Malaquais
Pont du Carrousel
Pont des Arts

Musée d'Orsay

r. de l'Université
r. du Bac

M

7e

Pont Neuf
Pont Neuf

M
pl. Dauphine

Pont Neuf
quai des Grands Augustins

r. de Bellechasse

r. de Varenne

blvd. St-Germain
Sts-Pères
r. Jacob
r. Bonaparte
r. de Seine
r. Mazarine
quai de Conti
Pont St-M.

① ③ carrefour de Buci
r. St-André des Arts

r. de Buci

blvd. f. de Grenelle
r. du Dragon
pl. St-Germain-des-Prés
M ②
④
r. de Buci

M

blvd. St-Germain
r. de l'École de Médecine

r. de Babylone
sq. Boucicaut
r. de Sèvres
r. du Four
r. Mabillon
r. de l'Ancienne Comédie
pl. de l'Odéon

r. Vaneau

r. du Bac

blvd. Raspail
M

M r. de Sèvres
r. du Vieux Colombier
⑤
pl. St-Sulpice

pl. de l'Odéon
⑩
Monsieur-le-Prince
pl. de la Sorbonne

r. de Sèvres

r. du Cherche-Midi
St-Placide
r. de Rennes
r. Madame
r. de Vaugirard
r. de l'Odéon

r. Mayet

M

M
r. de Vaugirard

r. de Fleurus
r. d'Assas

Palais du Luxembourg

6e
Jardin du Luxembourg

r. Soufflot

r. Gay Lussac

blvd. St-Michel

pl. du 18 juin 1940
M
r. de Montparnasse
r. Notre-Dame-des-Champs
r. Bonaparte
⑦
r. Auguste Comte

r. de l'Arrivée
M

Stanislas
r. Vavin
blvd. du Montparnasse
M

r. St-Jaques

⑥
r. du Départ
r. Delambre
blvd. Raspail
M

Gare Montparnasse
M
r. de la Gaité
blvd. Edgar Quinet

av. de l'Observatoire
blvd. de Port R.

Cimetière de Montparnasse
14e
⑧

av. D. Rochereau
r. du Faubourg St-Jacques

av. du Maine
r. Froidevaux
r. Daguerre
blvd. Schoelcher
⑨ pl. Denfert Rochereau
M
blvd. Arago
r. de la Santé

r. Gassendi
blvd. St-Jacques
M

Arènes de
Lutèce, **17**

Catacombes, **9**

Ecole Nationale des
Beaux-Arts, **1**

Eglise St-Etienne
du Mont, **15**

Eglise St-Germain-
des-Prés, **2**

Eglise
St-Séverin, **13**

Eglise St-Sulpice, **5**

Fondation
Cartier, **8**

Institut du Monde
Arabe, **18**

Jardin de
Navarre, **16**

La Mosquée, **19**

Musée de Cluny, **11**

Musée Delacroix, **4**

Musée National
d'Histoire
Naturelle, **20**

Musée Zadkine, **7**

Palais de l'Institut
de France, **3**

Panthéon, **14**

Sorbonne, **12**

Théâtre de
l'Odéon, **10**

Tour
Montparnasse, **6**

an unsuccessful press. On the other side of the Beaux-Arts school, Serge Gainsbourg had his Parisian digs at 5 bis rue Verneuil (today well covered with spray paint) until his death in 1991. Similar in style and impact to American Bob Dylan in his songwriting and general presence,

Exposed Art

Sure, you've heard that "Paris is like a museum" line a thousand times. There is some truth to the cliché, as works by the world's best-known artists decorate parks and traffic circles throughout the city. Here are some of the pieces living in Paris:

- In Montparnasse cemetery is Constantin Brancusi's The Kiss, a direct response to Rodin's work by the same name. The "primitivist" sculpture adorns the tombstone of Tanosa Gassevskaia, a classically tragic character who killed herself in 1910 over unrequited love.

- Two sculptures by Jean Dubuffet and Roy Lichtenstein sit at 3 quai Anatole France, just east of the Musée d'Orsay.

- Pablo Picasso sculpted the memorial bust of his poet friend Guillaume Apollinaire on square Laurent Prache, next to St-Germain-des-Prés. The two had a final falling out before the poet's death in 1918, but Picasso had time to let old wounds heal, taking over 40 years to complete the sculpture.

- Two tiny versions of the Statue of Liberty, a likeness of sculptor Frédéric Bartholdi's mom, found homes in Paris before the big one settled down in New York Harbor. The smaller of the two models is hidden in the bushes at the Jardin du Luxembourg, while the larger rests on the Allée des Cygnes (15e, Métro: Bir-Hakeim). Bartholdi also designed the lion at place Denfert-Rochereau.

- Marc Chagall crafted a likeness of friend Yvan Goll (across from Chopin) for his tombstone in Père Lachaise (see Dead Folk, above). When Yvan's wife, Claire, died in 1977, 27 years later, a different artist added her portrait.

- Sticking out of the ground close to the Cité des Sciences et de l'Industrie (see Technology and Science, in Not-So-Major Museums, above) are bits of a gargantuan bicycle by Claes Oldenberg. The sculpture is popular with children, who fortunately see no difference between a slide and "art."

- The promenade extending through La Défense (see Neighborhoods, above) is home to many expensive corporate-type installations, including a colorful, unnamed, oversize plasticine mess by Joan Miró, and Slat, a chunk of rolled steel stuck into the ground by Richard Serra.

- The grounds surrounding the UNESCO building (7 pl. de Fontenoy, 7e, Métro: Ségur) aren't always open, but when they are, you can see a large Alexander Calder mobile keeping company with a reclining figure by Henry Moore, a walking man by Giacometti, a Japanese garden, and an eerie angel that survived Nagasaki better than the church on which it hung.

Gainsbourg became a folk hero and national idol despite an imperfect voice. Turn right at the river and walk past the **Palais de l'Institut de France** (cnr of quai de Conti and Pont des Arts), the seat of the Académie Française, which Richelieu created in 1635 in an attempt to supervise the activities of Parisian intellectuals. The Académie is still around, defending the French language from foreign invaders—its latest stroke of brilliance was to *outlaw* the commercial use of non-French (read: English) words in France, though this was soon declared unconstitutional as violating the freedom of expression.

Walking along the Seine toward the Louvre, you'll pass **rue des Grands Augustins,** where at No. 5–7 Picasso enjoyed his last—and most luxurious—Parisian home from 1936 to 1955. Turn away from the river again on rue Dauphine, veering left at the fork a few blocks up, and you'll hit the **cour de Rohan,** where Dr. Joseph-Ignace Guillotin invented an execution device he described as a "puff of air on the neck" of the victim. Farther ahead, near Odéon, a statue of Danton marks where this great revolutionary once lived (Haussmann had his way with the actual building.) Great streets branch south off place Henri-Mondor, including the tiny **rue de l'Ecole de Médecine,** where Sarah Bernhardt was born at No. 5. To the west lies **rue Monsieur-le-Prince;** No. 14 was at various times home to American writer Richard Wright (from 1948 to 1959) and composer Camille Saint-Saëns (from 1877 to 1889). Head west a few blocks to **rue de Tournon,** whose 18th-century hôtels particuliers have housed too many celebrities to mention (read the plaques), among them Casanova (No. 27) and Balzac (No. 2). If you roam St-Germain with your eyes tilted upward, you'll find plenty of commemorative plaques to keep you busy.

Don't miss the **rue St-André-des-Arts,** a pedestrian street roughly between place St-Michel and carrefour de Buci, lined with crêperies, postcard shops, and a good experimental cinema. The nearby **cour du Commerce St-André** (an alley between rue St-André-des-Arts and boulevard St-Germain) was opened in 1776 and saw all sorts of revolutionary activity, including the printing of Marat's *L'Ami du Peuple* at No. 8, the beheading of subversives at No. 9, and the daily life of Danton in his seven-room apartment at No. 20.

Modern-day St-Germain is still a great place. Winding streets, wonderful markets, and upscale boulangeries (try Mulot, at the corner of rues de Seine and Lobineau) make this a posh residential neighborhood. It may be spruced up and overpriced, but the area hasn't quite lost the character that brought the counterculture here in the first place.

WHERE TO SLEEP   3

By Baty Landis

Unless you have well-placed friends, Paris is not the cheapest place to spend a night. Hotels start at 100F, and that's for a dingy fleabag room with a chenille bedspread. Even the hostels are more expensive here than elsewhere in France, charging up to twice as much as those just half an hour outside town. Paris hotels have learned some things over the centuries they've been catering to visitors, and if one of those lessons was that they could squeeze a lot of money out of guests, at least they've also learned—for the most part—how to treat those guests right. Provided you hit the 150F-plus range, checking into a hotel usually means you're laying your body on something clean, dealing with someone nice, and leaving your bags somewhere safe. Neighborhood has a lot to do with how far that "usually" goes; read our notes about a specific area and its quirks before you decide to settle in.

In summer, reserve as far in advance as possible, particularly for hotels in the Quartier Latin, St-Germain-des-Prés, the Marais, and the first arrondissement. Even hostels book up quickly in Paris, but if you arrive early in the morning your chances of finding space are much better. The tourist offices (*see* Visitor Information in Chapter 1, Basics) can find you something at the last minute, but you should use their service only as a last resort; they don't exactly specialize in cheap rooms. Places farther from the center—like Montmartre, Montparnasse, Belleville, and the Bastille—are less crowded, and public transport will give you easy access to the major sights.

For **long-term** stays, check out listings for private or shared apartments, studios, and au pair positions at the American Church in Paris (65 quai d'Orsay, 7e, tel. 1/47–05–07–99) and in *France-USA Contacts,* a free monthly bulletin found at most Anglophone-frequented cafés and bars. Expect to pay at least 1,800F per month in any situation that doesn't involve work, and that's if you're willing to share a bedroom or a one-room apartment. Otherwise, it'll cost 2,200F or more for your own room in a shared apartment, or 2,500F for your own studio. Tiny studios in the center can cost as much as 4,000F per month, one-bedroom apartments 5,000F and up. Be sure to read the fine print: If a listing specifies "t.c.c." (*toutes charges comprises*), you'll pay the listed rate and no more; otherwise, be ready for utility charges, which generally run 200F–300F a month for a tiny apartment.

Hotels

The French government bestows upon hotels a star rating, ranging from one to four, which indicates the percentage of rooms equipped with baths or other amenities. This rating may not be a good indication of how nice the place is. No-star and one-star hotels may have squeaky-clean rooms with character, or dingy closet-sized rooms with sticky carpet. Always ask to see a room before you take it. Room prices should be listed near the hotel's front door or on the wall behind the reception desk; the prices listed may or may not reflect room taxes, which run 1F–5F per person per night. Rooms marked "e.c." have a sink; rooms marked "douche" have a shower; and rooms marked "douche/WC" or "bain/WC" have a shower and a toilet, or a bath and toilet. Since French hotels almost invariably charge more for rooms with more plumbing, always ask for a room without toilet and shower, or simply for the *prix plus bas* (lowest price). The price categories in this book refer to the cost of a double room plus tax. If a hotel has doubles for a wide range of prices, our price category will generally refer to the less expensive (usually showerless) doubles. "Petit déjeuner compris" means that breakfast is included in the price of the room; otherwise, the price for breakfast should be posted, and it's usually a bad deal.

The Lost Generation Found Itself in Paris

Drawn to Paris by favorable exchange rates, the hypocrisy of Prohibition, and the disillusionment that followed World War I, many American writers, composers, and artists made the move to Paris in the 1920s and 1930s. Thus was formed the fabled and much-imitated group of American expatriates who drank a lot, kept to themselves, and never learned how to speak French. Here's where some of them lived, or at least passed through:

- *Djuna Barnes: 173 boulevard St-Germain*
- *Aaron Copland: 30 rue de Vaugirard*
- *Cole Porter: 269 rue St-Jacques*
- *James Baldwin: 170 boulevard St-Germain*
- *John Dos Passos: 45 quai de la Tournelle*
- *Ernest Hemingway: 44 rue Jacob, 39 rue Descartes, etc.*
- *William Faulkner: 26 rue Servandoni (entrance at 42 rue Vaugirard*
- *Gertrude Stein and Alice Toklas: 27 rue de Fleurus and 5 rue Christine*
- *Ezra Pound and Katherine Anne Porter: 70 bis rue Notre-Dame-des-Champs*
- *Henry Miller: all over the place, but especially at 100 rue de la Tombe-Issoire*

Although a few young Americans still try to live the expatriate life here, most have discovered that romance is cheaper by the koruna than the franc and have gone to Prague (see Eastern Europe on the Loose).

Right Bank

BASTILLE

Spreading over the 11th, 12th, and 4th arrondissements, the Bastille is a neighborhood on the rise. Cool cafés, reasonable restaurants, and cheap hotels make it one of the best areas to stay in town. Proximity to the Gare de Lyon is an added bonus: After lugging your pack out of the station, you'll find that most of the hotels listed below will have space long after similarly priced places in the Quartier Latin and the Marais are packed. To find a place on your own, walk along **rue de la Roquette** or **rue de Charonne** and check out the side streets.

UNDER 150F **Hôtel de la Nouvelle France.** Though this place is fairly squalid, it's hard to complain when rooms for one or two people start at 130F without shower. Given the place's location, right in the midst of the Bastille's bars and galleries, the holey bedspreads are bearable for a couple of days, and everything is cleaned almost daily. *31 rue Keller, 11e, tel. 1/47–00–40–74. Métro: Bastille or Voltaire. 47 rooms, 5 with bath. Showers free.*

Vix Hôtel. After a forebodingly dank entryway, the rooms here are a relief; far from luxurious, but large and clean enough. You can almost always get a room here, in the heart of the Bastille, at the last moment, especially since the friendly manager is reluctant to take reservations over the phone. Call anyway to see what's available. Some semipermanent residents also take advantage of the 100F nightly charge for singles. Couples pay 120F, 140F with private shower. *19 rue de Charonne, 11e, tel. 1/48–05–12–58. Métro: Ledru-Rollin or Bastille. 30 rooms, 7 with shower. Showers 15F.*

UNDER 200F **Hôtel Central Bastille.** This modest hotel sets you up in clean, simple rooms directly over some of Paris's busiest—and loudest—nighttime action and only a 15-second trot from the Opéra Bastille. Singles are 130F, doubles 150F, and doubles with private bath 200F. *16 rue de la Roquette, 11e, tel. 1/47–00–31–51. Métro: Bastille. 30 rooms, 5 with shower. Showers 15F.*

Hôtel Baudin. Big, colorful, comfortable rooms and a location across from the Bistrot du Peintre (*see* Bastille, in Restaurants in Chapter 4) make this hotel a great place to stay. Singles cost 120F, 210F with private shower; doubles start at 180F and go up to 280F for a deluxe room with full bath. Reservations are a good idea. *113 av. Ledru-Rollin, 11e, tel. 1/47–00–18–91. Métro: Ledru-Rollin. 19 rooms, 7 with shower. Showers 20F, breakfast 25F. AE, V.*

UNDER 300F **Pax Hôtel.** If you're sick and tired of low-budget lodgings, for 250F–280F you can live it up here in a double with full bath, phone, and color TV. It's no palace, but the rooms are meticulously maintained, and the staff is friendly. *12 rue de Charonne, 11e, tel. 1/47–00–40–98. Métro: Ledru-Rollin. 47 rooms, all with bath. Breakfast 30F.*

UNDER 350F **Centrotel.** On a street that has been Paris's furniture-store headquarters for hundreds of years, this splurge is particularly enticing for the vain or the indecisive: Every room has a hair dryer and identical decor. The facilities are sparkling, the mattresses firm, and a five-minute walk brings you to the Bastille. Rooms for one or two people with double bed, TV, and telephone go for 300F; an extra bed rolls in for 100F. Their credit-card machine is often mysteriously out of order; you may have to raise a ruckus if you really want to charge your stay. *117 rue du Faubourg St-Antoine, 11e, tel. 1/43–42–99–11. Entrance on passage de la Bonne Graine. Métro: Ledru-Rollin. 16 rooms, all with bath. Breakfast 25F. MC, V.*

UNDER 400F **Hôtel Daval.** An easy stumble home from the Bastille's bars is this modern hotel just off the rue de Lappe/rue de la Roquette intersection. The gray-toned rooms aren't exactly uplifting, but they are comfortable, and the location can't be beat. This is the kind of place where you could put your parents, who would appreciate the amenities and professionalism. Singles cost 330F–350F, doubles 380F and up, triples 480F. *21 rue Daval, 11e, tel. 1/47–00–51–23. Métro: Bastille. 20 rooms, all with bath. Breakfast 45F. AE, MC, V.*

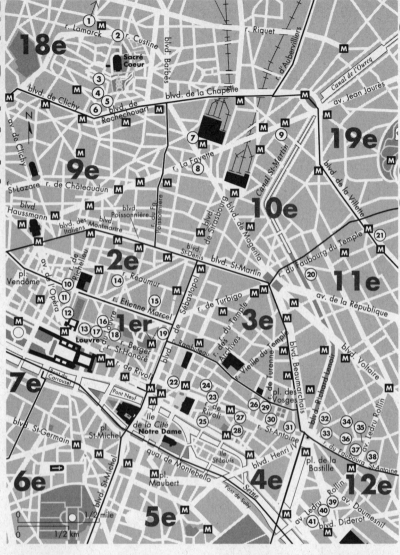

18e

r. Lamarck

r. Custine

blvd. Barbès

Sacré Coeur

blvd. de Clichy

blvd. de la Chapelle

blvd. de Rochechouart

av. de Clichy

N

9e

r. St-Lazare   r. de Châteaudun

r. La Fayette

Canal de l'Ourcq

av. Jean Jaurès

19e

blvd. de la Villette

blvd. Haussmann

blvd. des Italiens

blvd. Montmartre

blvd. Poissonnière

blvd. de Strasbourg

blvd. de Magenta

Canal St-Martin

10e

2e

pl. Vendôme

av. de l'Opéra

r. de Richelieu

r. Réaumur

r. Etienne Marcel

blvd. St-Denis

blvd. St-Martin

r. de Turbigo

r. du Temple

r. du Faubourg du Temple

11e

av. de la République

1er

Louvre

r. Berger

r. St-Honoré

r. de Rivoli

r. Rambuteau

r. des Archives

3e

r. Vieille du Temple

r. de Turenne

blvd. Beaumarchais

blvd. Richard Lenoir

blvd. Voltaire

7e

Pont du Carrousel

Pont Neuf

Île de la Cité

pl. St-Michel   Notre Dame

r. de Rivoli

r. St-Antoine

pl. des Vosges

pl. de la Bastille

r. du Faubourg St-Antoine

r. Ledru Rollin

blvd. St-Germain

6e

quai de Montebello

Île St-Louis

blvd. Henri IV

Seine

pl. Maubert

5e

Pont de Sully

4e

12e

av. Daumesnil

av. Ledru Rollin

blvd. Diderot

0   1/2 mile

0   1/2 km

BELLEVILLE

Loosely made up of the northern part of the 20th arrondissement above Père Lachaise, Belleville is not exactly a lodging mecca. Look around **place Gambetta** for hotels, but be careful wandering alone at night. Home to an eclectic mix of workers, artists, and immigrants, Belleville has a strong blue-collar character. North African and Asian markets and restaurants fill the streets leading off rue de Belleville.

UNDER 200F **Hôtel de Bordeaux.** A friendly propietor and his large hotel sit near the busy intersection of rue de Belleville and boulevard de Ménilmontant, close to more cheap restaurants than you could possibly try during your stay. The rooms are spartan, carpetless, and snug, but they're clean as can be and cost just 120F for a single, 160F for a double, or 200F for a larger double with bath and sometimes TV. The happy man at the desk can almost always squeeze you in with a day's notice. *3 rue Lemon, 20e, tel. 1/40–33-98-15. Métro: Belleville. 66 rooms, 20 with bath.*

Hôtel du Chemin de Fer. Though the cheapest rooms are dingy, all come with a TV to help cheer things up. You'll be in a relatively calm section of Belleville and just 60 seconds from the entrance to Père Lachaise. Singles or doubles go for 170F without a shower, 200F and up with. *233 rue des Pyrénées, 20e, tel. 1/43–58–55–18. Métro: Gambetta. 33 rooms, 26 with shower. Showers 18F. AE, MC, V.*

Nadaud Hôtel. The rooms at this hotel, some with gorgeous views of Paris, are well worth the price—180F and up (260F with private shower). The middle-age couple who run the place go out of their way to be helpful, and Père Lachaise is around the corner. *8 rue de la Bidassoa, 20e, tel. 1/46–36–87–79. Métro: Gambetta. 22 rooms, 13 with shower. Showers 20F, breakfast 27F. MC, V.*

UNDER 250F **Printana.** Right in the middle of bustling shops and restaurants, this hotel offers stark but respectable rooms in a safe part of Belleville. Tiny, dormlike singles go for

Have Wheelchair, Will Travel

Although parts of Paris are slowly beginning to accommodate visitors in wheelchairs, low-end hotels aren't making much progress. Unless you get a space in one of the accessible foyers, you're looking at 450F a night and up. Here's a list of accessible, if not exactly budget, hotels:

- *Grand Hôtel de France. Two double rooms are adapted (460F), though the entrance has one step. 102 blvd. de Latour-Maubourg, 7e, tel. 1/47–05–40–49. Métro: Ecole Militaire.*

- *Hôtel Campanile Italie Gobelins. Beyond the main entrance ramp, there are two steps to the reception, but several rooms and their bathrooms are adapted. Singles or doubles cost 420F. 15 bis av. d'Italie, 13e, tel. 1/45–84–95–95. Métro: Place d'Italie.*

- *Hôtel Urbis Jemmapes Louis Blanc. Two doubles with bath (430F) are adapted with bath, and the entrance and lobby have no steps. 12 rue Louis Blanc, 10e, tel. 1/42–01–21–21. Métro: Louis Blanc.*

- *Hôtel Urbis Lafayette. Everything is flat or reachable by elevator except for the back garden, which requires one step. Three adapted rooms with bath go for 440F. 122 rue La Fayette, 10e, tel. 1/45–23–27–27. Métro: Gare du Nord.*

140F; doubles cost 200F without shower, 240–290F with. Some rooms have balconies, but there are no hall showers—if you don't spring for a room with shower, you'll have to stay grubby. *355 rue des Pyrénées, 20e, tel. 1/46–36–76–62. Métro: Jourdain. 41 rooms, 24 with shower. Breakfast 25F.*

FIRST ARRONDISSEMENT

Anyone with a Napoleonic complex will want to stay here, smack in the historic heart of the city amid many of Paris's grandest monuments. It's certainly not the youngest or hippest of the city's neighborhoods; the cafés and restaurants here are among Paris's most expensive, and unless you stay in a BVJ *foyer* (a type of hostel; *see below*) or one of the hotels listed below, you'll shell out at least 500F for a room. The only affordable place on the Ile de la Cité, site of Notre-Dame, is the basic **Hôtel Henri IV** (25 pl. Dauphine, 1er, tel. 1/43–54–44–53), but it's *real* affordable: Singles start at 140F, doubles at 170F.

UNDER 250F **Hôtel de Lille.** The family running this welcome getaway on a quiet street offers worn yet well-tended rooms. If you reserve ahead, you'll enjoy the best deal in the quarter. Singles go for 170F, doubles for 200F–250F. *8 rue de Pélican, 1er, tel. 1/42–33–33–42. Métro: Palais Royal–Musée du Louvre. 14 rooms, 6 with shower. Showers 30F.*

Hôtel Richelieu Mazarin. This family-run hotel offers rooms fit for a cardinal at refreshingly common prices: singles from 190F, doubles from 230F, or 300F with private shower. You'll be five minutes from Garnier's Opéra and two from Molière's statue pointing the way to the Comédie Française. Reserve two weeks ahead for a room without shower, especially considering there are only two. *51 rue de Richelieu, 1er, tel. 1/42–97–46–20. Métro: Pyramides or Palais Royal–Musée du Louvre. 14 rooms, 12 with bath. Showers 10F, breakfast 25F.*

UNDER 300F **Hôtel Montpensier.** You probably thought you could never afford to stay 60 seconds away from the Louvre, right below the Opéra, and basically next door to the Comédie Française. Well, you can—by reserving ahead for one of the 250F singles or doubles without bath here (rooms with bath jump to 370F). The rooms themselves are comfortable, if unspectacular, but the place as a whole is high-class and run by a professional, English-speaking staff. *12 rue de Richelieu, 1er, tel. 1/42–96–28–50. Métro: Palais Royal–Musée du Louvre. 45 rooms, 37 with bath. Showers 25F, breakfast 30F.*

GARE DE L'EST AND GARE DU NORD

Gare de l'Est and Gare du Nord are close enough to merge; only a tiny block or two separates the rail lines stretching out behind each station. If you arrive late and want the first place out of the station, try one of the generally characterless places below. But don't stay in this area if you value peace and quiet. Or your wallet—foreign visitors frequently report thefts, some at gunpoint, in the neighborhood. To find all the hotels, head straight out the front of either station one block to **boulevard de Magenta,** which is chock-full of rooms in every price category.

UNDER 150F **Hôtel Métropole Lafayette.** Literally in the middle of the street, on an island between three busy avenues, this hotel is incredibly loud but also cheap: singles from 100F, doubles from 130F (from 150F with shower). Considering the smoky, slightly sinister entrance, the rooms are surprisingly clean and spacious, so at least you'll be comfortable while you're up all night listening to the traffic. *204 rue La Fayette, 10e, tel. 1/46–07–72–69. Métro: Louis Blanc. 29 rooms, 22 with bath. Showers 20F, breakfast 15F. MC, V.*

UNDER 200F **Hôtel Bonne Nouvelle.** A two-minute walk from the Gare du Nord, this clean, comfortable establishment will welcome you (in English, no less) with not only a bed but your own telephone and shower as well. The one single costs 150F; doubles cost 160F–220F, and reservations are recommended in summer. *125 blvd. de Magenta, 10e, tel. 1/48–74–99–90. Métro: Gare du Nord. 22 rooms, all with bath. Luggage storage, breakfast 20F.*

UNDER 250F **Hôtel du Brabant.** This is one of the more peaceful hotels near the stations, thanks to the little rue des Petits Hôtels, which takes you off the main drags. Singles start at 140F, doubles at 190F (240F with shower). Tour groups arrive in summer, so room availability tends to be tight—be sure to reserve ahead. *18 rue des Petits Hôtels, 10e, tel. 1/47–70–12–32. Métro: Gare du Nord or Gare de l'Est. 40 rooms, 11 with bath. Showers 18F, breakfast 20F.*

GARE DE LYON

If you arrive at Gare de Lyon and need a place to stay, walk 10 minutes down **rue de Lyon** and check out hotels around the Bastille (see above). Lodging around the train station itself is meager; only **rue d'Austerlitz**, off rue de Lyon to your left as you head toward the Bastille, has anything reasonable to offer. On the up side, the Gare de Lyon area is safer than those around most stations in town, though beware of pickpockets looking for lost tourists. Gare d'Austerlitz is just across the river, so if you arrive there the following spots might come in handy as well.

UNDER 150F **Modern's Hôtel.** The management is quite proud that the bathrooms are "almost as big as the rooms themselves. It's like having a second bedroom!" Not necessarily a sterling recommendation, but the place has clean, quiet quarters steps away from the station. Two people pay 140F for a simple room, 200F for a room with private shower. One person pays 10F less. *11 rue d'Austerlitz, 12e, tel. 1/43–43–41–17. Métro: Gare de Lyon. 29 rooms, 9 with bath. Showers 15F, breakfast 17F.*

UNDER 200F **Hôtel de Marseille.** You can easily lug the biggest of backpacks from the Gare de Lyon to this family-run establishment. At 160F–180F, the rooms aren't exactly being given away, but they're decent, and the staff is cordial. *21 rue d'Austerlitz, 12e, tel. 1/43–43–54–22. Métro: Gare de Lyon. Showers 20F, breakfast 23F.*

UNDER 250F **Hôtel du Midi.** Fresh rooms with wood furnishings and a location close to the Bastille might keep you here beyond that first night off the train. The whole place is sparkling and has free hall showers. Doubles start at 230F, 280F with private shower. Solo travelers pay 10F less. *31 rue Traversière, 12e, tel. 1/43–07–88–68. Métro: Gare de Lyon. 32 rooms, 22 with bath. Breakfast 30F. AE, MC, V.*

LE MARAIS

Onetime home to aristocrats, then to run-down ghetto housing, the Marais has once again become a quarter of the rich and hip. One of the best places to stay in Paris, this neighborhood is sandwiched between the Bastille, Les Halles, and the Seine, and the nightlife is great. Make your way into one of the quarter's famous *hôtels particuliers* (mansions) by staying at the fantastic foyers run by Maisons Internationales des Jeunes Etudiants (*see* Hostels and Foyers, *below*). The ritzy Marais population hasn't rid the place of all its cheap sleeps; look particularly in the streets just above **rue de Rivoli** near the Bastille.

UNDER 150F **Hôtel Rivoli.** This hotel is not big on decorative frills, but it's decent and cheap. The rooms facing rue de Rivoli can be noisy, so try to get one overlooking the smaller street instead. Singles and doubles with sink go for 130F and up, with shower for 150F–200F. *44 rue de Rivoli, 4e, tel. 1/42–72–08–41. Métro: Hôtel-de-Ville. 20 rooms, some with bath. Showers 20F, breakfast 20F.*

UNDER 200F **Grand Hôtel du Loiret.** This old hotel is appealing in its shabbiness. The lobby and stairway have been well maintained, and the wallpaper and bedspreads clash nicely in the cheap rooms. Singles start at 120F; doubles go for 160F with toilet, 210F with shower. *8 rue des Mauvais-Garçons, 4e, tel. 1/48–87–77–00. Métro: Hôtel-de-Ville. 30 rooms, some with bath. Showers 15F, breakfast 15F. MC, V.*

Hôtel de la Herse d'Or. If you weren't looking for the sign, you'd never know that the little door and cavernous entryway lead to a simple hotel that gets high marks, especially for the cozy lobby/dining area where the managers often chat with friends. Spacious singles and doubles cost 150F–190F, 250F with private bath. *20 rue St-Antoine, 4e, tel. 1/48–87–84–09. Métro: Bastille. 39 rooms, 15 with shower. Showers 10F, luggage storage, breakfast 25F.*

Sully Hôtel. Monochrome bedspreads and relatively fresh carpeting characterize the generously sized rooms of this hotel. You'll be around the corner from the place des Vosges and, as the name implies, right near the Sully hôtel particulier. The laid-back management will give you a key to the front door so you can take advantage of the Bastille and Marais nightlife. Rooms for one or two people go for 180F, 240F–280F with bath; triples with bath start at 300F. *48 rue St-Antoine, 4e, tel. 1/42–78–49–32. Métro: St-Paul or Bastille. 25 rooms, most with bath. Showers 10F, breakfast 20F.*

UNDER 250F **Hôtel Andréa.** Though most of the 350F doubles are spacious and come with your own telephone and TV, four or five more modest but inviting doubles rooms without bath go for 200F. Call far ahead to reserve the cheaper rooms. *3 rue St-Bon, 4e, tel. 1/42–78–43–93. Métro: Hôtel-de-Ville or Châtelet–Les Halles. 25 rooms, most with bath. Showers 15F, wheelchair access, luggage storage, breakfast 15F.*

Hôtel Pratic. If you have the refined sensibilities of an interior decorator, the mismatched decor here might offend you. Still, the rooms are clean and quiet, and some look out onto the little square in front of the hotel. Singles are 200F; doubles go for 230F without shower, 275F–340F with. It's best to reserve one week in advance. *9 rue d'Ormesson, 4e, tel. 1/48–87–80–47. Métro: St-Paul. Showers 10F, luggage storage, breakfast 25F.*

UNDER 350F **Grand Hôtel Jeanne-d'Arc.** This small hotel on a quiet street in the heart of the Marais is a good deal for couples; singles and doubles both start at 300F. The large, pretty rooms look like the guest rooms at a French grandma's house. All rooms have telephones, toilets, and either a bath or shower. *3 rue de Jarente, 4e, tel. 1/48–87–62–11. Métro: St-Paul. 40 rooms, all with bath. Wheelchair access, breakfast 30F. MC, V.*

LES HALLES AND BEAUBOURG

Les Halles is a tempting area to stay in because it's so central, lively, and cheap. Unfortunately, it is still a bit scary at night, despite recent police crackdowns on drug dealing in the area. Above rue Réaumur, streets like rue St-Denis host some serious red-light activity. Travelers who plan to stay out late and women traveling alone should think twice before checking into a hotel here, even if it's on a street that looks harmless by day.

UNDER 200F **Hôtel de France.** Though this hotel on the edge of Les Halles is drab, the surrounding neighborhood has recently been spruced up, sprouting cozy cafés and fun restaurants. Rooms cost 130F for a single, 175F–215F for a double without bath, and 225F for a double with bath. *11 rue Marie-Stuart, 2e, tel. 1/42–36–35–33. Métro: Châtelet–Les Halles or Sentier. 20 rooms, some with bath. Showers 20F.*

Hôtel de la Vallée. If you've come to Paris for a bohemian experience, try finding this hotel's front door amid all the prostitutes, punk rockers, and hustlers congregating on the sidewalk. Despite the entrance, the interior is actually pretty nice and the management impressively professional. Singles and doubles are a fair 150F–280F. *84 rue St-Denis, 1er, tel. 1/42–36–46–99. Métro: Châtelet–Les Halles. 30 rooms, some with bath. Showers 15F, breakfast 25F. MC, V.*

UNDER 250F **La Marmotte.** The Opéra, the Louvre, and the Marais are all a 10-minute walk away from this spot tucked in a quiet corner of Les Halles. The tidy rooms have telephones, saggy beds, and lots of closet space; singles run 180F–260F, doubles 200F–280F. In the evening, locals fill the bar downstairs. *6 rue Léopold-Bellan, 2e, tel. 1/40–26–26–51. Métro: Sentier. 16 rooms, most with bath. Showers 15F, breakfast 20F. AE, MC, V.*

MONTMARTRE

Montmartre is a crazy mix of sex shops, tourist traps, and old-style Paris. Although not centrally located, it's a great place to experience the city's diversity, and most of Paris's major attractions are only 10 minutes away by Métro. The nearer the sex shops of Pigalle, the cheaper and sleazier the rooms—be sure to specify one *night*, not one *hour*. The streets fanning out from **place des Abbesses** are full of cheap, sporadically respectable options.

UNDER 150F **Hôtel du Commerce.** A young clientele fills up the reasonably priced, reasonably clean rooms here. Amenities are few, but you get what you pay for: Singles or doubles are 100F, 130F with private shower. They don't accept reservations, so arrive by 10 AM to secure a spot. *34 rue des Trois Frères, 18e, tel. 1/42–64–81–69. Métro: Abbesses. 11 rooms, 2 with shower. Showers 15F.*

Hôtel Surcouf. A grim lobby belies the respectable rooms upstairs—yellowed but clean, and a steal at 120F, 160F with shower. The views of the street and the peeling interior courtyard are less than inspiring, but you can look out over all of Paris from Sacré Coeur, only five minutes away. *18 rue Houdon, 18e, tel. 1/46–06–41–30. Métro: Abbesses. 35 rooms, 11 with shower. Showers 20F.*

Société Modern Hôtel. Stay here if you're tired of all the tourists and want to be near cafés, cheap restaurants, and shops patronized by working-class folk who haven't considered going to a Left Bank bar in years. Sacré Coeur is a 10-minute walk to the south up the hill. The rooms, at 100F for a single, 130F for a double (170F with shower), are a bit spartan, but fresh paint and wallpaper help brighten them up. An extra bed for a third person costs 50F. *62 rue Ramey, 18e, tel. 1/46–06–29–40. Métro: Jules-Joffrin. From the Métro stop, walk up the hill; rue Ramey is on your left. 64 rooms, 18 with shower. Showers 20F, breakfast 20F.*

UNDER 200F **Hôtel Caulaincourt.** Behind the touristy mess of Sacré Coeur, in one of Paris's most unadulterated neighborhoods, this hotel has satisfactory, if institutional, rooms filled with businesspeople and families. Although far from the sights, it is close to friendly cafés. Singles start at 120F, doubles at 150F, triples with shower at 220F. *2 sq. Caulaincourt, 18e, tel. 1/46–06–42–99. Métro: Lamarck-Caulaincourt. 53 rooms, some with bath. 2 AM curfew. Showers 20F. MC, V.*

The Métro station Abbesses, near Sacré Coeur, has one of the few remaining art nouveau Métropolitain archways, as well as a seven-flight, curving stairway whose walls are decorated with murals by many different artists depicting Parisian life.

Idéal Hôtel. Despite the less-than-friendly management, this is one of the best values in Montmartre: A respectable room for one or two runs 170F, for three 230F. Stay here and you're essentially at the foot of the stairs to Sacré Coeur and near a number of lively restaurants. *3 rue des Trois Frères, 18e, tel. 1/46–06–63–63. Métro: Abbesses. 51 rooms, none with bath. Showers 20F.*

UNDER 250F **Hôtel André Gill.** The recently redone rooms at this two-star hotel are some of the nicest around place des Abbesses—your tired feet will love the plush carpet, and some rooms even have stained-glass windows. The hotel is set in a courtyard off the street, so if you try hard enough, you may forget the tons of sex shops two blocks away. Guests are free to play the piano in the breakfast room. Singles cost 210F, doubles 240F (300F–330F with shower). *76 rue des Martyrs, 18e, tel. 1/42–62–48–48. Métro: Abbesses or Pigalle. 32 rooms, 22 with bath. Showers 25F, breakfast 25F. AE, MC, V.*

Left Bank

MONTPARNASSE

Montparnasse spreads over the large 14th arrondissement, which stretches south below the Quartier Latin and St-Germain. Filled with students, Montparnasse has always been associated with intellectual life, particularly after Hemingway and company adopted its cafés. The area is a good, safe one in which to find a hotel, and rooms here are often less expensive than those in the Quartier Latin, only a 10-minute walk away. The streets immediately south of boulevard du Montparnasse, including **rue d'Odessa** and **rue Delambre,** and those around **place Denfert-Rochereau** are especially full of hotels.

UNDER 200F **Hôtel de l'Espérance.** The "Hotel of Hope" is on a small street in the southern, less touristed part of Montparnasse. Many of the comfortable rooms have views of the

Pont de l'Alma

Pont des Invalides

Pont Alexandre III

Pont de la Concorde

Pont Solférino

Seine

pl. de la Résistance

quai d'Orsay

quai d'Orsay

quai Anatole France

Seine

av. Rapp

av. Bosquet

av. de la Bourdonnais

r. St-Dominique

r. de Grenelle

av. de la Tour-Maubourg

r. de Bourgogne

bvd. St-Germain

r. de l'Université

Musée d'Orsay

av. G. Eiffel

Parc du Champ de Mars

Hôtel des Invalides

r. de Bellechasse

r. de Grenelle

r. du Bac

av. de Suffren

Ecole Militaire

av. de la Motte Picquet

av. de Lowendal

av. de Ségur

av. de Breteuil

av. de Villars

bvd. des Invalides

r. Vaneau

av. de Varenne

r. du Commerce

r. Frémicourt

blvd. de Grenelle

r. de Sèvres

7e

bvd. Raspail

r. de Rennes

r. de Sèvres

pl. du 18 Juin 1940

r. Lecourbe

r. de Vaugirard

15e

bvd. Edgar Quinet

Cimetière de Montparnasse

0 ___ 1/2 mile

0 ___ 500 meters

3e

N

1er

Louvre

r. de Rivoli

Pont Royal

Pont du Carrousel

Pont des Arts

Pont Neuf

4e

r. Beaubourg

r. de Rivoli

r. des Sts-Pères

r. Jacob

r. Mazarine

Ile de la Cité

Pont d'Arcade

quai des Célestins

M

blvd. Sébastopol

Pont au Change

Notre Dame

r. St-André des Arts

pl. St-Michel

blvd. St-Germain

r. du Four

r. de Rennes

pl. St-Sulpice

pl. de l'Odéon

quai de Montebello

Ile St-Louis

Pont de la Tournelle

Pont de Sully

r. St-Jacques

r. des Ecoles

pl. Maubert

r. Monge

quai St-Bernard

r. de Vaugirard

r. d'Assas

r. Guynemer

Jardin du Luxembourg

pl. du Panthéon

r. Cujas

r. Gay Lussac

blvd. St-Michel

5e

pl. de la Contrescarpe

r. Mouffetard

pl. Monge

Jardin des Plantes

6e

blvd. du Montparnasse

blvd. Raspail

14e

r. Claude Bernard

r. Monge

blvd. St-Marcel

6

7

8

9

10

11

12

13

15

16

17

20

21

22

23

24

25

26

27

28

29

30

31

32

33

34

35

36

Villa "Les Camélias," 15

Young and Happy Youth Hostel, 34

street toward place Denfert-Rochereau, where cafés and restaurants await you. Singles or doubles go for 180F, 255F with bath. *1 rue de Grancey, 14e, tel. 1/43–21–41–04. Métro: Denfert-Rochereau. 50 rooms, some with bath. Showers 20F, breakfast 25F.*

UNDER 250F **Celtic-Hôtel.** On a small and interesting street, the hotel has decent, quiet rooms with real wood armoires and carpets of questionable taste. Rooms for one or two people cost 200F with sink, 260F with shower and toilet. *15 rue d'Odessa, 14e, tel. 1/43–20–93–53. Métro: Montparnasse or Edgar Quinet. 36 rooms, some with bath. Breakfast 20F. Reserve at least 1 week ahead for cheaper rooms.*

Hôtel des Académies. Tucked right off boulevard du Montparnasse on a quiet street full of art stores and students, this hotel offers spacious, flowery singles from 180F and doubles from 240F (290F with bath). Smile a lot and the proprietress might even warm up after a while. *15 rue de la Grande-Chaumière, 6e, tel. 1/43–26–66–44. Métro: Vavin. 18 rooms, some with bath. Breakfast 27F.*

UNDER 300F **Hôtel Floridor.** This hotel in southern Montparnasse has become a kind of Bavaria West thanks to its connnection with a German travel agency. All the rooms are well tended and have TVs; some even have ugly stone balconies. The one room without bath is 180F; other rooms go for 250F–270F, with an extra bed costing 60F per night. Unfortunately, the 25F breakfast is *obligatoire*. *28 pl. Denfert-Rochereau, 14e, tel. 1/43–21–35–53. Métro: Denfert-Rochereau. 60 rooms, most with bath. Showers 20F.*

UNDER 350F **Hôtel Delambre.** The angle of the walls at the former home of the artist and writer André Breton (1896–1966) looks slightly surreal, but inside it's just a decent hotel. Doubles with TV go for 310F–350F, singles for 220F–240F. If you have a sensitivity to certain color schemes, let them know in advance. *14 rue Delambre, 14e, tel. 1/43–20–66–31. Métro: Edgar Quinet. 40 rooms, all with bath. Breakfast 24F. Reserve 2–3 weeks ahead.*

Villa "Les Camélias." The proprietress personally opens the door to welcome you into this wonderland of flowers and kitsch. The quiet, spacious rooms are lower octane than the lobby. Singles cost 300F, doubles 310F–360F. The hotel is east of the Gare Montparnasse, an easy walk from the Jardin du Luxembourg. *4 rue Jules-Chaplain, 6e, tel. 1/43–26–94–92. Métro: Vavin. 13 rooms, all with bath. Breakfast 30F.*

UNDER 400F **Hôtel des Bains.** A good splurge, this sparkling hotel on a small, lively street is managed by a friendly multilingual staff. The lobby and rooms are comfortable, peaceful, and new. All rooms have their own shower and toilet; most even have TVs. Doubles start at 350F, suites for two to four people at 450F. The place is especially economical for those traveling in groups and is pretty upscale for the price. *33 rue Delambre, 14e, tel. 1/43–20–85–27. Métro: Edgar Quinet. 41 rooms. Breakfast 42F. Reservations advised.*

NEAR THE EIFFEL TOWER

This quarter's reputation as one of the poshest parts of Paris means cheap lodging is tough to find here. Full of stately residential avenues, the seventh arrondissement invites hordes of tourists to the Eiffel Tower and Les Invalides and then takes advantage of them with expensive restaurants and cafés.

UNDER 250F **Grand Hôtel Lévêque.** Possibly the best deal in the seventh, this hotel occupies a small market street that feels actually lived in, unlike the rest of the neighborhood. The rooms are not luxurious but are still very nice, especially when you consider they cost only 200F a night, 300F with private shower. Hall showers are free. *29 rue Cler, 7e, tel. 1/47–05–49–15. Métro: Ecole Militaire. 50 rooms, 48 with shower. Breakfast 25F. MC, V.*

Rustic Hôtel. Midway between Les Invalides and the Eiffel Tower, this place has a musty lobby and staircase and worn but clean rooms. The rooms are the cheapest that solo travelers will find in the neighborhood: 150F, private shower included. Couples will pay 240F, groups of three 300F. *2 rue Duvivier, 7e, tel. 1/47–05–89–27. Métro: Ecole Militaire or Latour-Maubourg. 30 rooms, all with bath.*

UNDER 400F Hôtel du Centre. On a lively market-lined street about a 10-minute walk from the Eiffel Tower, this hotel offers quiet, well-worn rooms that come with funky decorative touches and a stern manager. Singles and doubles with sink start at 380F, making it a better bargain for a couple than a solo traveler. *24 bis rue Cler, 7e, tel. 1/47–05–52–33. Métro: Ecole Militaire. 30 rooms, all with bath. Breakfast 30F. AE, MC, V.*

Hôtel Résidence Orsay. Fans of impressionism should book far ahead and hope for one of the four 200F singles or 290F doubles kitty-corner from the Musée d'Orsay. Miss them and you'll pay 390F for two people, 480F for three, to stay in a really high-class joint. *93 rue de Lille, 7e, tel. 1/47–05–05–27. Métro: Assemblée Nationale. RER: Orsay. 27 rooms, all with shower. Breakfast 30F. MC, V.*

QUARTIER LATIN

With very few exceptions, if a hotel in the Quartier Latin seems too cheap, there's something wrong with it. Either the plumbing's kaput, the roof leaks, or the manager's such a grouch he scares most potential customers away—*something* is just not right. All the hotel proprietors in this area know they'll have no problems filling their rooms, so they don't have to sweet-talk you, or even give you a decent place to stay. And unless you've reserved at least a couple of weeks in advance, don't get your heart set on finding a room here. If you're determined and all the spots below are full, try **rue Gay-Lussac** and its side streets heading away from the Jardin du Luxembourg, or the area between **rue des Ecoles** and **boulevard St-Germain** (near the Maubert-Mutualité Métro). Things are better in the off-season, when the hotels are not as full and the proprietors are more tolerant of tourists. The neighborhood is a much nicer place to be then anyway.

UNDER 150F Hôtel du Commerce. This ramshackle establishment offers decent no-frills lodging close to the action of the quarter. The spartan furnishings, including a bed, Formica bedside table, and worn carpet, look like they came from a garage sale, but at these prices you could afford to redecorate your own room. Singles are 110F, 160F with shower; doubles are 130F, 160F with shower. Three people can share a room for 200F, four for 240F. *14 rue de la Montagne-Ste-Geneviève, 5e, tel. 1/43–54–89–69. Métro: Maubert-Mutualité. 32 rooms, 5 with bath. Showers 15F.*

UNDER 200F Hôtel des Alliés. At this clean operation in a working-class area on the far edge of the fifth arrondissement, the sunny, good-sized rooms have funky light fixtures and occasionally hideous wallpaper. The place fills up exceptionally fast in summer. Singles go for 110F–130F; doubles are 150F. *20 rue Berthollet, 5e, tel. 1/43–31–47–52. Métro: Les Gobelins. 43 rooms, 10 with shower. Showers 15F, luggage storage.*

Hôtel Médicis. This budget traveler's hangout has some of the cheapest (singles 80F–120F, doubles 150F–170F) and smelliest rooms in Paris. Solo travelers may be able to share a room with a stranger for a reduced rate. *214 rue St-Jacques, 5e, tel. 1/43–29–53–64. Métro: Luxembourg. 27 rooms, none with bath. Showers 10F.*

UNDER 250F Hôtel des Carmes. The helpful, English-speaking staff welcome you to this long-established hotel with large, well-kept rooms near the cinemas, bars, and frantic hype of place St-Michel. The 160F singles are the most coveted slots; doubles start at 210F without bath, 230F–450F with. Specify that you *don't* want breakfast; otherwise they might assume you do and charge you a whopping 30F. *5 rue des Carmes, 5e, tel. 1/43–29–78–40. Métro: Maubert-Mutualité. 40 rooms, 20 with bath. Showers 15F.*

Hôtel du Progrès. A British proprietress runs everything smoothly at this hotel right around the corner from the Jardin du Luxembourg. Spacious rooms, many with wood armoires and large windows leading to balconies, cost 240F for two people (330F with private bath) or 330F for three without bath. Single travelers can play the role of starving expatriate in tiny rooms with sinks for 150F–170F; the hall showers are free. The management asks that you send a deposit of 400F per couple, though rooms without shower are often available on short notice. *50 rue Gay-Lussac, 5e, tel. 1/43–54–53–18. RER: Luxembourg. 36 rooms, 6 with bath. Breakfast included.*

Hôtel Gay-Lussac. Only twosomes are likely to get a room here; the three 170F singles are usually occupied by residential students. Clean and spacious doubles with the occasional faux-marble faux fireplace or genuine wood armoire will set you back 220F–400F; add 50F for an extra bed. *29 rue Gay-Lussac, 5e, tel. 1/43–54–23–96. RER: Luxembourg. 44 rooms, 30 with bath. Showers 15F, breakfast 25F.*

Hôtel le Central. This small hotel run by a friendly Portuguese family offers tidy, small rooms with showers for a song. Although the halls are musty and the rooms worn, an excellent location in a tiny square near rue Mouffetard and the Panthéon compensates for the hotel's faults. Singles and doubles go for 150F–240F. *6 rue Descartes, 5e, tel. 1/46–33–57–93. Métro: Maubert-Mutualité. 16 rooms, all with bath.*

UNDER 300F **Les Argonautes.** Though the Greek restaurant of the same name downstairs hosts boisterous Greek musicians almost every night, a peaceful night in this hotel on a little pedestrian street a few steps from the Ile de la Cité is not out of the question. After the band packs up around midnight, only an occasional Greek-island print on the walls will remind you of the ruckus. Singles with bath go for 200F, and doubles start at 250F; an extra bed for a third person (if it'll fit) is 50F more. *12 rue de la Huchette, 5e, tel. 1/43–54–09–82. Métro: St-Michel. 25 rooms, all with bath. Breakfast 25F. AE, MC, V.*

Hôtel Cujas. In the thick of the university fray, this dingy joint houses both travelers and students. Staff members are a bit abrupt and speak little English, but the old-fashioned rooms are decent. They often have rooms here when other places are filled, and you can almost always get one with two days' notice. Singles are 170F–180F with shower; doubles with shower start at 250F; and triples are 300F. *18 rue Cujas, 5e, tel. 1/43–54–58–10. Métro: Cluny–La Sorbonne. 55 rooms, 30 with shower. Showers 20F.*

Hôtel Marignan. The prices here are a bit high but justifiable when you figure that hall showers are included. A British family runs the place, and the rooms are well maintained though spartan—you could call the singles dormlike. In true British style, breakfast is *not* optional. One person pays 180F; for two it's 290F, for three 390F, and for four 460F. *13 rue du Sommerard, 5e, tel. 1/43–54–63–81. Métro: Cluny–La Sorbonne or Maubert-Mutualité. 30 rooms, none with bath.*

UNDER 400F **Hôtel Esmeralda.** If you've had it with cramped hotel rooms and have the foresight to reserve a couple of months in advance, treat yourself to a night at this 17th-century hôtel, five steps away from Notre-Dame. In addition to an attractive country-style lobby and welcoming management, the place offers rooms with views, gauzy curtains, and wood furniture. In a gesture of stunning largesse, the owners have reserved several singles for a mere 160F per night, although showers will set you back another 10F. Doubles, all with showers, are 320F–420F. *4 rue St-Julien-le-Pauvre, 5e, tel. 1/43–54–19–20. Métro: St-Michel. 19 rooms, 16 with bath. Breakfast 40F.*

ST-GERMAIN-DES-PRES

St-Germain-des-Prés is centered around the oldest church in Paris (Eglise St-Germain) and bordered by the Seine. Although the area around it has been gentrified into unconsciousness, a few cheap hotels have stubbornly held on, helping to retain a bit of the atmosphere that originally attracted poor bohemians. This is certainly one of Paris's safest neighborhoods, and provided you reserve far, far in advance, you can have a room near good shopping, a big park, tons of young foreigners, and plenty of well-dressed French people.

UNDER 250F **Hôtel Jean Bart.** Thirty-six frumpy, old-fashioned rooms, many with wood armoires and high beds, make up this hotel near the Jardin du Luxembourg. The prices are quite reasonable in August, when they drop 30F a person because breakfast is not required (or offered); the rest of the year you'll pay 190F–230F for one person, 210F–300F for two. *9 rue Jean Bart, 6e, tel. 1/45–48–29–13. Métro: St-Placide. 36 rooms, 19 with shower. 1 AM curfew, showers 10F.*

Hôtel St-Michel. Tiny, clean, slightly tacky, and right next to place St-Michel, this hotel is an especially good deal for couples: Basic doubles start at 230F, 330F with bath. Singles run 210F–350F. All rooms have a sink, and breakfast is included. The management will welcome you with big smiles—assuming you've made your reservation three to four weeks in advance. *17 rue Gît-le-Coeur, 6e, tel. 1/43–26–98–70. Métro: St-Michel. 25 rooms, some with bath. Showers 25F, luggage storage.*

UNDER 300F **Hôtel de Nesle.** A bohemian backpacker haven with a Turkish bath and a duck-inhabited garden, this place has more character than most other Parisian hotels combined. Each room has an enthusiastically executed historical theme, including an Egyptian room and one dedicated to Molière. Solo travelers can sometimes share a double for 130F; singles cost 220F; and doubles are 270F. All prices include breakfast. They don't accept reservations, so arrive around 10 AM to see what's available. *7 rue de Nesle, 6e, tel. 1/43–54–62–41. Métro: Odéon. 20 rooms, 10 with bath. Showers 25F.*

Hôtel Stella. This hotel is a good deal for groups of all sizes: Singles cost 140F, doubles are 270F, and sprawling rooms that can hold up to five visitors go for about 600F. The rooms are clean, if plain. The location, on a small street filled with restaurants near the Jardin du Luxembourg, is great. *41 rue Monsieur-le-Prince, 6e, tel. 1/43–26–43–49. Métro: Odéon. 20 rooms, all with shower.*

UNDER 350F **Hôtel du Globe.** Adorably rustic rooms and redone bathrooms make this two-star hotel a good splurge for anyone wanting to stay in the heart of the sixth arrondissement. The cheapest rooms are a bit cozy, but not uncomfortably small. Singles or doubles run 280F–380F. For something a step up, the same owners run the cheapest three-star in the neighborhood, the **Hôtel St-Louis,** around the corner on rue St-Sulpice. *15 rue des Quatre-Vents, 6e, tel. 1/46–33–62–69. Métro: Mabillon. 15 rooms, all with bath. Breakfast 30F. Reserve at least 2 weeks ahead. Closed Aug.*

Hôtel du Petit Trianon. This amazingly located, ramshackle gem serves up all the shabby street life you can stand right outside your front door. The rooms are threadbare, clean, and sometimes noisy. Doubles cost 330F–360F with bath; singles cost 180F without. *2 rue de l'Ancienne Comédie, 6e, tel. 1/43–54–94–64. Métro: Odéon. 13 rooms, some with bath. Showers 25F.*

UNDER 400F **Hôtel Récamier.** Tucked into a corner beside the Eglise St-Sulpice, this hotel offers calm, classy rooms and attentive service. The Jardin du Luxembourg is two blocks away on one side, the restaurant- and bar-filled rues des Canettes and Princesse a block away on the other. Singles are 300F, doubles 360F without shower or 410F with. *3 bis pl. St-Sulpice, 6e, tel. 1/43–26–04–89. Métro: St-Sulpice or Mabillon. 30 rooms, 21 with bath. Showers 20F, breakfast 30F. Reserve a few weeks ahead. MC, V.*

Hostels and Foyers

Even at the height of tourist season you ought to be able to find a room in one of Paris's many foyers—places that usually offer a few single and double rooms as well as dorm accommodations—or hostels. Hostels are a few francs cheaper than foyers but tougher to find space in at the last minute; both are good options if you want to meet other adventurers or are traveling solo and tired of being charged for a double room. Those traveling in groups won't necessarily save money, but the facilities are almost always scrupulously cared for. Just be prepared to rub elbows with lots of noisy student groups. Some hostels and foyers have a curfew, others don't, but all have free showers for guests.

HOSTELS

Hostelling International and private hostels don't differ greatly in price and quality, so you might want to decide which to stay in on the basis of location or availability.

HI HOSTELS Three hostels in Paris are run by the **Fédération Unie des Auberges de Jeunesse (FUAJ),** the French branch of Hostelling International (HI). The price of a bed, about 105F–110F, includes sheets, showers, and breakfast, and none of the HI hostels has a curfew. Most rooms are single-sex, unless it's really crowded, in which case they might start sticking people wherever they can. To reserve a space ahead of time at Cité des Sciences or d'Artagnan (*see below*), mail them a check covering the first night. If you want to stay at Jules Ferry, which accepts no reservations, show up well before 10 AM to secure a spot. All three HI hostels require a hostel card; if you don't have one, they'll make you pay 114F for the card, which gives you an HI membership for a year. You can also buy a card at most budget-travel agencies at home for about $16, or for 100F at one of Paris's three FUAJ offices: *FUAJ Centre National: 27 rue Pajol, 18e, tel. 1/46–07–00–01, Métro: La Chapelle. FUAJ Ile de France: 9 rue Notre-Dame de Lorette, 9e, tel. 1/42–85–55–40, Métro: Le Peletier. FUAJ Beaubourg: 9 rue Brontôme, 3e, tel. 1/48–04–70–40, Métro: Châtelet–Les Halles or Rambuteau.*

If you want to assure yourself of a room in the Cité des Sciences or d'Artagnan hostels (*see below*), take advantage of Hostelling International's new computerized booking network. Just call the HI-AYH office in Washington, D.C. (tel. 202/783–6161), give them your credit card number, and tell them when and where you want to stay. They'll charge you for the price of a night's stay plus a $5 booking fee, but it may be worth it if you want to avoid the hassle of finding a room your first night in Paris during high season.

Auberge de Jeunesse Cité des Sciences. Technically in the Parisian *banlieue* (suburbs), this hostel is nonetheless well served by the Métro. The mellow staff welcome you to cramped, typically boring dorm rooms of four to six beds. Just opened in 1993, the hostel is too new to have gotten grimy yet. Though the rooms close for a few hours in the middle of the day, the small common area remains open, so you can transfer your nap to the couch. Beds cost 105F per night, including sheets, showers, and breakfast. *24 rue des Sept-Arpents, 93000 Le Pré-St-Gervais, tel. 1/48–43–24–11. Métro: Hoche. 128 beds. Laundry, wheelchair access, luggage storage 10F.*

Auberge de Jeunesse d'Artagnan. This enormous, spotless hostel is only steps away from Père Lachaise. It gets loud and packed in summer; three meals are served daily at the very social bar and cafeteria. A dorm bed with breakfast, sheets, and showers is 110F; beds in double rooms cost 130F. *80 rue Vitruve, off rue Davout, 20e, tel. 1/43–61–08–75. Métro: Porte de Bagnolet. 425 beds. Lockout 10–2, laundry, wheelchair access, luggage storage 10F.*

Auberge de Jeunesse Jules-Ferry. Come early and be ready to socialize, because this hostel is extremely popular and often full. Overlooking a canal of the Seine and close to place de la République and the Bastille, the hostel couldn't be better located. Cheap food and groceries are close by, but breakfast and showers are included in the 105F price (115F per person for the few doubles). *8 blvd. Jules-Ferry, 11e, tel. 1/43–57–55–60. Métro: République. 100 beds in rooms of 2–8. Lockout 10–2, luggage storage 5F.*

PRIVATE HOSTELS Three Ducks Hostel. No hostel card is required at this boisterous spot where 90F will get you a bed in a room of two to five. The TV room, bar, barbecue, patio, and balcony on the second floor are at your disposal, if you can squeeze in with the large American contingent. Book ahead between May and October by sending payment for the first night. No meal service is available, but the kitchen is open to guests. You can rent mountain bikes here or join one of their guided bike tours of Paris (*see* Getting Around By Bike, in Chapter 1). *6 pl. Etienne-Pernet, 15e, tel. 1/48–42–04–05. Métro: Commerce. 70 beds. 1 AM curfew, lockout 11–5, laundry next door, luggage storage.*

Young and Happy Youth Hostel. Despite its redundant (and slightly silly) name, this place has become such an establishment in Paris that it now has its own T-shirt. Spectacularly located amid cafés, shops, and restaurants in the Quartier Latin, the hostel is well-known by American and Japanese travelers. The rooms of two to five beds are standard yet spotless. A bed in any room costs 100F, breakfast included. Sheets are 12F. Arrive before 11 AM or, to reserve, send a deposit for the first night. *80 rue Mouffetard, 5e, tel. 1/45–35–09–53. Métro: Monge. 75 beds. 1 AM curfew, lockout 11–5.*

FOYERS

Foyers are similar to hostels in price and quality but often have a larger selection of room sizes and tend to be less social. Hostel cards are not needed, but age limits are sometimes enforced.

BVJ FOYERS These foyers for travelers under age 35 have smashing locations and characterless but immaculate rooms. Breakfast, sheets, shower, and a bed cost 120F per night, and all four locations have kitchen facilities and a reception desk staffed from 6 AM until the 2 AM curfew. You can't reserve—except at the Quartier Latin branch if you plan to stay at least two weeks. Just show up at any of them in the morning; you should get a space in any season, and if one place is filled they'll call another for you. The Louvre location has a restaurant where guests at any of the four foyers can eat for 50F.

BVJ Centre International de Paris/Les Halles. The smallest BVJ center is less lively than the others, but the facilities are just as well tended. Meals at the Louvre location are around the corner. *5 rue du Pélican, 1er, tel. 1/40–26–92–45. Métro: Louvre-Rivoli or Palais Royal–Musée du Louvre. 55 beds in rooms of 1–8. Closed Nov.–Jan.*

BVJ Centre International de Paris/Louvre. This is probably the nicest-looking of the BVJs, and since this is the reservation center for all of them, you may have to wait in line behind student herds. *20 rue J.-J. Rousseau, 1er, tel. 1/42–36–88–18. Métro: Louvre-Rivoli. 200 beds in rooms of 2–10. Luggage lockers 10F, meals 50F.*

BVJ Centre International de Paris/Opéra. If you came to Paris to eat Japanese food, you'll find a ton of restaurants nearby. *11 rue Thérèse, 1er, tel. 1/42–60–77–23. Métro: Pyramides. 68 beds in rooms of 1–8. Closed Nov.–Jan.*

BVJ Centre International de Paris/Quartier Latin. This is the one BVJ branch that hosts year-round students, so the atmosphere is especially comfortable. They are a cheerful if studious bunch—and not afraid to remind you of their territorial rights to the study lounge. The 10-bed rooms are institutional and spotless. One- or two-person rooms are comfortable, modern, and amply furnished. Singles cost an extra 10F here. *44 rue des Bernardins, 5e, tel. 1/43–29–34–80. Métro: Maubert-Mutualité. 138 beds in rooms of 1–10. Luggage lockers 10F.*

MIJE FOYERS Set up in medieval aristocratic palaces and 18th-century hôtels particuliers in the Marais, **Maisons Internationales des Jeunes Etudiants (MIJE)** foyers are more comfortable than many hotels you're likely to stay in, though unlike hotels they give you the boot after five nights. The dorm rate of 115F per night (in rooms of up to eight) includes sheets, breakfast, and showers. Double rooms with private bath cost 280F. The MIJE foyers don't take reservations, so during high season show up at any location between 8 and 8:30 AM for a shot at one of the 450 beds. All three enforce a 1 AM curfew and offer free luggage storage. A restaurant in the Fourcy location offers meals to visitors at 25F for lunch, 50F for dinner. Guests must be between the ages of 18 and 30.

Hôtel le Fauconnier. *11 rue du Fauconnier, 4e, tel. 1/42–74–23–45. Métro: St-Paul or Pont-Marie.*

Hôtel le Fourcy. *6 rue de Fourcy, 4e, tel. 1/42–74–23–45. Métro: St-Paul.*

Hôtel Maubuisson. *12 rue des Barres, 4e, tel. 1/42–72–72–09. Métro: St-Paul, or Hôtel-de-Ville.*

INDEPENDENT FOYERS **Association des Etudiants Protestants de Paris.** This large old foyer across the street from the Jardin du Luxembourg is one of the cheapest options in Paris, at 70F for a dorm bed, 90F per person for a double or single, breakfast and sheets included. Better yet, you can stay here for five whole weeks, even in the summer, without dealing with a lockout or a curfew. The top floors accommodate full-time students, and although the residence claims to cater only to students ages 18–25, they may be flexible. Show up early in the morning to get a bed for the night; the office opens at 8:45, and they don't take reservations. *46 rue Vaugirard, 6e, tel. 1/46–33–23–30. Métro: Mabillon or St-Sulpice. Kitchen facilities.*

Foyer International d'Accueil de Paris Jean Monnet. This sleek, friendly foyer is extremely popular, not least of all because the food served in the cafeteria is actually not bad; a meal ticket costs 60F. The bar downstairs stays open and crowded until midnight. Beds in rooms of eight cost 125F per night, in rooms of four 150F, in doubles 170F, and in singles 250F. Breakfast and sheets are included in all cases. The foyer also has several rooms and bathrooms adapted for disabled visitors; book way ahead for them in high season. *30 rue Cabanis, 14e, tel. 1/45–89–89–15. Métro: Glacière. 500 beds. 2 AM curfew.*

Maison des Clubs UNESCO de Paris. Single dorm-style rooms cost 155F, doubles 130F per person, and dorms 115F per bed, breakfast and sheets always included. *43 rue de la Glacière, 13e, tel. 1/43–36–00–63. Métro: Glacière. 100 beds. 1:30 AM curfew.*

Maison des Etudiants. This fabulous mansion with a flowered courtyard has dorm beds for 120F a night, including breakfast, shower, and sheets. This is a perfect place to stay if you'll be spending days on end at the Louvre—there is a three-night minimum stay. Sunny single rooms cost 200F per night. Call ahead to reserve. *18 rue J.-J. Rousseau, 1er, tel. 1/45–08–02–10. Métro: Palais Royal–Musée du Louvre. 80 beds. Closed Sept.–May.*

Université de Paris Foyer International des Etudiantes. Staying in this old wood-and-iron building with a rooftop terrace, theater, and cafeteria will tempt you to stay put all day, but don't: You'll be right by the Quartier Latin and the Jardin du Luxembourg. In July and August, single rooms cost 155F, doubles 105F per person, both with bath and breakfast; the rest of the year prices drop by 20F per person. *93 blvd. St-Michel, 5e, tel. 1/43–54–49–63. RER: Port Royal. 150 beds. 1:30 AM curfew Sun.–Fri.*

Down and Out in Paris

So you're an innocent, freeloading traveler who just wants to sleep under the smog? Think again. Métro stations close between 1 AM and 5 AM, so you can't catch any free z's on their benches. Bus and train stations pull a similar trick. Most of Paris's parks are well-fenced and guarded, not to mention sometimes populated with people you wouldn't necessarily want to spend the night with.

The Trocadéro gardens and the lawns around the Eiffel Tower are two fenceless, accessible spots, but unfortunately everyone knows this, including the police. If you're caught snoozing you'll likely be carted away and charged for vagabondage. Near the banks of the Seine you're less likely to be caught, and even less likely to be comfortable. Basically, sleeping outside in Paris is difficult and risky, not a good idea even in the city's best neighborhoods. Find an all-night bar or dance at a nightclub until morning, and find a nap-friendly bench or lawn during safer daytime hours.

FOOD

By Baty Landis and Oliver Schwaner-Albright

When Catherine de Médicis moved to France in 1533 to marry the duc d'Orléans, the future Henri II, she brought along her entourage of Italian chefs. By the end of the century, other prestigious Italian cooks had flocked to France, bringing along the fresh spices of their home country and adding a Mediterranean flair to what was otherwise a rather heavy cuisine. French food has been a serious art form ever since. Antoine Beauvilliers developed the art by opening Paris's first modern restaurant in 1782, on the rue de Richelieu. Called the Grande Taverne de Londres, it was the first eating establishment to list items on a menu and serve meals at individual tables. Today a wide variety of Parisian eating places cater to the French people's passion for dining among friends, and we can thank Catherine's picky eating habits and Beauvilliers's menu of calves' sweetbreads and carp-roe pie for helping to turn the city into one of the culinary capitals of the world.

First-time visitors to France may be confused by the variety of names given to different types of eating establishments. A restaurant traditionally serves a three-course meal at both lunch and dinner; distinctions among bistrots, cafés, and brasseries are a little hazier. Technically, a *bistrot* is a wine bar offering plates of cheese or *charcuterie* (cold cuts) or even full meals as accompaniments, though wine is definitely the focus. Bistrots that fit this description are listed after all the restaurants in this chapter; places that call themselves bistrots but actually emphasize food over drink are included with the other restaurants. *Brasserie* literally means brewery—a brasserie is the French version of a pub, offering plain, single-course dishes that are traditionally, but not necessarily, served with a beer. Cafés, again, may offer solid food, but the focus is on drinks, whether coffee, beer, soft drinks, or wine.

Most restaurants and many brasseries and bars offer prix-fixe menus, which include an *entrée* (appetizer), a *plat* (main course), and usually dessert in the price (usually 60F and up). Other restaurants offer a *plat du jour* (daily special), which includes meat, veggies, and pasta or potatoes, often for as little as 40F. *Déjeuner* (lunch) is normally served from noon until 2 or 2:30 and *dîner* (dinner) from 7 to 10 or 11—evening meals are meant to be lingered over. Although you might want to eat out at dinner just for the leisurely social experience, meals often cost about a third less at lunch. *Petit déjeuner* (breakfast) usually consists of no more than coffee and bread or croissants. Service is almost always included in the bill; if your waitperson was extra friendly, leave an extra 2F–5F, but it's not an insult to leave nothing.

Be forewarned that nearly everyone who isn't a tourist vacates Paris during the month of August; it's a lonely time to visit. Many cafés, bars, and restaurants close for a few weeks during this time (and sometimes for a week or two in winter, too).

When the high price of Parisian cuisine gets you down, consider the fact that over two million people live, work, and shop in Paris and eat very well, thank you. To find out how, stop at the *boulangeries* (bakeries), *boucheries* (butcher shops), *pâtisseries* (pastry shops), *traiteurs* (delicatessens), and *fromageries* (cheese shops) found in every residential area of the city—then finish off your shopping at the outdoor markets. *See* Markets and Specialty Shops, *below,* for tips on finding everything from pâté de foie gras to Pop Tarts in Paris's shops.

Restaurants

The following restaurants are arranged by neighborhood and price. If you're looking for a specific type of cuisine, flip to the Reference Listings at the end of this chapter. While French food (not surprisingly) dominates the scene, you'll also find Middle Eastern, African, Greek, Italian, and Asian restaurants aplenty in many of the city's districts. The price categories listed generally refer to the price of a three-course meal and a drink.

BASTILLE

It's only fitting that a great nighttime area would have a great selection of restaurants. Take-out joints of all stripes, serving mostly cheap falafel and sandwiches, line **rue de la Roquette;** on the rue's first block off place de la Bastille, homesick Americans take comfort from the thick pizza at **Slice.** Otherwise, you'll find plenty of cafés open late and many opportunities for a quality meal, often served in converted art galleries. Finally, one of the best crêpe makers in Paris, Eddie, sets up near the north corner of rue du Faubourg St-Antoine and rue Trousseau.

UNDER 60F **Le Bistrot du Peintre.** This popular café and bar serves food until midnight and closes at 2 AM. The standard French cuisine includes a great *soupe à l'oignon* (onion soup; 30F) and the best *salade au chèvre chaud* (warm goat cheese salad; 32F) in the city. The waiters are friendly, and loyal regulars dominate the crowd. Authentic, well-worn art nouveau decor makes the setting that much more pleasant. *116 av. Ledru-Rollin, 11e, tel. 1/47–00–34–39. Métro: Ledru-Rollin. Closes at 10 PM Sun. MC, V.*

UNDER 80F **Le Temps des Cerises.** This tiny lunch-only restaurant has been around since 1900, and from the convivial atmosphere and the photos of old Paris, you might think you've jumped back in time. The place is named after "The Time of Cherries," a song whose words you can read off the walls. Get here early (not too long after noon) and squeeze in with the locals for a 60F menu or one of the many meat or salad specials. *31 rue de la Cerisaie, 4e, tel. 1/42–72–08–63. Métro: Sully-Morland or Bastille. Closed weekends and Aug.*

Zagros. Though north of the Bastille district proper, this restaurant warrants a trip when you have a hankering for "Greco-Kurdish" cuisine. The cozy dining room almost feels like a real Greek home, and the food is even more authentic; you can order excellent moussaka (56F) with rice and a mixed salad or a generous appetizer platter (40F) with plenty of *tsatziki* (cucumber-and-yogurt dip) and hummus. At lunch, a three-course menu goes for 55F. *21 rue de la Folie-Méricourt, 11e, tel. 1/48–07–09–56. Métro: St-Ambroise. Closed Sun. MC, V.*

UNDER 100F **Naz Restaurant.** A laid-back crowd lingering over long meals fills this Indian-Pakistani place nightly for curry and tandoori specials. *Poulet palak* (chicken curry with creamed spinach) runs 75F; the three-course menu costs 70F for lunch, 100F for dinner. Indian music plays softly in the background, and the whole experience is soothing enough to lull you out of your urge to party on nearby rue de Lappe. *19 rue de la Roquette, 11e, tel. 1/48–05–69–19. Métro: Bastille. Closed Fri. lunch. AE, MC, V.*

Tapas Nocturne. Not to be confused with the considerably less enticing tapas place a few doors down, this tiny joint is a loud, crowded, congenial place with a live guitarist most nights. Come on a weekend around 10 PM if you want the longest wait, which can easily run an hour. At least the sangria (20F) is flowing as you crowd in what little there is of a bar area. Tapas run 30F–50F. *17 rue de Lappe, 11e, tel. 1/43–57–91–12. Métro: Bastille. Service Mon.–Sat. until 1:30 AM. MC, V.*

SPLURGE **Chez Paul.** A modest sign welcomes you to the best splurge in the Bastille. You've seen these dishes before, but here they're much better: The grilled salmon (80F), rabbit with goat cheese sauce (75F), and escargots (40F) are delectable. Bottles of wine start at 100F. The whole place is crowded with locals and clued-in visitors, so make reservations. If you didn't plan ahead, you can get a drink at the bar or head over to Les Portes (*see* Bars, in Chapter 5) across the street during your long, long wait. *13 rue de Charonne, 11e, tel. 47–00–34–57. Métro: Bastille. Open daily, seatings until midnight. MC, V.*

Les Voyageurs. A constant stream of fashionably bespectacled local artists, writers, and furniture designers comes to try the three-course French menu (110F), including such dishes as rabbit in mustard sauce, served in this art gallery cum dining room. The wine list offers several inviting selections for under 90F and a house liter for 60F. *1 rue Keller, 11e, tel. 1/48–05–86–14. Métro: Ledru-Rollin or Bastille. Closed Sun. AE, MC, V.*

BELLEVILLE

The Africans, Asians, and Eastern Europeans who inhabit Belleville don't munch on escargots every night; rue de Belleville, rue des Pyrénées, and the streets stretching south from them offer some of the most varied and affordable dining in town, often in the front room of the owner's home. Unfortunately, the recent "improvements" in Belleville mean that such places are liable to fall under the wrecking ball at any time, so try not to fall in love. The scads of good Chinese restaurants on rue de Belleville are relatively permanent, as are Chinese grocers like the well-stocked **Wing An** (7 rue de Belleville, 19e, tel. 1/42–38–05–24); pick up an egg roll or other snacks to go. The Sephardic Jews in the area have opened up a kosher shop here and there; try **Maison du Zabayon** (122 blvd. de Belleville, 20e, tel. 1/47–97–16–70), a kosher bakery with good pastries for about 8F–10F.

UNDER 60F **Restaurant Lao Siam.** Lao and Thai specialties mark the vast menu of this Belleville institution, which focuses on basics like chicken with bamboo shoots (35F) and sautéed rice with spicy Thai sauce (40F). The *omelette fou-yong* (27F) is a tasty option if you want to get filled up cheaply. Last orders are at 11:30 PM. *49 rue de Belleville, 19e, tel. 1/40–40–09–68. Métro: Belleville.*

Le Soleil. When the Bastille became too well known, Belleville joints like this one became popular with the beat crowd looking for something new. You can have a three-course French meal here for 40F—it's not haute cuisine, mind you, but the food's cheap and good. The front bar area often stays crowded until after midnight; a *pression* (half pint of draft beer) is 12F. *136 blvd. Ménilmontant, 20e, tel. 1/46–36–47–44. Métro: Ménilmontant.*

UNDER 80F **Restaurant Tai-Yien.** You know it's a good sign when 80% of a Chinese restaurant's clientele is Asian. This place serves up some of Paris's best Chinese food to a stream of customers who don't mind the dull dining room. The simple stuff—like roast chicken with rice (36F)—is best, but it's all good. The more adventurous will want to try the curried frog legs (44F) or daily specials like lamb with ginger and onions (60F). The 63F menu includes three courses and rice. *5 rue de Belleville, 19e, tel. 1/42–41–44–16. Métro: Belleville. Open daily 10 AM–1 AM. MC, V.*

UNDER 100F **Chez Justine.** Though only one of many trendy, buffet-style restaurants, Chez Justine is perhaps the only with log-cabin decor. The 70F lunch menu and 85F dinner menu come with an all-you-can-eat appetizer buffet, a meat dish, dessert, and wine. Salads are 40F. *96 rue Oberkampf, 11e, tel. 1/43–57–44–03. Métro: St-Maur or Ménilmontant. Closed Mon. lunch, Sun., and Aug. AE, MC, V.*

Resto La Pirogue. This is one of the area's better African restaurants, serving good meals in a cafeteria-like setting under the gaze of modern African artwork. Appetizers run 30F–35F, meat dishes 50F–65F; try the 55F *xinxin* (chicken in a sauce of coconut milk and palm and peanut oil). All dishes come with rice; side orders of vegetables are 20F each. *8 rue Rampal, 19e, tel. 1/40–18–33–00. Métro: Belleville. Open Mon.–Sat. 7 PM–midnight.*

SPLURGE **A la Courtille.** This brasserie thrives in a spectacular location overlooking the Jardin de Belleville. Businesspeople fill it up at lunch, neighborhood regulars on evenings and weekends. The outdoor terrace is covered, so you can enjoy the view even in the rain, though the spacious interior with high ceilings is also enjoyable. Appetizers such as the house terrine run 40F; main courses like steak tartare are 75F–85F. Stop in for drinks between mealtimes. *1 rue des Envierges, 20e, tel. 1/46–36–51–59. Métro: Pyrénées. Open daily noon–2 and 8–10:45. MC, V.*

GARES DE L'EST AND DU NORD

A jazzy, post–World War II expatriate crowd ushered in new life to this inconspicuously cool neighborhood spreading southwest of the the Gares de l'Est and du Nord. These were not the intellectual types who had previously run to the shelter of Montparnasse cafés, but restaurateur Leroy Haynes and his swingin', boppin' followers. Their spirit has been quietly maintained in a few restaurants near **place St-Georges,** as well as in the hidden jazz joints sprinkled around the area. With a large Jewish population, this area is an even better, and cheaper, neighborhood than the Marais for a kosher meal; check especially right around **rue de Montyon.**

UNDER 60F **Restaurant Chartier.** Since the mid-1800s this restaurant has served good, cheap meals to workers, bankers, students, and, more recently, tourists. The place is big and old, with touches of brass and stained glass. The old revolving door is a fitting introduction to the whirlwind you're in for. Erratic, near-frantic service demands that you assert yourself at times, but the waiters remain jovial through it all. The menu changes daily; main dishes may include grilled steak with fries (40F) or frog legs provençale (33F). Desserts are 5F–20F, and half a carafe of passable red wine is 8F. Dinner is served only until 9:30. *7 rue du Faubourg-Montmartre, 9e, tel. 1/47–70–86–29. Métro: Rue Montmartre. AE, MC, V.*

UNDER 80F **A la Ville de Belgrade.** Here you'll find hearty, traditional Eastern European food in dark surroundings near the Gare de l'Est. A 52F lunch menu includes an appetizer, a main dish, and cheese or dessert. Order à la carte moussaka for 65F or a *cassoulet* (white-bean-and-meat stew) for 60F, but save room for homemade baklava (27F). *153 quai de Valmy, 10e, tel. 1/46–07–60–93. Métro: Gare de l'Est. Closed Tues. and Aug. AE, MC, V.*

Bhai Bhai Sweets. Ten minutes south of the Gare de l'Est is an old *passage* (passageway) that hasn't received the restorative attention of other Paris passages (*see* box Parisian Passages, in Chapter 6). Nearly a dozen Indian restaurateurs aren't worried about it crumbling and maintain cramped eateries within its walls. Though all offer similarly greasy fare, Bhai Bhai's is slightly better. The 70F lunch or dinner menu includes three courses, such as *bharta* (eggplant puree with onions, tomatoes, and spices) and *dall* (lentils); all kinds of vegetable beignets cost 16F. *77 passage Brady, 10e, tel. 1/42–46–77–29. Métro: Château d'Eau. MC, V.*

Chez Bruno. Arrive well before 9 PM, when Bruno stops serving the 60F menu, and bring an ear for mellow jazz, performed live most nights. The musical theme continues on the memorabilia-packed walls, home to portraits of jazz greats. This is one of the most civilized meals in Paris for the price; the veal dishes are especially nice. If you miss the cheap menu, consider one of Bruno's mammoth salad plates (60F). *5 rue Bergère, 9e, tel. 1/45–23–24–42. Métro: Rue Montmartre. Closed Sat. lunch and Sun. MC, V.*

Paparazzi. This boisterous spot just north of some of the ninth arrondissement's best nighttime action sees a young, good-natured crowd diving into varied plates of pasta (50F–60F) and megapizzas. Lunchtime brings a good 60F menu. *7 bis rue Geoffroy-Marie, 9e, tel. 1/48–24–59–39. Métro: Rue Montmartre. Closed Mon. night and Sun. MC, V.*

UNDER 100F **Chalet Maya.** Handsome waiters serve inventive dishes to a largely gay clientele. Hot, gay French actor Jean Marais, the godfather of the establishment's *patron* (proprietor), was the heartthrob of many unknowing teenage girls in the '40s and is now immortalized in artsy photos on the walls. The place fills up after 10:30, when people file in to try the 85F two-course menu, including starters like fish terrine and main courses like duck baked with peaches. *5 rue des Petits-Hôtels, 10e, 1/47–70–52–78. Métro: Gare de l'Est. Closed Mon. lunch and Sun. MC, V.*

Haynes. If you're going to succumb to cravings for American food, make this the place you run to. Opened in 1950 by Leroy Haynes, it immediately became a Parisian hot spot, showcasing jazz greats who were flocking to Paris to cash in on the postwar boom. The "New Orleans cuisine" tickled expatriates and gastronomically open-minded Parisians, and it still does, in a low-lit atmosphere with live piano music in the background and photos of American music greats on the walls. Fried chicken costs 65F, barbecued ribs 70F, and gumbo 90F. *3 rue Clauzel, 9e, tel. 1/48–78–40–63. Métro: St-Georges. Closed Sun. and Mon. MC, V.*

Van Gölu. Though the food is excellent, it's not the main reason to come to this Turkish institution. The nightly show features a belly dancer who, to the accompaniment of a *saz* (Turkish lute), flings her sequins as she shimmies expectantly near each man, most of whom oblige with

Restaurant Chains

Let's face it: You can't eat at Maxim's every night. Several reliable restaurant chains have infiltrated the city, so get over the standardized decor and mass-consumer guilt and sit yourself down next to the hundreds of Parisians who are doing the same. You may even come to regard these restaurants with some tenderness. Warning: Just because it's a chain doesn't mean the prices are set in stone, so if you choose the Champs-Elysées version of any of the following restaurants, be prepared to pay a good 20F–30F more than you would in Les Halles.

- *Hippopotamus. Not for vegetarians. The best deal is "Hippo Malin," a 60F plate with steak and all the fries or salad you can eat. The branch on the Champs-Elysées (Métro: Franklin D. Roosevelt) also sells Citroën cars. There's one on place de la Bastille, another on place de l'Opéra.*

- *Hollywood Canteen. Step up to the 1950s-style counter for a burger and an authentic cherry Coke. The Sunday brunch menu (60F) is complete with bacon and eggs, pancakes, and waffles. A couple Canteen locations: 18 boulevard Montmartre (9e) and the corner of boulevard St-Germain and rue Boutebrie (5e).*

- *Léon de Bruxelles. The place for beer, mussels, and Belgian-style fries served in massive portions; count on 60F–80F for a good meal. Léons can be found at 120 rue Rambuteau (1er), near Les Halles; 3 boulevard Beaumarchais, off place de la Bastille (4e); and 82 boulevard Montparnasse (14e).*

- *Lina's Sandwiches. Deli-style food is served with a flair at these spacious, upscale lunch counters. The sandwiches are variations of American and French standards, like roast beef with a mustard/mayonnaise vinaigrette (36F) and oeuf mayonnaise (egg salad) on whole-wheat bread (19F). The International Herald-Tribune is kept out for customers at the 27 rue St-Sulpice (6e) location; other addresses include 50 rue Etienne Marcel (2e) and 8 rue Marbeuf (8e).*

- *Pizza Pino. Come for pretty good pizzas (35F–55F) and impressively fresh, meal-size salads (around 45F). There's one on place des Innocents (1er) that stays open 11 AM–5 AM seven days a week and another at 57 boulevard Montparnasse (6e).*

a 50F bill. This is not a crowd of people who just happened upon this place; judging by the diners' ability to sing along, most have been here before. *3 rue d'Enghien, 10e, tel. 1/47–70–41–01. Métro: Strasbourg–St-Denis. Closed Sun. lunch.*

SPLURGE **Julien.** This grand 1879 brasserie stands out from its humble 10th-arrondissement surroundings. High ceilings, mirrors, and tuxedoed waiters all take you back to a golden era when fashionable theatergoers frequented the place. On theater nights you'll still see decked-out dandies, playbill in hand, coming for the fantastic desserts (from 30F) served until 2 AM. The profiteroles (51F)—ice cream inside a puff pastry smothered in chocolate—are Julien's specialty. Real food is good but expensive; try to come after 10 PM, when a night menu costs 110F for two courses and a drink, or just linger over a 36F soup. *16 rue du Faubourg St-Denis, 10e, tel. 1/47–70–12–06. Métro: Strasbourg–St-Denis. Open daily until 2 AM. AE, MC, V.*

LES HALLES

Les Halles has the unique distinction of having the worst crêpe stands in town, a trait indicative of the eating scene here as a whole. Though some restaurants have been doing the same great stuff for ages, there are also a lot of operations, particularly south of the Forum des Halles, happy to take your francs for a plate of crap. It's not that you *can't* eat well here—just be careful and take recommendations instead of going by instinct. Perhaps the best thing about the restaurants here is that many stay open until morning (*see* box 24-hour Eateries, *below*), including the reasonable **Pizza Pino** (*see* "Restaurant Chains" *box, above*) on place des Innocents.

UNDER 40F **Panini Sandwiches à Emporter.** For a quick, cheap take-out meal a step above street fare, try Panini's fresh, hot sandwiches. The Napoli (14F) is grilled with mozzarella cheese and tomatoes; the Florence (22F) has tomatoes, eggplant, mozzarella, and basil. *65 rue Rambuteau, 3e, tel. 1/42–77–60–45. Métro: Rambuteau.*

UNDER 60F **Dame Tartine.** Next to Centre Georges Pompidou and facing place Igor Stravinsky, this restaurant-cum-art-gallery displays works by local artists and serves inspiring glasses of Bordeaux (15F). Another specialty is *tartines* (hot or cold open-faced sandwiches)—try the 30F *poulet aux amandes* (chicken with almonds). You may have to wait for a few yuppies to clear out before you get a spot at one of the indoor or outdoor tables. *2 rue Brisemiche, 3e, tel. 1/42–77–32–22. Métro: Rambuteau or Les Halles.*

Japanese Barbecue. Some of the cheapest sushi·in Paris passes over the counter at this friendly restaurant. The dining room is simple—some might say characterless—but crowds of workers fill the tables for the 45F lunch menu of soup, salad, and brochettes on rice. Satisfactory sushi rolls start at 25F, regular sushi at 30F a pair, and dinner menus at 60F. The counter is a comfortable spot for a solo meal; the guy at the grill is a big-time small talker. *60 rue Montorgueil, 2e, tel. 1/42–33–49–61. Métro: Sentier or Les Halles. Open Mon.–Sat. noon–2:30 and 7–10:45. MC, V.*

UNDER 80F **Au Petit Ramoneur.** At this crowded, family-run restaurant the 65F menu comes with half a liter of wine or beer and includes goodies like fried potatoes and sausage, tripe cooked in Calvados brandy, and salads. At lunch the place is packed with working-class regulars who schmooze with the staff and whoever is sitting nearby. If you sit outside, you get to watch the people going into the nearby cine-sex shops. *74 rue St-Denis, 1er, tel. 1/42–36–39–24. Métro: Les Halles or Etienne Marcel. Closed weekends and end of Aug.*

UNDER 100F **Chez Max.** Take the mural-bedecked staircase up from the street find a much more tasteful, subdued dining room. The 90F three-course menu includes wine and is excellently prepared by a chef from Bayonne. A la carte dishes include rabbit pâté and a bacon-and-poached-egg salad (45F). *47 rue St-Honoré, 1er, tel. 1/45–08–80–13. Métro: Châtelet or Louvre. Closed Mon. lunch and Sun. AE, MC, V.*

Entre Ciel et Terre. A scarecrow holding the menu points you into this happy, crunchy place focusing on the basics: meals of fruits and vegetables, and walls of wood and stone. The three-course vegetarian menu runs 90F, but you can get tasty meal-size specials like veggie lasagna for 55F with a 15F glass of organic grape juice. *5 rue Hérod, 1er, tel. 1/45–08–49–84. Métro: Les Halles or Louvre-Rivoli. Closed weekends. MC, V.*

LOUVRE TO OPERA

Just the names "Louvre" and "Opéra" should clue you in to the fact that most of this neighborhood is going to be out of your range. But when you find a place you *can* afford, this area, with all its poshness, is great for a meal. Check out **rue Ste-Anne**, packed with Japanese restaurants and stores, and, across the avenue de l'Opéra, **rue St-Roch,** with some of the best sushi in town at **Foujita** (41 rue St-Roch, tel. 1/42–61–42–93); a sushi sampler costs 100F. **Rue du Faubourg-St-Honoré** has some good lunch deals; workers from all the ritzy shops find refuge here.

UNDER 60F **Higuma.** Primarily a lunch place for Japanese and French businesspeople in the area, Higuma offers either tables in the back or ample counter space where you can watch the chefs' butcher knives flailing around. The 60F menu, which includes a minisalad, soup, and Japanese ravioli, isn't fancy but is surprisingly hearty. *32 bis rue Ste-Anne, 1er, tel. 1/47–03–38–59. Métro: Pyramides.*

UNDER 80F **Country Life.** For health nuts, this may be the best deal in town: 65F gets you unlimited access to the quality pickings of both a hot and a cold vegetarian buffet; drinks are extra. The health food store in the front sells lots of dried fruits, nuts, organic vegetables, and tempting items like a soy dessert (11F). *6 rue Daunou, 2e, tel. 1/42–97–48–51. Métro: Opéra. Closed Fri. dinner and weekends.*

L'Incroyable. A tiny rustic dining room and private courtyard fill up with regulars. The fare is French and a great deal at 60F for lunch, 70F for a three-course early dinner. The name refers to the self-proclaimed "Incredibles," a vulgarly egotistical group of nouveaux riches who sprang up after the Revolution under the Directory. *26 rue de Richelieu or 23 rue de Montpensier, 1er, tel. 1/42–96–24–64. Métro: Palais Royal–Musée du Louvre. Open noon–2:15 and 6:30–9. Closed Mon. dinner, Sat. dinner, and Sun.*

Le Palet. Reserve ahead if you want to join the lunchtime professional crowd in this adorably homey room for a filling 65F menu that includes tomato-and-mozzarella salad and steak; a slightly more elaborate 95F menu offers dishes like goat cheese salad and *St-Pierre gratinée* (a white fish baked with cheese on top). The restaurant sits just above the Jardin du Palais Royal, so you can recover from your meal on a shady bench. *8 rue de Beaujolais, 1er, tel. 1/42–60–99–59. Métro: Palais Royal–Musée du Louvre. Closed Sat. lunch and Sun. MC, V.*

UNDER 100F **Jhelum.** A block from the Opéra Comique, this dim, slightly upscale restaurant serves Indian and Pakistani specialties to a small, slightly upscale clientele. The flavorful chicken tandoori appetizer costs 35F; main-course versions start at 70F. At lunch there's an 80F menu; otherwise, you have to order à la carte. *30 rue St-Marc, 2e, tel. 1/42–96–99–43. Métro: Richelieu-Drouot. Closed Sun.*

Yamamoto. Yamamoto is a crowded place that serves excellent food to a largely Japanese clientele. Start off with a simple miso soup (20F), then try filling sushi rolls like *futo maki* (55F) or a sampler of six different kinds of sushi (95F). Wash it all down with a large, cold can of Sapporo (35F) or a warm sake (25F). *6 rue Chabanais, 2e, tel. 1/49–27–96–26. Métro: Quatre-Septembre or Pyramides. Closed Sun. MC, V.*

MARAIS

The best restaurants in the Marais cater to the Jewish population or the hip gay crowd, meaning there are plenty of Middle Eastern places (especially along **rue des Rosiers**), as well as artsy, trendy, vegetarian joints. The café scene is thriving, with newer and hipper ones popping up all the time and charging more and more for a cup of coffee. Restaurants like Le Gamin de Paris (*see below*) now stay open during the afternoon for tea, while many bars like **Au Petit Fer à Cheval** (*see* Bars, in Chapter 5) serve great full meals. The gay scene centers on **rue Ste-**

Croix-de-la-Brétonnerie and **rue Vieille-du-Temple,** where you'll find tons of gay bars, restaurants, and cafés, plus the main gay bookstore in the city (*see* Bookstores, in Chapter 6).

UNDER 40F **Sacha et Florence Finkelsztajn.** Eastern European and Russian snacks and specialties fill the shelves of this store/deli, open since 1946. Small *pirojki* (pastries filled with fish, meat, or vegetables) cost 10F, 20F for a large, almost meal-size version. Definitely meal-size sandwiches are 30F–40F; blinis, gefilte fish, and blueberry muffins are also sold. *24 rue des Ecouffes, 4e, tel. 1/48–87–92–85. Métro: St-Paul. Open Thurs.–Mon. noon–7ish.*

UNDER 60F **Chez Rami & Hanna.** In addition to serving hearty meals in the small, friendly dining room, this place just happens to have the best falafel in Paris and probably in France. Get a falafel special to go for 22F, or stick around for dishes like the Israeli Platter (hummus, tahini, and falafel balls; 35F), spicy Moroccan salad (40F), and chicken liver with onions (55F). The owners take a lot of pride in making their customers full and happy. *54 rue des Rosiers, 4e, tel. 1/42–78–23–09. Métro: Hôtel-de-Ville. Open daily 11–3 and 6–1:30.*

Le Petit Gavroche. All kinds install themselves at the bar of this tiny and congenial bistrot for a nightly glass of Bordeaux. Happy diners take themselves upstairs for a filling 45F meal served at lunch and until midnight. Don't expect fancy cuisine or reverent service; this place has remained basic and casual, like the rest of the quarter once was. *15 rue Ste-Croix-de-la-Brétonnerie, 4e, tel. 1/48–87–74–26. Métro: St-Paul. Closed Sat. lunch and Sun. MC, V.*

UNDER 80F **Café de la Cité.** Only a few minutes from Centre Georges Pompidou and just northwest of the Marais, this tiny brasserie accommodates a crowd of lunchtime regulars with good, hearty meals. At lunch all appetizers (including escargots and avocado salad) are 15F, all main dishes 40F, and desserts only 15F. Prepare to wait in line or come on the weekend. At dinner your only option is the 62F two-course menu, which includes appetizers like goat cheese salad and plenty of main-course steak dishes. *22 rue Rambuteau, 3e, tel. 1/42–78–56–36. Métro: Rambuteau.*

Chez Marianne. You'll know you've found Marianne's place when you see the line of people reading the bits of wisdom painted across her windows. The restaurant/deli serves excellent Middle Eastern and Central European specialties. Try one of the platters that lets you sample four items for 55F, five for 65F, or six for 75F. Choices include egg salad, hummus, and babaganoush. Make reservations for dinner, grab something to go from the deli (featuring piles of dried fruits and nuts in bulk), or get a fabulous 22F Israeli-style falafel (with beets and cabbage) from the window outside. *2 rue des Hospitalières-St-Gervais, 5e, tel. 1/42–72–18–86. Métro: St-Paul. MC, V.*

UNDER 100F **La Canaille.** *Canaille* means rascal or rabble-rouser, and that's exactly who came to this artsy joint to eat, drink, and sing protest songs in the early 1970s. Ever since, the place has stayed true to the ideals of fine food and drink, but the singing, sadly, is on the wane. Both the 70F lunch menu and the 85F dinner menu offer lots of choices; the 65F lunch menu comes with an entrée, main dish, and dessert. Meat portions are huge; for something light, try the 38F goat cheese salad. *4 rue Crillon, 4e, tel. 1/42–78–09–71. Métro: Sully-Morland or Quai de la Rapée. Closed Sat. and Sun. lunch.*

The Studio. Come on a nice night, when the romantic courtyard is filled with dozens of candlelit tables. The food is classic American West: spare ribs for 85F and a hickory-smoked beef sandwich plate with cole slaw, green beans, and fries for 70F. Margaritas are 50F, draft beers 25F. The secluded setting makes you feel like the holder of a great secret, if you can ignore the other diners who are in on it, too. *41 rue du Temple, 4e, tel. 1/42–74–10–38. Métro: Rambuteau. Open daily until midnight. AE, MC, V.*

SPLURGE **Le Gamin de Paris.** It may be a big splurge, but you can't eat baguettes out of your backpack forever. The waitstaff here is happy to give recommendations; if you don't want to follow them, be prepared to stick to your guns. Candlelight accompanies appetizers like escargots (40F) and salmon pasta (50F). Main dishes include beef fillets with shallots (90F) and roast duck with figs and raisins (90F). A weekday lunch special goes for 45F. Between mealtimes, you can come for just a drink or a luscious dessert (around 30F). *49 rue Vieille-du-Temple, 4e, tel. 1/42–78–97–24. Métro: St-Paul. Reservations required for dinner. MC, V.*

The first rule of eating in Montmartre is to stay away from the streets right behind Sacré-Coeur, which are absolutely overflowing with tourist traps. Go down the hill a bit—toward the city for good French meals, away for African and other non-French specialties. **Rue des Trois Frères** is a good street for exploration, though Chez les Fondus (*see below*) can often seem like a vacuum stealing customers from all the neighboring joints. The adjacent neighborhood, Pigalle, doesn't have much to offer—mostly chains and café fare.

UNDER 40F **La Pignatta.** This "Italian pizzeria" sells not only fresh and prepared pastas and *panini* (sandwiches with mozzarella, basil, and tomato; 16F) to go, but also some items you probably didn't realize were Italian: Hummus and tabbouleh go for 70F per kilo, or try a loaf of poppyseed bread for 4F. A table or two out front can handle an immediate picnic; you can also get rather sad pizzas out there. *2 rue des Abbesses, 18e, tel. 1/42–55–82–05. Métro: Abbesses. Open daily 9:30–11.*

UNDER 60F **Au Grain de Folie.** This vegetarian restaurant has been around for 15 years, serving up the same tantalizing tarts and salads to the loyal customers who fill the cozy five or six tables (a couple more when it's nice outside). You can get soup and a tart for 60F or a couple of items à la carte—vegetable soup, crudités—for 20F each. Wash it all down with the 12F organic apple juice for good luck. *24 rue la Vieuville, 18e, tel. 1/42–58–15–57. Métro: Abbesses. Closed Mon. lunch.*

Cambodiana. This neighborhood hangout serves homemade food in the back room of Madame Sisowadh's house. Don't expect anything fancy, just heaps of savory Cambodian specialties, including a variety of vegetarian dishes. A full meal costs around 50F, though prices don't seem to be set in stone. At lunch, tell your hostess how much you'd like to spend and on what, and she'll fix you a generous little box to take to one of the parks or to Sacré-Coeur, a couple of blocks away. Dinner time brings more sit-down guests, often including Madame Sisowadh's family. Lining the walls are items for your shopping pleasure—dresses, tea sets, condiments, and alcohol. *35 rue Lamarck, 18e, tel. 1/42–52–20–86. Métro: Lamarck-Caulaincourt.*

Le Fouta Toro. Some of the Senegalese dishes here are terrific (*mafé au poulet,* chicken in peanut sauce; 47F), some so-so (fish dishes), but warm, cheery surroundings, jolly service, and

University Cafeterias Offer a Full Load of Courses

You'll hear mixed reviews of the university cafeteria-style restaurants, but dig this: You can get a three-course meal for about 15F. If you've been gnawing on bread and cheese for a week, this is nirvana. They're supposed to ask to see a student ID card (if you don't have one, the price gets jacked up slightly), but many times they don't. Some have better food than others, so shop around; you can also call 1/40–51–37–13 for general information. The "resto-u" at 115 boulevard St-Michel (RER: Luxembourg) has all-you-can-eat couscous with vegetables, meat, salad, and bread for 15F; some nights you get lentils or beans instead. Other addresses include:

- 3 rue Mabillon, 6e. Métro: Mabillon.

- Cours de la Reine, 8e. Métro: Champs-Elysées.

- 92 rue d'Assas, 6e. Métro: Notre-Dame des Champs.

- 13–17 rue Dareau, 14e. Métro: St-Jacques.

huge servings make this a great spot if you want a day's worth of food for just 50F. The restaurant, in the working-class area behind touristy Montmartre, is small and very popular. *3 rue du Nord, 18e, tel. 1/42–55–42–73. Métro: Marcadet-Poissonniers. Open Wed.–Mon. until after midnight.*

Le Pic à Vin. Come here for one of the cheapest snazzy meals around. Hanging plants decorate the dining room, the music is classical, and the crowd verges on sophisticated. Still 50F brings you a two-course meal that could include a raw salmon fillet with lemon and herb-roasted chicken. *108 rue Lepic, 18e, tel. 1/46–06–19–29. Métro: Abbesses. AE, MC, V.*

Rayons de Santé. So you've finally had too much crème fraîche and brie, and you're crying: "I just want something healthy"? The entirely vegetarian menu here, featuring 20F–30F appetizers like vegetable pâté and artichoke mousse, will do you right. Main courses include spicy couscous with vegetables and soy sausage, and vegetarian goulash. For dessert we and the proprietress recommend the coconut flan. Main dishes run 30F–35F and desserts 10F–20F. *8 pl. Charles-Dullin, 18e, tel. 1/42–59–64–81. Métro: Abbesses. Open Sun.–Thurs. 9–3 and 6:30–10, Fri. 9–3.*

UNDER 80F **Chez les Fondus.** Tourists and locals alike line up to share a table at this lively fondue spot—don't come if you value elbow room. Decisions are kept to a minimum; the waiter simply asks "*viande ou fromage?*" (meat or cheese?) and "*rouge ou blanc?*" (red or white wine), then sets you up with an aperitif, appetizers, your fondue, or a large baby bottle (no joke) filled with wine. Not bad for 85F. Dessert is included, but for an extra 10F you can get homemade lemon or orange sorbet. *17 rue des Trois-Frères, 18e, tel. 1/42–55–22–65. Métro: Abbesses. Reservations advised.*

Le Kezako. This self-proclaimed hangout of Montmartre "professors, plumbers, and engineers" is one of Paris's best new tapas joints: Sophie and Miquel serve cheap eats in their tiny, oddly mirrored rooms, and, as is proper, their sangria (65F per liter) has nothing in common with fruit punch. A glass of sangria and a small tapa (22F) make for a perfect mid-evening snack, while a filling collection of four larger tapas costs 75F. *12 rue Veron, 18e, tel. 1/42–58–22–20. Métro: Abbesses. MC, V.*

UNDER 100F **L'Eté en Pente Douce.** This unassuming spot on a darling little corner east of Sacré-Coeur sees regulars filing in for fantastic dinners. The asymmetrical dining room feels like a simple country house, and a covered porch lets you look out over the park next door. Large salads cost 45F–60F, meat dishes 60F–80F, and a delicious pear dessert with nuts 30F. Reserve for dinner or come for lunch, when things are considerably calmer. *23 rue Muller, 18e, tel. 1/42–64–02–67. Métro: Château Rouge. MC, V.*

MONTPARNASSE

The Montparnasse area is close to St-Germain-des-Prés and, by association, gets to charge high prices. But since there's also a train station here, you'll find lots of fast food. Many people from Brittany settled in this area after arriving at the Gare Montparnasse, so crêperies are popular; it's incredible that all the ones along rues Montparnasse and Odessa can stay in business simultaneously.

UNDER 60F **Chez Papa.** Rowdy waitresses serve southwestern French food at this crowded restaurant across from the cemetery. Mongo salads packed with potatoes, egg, ham, cheese, and tomato are known as "Boyardes" and cost a piddling 35F. Escargots "Papa" (70F) come piping hot in a bright orange pot. Set menus go for 50F and 55F day and night until 1 AM. Their other location is at 206 rue La Fayette (10e, tel. 1/42–09–53–87, Métro: Louis Blanc). *6 rue Gassendi, 14e, tel. 1/43–22–41–19. Métro: Denfert-Rochereau. Open Mon.–Sat. 7 AM–2 AM, Sun. 10 AM–2 AM. MC, V.*

UNDER 80F **Aux Artistes.** This restaurant is as artsy as its name suggests: worn, covered in paint and posters from top to bottom, and inhabited by cool people who were born halfway through a cigarette. The dining room is just loud enough to keep conversations intimate. Best of all is the menu: 75F lets you choose among 29 appetizers, 35 main dishes, and several cheeses or simple desserts. The food is French, and the chicken dishes are especially good. A bottle of house wine costs 32F. *63 rue Falguière, 15e, tel. 1/43–22–05–39. Métro: Pasteur. Dinner served until midnight. Closed Sat. lunch and Sun. MC, V.*

Mustang Café. This is the most popular of the many Tex-Mex café/bars in Montparnasse, drawing foreign students and Parisians who want to meet foreign students. You won't exactly be soaking up French culture, but you can have a respectable meal at almost any hour—they're open daily 9 AM–5 AM. Taco salads cost 50F, quesadillas 40F, enchiladas 60F, and Dos Equis 30F. Weekdays 4–7, margaritas and cocktails go half-price. Expect it dark, loud, and cramped all night. *84 blvd. Montparnasse, 14e, tel. 1/43–35–36–12. Métro: Montparnasse. MC, V.*

Olivier-Ouzerie. When Parisians decide to do Greek food right, they *really* do it right. This comfortable joint serves delicious dishes in an airy, minimally decorated dining room. The 95F menu could include dolmas, moussaka, and cheese or dessert; the calamari in wine (50F) will be a jolt for anyone not used to dealing with squid with their entrails still intact. At lunch, a similar menu costs 60F. *9 rue Vandamme, 14e, tel. 1/43–21–57–58. Métro: Gaîté or Montparnasse. Closed Sun. MC, V.*

Pont Aven. Of the legions of crêperies below boulevard Montparnasse, this very small, very red one is among the best. Lively crowds of neighborhood students come for the *galette* (buckwheat crêpe) du jour plus cider at 45F; à la carte, galettes go for 15F–50F, crêpes for 15F–36F. The lunch menu (62F) includes salad, galette, and crêpe; the dinner menu (76F) galette, crêpe, and cider. *54 rue Montparnasse, 14e, tel. 1/43–22–23–74. Métro: Vavin.*

NEAR THE CHAMPS-ELYSEES

Even the chains charge more on the Champs-Elysées. Though it's one of Paris's best-known boulevards, the area around it is possibly the worst neighborhood in which to seek out a decent meal for under 200F. But because of all the theaters and clubs here, you may find yourself on the Champs and in need of a bite.

UNDER 60F **Chicago Pizza Pie Factory.** Some deep-dish pizza and a visit to the loud sports bar for half-price happy-hour drinks (Monday–Saturday 6–7:30) could cure you of any nostalgia for the Windy City. In addition to pizzas (80F for a two-person cheese pizza, 200F for the four-person everything-on-it), you can order all sorts of big salads (20F–55F), garlic bread (21F), and good ol' California wine. The video screen behind the bar features American baseball and football games. *5 rue de Berri, 8e, tel. 1/45–62–50–23. Métro: George V. Open daily until 1 AM. MC, V.*

24-Hour Eateries

- *Chez Robert Vattier. About the nicest all-night joint in Les Halles, this place serves French dishes at 100F per menu. 14 rue Coquillière, 1er, tel. 1/42–36–51–60. Métro: Les Halles.*

- *Le Dépanneur. This diner near Pigalle is styled in wood, with comfy chairs and artsy touches like chrome. Big salads, hamburgers, and sandwiches run 40F–70F, a small carafe of wine 25F (15F during the day). 27 rue Fontaine, 9e, tel. 1/40–16–40–20. Métro: Blanche.*

- *Pub St-Germain. On place de l'Odéon, this pub is always packed with foreigners and students. Dozens of beers on tap and more in bottles accompany French pub food— large salads are 65F—and occasional live jazz. 17 rue de l'Ancienne Comédie, 6e, tel. 1/43–29–38–70. Métro: Odéon. AE, MC, V.*

SPLURGE **Minim's.** If you're dying to eat at a big-name establishment but can't justify the expense, consider a stop at this lunch-only spin-off of Maxim's, catercorner from the Elysée Palace. Large salads run 62F and up, desserts 30F–40F, and a full menu 160F; after mealtime, a salon de thé serving 20F cafés opens. In the off-season, an ice creamery by the same name opens down the street. *76 rue du Faubourg St-Honoré, 8e, tel. 1/42–66–10–09. Métro: Concorde. Closed Sun. MC, V.*

QUARTIER LATIN

The Quartier Latin has more or less stuck to its role as a student district, offering many possibilities for an affordable meal. For reasonable Asian specialties, try the restaurants behind **square Viviani**, near the quai de Montebello. French fare is best and most reasonable around the Panthéon. Of course, there's always **rue Mouffetard** and surroundings, with dozens of French, Greek, and Mexican places offering a full meal for less than 70F. A serious crêpe duel goes on in the area between the stand at 61 rue Mouffetard and the one on place de la Contrescarpe. Nutella (chocolate-hazelnut paste) crêpes go for 11F at the first, for 12F at the second, and are great at both.

UNDER 40F **Al Dar.** The deli side of this otherwise expensive Lebanese restaurant offers delicious sandwiches (20F) and small plates (30F) featuring falafel and spicy chicken sausage, among other things. A whole slew of varied goodies costs 65F if you take it on the picnic tables outside, 60F if it's packed to go. The lack of a menu and hurried counter people can make it difficult to order, but pointing ought to do the trick. *8–10 rue Frédéric Sauton, 5e, tel. 1/43–25–17–15. Métro: Maubert-Mutualité. Open daily until midnight. AE, MC, V.*

Mouff'Tartes. Maybe this place opened only because the name was too cute to pass up, but the quiche and pizza (both around 15F) this place doles out are a tasty value. There are a few drab tables you could use in back of the store, but it would be a shame with such great plazas all around you. *53 rue Mouffetard, 5e, tel. 1/43–37–64–64. Métro: Monge. Open daily about noon–1 AM.*

UNDER 60F **Le Boute Grill.** A certain faction of Maghrebian expatriates feels this Tunisian restaurant serves the best couscous in Paris. The servings are enormous and include your choice of 14 meats; a house specialty is large pieces of tripe stuffed with herbs, or with lamb (55F). There's a three-course menu at 72F, but even the ravenous men hunched over their plates shudder at the thought of finishing it all. The decor is simple, the waiters patient with newcomers. *12 rue Boutebrie, 5e, tel. 1/43–54–03–30. Métro: Cluny–La Sorbonne.*

La Petite Légume. This small restaurant near the Jardin des Plantes takes its status as a vegetarian restaurant seriously—most dishes use no dairy products, and several of the desserts don't even have any fat. Portions are generous and tasty and relatively cheap. Grains with mixed vegetables cost 35F–40F, miso soup 30F, the vegetarian platter (tofu galette, vegetables, rice, and dried fruits) 60F. Pastries range from 16F to 32F. *36 rue des Boulangers, 5e, tel. 1/40–46–06–85. Métro: Jussieu. Closed Sun.*

Taco Mucho. Finally someone realized what's wrong with most Parisian restaurants of this genre: Mexican food is supposed to be *cheap*. Or at least cheap for Paris, which means free chips and dip, 25F appetizers like nachos with guacamole, 30F–38F main dishes, and 20F Dos Equis. Neighborhood students and the odd professor linger over their lunches deep in conversation, though you can also get food to go for a picnic in the Jardin du Luxembourg. The food's not great, but no worse than that at any of the other Tex-Mex joints in town. A 50F two-course menu is offered at lunch only. *206 rue St-Jacques, 5e, tel. 43–29–96–14. RER: Luxembourg. Closed Sun. MC, V.*

UNDER 80F **L'Apostrophe.** Early diners get a deal at this country-style place near the Panthéon. A 50F two-course menu (add 10F for dessert), served only until 8 PM, features appetizers like calamari salad and French onion soup, main courses like pepper steak or shish kebabs, and ice cream or bananas flambées to finish it all off. The 65F two-course menu is served until 9. Miss both of those and you're stuck with the 85F menu, featuring subtler French cuisine and an all-you-can-eat salad bar. *34 rue de la Montagne-Ste-Geneviève, 5e, tel. 1/43–54–10–93. Métro: Maubert-Mutualité. MC, V.*

Bistrot de la Sorbonne. Underpopulated and underdecorated (the wall murals were left unfinished), this university-area restaurant cooks up some tempting dishes: The "Délices de la Sorbonne" (70F) is, as promised, a delicious deep casserole packed with vegetables and meat and baked with cheese on top. Evenings, the prix-fixe menu offers plenty of traditional French options starting at 60F. *4 rue Toullier, 5e, 1/43–54–41–49. Métro: St-Michel. RER: Luxembourg. Closed Sun. MC, V.*

Le Jardin des Pâtes. The "Garden of Pasta" serves fresh pasta made from organic grains, along with sublime sauces. Vegetarians will enjoy the tomato-basil sauce or the mixed vegetables with ginger and tofu; for carnivores there's smoked duck with cream and nutmeg, or smoked salmon with leeks. Pasta dishes range from 40F to 70F; appetizers, including cucumber with mint in yogurt sauce, go for 20F–45F. Young locals fill the sleek dining room most nights. *4 rue Lacépède, 5e, tel. 1/43–31–50–71. Métro: Monge. Closed Mon. MC, V.*

UNDER 100F **Surma.** Across from the east wall of La Mosquée, this Indian restaurant fills its small dining room with regulars every night. The three-course menu is 100F, but you may do better ordering á la carte from among the 11 tandooris or 21 curries, which run 50F and up. Add on the 30F *begun barta* (spicy roasted eggplant spread), fluffy cheese *nan* (16F), and a tiny 24F pitcher of *citron lassi* (lemon yogurt drink), and you will be pleasantly stuffed. *5 rue Daubenton, 5e, tel. 1/45–35–68–60. Métro: Censier-Daubenton. MC, V.*

SPLURGE **L'Ange Gourmand.** This high-class restaurant feels like more of a splurge than it really is—provided you stick to the 100F three-course menu. The *chèvre chaud* (warm goat cheese salad) with walnuts and the *rillettes de saumon fumé* (smoked salmon spread) are wonderful, but the real highlight is the best chocolate mousse in Paris, served in an immense casserole dish. Add posh decor and a Seine-side location, and you've got a combination that many places would charge triple the price for. Dress up, reserve ahead, and bring someone you want to impress. *31 quai de la Tournelle, 5e, tel. 1/43–54–11–31. Métro: Maubert-Mutualité.*

ST-GERMAIN

St-Germain may not be the hipster stronghold it once was, but it remains a terrific restaurant neighborhood; lots of little restaurants are tucked away among the abundant galleries and boutiques. **Rue Monsieur-le-Prince** is one of the best restaurant streets in the city, featuring Asian eateries with three-course menus for as little as 40F. **Rue des Canettes** and the surrounding small streets are best for crêpes and other fast eats; the classic French restaurants here often fall flat.

UNDER 60F **Auberge des Deux Dragons.** The food at this always-crowded Chinese/Vietnamese restaurant ranges from good to great, depending on which menu you order from. For 35F you get soup like hot-and-sour or vermicelli-chicken, a main course (including roast duck or pork and Szechuan vegetables), and a piece of fruit for dessert. The 47F menu will get you Thai specialties, better sauces, and exotic fruits for dessert. *24 rue Monsieur-le-Prince, 6e, tel. 1/43–54–66–73. Métro: Odéon. MC, V.*

Have you noticed those signs on many brasserie windows boasting that they serve Poilâne bread? It's all coming from a sublime St-Germain bakery (8 rue du Cherche-Midi, 6e, tel. 1/45–48–42–59), where specials include a 21F wheat loaf with nuts, and old-fashioned apple tarts for 10F.

Cosi. Leave it to the French to make a delicatessen chic. This fancy sandwich shop serves your choice of ingredients—including chèvre, spinach, salmon, mozzarella, tomatoes, and curried chicken—on fresh focaccia bread for 35F–46F. Add to this a glass of wine (20F), modern decor with photos of opera greats, and a changing selection of opera music, and voilà: French deli. *54 rue de Seine, 6e, tel. 1/46–33–35–36. Métro: Odéon. Open daily noon–midnight.*

La Crêpe Canettes. This simple crêperie, decorated with posters from neighborhood art galleries, is a popular lunch spot; come alone and you may find yourself sitting across from someone you don't know. The 52F menu includes a salad with walnuts, a galette, and Breton cider. Choose a dessert crêpe and tack 20F–40F more onto your bill. *10 rue des Canettes, 6e, tel. 1/43–26–27–65. Métro: Mabillon. Closed Sun. and Mon. dinner. MC, V.*

Orestias. Come here only if you're in the mood for a boisterous meal; otherwise, the haphazard service may drive you nuts. Owned by a Greek family who communicates by shouting (they shout at you to take a seat, they shout your order to the kitchen), the restaurant serves a passable three-course meal for 45F, featuring a variety of grilled meats and desserts like baklava. This place is not for vegetarians: Not only are the dishes meaty, but animal heads on the wall gaze down at you while you eat. *4 rue Grégoire-de-Tours, 6e, tel. 1/43–54–62–01. Métro: Odéon. Closed Sun. MC, V.*

UNDER 80F **Le Coffee Parisien.** This popular spot, frequented by the young leisure class of the St-Germain area, specializes in brunch, served at the diner-style counter or at tables. We're talking *real* brunch, like eggs Benedict (65F), pancakes (45F), and eggs Florentine (65F). The place also serves burgers and big salads (spinach salad 45F). The lunchtime café across the street has bagels and hot sandwiches to go and sells hard-to-come-by American products at jacked-up prices. *5 rue Perronet, 7e, tel. 1/45–44–92–93. Métro: St-Germain-des-Prés. Open daily 10 AM–11:30 PM.*

Les Jardins de St-Germain. This eatery near the Cathédrale St-Germain fills up at lunch with well-dressed professionals and students visiting from the Quartier Latin. The menu costs 65F at lunch, 75F at dinner, and includes a kir, a generously garnished main course such as grilled salmon, your choice of veggies, and a dessert. The typical French food is artfully presented, and there are many dishes from which to choose. If all the tables are taken, go across the street to the very similar **La Ferme St-Germain.** *14 rue du Dragon, 6e, tel. 1/45–44–72–82. Métro: St-Germain-des-Prés. MC, V.*

Le Petit Vatel. This tiny, tiny restaurant has long served as headquarters for hungry budget travelers and romantics. A healthy-size main course with two vegetables (your choice) costs 55F. They serve lots of meat dishes, including turkey with olives or pork with carrots, but you can also get a vegetarian plate for 45F. *5 rue Lobineau, 6e, tel. 1/43–54–28–49. Métro: Mabillon. Closed Sun. lunch and end of Dec. AE, MC, V.*

Restaurant des Beaux-Arts. Students and professors painted the frescoes on the walls of this bustling, old-time establishment near the Ecole des Beaux-Arts. The 75F menu is refreshingly varied, featuring no fewer than eight choices among appetizers, main courses, and desserts, and it includes wine. *11 rue Bonaparte, 6e, tel. 1/43–26–92–64. Métro: St-Germain-des-Prés.*

UNDER 100F **Chassagne Restaurant.** This classic French restaurant is one of the best values in the quarter: For 85F you can have a scrumptious three-course meal, including the house terrine, lamb brochettes, and a fabulous dessert. Plenty of regulars fill the vast, dark, almost rustic interior, but you can also sit outside on clear nights. The low-key waitstaff will attempt timid English translations if you need help with the menu. *38 rue Monsieur-le-Prince, 6e, tel. 1/43–26–54–14. Métro: Odéon. RER: Luxembourg. Closed Sun. AE, MC, V.*

Le Petit Mabillon. In a section of St-Germain where restaurants are prohibitively expensive, this friendly Italian spot puts them all to shame with a delicious, filling 80F three-course menu. In good weather, use the outside tables to watch the crowds pass by. Try the daily pasta specials, included with the menu or around 50F à la carte. *6 rue Mabillon, 6e, tel. 1/43–54–08–41. Métro: Mabillon. Closed Mon. lunch, Sun. MC, V.*

Village Bulgare. Not far from Pont Neuf, this place is a bit too hidden to be terribly popular, but the dimly lit dining room is fun, the food is good, and crowds come on the weekends. Expect all those Bulgarian specialties you're used to, like *kebabtcheta* (a grilled meat roll) and *banitza* (a baked pastry filled with cheese or spinach); the three-course menu costs 80F. "Une cuisine qui chante" (Cooking that sings), as their flyers claim. *8 rue de Nevers, 6e, tel. 1/43–25–08–75. Métro: Pont-Neuf. Open Mon.–Sat. 11–3 and 6–1:30 AM, Sun. 11–3.*

SEVENTH ARRONDISSEMENT

The restaurants in this area cater primarily to diplomats and politicians. In other words, you won't be eating many meals here. However, moderately priced lunches at tiny restaurants where the ministers escape when they want to "go local" do exist: **Rue de Babylone,** though long and boring, is a promising walk for a good lunch. The cafés, often filled with students from the nearby campuses, can also be fun.

UNDER 60F **Le Babylone.** The proprietress hustles her family around the tables of this lunch-only restaurant, serving grilled specials to everyone from political bigwigs to college intellectuals. Salmon in cream sauce (50F) is devoured under the watchful gaze of ceramic Pope plates, and the appetizers are inexpensive (20F for pâté Basque). The best deal is the wine: 13F for a tasty half-bottle of house red. *13 rue de Babylone, 7e, tel. 1/45–48–72–13. Métro: Sèvres-Babylone. Closed Sun. and Aug.*

UNDER 80F **Bar de la Maison de l'Amérique Latine.** You walk through a gallery of Latin American art (and *past* the expensive restaurant) to reach this cultural center's café-style restaurant. A la carte dishes include Mexican chili con carne (62F) and Argentinean empanadas (25F); a changing 65F menu includes appetizer, main course, and a glass of wine. The clientele tends to be yuppie-ish. *217 blvd. St-Germain, 7e, tel. 1/45–49–33–23. Métro: Rue du Bac. Closed dinner and weekends. AE, MC, V.*

Chez l'Ami Jean. Checkered tablecloths and a sawdust-littered floor pretty well set the tone for this Basque restaurant. It's an informal family joint with tremendous specialties like *pâté campagne* (country-style pâté; 20F), trout meunière (50F), and pepper steak; equally tempting desserts run 20F–25F. You'll share the ambience with well-behaved kiddies and their well-behaved parents (this is the seventh, remember). *27 rue Malar, 7e, tel. 1/47–05–86–89. Métro: Latour-Maubourg. Closed Sun. MC, V.*

SPLURGE **La Fontaine de Mars.** You know a place is gonna cost a lot when there's a guy in a tux standing out front, but for a well-presented meal in the neighborhood, you can't do better than this. This snazzy restaurant near the Champ de Mars will charm you and fill you up with a delicious selection of classic French fare like terrine (50F) or lamb chops with country herbs (80F). The 85F lunch menu offers a choice of two appetizers and two main courses; otherwise, count on spending at least 100F à la carte. *129 rue St-Dominique, 7e, tel. 1/47–05–46–44. Métro: Ecole Militaire. Closed Sun. MC, V.*

Bistrots

Often confused with their more expensive and largely British-run cousins, the *bars à vins,* or wine bars, bistrots are an obstinately traditional Parisian institution. Wine is the reason to come here—although you can order food from a limited menu. Bistrots usually sell wine by the bottle, often specializing in obscure regional wines, and sometimes buy grapes from the vineyards to blend themselves. They're a lot of fun and a fairly inexpensive way to try France's wide array of wines.

According to one theory, the word "bistrot" dates back to the early 19th century. After the fall of Napoléon, the Russian soldiers who occupied Paris supposedly banged on zinc-topped café bars yelling "buistra"—"hurry" in Russian.

Le Baron Rouge. Refreshingly mellow, the Red Baron has enough varieties of cheap wine to keep its poststudent crowd happy. Glasses of white start at 6F, meat plates at 35F; smoked duck is 18F. You'll eat in a room whose decor, though named after Snoopy's nemesis, is more red than "Peanuts"-based. About twice a week a live rock or blues band takes over and forces some patrons out onto barrels set up on the sidewalk—stop by to pick up a monthly performance schedule. *1 rue T. Roussel, 12e, tel. 1/43–43–14–32. Métro: Ledru-Rollin. Open daily until 10 PM.*

Bistrot-Cave des Envierges. A cozy room and a few scattered sidewalk tables mark this casual bistrot just above the Jardin de Belleville. Ten wines—five whites and five reds—are offered daily at 8F–12F a glass, and the list always features at least a couple of Loires. Snacks like gazpacho or cheese cost 30F, the few heftier dishes around 60F. A cool, hang-loose crowd—not that there's ever much of one—makes this a great place to unwind, even if you have to climb the hill to do it. *11 rue des Envierges, 20e, tel. 1/46–36–47–84. Métro: Pyrénées. Closed Mon. and Tues.*

Bistrot des Augustins. One of several bistrots along the St-Germain Seine, this spot has a worn wood-and-brass bar, aging mirrors, and shelves cluttered with dried flowers. When the weather is nice, the front doors open onto the street and tables dot the sidewalk, which is not necessarily a good thing given the heavy traffic and loud noise of the busy street. The devoted clientele have a blast anyway, drinking wine by the glass (13F and up) and munching on snacks like terrine (32F). *39 quai des Grands Augustins, 6e, tel. 1/43–54–41–65. Métro: St-Michel. MC, V.*

Le Bouchon du Marais. For a relatively quiet meal at this bistrot, grab a table downstairs. For something more boisterous, reserve ahead for a table *à l'étage* (on the second floor). The patron specializes in Touraine wines and offers a wide selection by the glass: Sauternes is 30F. To accompany your wine, have a meat plate or fondue (65F–120F per person); a three-course menu runs 90F. The walls are full of snapshots of the patron and his friends, all conspicuously drunk. *15 rue François Miron, 4e, tel. 1/48–87–44–13. Métro: St-Paul. Seatings past midnight. Closed Sun. AE, MC, V.*

Le Brin de Zinc. This friendly place above Les Halles is perfect for enjoying an afternoon glass of wine (25F) at either the smoky bar or an airy sidewalk table. Munch on platters of cheese (50F) or selected meats (65F), and choose a bottle of wine (90F and up) from the thoughtfully assembled cellar. Every day from 5 to 9, beer (14F and up) and other drinks are two-for-one; nurse a brew long enough for the late-night music to get going downstairs. *50 rue Montorgueil, 2e, tel. 1/42–21–10–80. Métro: Etienne Marcel. Closed Sun.*

Each fall, when the grapes on the vines outside Jacques Mélac's windows ripen, he closes off the street and holds his own private harvest festival. Everyone picks, the young'uns stomp, and the drinking goes on through the night.

Jacques Mélac. This is one of a handful of Paris bistrots where the proprietor makes the wine. Even though he offers a large selection of other labels, you should try what award-winning Jacques has produced (bottles start at 70F), though the results are not uniformly impressive. The bar and dining rooms are packed with locals who aren't afraid to serve themselves when the waiters are a little slow. Omelettes (20F–50F) and plates of meats and cheese (20F–60F) may accompany the wine, but the waiters refuse to serve water with the food. *42 rue Léon Frot, 11e, tel. 1/43–70–59–27. Métro: Charonne. Closed weekends. AE, MC, V.*

Le Relais du Vin. This is the perfect place for budding viticulturists. Ten years ago, Mr. Beaugendre transformed his bar into a restaurant specializing in wines, which range from 13F to 30F per glass. The long list of bottles starts with a 65F Château Coquille 1992 rosé and winds up at a 1,400F Château Margaux 1976 Premier Grand Cru Classé. For 40F you can compare small glasses of three different Burgundies. The menu runs 65F for two courses and a drink, 85F for three courses, and the 35F onion soup is available until past midnight. Outdoor seating affords you a view of frazzled patrons emerging from the sex shops across the street. *85 rue St-Denis, 1er, tel. 1/45–08–41–08. Métro: Les Halles. Closed Sun. MC, V.*

Le Rouge Gorge. Sedate, sophisticated surroundings and company accompany your glass at this southern Marais wine bar. The light, airy rooms are a good place to bring that new edition of *War and Peace* and mull over life and a glass of white (from 15F) or red (from 12F). Desserts and cheeses cost around 30F, and the whole show stays open late (until 2 AM) for all those smooth talkers with the midnight munchies. *8 rue St-Paul, 4e, tel. 1/48–04–75–89. Métro: Sully-Morland. Closed Aug. MC, V.*

Cafés

Along with air, water, and the three-course meal, the café remains one of the basic necessities of life in Paris. You'll find a café on every corner and around every bend, and after a while you may notice . . . hey, they all look the same! Cafés in Paris have an almost institutional uniformity that you may find comforting or romantic for a while, but eventually, like too many visits to the post office, it gets kind of old. Thankfully, once in a while you'll duck past that facade to find some pleasant surprises. Those on the *grands boulevards* (such as boulevard St-Michel, boulevard St-Germain, and the Champs-Elysées) and in the big tourist spots (near the Louvre, the Opéra, and the Eiffel Tower, for example) will almost always be the most expensive and the least interesting, although most have terraces from which you can watch the entire Tourist World go by. Step into the smaller, less flashy establishments on the smaller, less flashy streets for a cheaper cup of coffee and a feeling of what real French café life is like.

Cafés are required to post a *tarif des consommations,* a list that includes prices for the basics: *café* (espresso-like coffee), *café crème* (the same with hot milk), *bière à la pression* (beer on tap), *vin rouge* (red wine), *citron* or *orange pressé* (fresh-squeezed lemonade or orange juice), etc. They list two prices, one *au comptoir* (at the counter) and the other *à terrasse* or *à salle* (seated at a table). Below we list the seated prices. If you just need a quick cup of coffee, take it at the counter and save yourself a lot of money. If you have a rendezvous, take it at the table, remember you're paying rent on that little piece of wood, and hang out as long as you like. People have written entire masterpieces in cafés over one tiny little cup of coffee. Or maybe two.

Cafés listed here under the heading "Midi" (midday) thrive before the dinner hour, while those listed under "Soir" (evening) only get more popular as the night progresses. Expect Midi cafés to close around 7 PM. Soir cafés are usually open until midnight or later and charge about 5F more per drink after 10 PM or so.

MIDI

L'Allée Thorigny. A bright, simple café a few steps from the Musée Picasso provides everything you need: temporary shelter (or simply a seat outside), a cup of coffee (9F), and the *International Herald-Tribune* (9F). In fact, a full press shop takes up a corner of the café, which might

Left Bank Literary Cafés

If you really want to sink a lot of money into a cup of café crème, stop by one of the cafés made famous by their artsy patrons of the 19th and early 20th centuries. On place St-Germain-des-Prés is Les Deux Magots, named after the grotesque Chinese figures, or magots, inside. Still milking its post–World War II reputation as one of the Left Bank's prime meeting places for the intelligentsia, Deux Magots charges hordes of tourists 35F for a cup of coffee. Although Jean-Paul Sartre and Simone de Beauvoir can take a lot of credit for making the place famous (they supposedly met here), they probably spent more time two doors down at the Café de Flore, hanging with their fellow graduates from the Ecole Normale Supérieure.

Perhaps the most famous bastion of Left Bank café culture (and certainly one of the most expensive, having been turned into a pricey bar/restaurant), Closerie des Lilas (171 blvd. du Montparnasse) marks its bar seats with plaques indicating who once sat there. For the price of an expensive drink, you can rest your buns where Baudelaire, Apollinaire, and Hemingway once sat. Finally, Le Procope (13 rue de l'Ancienne Comédie), Paris's first café, was founded in 1686 and supplied coffee and booze to Voltaire, Oscar Wilde, Napoléon, Robespierre, and Ben Franklin, though probably not all on the same day and certainly not all at the same table.

explain the predominance of readers here. If the 114-year-old waiter is still around, order loudly and don't ask questions. *2 pl. Thorigny, 3e, tel. 1/42–77–32–05. Métro: St-Paul or Chemin-Vert.*

A Priori Thé. This small salon serves up large pots of tea (22F) in its comfortably worn room in the Galerie Vivienne, a renovated passage near the Bibiliothèque Nationale. Tables line the old glass-roofed galleria, making the place feel like a sidewalk café, only without the traffic and gloomy weather. Don't worry; Parisians will still promenade past with their dogs. Older women sip tea and nibble on divine, though expensive, pastries (30F). *35–37 Galerie Vivienne, 2e, tel. 1/42–97–48–75. Métro: Bourse. Closed Sun.*

Brûlerie de l'Odéon. When you enter this old-fashioned café specializing in gourmet coffees and teas, the friendly proprietress might engage you in conversation about the weather, even if you don't speak any French. The decor (teak tables and coffee paraphernalia) is as low-key as the service, and the coffee is cheap and good. Café is 9F, café crème 16F–20F, and pastries 12F–16F. *6 rue Crébillon, 6e, tel. 1/43–26–39–32. Métro: Odéon. Closed Sun.*

If you're wandering around the city and need to find a bathroom, one of the city's ubiquitous cafés may be your best bet. Not only are they on almost every street corner, but proprietors are required by law to let anyone use their bathroom, whether they're a patron or not.

Café au Petit Suisse. At the edge of the Quartier Latin and across the street from the Jardin du Luxembourg, this café nurtures students, starving writers, and other locals who sit in the cozy little room when the weather is rotten and on the sunny terrace when it isn't. With private booths and an indoor balcony, the Petit Suisse manages to draw you in without being flashy or touristy. Café is 8F, café crème 12F, and cold drinks 15F. *9 rue Corneille at rue Vaugirard, 6e, no phone. Métro: Odéon. RER: Luxembourg. Closed Sun.*

Café des Enfants Gâtés. Finally, a café whose staff realizes that it doesn't cost any more to give you jugs of hot water with your tea. That's not to say this place is any bargain basement; coffee costs 15F, loose-leaf, flavored teas 25F, and pastries a whopping 40F. The low lights, tattered leather chairs, ceiling fans, and old movie posters offer a great background for literary types on rainy days. *43 rue des Francs-Bourgeois, 4e, tel. 1/42–77–07–63. Métro: St-Paul.*

Mariage Frères. This is the most reputable tea house in Paris; the shop up front sells hundreds of varieties of loose leaves by the gram, as well as every device imaginable in which to brew them. A pot will run you 34F; desserts go for 45F–55F. Tea leaves aside, indulge in the decadent brunch (120F), served daily noon–6. *30 rue du Bourg-Tibourg, 4e, tel. 1/42–72–28–11. Métro: St-Paul or Hôtel-de-Ville.*

La Mosquée. Inside the main mosque in Paris, this salon de thé is intricately tiled and decorated with Moroccan wood carvings and tapestried benches. Once you're inspired by the Middle Eastern music, visit the Turkish baths next door for a really decadent afternoon (*see box* Steam Baths Are a Turkish Delight, in Chapter 2). Coffee or a teeny glass of sweet mint tea is 10F; baklava and other pastries cost 11F–15F. *19–39 rue Geoffroy-St-Hilaire, 5e, tel. 1/43–31–18–14. Métro: Censier-Daubenton.*

Pâtisserie Viennoise. A scaled-down version of its Austrian counterparts, this cramped local institution keeps potential doctors from the nearby Ecole de Médecine caffeinated. Pastries are created in the kitchen downstairs, including several variations on the chocolate torte (16F), each one named for a famous composer; lesser pastries start at 6F. Café is 8F and café crème 11F. The daily lunch specials are a good deal. *8 rue de l'Ecole de Médecine, 6e, tel. 1/43–26–60–48. Métro: Odéon. Closed weekends and Aug.*

La Pause. This café in the Bastille has an outdoor terrace overlooking the rue de Charonne, one of the most interesting streets in the neighborhood. Sandwiches cost 19F–29F, salads 19F–39F, and full meals 55F. Bargain coffee is 7F50, crème 12F. The crowd is of mixed ages and mostly French, with a significant but not overwhelming contingent of types who ride their motorcycles on the sidewalk. *41 rue de Charonne, 11e, tel. 1/48–06–80–33. Métro: Bastille or Ledru-Rollin.*

Sydney Coffee Shop. A tiny little counter and two tables welcome you to this low-key Australian hangout where Foster's is 35F a pint, Melbourne bitter 25F. It's too cramped not to be sociable, so don't come expecting a quiet, contemplative beer. A meat pie with salad is 35F, making it a good lunch spot as well. *27 rue Lacépède, 5e, tel. 1/43–36–70–46. Métro: Monge or Cardinal Lemoine.*

SOIR

amnésia café. The music is just loud enough to keep conversations *à deux* at this modern, dimly lit, potentially intimate gay café. To call the scrumptious salad plates (45F–65F) meal-size hardly does them justice; very few cows could munch that much greenery in one sitting. A café costs 9F, café crème 12F, and a jumbo crème 16F; beers run 20F–30F. Nightfall ups both the prices and the crowd. *42 rue Vieille-du-Temple, 4e, tel. 1/42–72–16–94. Métro: St-Paul or Hôtel-de-Ville.*

Au Soleil de la Butte. A good cup of coffee in an untouristy café near Sacré-Coeur is a rare, rare commodity, but this place manages to serve it up. A small but cool crowd hangs out on the covered terrace on a blessedly quiet corner sipping café (10F) and beer (17F). The menu is long and includes salads from 22F. Just be sure to walk down the hill to the *east* side of the basilica, away from place du Tertre. *32 rue Muller, 18e, tel. 46–06–18–24. Métro: Château Rouge.*

Café Beaubourg. Its name may not carry the weight that Café Costes's (*see below*) does, but the Café Beaubourg is stylish enough to make it a worthy Les Halles rival. The large café sits in the shadow of the Centre Georges Pompidou and serves large salads (around 50F), small meals, and desserts. Best of all are the bookshelves filled with French titles that you can borrow during your stay. *100 rue St-Martin, 4e, tel. 1/48–87–63–96. Métro: Châtelet or Hôtel-de-Ville.*

Café Costes. This café right in the center of Les Halles is one of the few Parisian projects of French architect and designer Philippe Starck. Inside seating is recommended to better take in Starck's streamlined, postmodern design. But even if you can't afford a 16F café or 24F crème, run in just to see the cool bathrooms, where little boys can gleefully whiz on an illuminated glass wall. *Pl. des Innocents, 1er, tel. 1/45–08–54–39. Métro: Châtelet.*

Café de l'Industrie. Every 20-something in town flocks to these large rooms where funky art hangs from the red walls. This is a great place for a light dinner and drink before hitting the Bastille scene; unfortunately, it's closed Saturdays. Beers are 16F, salads around 40F. *16 rue St-Sabin, 11e, tel. 1/47–00–13–53. Métro: Bastille or Bréguet-Sabin. MC, V.*

Freshly Baked Bread from Paris? Maybe Not

Hate to burst your bubble, but most of the boulangeries in Paris aren't allowed to make their own bread because you need a special permit to own an oven. That bread you're eating was probably mass-produced in the suburbs and shipped in. To have a real loaf of Paris-baked bread, look for a sign in front of the boulangerie saying ARTISAN BOULANGER.

Each year, the mayor gives a 20,000F prize to the Paris boulangerie that bakes the best baguette. The winner of the 1994 award was Au Pain Bien Cuit (111 blvd. Haussmann, 8e, Métro: Miromesnil), whose owner claimed that the sign of real baguette excellence was in the bread's texture several hours after baking—only inferior bread need be eaten when still warm. Second place went to Daniel Dupuy (13 rue Cadet, 9e, Métro: Cadet), and third to Phillippe Thilloux (24 rue du Commerce, 15e, Métro: La Motte-Piquet–Grenelle).

Café Marly. Owned by the same brothers who run the Costes and Beaubourg cafés (*see above*), this upscale, indulgently decorated, and unabashedly sophisticated café overlooks the Cour Marly in the Louvre's new Richelieu wing. The stunning view, clientele (designer Jean Nouvel has been seen here), and reputation (the *International Herald-Tribune* did an article on the place) might justify paying 16F for a café and 35F for a chocolate tart, at least once. The extra-long hours—8 AM to 2 AM—are a bonus, too. *Cour Napoléon, 1er, tel. 1/49–26–06–60. Métro: Palais Royal–Musée du Louvre. MC, V.*

Café Wah-Wah. This grungy Bastille café with asymmetrical tile decor looks like it was lifted straight out of San Francisco's Haight district or London's Camden Town: The customers sit around being beaten to death by the music. The bar folks are nice but may look at you funny if you smile too much. Café is 6F, a pression 12F. *11 rue Daval, 11e, tel. 1/47–00–26–06. Métro: Bastille.*

La Palette. This old café on a little street in the St-Germain area offers much in the way of atmosphere: garrulous waiters, an old mirrored bar, outdoor seating among the cherry trees, and palettes on the walls. It's pretty much an evening/night café; lots of university students come here to unwind. Café is 11F and a glass of wine 20F. *43 rue de Seine, 6e, no phone. Métro: Mabillon. Open until 2 AM.*

Markets and Specialty Shops

Besides its stunning array of open-air markets (*see below*), Paris has a variety of options when you need to buy food at odd hours or need certain specialty items. Supermarkets offer the distinct advantage of having longer hours, as well as offering products that street markets just don't have. **Monoprix** and **Prisunic**, two large budget department store chains, have supermarkets inside. Monoprix is all over and usually open until 8 or 9; the Prisunic (109 rue de la Boétie, 8e, tel. 1/42–25–10–27) just off the Champs-Elysées stays open until midnight but closes Sundays.

A lifesaver for anyone on a budget, **Ed l'Epicier** is the cheapest supermarket in Paris. Although it's an outlet with a varying selection, you can always find the basics (pasta, rice, beans, meat, cheese, wine, chocolate) for way less than anywhere else. Bring your own grocery sacks. *Branches include: 84 rue Notre-Dame-des-Champs, 6e, Métro: Notre-Dame des Champs; 123 rue de Charonne, 11e, Métro: Bastille; 80 rue de Rivoli, 4e, Métro: Hôtel-de-Ville.*

Need kiwis and raspberries in January? Truffles and caviar for that party you're planning? To see French connoisseurship at its most prestigious and pretentious, check out the famous **Fauchon** (pl. de la Madeleine, 8e, tel. 1/47–42–60–11). You won't be able to afford anything, but you can at least browse amid jars of caviar, olive oil, and foie gras. Neighboring grocer **Hédiard** (21 pl. de la Madeleine, 8e, tel. 1/42–66–44–36) also merits a glance.

OPEN-AIR MARKETS

They're fun, they're packed, and they just might save you from starvation. Paris has legions of open markets, feeding millions of families who have decided to bypass the city's many restaurants for the evening. Stands and permanent shops are set up at the south end of **rue Mouffetard** (5e). **Rue de Buci** (6e), near St-Germain, and **rue Lepic** in Montmartre (18e) also offer an astounding array of produce, cheeses, meats, breads, candies, and flowers. There's a big outdoor food market on **rue Daguerre** (14e) in Montparnasse. Cheaper yet are the markets at **place Monge** (5e) and on **rue d'Aligre** (12e), near Bastille. Try also the excellent daily **Chinese market** (Métro: Porte de Choisy), near Paris's stab at a Chinatown in the 13th arrondissement. The markets are usually open Tuesday through Sunday 8 AM–1 PM. Come in the early morning to watch chefs and housewives preparing for the day, or around noon to get incredible bargains on the day's remains.

NON-FRENCH FOODS

If you shop only at Monoprix, it's easy to become frustrated by the limited range of non-French foods offered. Luckily, specialty stores fill in the gaps. American and British goods are most common in central neighborhoods like St-Germain and the Marais, while Asian and Middle Eastern supplies are more plentiful around Belleville, Chinatown, and the 15th arrondissement.

La Grande Epicerie. Perhaps the best part of the department store Au Bon Marché (*see* Grands Magasins, in Chapter 6) is the gourmet grocery attached. Other than the best brands and the highest prices on all your usual French supplies, this place has sections devoted to British, American, Italian, Indian, kosher, and "exotic" goods. Wishbone Ranch dressing is 25F, Nutter Butters 23F, and Diet Dr Pepper 6F a can. *38 rue de Sèvres, 7e, tel. 1/44–39–81–00. Métro: Sèvres-Babylone.*

Izraël. This small, packed (both with food and with customers) shop in the Marais specializes in hard-to-find goods from all over the world, including huge bins of rices, grains, and olives, some prepared dishes, and shelves of prepackaged goods. Pick up anything from Kraft marshmallow spread (30F), Indonesian soya sauce (15F), and Italian Modena vinegar (30F) to a honey bear (35F). The selections of olive oils, honeys, and jams are especially varied. *30 rue François-Miron, 4e, tel. 1/42–72–66–23. Métro: St-Paul.*

Kong Thai. This Belleville establishment sells fruit, vegetables, and dried goods from Africa, the Americas, and southern Europe. *64 blvd. de Belleville, 20e, tel. 1/44–62–99–12. Métro: Couronnes.*

Mexi & Co. If you're tired of faux Mexican food, you might just want to cook up a real fajita de pollo that doesn't taste like coq au vin. This teeny specialty store sells your basic Mexican and Latin American specialties at high prices: A can of refried beans costs 13F, a kilo of flour tortillas 36F. At several sidewalk tables or the inside bar you can sip on a Tecate (18F) while munching on chips and salsa, or order a dish like the chicken burrito plate (29F) from the simple menu. *10 rue Dante, 5e, tel. 1/46–34–14–12. Métro: Maubert-Mutualité or Cluny–La Sorbonne.*

Ste-Kioko. Come here for fresh and packaged Japanese foods and ingredients. *46 rue des Petits-Champs, 1er, tel. 1/42–61–33–66. Métro: Pyramides.*

Picking Your Picnic-Packing Stop

The best way to choose a market is to find the one closest to you; quality doesn't vary enough to warrant trips across town. If you need more romantic incentives, consider these:

- To survive on 10F a day: Go to the Marché d'Aligre, on rue d'Aligre in the 12th. Besides wonderful fruits from all over the world, this market features the cheapest prices in Paris.

- To be knocked down by a wayward backpack: The market at the bottom of rue Mouffetard (5e) is small but very good—as the entire tourist world seems to already know.

- To meet a rich widow: The best of the sixth come out to this pretty market on rue de Buci, which, despite its appearance, offers reasonable deals on all kinds of fruits, vegetables, and flowers.

Tang Frères. In addition to stocking a hearty produce selection and some basic French ingredients, several Chinatown locations of Tang Frères sell Chinese wines and beers, spices, and packaged goods, including frozen prepared foods. *168 av. de Choisy, 13e, tel. 1/44–24–06–72. Métro: Place d'Italie or Tolbiac.*

Thanksgiving. Don't do major shopping here; it would be cheaper to have mom Federal Express a care package from home. But when you *really* need Oreos, 50F for a package suddenly doesn't seem so outrageous. Other finds include Wheat Thins (40F), Pop Tarts (35F), and Duncan Hines chocolate chip cookie mix (40F). The attached pâtisserie sells "New York" bagels and Philadelphia Cream Cheese. *20 rue St-Paul, 4e, tel. 1/42–77–68–29. Métro: St-Paul.*

CHOCOLATE

Parisians have to admit that Belgian chocolates are better than French ones. Accept this fact and be glad that Belgium isn't far away, ensuring easy access to their celebrated *pralines* (filled chocolates). Not that the French are completely inept. Shop at some of the places below to find some of the best chocolates the French have to offer.

Chocolate was believed to have medicinal value in the 18th century. Doctors prescribed chocolate candy for indigestion, coughing, fever, and inflammation, among other ailments.

A la Mère de Famille. This *confiserie* (sweets shop) founded in 1761 was the first in Paris. It sells divine house-made chocolates at 86F for 250g (if you just want a taste, get a large piece for 12F), as well as brand-name candies, dried fruits, and gourmet coffees. *35 rue du Faubourg Montmartre, 9e, tel. 1/47–70–83–69, Métro: Rue Montmartre; 1 rue Montmartre, 1er, Métro: Les Halles. MC, V.*

Le Chocolatier de Paris. This place proves the French can do chocolate cheaply: A kilogram (2.2 lbs) costs just 100F. *71 rue de Tolbiac, 13e, tel. 1/45–86–38–39. Métro: Nationale.*

Jeff de Bruges. Jeff isn't far behind Léonidas (*see below*) in the popularity contest, though his stuff is a bit more expensive. *Branches include: 55 rue St-Antoine, 4e, tel. 1/42–71–97–74, Métro: St-Paul; 13 rue Daguerre, 14e, tel. 1/40–47–01–32, Métro: Denfert-Rochereau.*

Léonidas. Judging by the number of branches throughout the country, this is France's favorite chocolate shop. Get a 33F, 250-gram box (about 12 chocolates) to try for yourself, and be sure to ask for plenty of the white ones. *Branches include: 66 blvd. St-Germain, 6e, tel. 1/43–84–55–60, Métro: Cluny–La Sorbonne; 7 rue des Innocents, 1er, tel. 1/42–36–11–92, Métro: Châtelet–Les Halles.*

Reference Listings

BY TYPE OF CUISINE

AFRICAN

UNDER 60F
Le Boute Grill (Quartier Latin)
Le Fouta Toro (Montmartre)

UNDER 100F
Resto La Pirogue (Belleville)

AMERICAN

UNDER 60F
Chicago Pizza Pie Factory (Champs-Elysées)

UNDER 80F
Le Coffee Parisien (St-Germain)

UNDER 100F
Haynes (Gares de l'Est and du Nord)
The Studio (Marais)

CRÊPERIES

UNDER 60F
La Crêpe Canettes (St-Germain)

UNDER 80F
Pont Aven (Montparnasse)

DELIS

UNDER 40F
Al Dar (Quartier Latin)
Sacha et Florence Finkelsztajn (Marais)

UNDER 60F
Cosi (St-Germain)

UNDER 80F
Chez Marianne (Marais)

EASTERN EUROPEAN

UNDER 40F
Sacha et Florence Finkel-sztajn (Marais)

UNDER 80F
A la Ville de Belgrade (Gares de l'Est and du Nord)

UNDER 100F
Village Bulgare (St-Germain)

FRENCH

UNDER 60F
Le Babylone (Seventh Arrondissement)
Le Bistrot du Peintre (Bastille)
Chez Papa (Montparnasse/Gares de l'Est and du Nord)
La Crêpe Canettes (St-Germain)
Dame Tartine (Les Halles)
Le Petit Gavroche (Marais)
Le Pic à Vin (Montmartre)
Restaurant Chartier (Gares de l'Est and du Nord)
Le Soleil (Belleville)

UNDER 80F
L'Apostrophe (Quartier Latin)
Au Petit Ramoneur (Les Halles)
Aux Artistes (Montparnasse)
Bistrot de la Sorbonne (Quartier Latin)
Café de la Cité (Marais)
Chez Bruno (Gares de l'Est and du Nord)
Chez l'Ami Jean (Seventh Arrondissement)
Chez les Fondus (Montmartre)
L'Incroyable (Louvre to Opéra)
Les Jardins de St-Germain (St-Germain)
Le Palet (Louvre to Opéra)
Le Petit Vatel (St-Germain)
Pont Aven (Montparnasse)
Restaurant des Beaux-Arts (St-Germain)
Le Temps des Cerises (Bastille)

UNDER 100F
La Canaille (Marais)
Chalet Maya (Gares de l'Est and du Nord)
Chassagne Restaurant (St-Germain)
Chez Justine (Belleville)
Chez Max (Les Halles)
L'Eté en Pente Douce (Montmartre)

SPLURGE
A la Courtille (Belleville)
L'Ange Gourmand (Quartier Latin)
La Fontaine de Mars (Seventh Arrondissement)
Chez Paul (Bastille)
Le Gamin de Paris (Marais)
Julien (Gares de l'Est and du Nord)
Les Voyageurs (Bastille)
Minim's (Champs-Elysées)

GREEK

UNDER 60F
Orestias (St-Germain)

UNDER 80F
Olivier-Ouzerie (Montparnasse)
Zagros (Bastille)

INDIAN

UNDER 80F
Bhai Bhai Sweets (Gares de l'Est and du Nord)

UNDER 100F
Jhelum (Louvre to Opéra)
Naz Restaurant (Bastille)
Surma (Quartier Latin)

ITALIAN

UNDER 40F
Panini Sandwiches à Emporter (Les Halles)
La Pignatta (Montmartre)

UNDER 80F
Le Jardin des Pâtes (Quartier Latin)

Paparazzi (Gares de l'Est and du Nord)

UNDER 100F
Le Petit Mabillon (St-Germain)

JAPANESE

UNDER 60F
Higuma (Louvre to Opéra)
Japanese Barbecue (Les Halles)

UNDER 100F
Yamamoto (Louvre to Opéra)

LATIN AMERICAN/ TEX MEX

UNDER 60F
Taco Mucho (Quartier Latin)

UNDER 80F
Bar de la Maison de l'Amérique Latine (Seventh Arrondissement)
Mustang Café (Montparnasse)

NORTH AFRICAN/ TURKISH/ MIDDLE EASTERN

UNDER 40F
Al Dar (Quartier Latin)

UNDER 60F
Le Boute Grill (Quartier Latin)
Chez Rami & Hanna (Marais)

UNDER 80F
Chez Marianne (Marais)
Zagros (Bastille)

UNDER 100F
Van Gölu (Gares de l'Est and du Nord)

SOUTHEAST ASIAN/ CHINESE

UNDER 60F
Auberge des Deux Dragons (St-Germain)
Cambodiana (Montmartre)
Restaurant Lao Siam (Belleville)

153

UNDER 80F
Restaurant Tai-Yen (Belleville)

SPANISH

UNDER 80F
Le Kezako (Montmartre)

UNDER 100F
Tapas Nocturne (Bastille)

VEGETARIAN

UNDER 60F
Au Grain de Folie (Montmartre)
La Petite Légume (Quartier Latin)
Rayons de Santé (Montmartre)

UNDER 80F
Country Life (Louvre to Opéra)

UNDER 100F
Entre Ciel et Terre (Les Halles)

SPECIAL FEATURES

DINNER AND ENTERTAINMENT

UNDER 80F
Chez Bruno (Gares de l'Est and du Nord)

UNDER 100F
Haynes (Gares de l'Est and du Nord)
Tapas Nocturne (Bastille)
Van Gölu (Gares de l'Est and du Nord)

OUTDOOR DINING

UNDER 60F
Dame Tartine (Les Halles)

UNDER 80F
Au Petit Ramoneur (Les Halles)
L'Incroyable (Louvre to Opéra)

UNDER 100F
Chassagne Restaurant (St-Germain)
Le Petit Mabillon (St-Germain)
The Studio (Marais)

SPLURGE
A la Courtille (Belleville)

TAKEOUT

Al Dar (Quartier Latin)
Cambodiana (Montmartre)
Chez Marianne (Marais)
Chez Rami & Hanna (Marais)
Mouff'Tartes (Quartier Latin)
Panini Sandwiches à Emporter (Les Halles)
La Pignatta (Montmartre)
Sacha et Florence Finkelsztajn (Marais)
Taco Mucho (Quartier Latin)

AFTER DARK

5

By Baty Landis and Oliver Schwaner-Albright

If you don't go out at night during your stay in Paris, you're depriving yourself big time. Even if you don't want to dress up or spend a lot of money, there's plenty to fill an evening, from listening to a lone saxophonist wail away by the river to just running around the streets made mystical by that peculiar glow emitted by streetlamps at 3 AM.

Of course, if you *do* have money, Paris offers almost endless options for nightlife: every film you ever wanted to see; discos that don't close until sunrise; and the more traditional activities to be found in theaters, concert halls, and the legendary cabarets. The city is known for its jazz and up-and-coming world music scene, and posters plastered everywhere tell you about the best shows. Every couple of weeks, "private" parties for which you can buy entrance are thrown on various boats in the Seine; keep an eye out for flyers, or check in *Pariscope,* a weekly publication listing nighttime activities all over the city. *Lylo,* short for "les yeux les oreilles," is a new, small monthly detailing the goings-on around town for each day of the month, including info about cover charges, types of music, and wheelchair accessibility.

Parisian cafés, bars, and *boîtes* (dance clubs) tend to mutate over the course of an evening—something that was a restaurant at lunch could become a bar at 8 PM and then a dance club until sunrise. This means that a place we call a café could wind up being a great place to have a drink after dinner or to listen to live music on certain nights.

Gay life in Paris has its geographic base in the Marais, though it's not the raging scene big-city kids from the United States might be used to. Lesbian life is still less visible and more subject to the whims of fashion. Try contacting the **Maison des Femmes** (8 cité Prost, 11e, tel. 1/43–48–24–91), a feminist/lesbian resource center and cafeteria for info on events. The free monthly *Illico,* found in gay bars and cafés, has a calendar of gay events, including tea dances, lectures, and concerts, as well as essays on topics like AIDS research or gays in the media; risqué pretty-boy pictures are included for your viewing pleasure.

Bars

Most Parisian bars (at least the ones that aren't open as cafés earlier in the day) open around 10 PM and close at 2 AM, even on weekends. Law requires that prices be posted, but if they're not, expect to pay 20F–35F for a draft beer, referred to as *une pression, une demi-pression,* or simply *une demi* (all mean a half-pint on tap). If beer isn't your thing, try a *kir* (white wine flavored with crème de cassis), a *diabolo* (tonic water flavored with grenadine), a *kriek* (black-cherry flavored beer), or a *panaché* (half beer, half lemonade). Wine costs about the same as beer, and cocktails are generally too expensive to bother with.

155

BASTILLE

The Bastille is still riding the crest as the hottest nightlife area in town, welcoming hordes of Parisians, knowing visitors, and new arrivals who have discovered that the Left Bank is no longer where it's at. The block-long **rue de Lappe** has more bars per meter than any other street in Paris, while **rue de la Roquette** starts off crowded at place de la Bastille and grows desolate to the north. Side streets like **rue de Charonne** and **rue Keller** harbor low-key joints. If you're in the area, visit **L'Iguana** (15 rue de la Roquette, 11e, tel. 1/40–21–39–99), a rather upscale, modern, two-story bar where you can relax over a 30F beer, or **Le Bar Sans Nom** (39 rue de Lappe, 11e, tel. 1/48–05–59–36), a heavily draped bar with a mellow crowd lounging on big cushions.

La Bastide. This cramped, funky bar in the heart of the Bastille serves some of the cheapest beer (14F–20F) in the neighborhood, making it a haven for young scruffy types and smart shoppers. The steady flow of jazz and blues (with the occasional '60s tune thrown in) and cheap beer encourage all kinds of sing-alongs. *18 rue de Lappe, 11e, tel. 1/47–00–26–72. Métro: Bastille.*

Café de la Plage. Soul, funk, blues, and jazz tracks accompany drinks (beers 20F–35F, aperitifs 30F) and idle chat at this Franco-British bar. Drinks cost more in the *cave* (cellar) during the weekend DJ shows, when the place becomes one of the downest, coolest dance scenes in town (cover 50F). The crowd is young and congenial and aspires to be in a band. *59 rue de Charonne, 11e, tel. 1/47–00–91–60. Métro: Charonne.*

Le China Club. Haute sophistication reigns in this big establishment done up in colonial Hong Kong style. The ground floor is sprawling and candle-lit; upstairs, a more intimate garden setting invites hushed intrigues. Drink prices are outrageous; the cheapest is the 35F coffee. *50 rue de Charenton, 12e, tel. 1/43–43–82–02. Métro: Ledru-Rollin.*

Le Leche Vin. Jesus and Mary watch as you down drafts in this small place lined with Christmas-tree lights and religious paraphernalia. The crowd is casual—much less image-conscious than in most of the Bastille. A pression or *orange-pressé* (fresh-squeezed orange juice) goes for around 20F. *13 rue Daval, 11e, tel. 1/48–05–16–75. Métro: Bastille.*

Les Portes. If the madness of rue de Lappe and rue de la Roquette gets to be too much, take a break at this laid-back bar with jazz in the cellar many weeknights (except in summer). Prices hover at about 22F for a kir and 25F for draft beer; the best deal is the giant 30F kriek. Incredibly, prices *don't* go up during performances. *15 rue de Charonne, 11e, tel. 1/40–21–70–61. Métro: Bastille.*

CHAMPS-ELYSEES

The streets branching off from the Champs-Elysées (coolly referred to as Les Champs by regulars) harbor bars filled with models, foreigners, and diplomats. The **Chicago Pizza Pie Factory** (*see* Restaurants, in Chapter 4) is a good place to socialize with Americans and the French people who want to meet them while sipping a 35F beer and watching sports on TV.

Doobie's. To experience all the stress of getting into an exclusive club when you're just going to a plain old bar, ring the doorbell at Doobie's. Ever since tennis star Yannick Noah opened the place several years ago, it's been a magnet for agents, models, and cool businessmen. The atmosphere is too sleek for words, and the bartender may not notice you if you're under five foot ten. Not that you wanted to spend 50F on a beer, anyway. *2 rue Robert Estienne, 8e, tel. 53–76–10–76. Métro: Franklin D. Roosevelt.*

LES HALLES

Though Les Halles is most frequented for its live-jazz bars, a number of watering holes cater to those who'd just as soon pay 80F less for a beer and listen to a record. At night the area is almost as touristy as during the day, but it catches some gay nightlife from the nearby Marais and still lures a fair number of Parisians with relatively cheap drinks and plenty of late-night eateries. Unaccompanied women should be careful at night, especially around the deserted streets of northern Les Halles.

Banana Café. A supremely hip gay crowd gathers at this Les Halles bar, which welcomes a mixed crowd and serves 20F beers. The interior is sleek and dim, while the terrace just off place des Innocents is prime people-watching territory. Most nights, the downstairs area becomes a small, sweaty boîte. *13 rue de la Ferronnerie, 1er, tel. 1/42–33–35–31. Métro: Châtelet. Open nightly until 5 AM.*

Le Baragouin. This friendly northern Les Halles joint features bizarre decor (a backdrop of aluminium foil behind the bar, for instance) and reasonable drinks. Come before 9 PM for happy hour, when a beer at the bar costs just 5F. Wooden tables in the back room allow for intimate talks or raucous drinking games. *17 rue Tiquetonne, 2e, tel. 1/42–36–18–93. Métro: Etienne Marcel.*

Le Champmeslé. Come to this mixed bar several blocks northwest of Les Halles on a Thursday night for live concerts—solo guitarists, quiet jazz, that kind of thing. On any night, the comfortable back room hosts an intimate crowd, including members of Paris's B.C.B.G. (Bon Chic Bon Genre, or French yuppie) lesbian set. Drinks are 30F–40F. *4 rue Chabanais, 2e, tel. 1/42–96–85–20. Métro: Pyramides.*

Flann O'Brien. Between Les Halles and the Louvre, Flann O'Brien might be the only bar commemorating an Irish writer that contains no posters, not even a single cocktail napkin, with any reference to James Joyce. Live, potentially obnoxious rock or blues music (you are strongly encouraged to sing along) accompanies pints of frothy Guinness (17F–32F). *6 rue Bailleul, 1er, tel. 1/42–60–13–58. Métro: Louvre-Rivoli.*

The Frog and Rosbif. Paris's newest Irish pub is a hit with both Parisians and Anglophones, who come for pint of Guinness (35F) or the bar's own bitter Real Ale (35F–40F); call ahead for a free tour of the microbrewery downstairs. The high-ceilinged, airy room with wooden booths, dartboards, and weekly events like Tuesdays with Gary the Magician make this place hard to pass up. *116 rue St-Denis, 2e, tel. 1/42–36–34–73. Métro: Les Halles.*

MARAIS

An artsy, hip, gay neighborhood, the Marais is filled with all kinds of people and all kinds of nocturnal possibilities. Rue Vieille-du-Temple is the main nightlife street; in addition to the bars listed below, check out **Majestic Café** (34 rue Vieille-du-Temple, 4e, tel. 1/42–74–61–61), a loose, fun place to hang out. At **Le Pick-clops** (cnr rue Vieille-du-Temple and rue du Roi-de-Sicile, 4e, tel. 1/40–29–02–18) a boisterous crowd stands under colored lights. After your revelries, head over to **Chez Rami & Hanna** (*see* Chapter 4, Food), serving great falafel until 1:30 AM.

Tuesday through Saturday, come to the tiny, nondescript Café au Vieux Paris (72 rue de la Verrerie, 4e) after midnight, when song lyrics are handed out and the resident accordion player gets going. Audience participation is not optional. Drinks are 20F.

Au Petit Fer à Cheval. A mixed and mingly bunch of locals fills this tiny bar all day and into the night. It's got an impressive range of seating options for such a small place, but the best spot is right up against the bar, where the drinks are cheaper (*café crème* 12F, beer 22F). *32 rue Vieille-du-Temple, 4e, tel. 1/42–72–47–47. Métro: St-Paul or Hôtel-de-Ville.*

Bar d'Arts/Le Duplex. Changing art exhibitions and loud alternative music distinguish the dim, cool atmosphere of this gay men's bar full of sexy young tortured-artist types. Women are welcome but are usually few and far between. A pression costs 20F. *25 rue Michel le Comte, 3e, tel. 1/42–72–80–86. Métro: Rambuteau.*

Le Piano Zinc. A primarily gay crowd packs into this multilevel hot northern Marais piano bar to sing, scope, and drink 20F pressions. The self-proclaimed theme is "sho-biz"—perhaps because everyone here wants to be in it. Anyone with an itch sings, whether it's the piano man, the loud clientele, the bartenders, or everyone at once. It may be stifling and smoky, but don't pass up the chance to see a man in a skirt singing "*Je suis une fille de Provence*" (I'm a girl from Provence). *49 rue des Blancs-Manteaux, 4e, tel. 1/42–74–32–42. Métro: Rambuteau.*

Subway. Subtle decorative touches, like hanging tires, chains, and iron bars make this gay men's bar feel just like home. The place has everything your teen-fantasy basement might have—pool tables, MTV, and pinball machines. A fairly young, trendy crowd frequents this industrial wonderland all day and night. They might not let you in if they don't like your looks; women are welcome only with a man—and a hip man at that. *35 rue Ste-Croix-de-la-Bretonnerie, 4e, tel. 1/42–77–41–10. Métro: St-Paul.*

MONTMARTRE AND PIGALLE

The modest collection of neighborhood bars and pubs that see nightly gatherings of *Montmartrois* stops abruptly at rue Pigalle, the most outrageous street in the outrageous Pigalle area. In Montmartre, customers are either neighbors or cousins of the bartender; in Pigalle, where sex shops, strip shows, and prostitution houses crowd the streets, anonymity is key. To avoid the neon sleaze, head south of place Blanche along rue Blanche and rue Fontaine.

Le Gerpil. Though only a few steps north of Pigalle, this simplest of bars is wholly Montmartre. The proprietor alternates sips of gin with *bises* (kisses) for all his regulars filing in and vows he has "only good music" for his admirably powerful cassette player. Try requesting a little old-time French accordion or some flamenco guitar. Pressions run 15F–20F. *14 rue Germain-Pilon, 18e, tel. 1/42–64–16–78. Métro: Pigalle.*

Lily la Tigresse. For a mild taste of Pigalle's traditional charms, come to this large, red-velvet-lined space with bar-top dancers. The crowd is surprisingly wholesome, and there's plenty of plush seating, though most people stand around the bar sipping 35F beers. *98 rue Blanche, 9e, tel. 1/48–74–08–25. Métro: Pigalle.*

Le Moloko. All kinds, from sophisticated models to giggly high schoolers, fill this *branché* (hip) bar/boîte until 6 AM. The three rooms include a dance floor, a smoky sitting room, and a brighter "salon." *26 rue Fontaine, 9e, tel. 1/48–74–70–76. Métro: Pigalle.*

Le Sancerre. A nightly gathering of jovial Montmartrois fills up this established neighborhood bar, which can be unbearably smoky when they close the front windows in bad weather. The 9F pression doubles in price after 10 PM. *35 rue des Abbesses, 18e, tel. 1/42–58–08–20. Métro: Abbesses.*

QUARTIER LATIN

Though most spots near the river are intolerably touristy and expensive, above boulevard St-Germain near Maubert-Mutualité and rue Mouffetard are some lower-key bars where you can still get an affordable beer with crowds of students. English-speaking folks tend to hang out around here, so it's a good place to meet Brits, Aussies, Canadians, or—if you've had any trouble finding them—Americans.

Café Oz. A bunch of Aussies has opened up this small, convivial bar serving Foster's on tap for 32F a pint. The sign outside claims ON PARLE FRANÇAIS (we speak French), but they must not get much practice; American college students have taken over, though foreign students from other countries also adopt the place from semester to semester. *184 rue St-Jacques, 5e, tel. 1/43–54–30–48. Métro: Cluny–La Sorbonne. RER: Luxembourg.*

Le Manhattan. Only men are admitted to this cool weekend bar/dance club. The boys arrive after 1 AM, then hang around and boogie until dawn drinking 37F beers. The club's business card doubles as a date card—on the back you can write your name and number and hand it to that hot man you've been watching all night. *8 rue des Anglais, 5e, tel. 1/43–54–98–86. Métro: Maubert-Mutualité. Closed Mon.–Thurs.*

Le Piano Vache. University students come here in groups to rest heavy elbows on the tables, chain-smoke, and solve the world's problems. The bar is sufficiently dark and the music sufficiently angst-inspiring to keep you from getting too optimistic. Beer is 20F–30F. *8 rue Laplace, 5e, tel. 1/46–33–75–03. Métro: Cardinal Lemoine.*

Polly Maggoo. This little bar harbors refugees when everything else in the neighborhood closes down—hence the bad wine (20F), since by the time patrons arrive, they don't care what they're drinking anymore. The clientele is mostly young Frenchmen who do their best to impress the few young, foreign women. *11 rue St-Jacques, 5e, tel. 1/46–33–33–64. Métro: St-Michel.*

ST-GERMAIN-DES-PRES

For a neighborhood that used to be the hippest, swingingest *quartier* around, St-Germain's nightlife has fallen pretty flat. Most of the jazz bars have tried unsuccessfully to go upscale, and the bars are overrun by foreigners about 20 years behind the times. The spots that have managed to keep a low profile have done the best, holding on to a loyal clientele and almost justifying the 30F and up you'll pay for your beer. Most of the good bets are between boulevard St-Germain and the Jardin du Luxembourg.

Le Birdland. A mellow, well-lit bar with a big recorded-jazz collection, the Birdland caters to a crowd of varying ages with cocktails (65F), beer (35F), Monk, and Bird every night until 6:30 AM, except Sunday, when they quit early. *20 rue Princesse, 6e, tel. 1/43–26–97–59. Métro: Mabillon.*

Chez Georges. Upstairs, this bar has been serving glasses of red wine, *pastis* (a licorice-flavored liqueur), and beer (20F–30F) to old men in work clothes for the last 60-odd years, as the ancient decor and patrons attest. Down in the basement, local students crowd around tiny tables. Don't be intimidated if the place looks packed—there's always room to squeeze in somewhere, and even the staunchest regulars are ready to make new friends. *11 rue des Canettes, 6e, tel. 1/43–26–79–15. Métro: Mabillon. Closed Sun.–Mon. and mid-July–mid-Aug.*

On pretty evenings, there's nothing more romantic than a drink at St-Régis (6 rue Jean du Bellay, 4e, tel. 1/43–54–59–41), an Ile St-Louis bar that serves 12F beers in plastic cups that you can take onto the bridge just ouside, where musicians, magicians, and their admirers tend to gather behind Notre-Dame.

Le Mazet. Come to this bright bar quickly, before cirrhosis does in the little red-nosed proprietor. On an especially cheery day, he might sneak you samples of his varied beers, all of which—from *pêcheresse* (peach-flavored) to kriek to the classics—are delicious and go for about 45F a pint. *61 rue St-André-des-Arts, 6e, tel. 1/43–54–68–81. Métro: Odéon.*

La Paillotte. Nurse a carefully chosen cocktail (45F) and gaze deep into somebody's eyes until dawn in this dark, smoky joint in St-Germain. The owner stations himself at the bar to greet you and keeps a close eye on the turntable, where he plays one of the best jazz collections in Paris. Beers are 25F at the bar, 40F seated. *45 rue Monsieur-le-Prince, 6e, tel. 1/43–26–45–69. Métro: Odéon. Closed Sun.*

Dance Clubs

Hefty covers, absurd door policies, frequent "private soirées," lousy music . . . At worst, Paris's *boîte de nuit* (nightclub) circuit is a complete mess; at best, it's a tough scene to break into. Once you plunge in, though, it can be a lot of fun, especially if you have the stamina to start after midnight and keep hopping until at least 4—though by no means do you have to head home right after that. Many clubs also host weekly afternoon "tea dances," gatherings where couples often dance the swing and more traditional steps. Tea dances are often men- or women-only; check *Pariscope.*

In gaining admission, women have an advantage over men; at heterosexual places, guys are better off finding a woman or two to accompany them. Following these guidelines will also up your chances: (1) Dress well. (2) Arrive early (before midnight); until you become known at a particular disco door, this little trick greatly improves your shot at getting in—and of getting in free. (3) Try to find a club featuring a guest—and preferably foreign—DJ; otherwise, you might be subjected to badly remixed techno all night. Two big-name clubs to avoid are **La Locomotive** (90 blvd. de Clichy, 18e, tel. 1/42–57–37–37, Métro: Blanche) and **La Scala** (188 bis rue de Rivoli, 1er, tel. 1/42–60–45–64, Métro: Palais Royal–Musée du Louvre), which play mostly mainstream house music for young and pouty crowds.

Les Bains. This former municipal bath turned exclusive disco is one of the most desirable clubs in which to be seen, with the highest ratio of models to real people found anywhere outside the pages of *Vogue*. If the extremely choosy doorwoman decides that you look okay, and if you decide to fork over 140F, you'll find rooms full of people who are way too preoccupied with what everyone else is doing to have a good time and a DJ who couldn't mix his way out of a paper bag. Most people have a blast the first time, an okay time the second, and it gets worse from there. *7 rue du Bourg-l'Abbé, 3e, tel. 1/48–87–01–80. Métro: Etienne Marcel.*

Le Balajo. The granddaddy of the Paris discos keeps 'em coming back, decade after decade, to the same hyper-kitschy decor and tempo: from rock and roll to salsa to mainstream disco. It's a good standby if you're in the neighborhood and have 100F to blow, though women should be warned that the male-dominated crowd can be revoltingly clingy. *9 rue de Lappe, 11e, tel. 1/47–00–07–87. Métro: Bastille. Closed Mon.–Tues.*

Chez Moune. This old, dark cabaret in Pigalle is a women's disco during the week, while Friday and Saturday nights bring a cabaret performed by women for women: Cover is a compulsory 130F drink. The club also has a 75F women-only tea dance on Sunday afternoon. *54 rue Pigalle, 9e, tel. 1/45–26–64–64. Métro: Pigalle.*

L'Escale. Underneath a stuffy ground-floor bar hides one of Paris's best salsa dance floors. There's a minimum of unwanted groping—no matter what the music may encourage. It's open weekends only, and drinks start at 90F. *15 rue Monsieur-le-Prince, 6e, tel. 1/43–25–55–22. Métro: Odéon.*

Les Folies Pigalle. Decorated like a 1930s bordello, this small, red-hot gay club plays techno and hip hop for a crowd crammed onto the two-level dance floor. Frequent drag shows might spotlight a faux Cher, Barbra Streisand, or Boy George, and weekends feature giddy theme nights. Some nights are more mixed than others: Thursdays see some heteros and women. Weekend mornings, the party often goes on until noon. Entry costs 100F, drinks 50F. *11 pl. Pigalle, 9e, tel. 1/48–78–25–56. Métro: Pigalle.*

Kat Privilège. This hopping disco lays down house and funk for a stylish lesbian crowd. Weekends are the most fun—and the toughest nights for men to gain admission. Cover is 100F, one drink included. Saturday and Sunday mornings, this becomes the after-hours spot of choice for hedonistic homosexuals with dance fever. *3 cité Bergère, 9e, tel. 1/42–46–50–98. Métro: Rue Montmartre. Closed Sun.–Mon.*

Keur Samba. Your chances of meeting the son or daughter of an African ambassador are unusually high in this pumping, expensive disco near the Champs-Elysées. The music ranges from reggae to African soukous and American hip hop and house. Dress up and bring generous funds for the 120F entrance and first drink. *79 rue la Boétie, 8e, tel. 1/43–59–03–10. Métro: St-Philippe du Roule.*

Le Monocle. A fun lesbian crowd converges nightly at this boîte that features sporadic sexy "*spectacles.*" It's open early for intimate drinks and later becomes one of the best places to dance among women. Men are few. Drinks start at 100F. *60 blvd. Edgar Quinet, 14e, tel. 1/43–20–81–21. Métro: Edgar Quinet. Closed Sun.*

Le Palace. This super '80s extravaganza, housed in a historical monument that was once the theatrical venue for the likes of Maurice Chevalier and Jean Gabin, remains popular through flights of fashion and the fickleness of disco patrons. The doormen charge 100F and let in all styles—just be sure you have one—ensuring a variety of groovers inside. Many nights DJs from London play everything from disco to house to Motown. The Sunday-afternoon tea dance (5–10 PM; cover 60F) has become an institution in the gay community. *8 rue du Faubourg Montmartre, 9e, tel. 1/42–46–10–87. Métro: Rue Montmartre. Closed Mon.*

Le Queen. This high-profile, super-cool gay nightclub on the Champs admits most women accompanied by a man, except on Thursdays. Everyone gyrates happily to house music (Monday is '70s night) on the vast dance floor, and the whole scene is extremely cutting-edge, right down to New Age cocktails like the Love Bomb, created with plant extracts. Cover is free during the week, 80F on the weekend. *102 av. des Champs-Elysées, 8e, tel. 1/42–89–31–32. Métro: George V.*

Rex Club. A disco and live-music venue featuring a variety of garage/rock bands, the Rex provides a much-needed outlet for all those rockers who are about to be genteeled to death. Different nights feature different types of music, including soul, thrash funk/rock, and "exotic." Couples of all ages come to the afternoon tea dances (30F) to twist and tango. *5 blvd. Poissonnière, 2e, tel. 1/42–36–83–98. Métro: Bonne-Nouvelle. Cover: 50F, 70F weekends. Closed Sun.–Tues.*

Live Music

This town has loved jazz for as long as jazz has been around. American artists flocked here during the post–World War II boom and fostered an appreciative and innovative atmosphere for their music-making. Though there's still some fine music being played in Paris, and though young French groups try earnestly to catch the beat, these days it's hard to find truly jazzy dives. For some time now, African, Caribbean, and South American music has been moving in, spicing up the music club circuit, and many "jazz" clubs have a weekly *zouk* (Caribbean dance music) or salsa night.

Most jazz clubs are in Les Halles, St-Germain, or the Quartier Latin, and in most places you can stay all night for the price of a drink—a 50F–100F drink, that is. For cheaper shows, keep an eye on some of the museums and cultural centers around town (the Musée Guimet and Institut du Monde Arabe, for example); they occasionally host free or almost free concerts. One particularly good venue for world music and jazz is the café/cinema Passage du Nord-Ouest (*see* Cinemas, *below*). **Radio Nova** (101.5 FM) is an excellent multicultural radio station, while the free monthly *Paris Boum-Boum* (available at cafés) has a section on world music happenings around town.

Au Duc des Lombards. Quality European blues and jazz acts regularly fill up this Les Halles club for 10:30 shows. The secret to this place, though, is attending the jam sessions played by local groups most nights between 8 and 9:30, when beers cost only 30F. Get here even earlier for 8F beers and hang out with the bar crew. Beers also drop back down to 10F or so between jam sessions and headliners, though they then shoot up to around 50F for the main act. The restaurant upstairs serves passable meals for around 100F until 4 AM every night but Sunday. *42 rue des Lombards, 1er, tel. 1/42–33–22–88. Métro: Châtelet.*

Le Baiser Salé. This bar's small, potentially hot upstairs room is the perfect venue for small, potentially hot ensembles. Sit back on your velvety turquoise seat and listen to music ranging from blues to fusion to Afro-jazz. The first drink is 90F, and with each new set you have to buy another one for 40F. *58 rue des Lombards, 1er, tel. 1/42–33–37–71. Métro: Châtelet.*

Le Bistrot d'Eustache. This small, classic café/bar across from its eponymous cathedral is well loved by young Parisians without a lot of money. Singers somewhere between Martha Washington and your local lounge lizard perform weekend nights from 10:30 until 4. A frustrating column in the middle of the room means that only three tables and the bar have an unobstructed view of the musicians. Beers cost 15F at the bar, around 30F seated; snacks run 30F and up. *37 rue Berger, 1er, tel. 1/40–26–23–20. Métro: Les Halles.*

Les Bouchons. Below a classy restaurant, this versatile joint hosts jazz and rock groups Monday through Thursday and becomes a good disco on weekends. The atmosphere is intimately dim, the crowd mellow, and the drinks 50F and up. *19 rue des Halles, 1er, tel. 1/42–33–28–73. Métro: Châtelet.*

Le Caveau de la Huchette. This classic caveau has been serving up swing and Dixieland to boppin' cats since the 1950s, and the young, wholesome crowd of tourists and students still swing dances here like it's going out of style. Entrance costs 60F, 70F on weekends; students pay 5F less. *5 rue de la Huchette, 5e, tel. 1/43–26–65–05. Métro: St-Michel.*

La Chapelle des Lombards. This hot bar often has high-quality live Latin music, zouk, and African music. The crowd is as "world" as the music and really gets into the shows, making a dance floor out of everything. Entrance for concerts costs 100F, 120F weekends, one drink included. *19 rue de Lappe, 11e, tel. 1/43–57–24–24. Métro: Bastille.*

Every June 21, France comes alive with free music in celebration of the summer solstice. During this Fête de la Musique, Paris's churches, clubs, parks, and squares fill with musicians and onlookers. You owe it to yourself to stay out all night.

La Cigale. The big names who come through this place fashioned like a small opera house belt blues, rock, and anything current. Float between upstairs theater-style seating and the orchestra dance floor; a small bar in the basement keeps you fueled with 20F beers. Tickets run around 150F; for the really popular groups, buy your ticket in advance at Fnac or Virgin Megastore. *120 blvd. Rochechouart, 18e, tel. 1/49–25–81–75. Métro: Pigalle.*

Méridien-Jazz-Club Lionel Hampton. This club in a luxury hotel on the edge of town manages to lure some big names, perhaps with the help of the 130F you hand over for a drink. The atmosphere is less than dynamic and can even drag down some normally upbeat performers, but if your favorite group from home is passing through, here's a trick: Dress other than as a street urchin, sit in the large lobby separated from the lounge by shrubbery, and enjoy partial visibility for free. *81 blvd. Gouvion St-Cyr, 17e, tel. 1/40–68–30–42. Métro: Porte Maillot.*

New Morning. This is *the* big-time Paris jazz club. All the greats have sweated on its stage at one time or another: Archie Shepp, Dizzy Gillespie, Miles Davis, Celia Cruz. The quality and reputation remain exceptional, and the repertoire now also includes reggae, salsa, and Latin jazz. Admission to the dark, 600-seat club costs 130F–150F; drinks are 30F. *7–9 rue des Petites-Ecuries, 10e, tel. 1/45–23–51–41. Métro: Château d'Eau.*

Péniche B.B. Antillais. This restaurant/bar/disco on a boat hosts live Caribbean music in the piano bar Thursday through Saturday nights. Drinks cost 60F–80F and include cover. *Docked at 23–26 quai Alphonse Le Gallo, just west of town, tel. 1/48–25–92–85. Métro: Pont de Sèvres.*

Slow Club. This classic swing/jazz dance hall has been around for decades, seducing jazz greats such as Miles Davis into a show or two. Every night, way underground, bands play Dixieland, bebop, blues, and more until the wee hours to an older crowd of swing dancers. Admission is 55F–75F, and optional drinks are 30F and up. *130 rue de Rivoli, 1er, tel. 1/42–33–84–30. Métro: Châtelet.*

Cabaret

That great old institution the Paris cabaret, which hit its peak early this century, is seeing something of a revival these days after too many years devoted to sleazy Pigalle-style shows. Shows most often involve a series of solo musicians, singing quartets, and other groups. If you find yourself in the Marais, check out **Le Piano Zinc** (*see* Bars, *above*). Otherwise, the greatest concentration of cabarets is still up on Montmartre hill—just be sure you choose the right kind of club.

Two of the tackiest, most famous shows in town—**Le Moulin Rouge** (pl. Blanche, 9e, tel. 1/46–06–00–19), named for the windmills that used to cover Montmartre hill, and **Les Folies-Bergère** (32 rue Richer, 9e, tel. 1/44–79–98–98)—manage to draw a crowd despite the admission price of about 465F. The Folies reopened a few years ago under a new director, who is trying to give cabaret a more contemporary, intellectual flair.

Au Lapin Agile. This unassuming joint on Montmartre's back side has been around since 1860, including a stint under the ownership of Aristide Bruant, the famous songwriter who introduced a new form of satirical song to the Paris music scene. Today it's still serving up classic French oldies, largely to French tourists, in a dark, close room. Any evening sees solo pianists, singers, and other musicians, who rotate from 9 to 2. Entrance with a drink is 110F, 80F for students. *22 rue des Saules, 18e, tel. 1/46–06–85–87. Métro: Lamarck-Caulaincourt. Closed Mon.*

Au Pied de la Butte. It's everything you ever hoped for from a Paris cabaret, staging glittery, flashy numbers interspersed with Edith Piaf favorites. Though the focus is on solo singers and groups, you'll also see comedians, magicians, balloon artists, and more. Grab a spot at one of the small tables, pay 80F for a drink, and stay as long as you like—things usually wind up around 3 AM, later on weekends. *62 blvd. Rochechouart, 18e, tel. 1/46–06–02–86. Métro: Anvers.*

Cinema

On any given night, the range of films showing in Paris is phenomenal. That incomprehensible documentary that lasted a week at your local artsy cinema seven years ago plays here on a regular basis, even if the attendance rarely hits double digits. You'll also find low-budget films in a dozen or so languages, often making that documentary seem mainstream. The small, funky cinemas that like this kind of thing tend to congregate in and around the Quartier Latin. Often they have a limited but obscure collection and show the same 40 or so films over and over—which means that if you miss the last screening of *Prospero's Books,* it'll probably be back in a week or two.

On the other hand, you have big flashy cinemas that offer blockbuster films, plush seats, and good sound. Two of the biggest and flashiest are **Gaumont Grand Ecran** (30 pl. d'Italie, 13e, tel. 1/45–80–77–00) and **Max Linder Panorama** (24 blvd. Poissonnière, 9e, tel. 1/48–24–88–88), both of which have immense screens and seat hundreds and hundreds of people; Max Linder is also wheelchair accessible. The Champs-Elysées is a good drag to cruise for new, expensive showings.

Almost all foreign films are played in the *version originale* (original language) with French subtitles, marked "v.o." in listings; the abbreviation "v.f." (*version française*) means a foreign film is dubbed in French. Occasionally, French films show with English subtitles; look for the words "*sous-titres anglais*" in the listing. Both Paris entertainment weeklies, *L'Officiel des spectacles*

The Little Sparrow

Born in Belleville in 1915 (and shortly thereafter abandoned on someone's doorstep), Edith Piaf began singing in cafés and on the streets of Paris at the age of 15. Often called "the Little Sparrow," Piaf soon became famous for her expressive, tremulous voice, performing in many cabarets and even a few plays and films. One look at a photo of this waifish, saucer-eyed singer, though, and you'll know that life was not all song and dance for this troubled woman; Piaf's life was filled with tragic relationships and drug addiction. After a serious illness, she made a comeback in 1961, but died two years later. Despite her troubled life (or perhaps because of it), Parisians have passion for Piaf, and the songs she made famous, including "La vie en rose," "Je ne regrette rien," "Milord," and "Mon Dieu," are likely to pop up in any cabaret show.

and *Pariscope,* have comprehensive film listings that include prices, which normally run 35F–45F with discounts for students. Different theaters also offer price breaks on certain days of the week, most often Monday.

Cinémathèque Français. Founded in 1936 by Henri Langlois, this is a cinephile heaven, with different classic french and international films playing every day. Often film schedules pay homage to a certain filmmaker, with a few unrelated pieces thrown in for variety. Tickets are 25F, 15F students. The Chaillot location has a tiny film museum. *Palais de Chaillot at Trocadéro, 16e; 18 rue Faubourg du Temple, 11e. Tel. 1/47–04–24–24.*

L'Entrepôt. This cinema cum café/bar/restaurant and bookstore is a must for film lovers. The three cinemas host a variety of festivals and show some great art and international films. Hang around the bar with other types who are suffering for their art, and maybe an independent filmmaker will discover you. Film tickets are 36F, 27F for students. *7 rue Francis-de-Pressensé, 14e, tel. 1/45–43–41–63. Métro: Pernety.*

Le Grand Rex. The grandest of Paris's cinemas, this movie palace should not be confused with the other little Rexes that don't have the painted ceiling, the cloud machine, or the capacity (2,750 seats) of this Rex. The memorable and much-photographed facade was designed in 1932; unfortunately, much of the interior has been chopped up into smaller screens, each showing mainstream films. Seats are 42F, 35F for students and on Mondays. *1 blvd. Poissonnière, 2e, tel. 1/36–65–70–23. Métro: Bonne-Nouvelle.*

Le Lucernaire. This multimedia supercenter has two stages, three cinemas, occasional concerts, art expositions, a restaurant, and a café. The film selection is eclectic, specializing in the foreign and the rare. Seats cost 39F, 28F for students. On one of the stages, *Le Petit Prince* has been running for seven years; shows cost 120F–140F, 70F–90F for students, and still less if you spring for a 100F membership card. *53 rue Notre-Dame-des-Champs, 6e, tel. 1/45–44–57–34. Métro: Notre-Dame des Champs.*

> *The Lumière brothers showed their first film—the first public showing of any projected film ever—in 1895 in a café at 14 boulevard des Capucines.*

La Pagode. Although the selection of first-run French and international films is pretty standard, you've never seen another theater like this in your life. In 1896, the wife of the owner of Au Bon Marché built what was to become the most fashionable salon in Paris; it became a theater in 1931, and filmmaker Louis Malle rescued it from wreckers 40 years later. The silk-and-gilt Salle 1 is the best place to watch a film. A tiny café takes over the garden in summer. Tickets are 44F, 36F for students. *57 bis rue de Babylone, 7e, tel. 1/36–68–75–07. Métro: St-François Xavier.*

Passage du Nord-Ouest. This café/cinema screens artsy flicks to accompany your café crème. The schedule is very erratic: One week may see only one or two showings, the next a miniature film festival. Entry costs around 30F. Most films play in the afternoon, to make way for the jazz and world music concerts that happen at night. *13 rue du Faubourg Montmartre, 9e, tel. 1/47–70–81–47. Métro: Rue Montmartre.*

Vidéothèque. While hard-core movie goers may scoff at the idea of videotapes, the Vidéothèque is one of Paris's most important resources for moving images. A full day of audiovisual stimulation costs just 30F; the daily program can vary from a score of avant-garde shorts to a handful of '30s feature-length films, all screened either in an immaculate projection room or on private consoles. The auditorium is also a forum for symposia and lectures, drawing a host of international critics and filmmakers eager to argue about the *meaning* of the tracking shot. *2 Grande Galerie des Halles, 1er, tel. 1/40–26–34–30. Métro: Les Halles. Open Tues.–Sun. 12:30–8:30 PM.*

Performing Arts

The performing arts scene in Paris is overwhelming, with two of the world's greatest opera houses, over 150 theaters, and at least a dozen classical concerts performed daily. While many opera houses hold music concerts, the best place to catch classical performances is in Paris's churches. Scan the first 70 pages of *Pariscope* each week for listings, looking especially for the words *"entrée gratuite"* or *"entrée libre,"* meaning this is a freebie in the otherwise costly arts world. The posters and notices pasted on the walls of Métro stations are not a bad way to keep up with the calendar either. To find out what is being performed during the 1995 season in many of the major venues listed below, *see* Performing Arts Schedules, *below*.

Though opera is the queen of Parisian performing arts, the dramatic tradition established by Racine and Molière has also been packing in crowds for 300 years. Traditional productions by these playwrights and others like Beckett and Ionesco generally fill the schedules, although more innovative, experimental theater is easily found out toward the suburbs. A surprising number of English-language troupes also call the city home.

Tickets to performances are not impossible to get, if you use a little foresight. At most venues, box offices start selling tickets two weeks before a performance, though a limited number of tickets are available one month in advance if you charge by phone. Day-of-performance tickets are often available for students ages 25 and under; depending on the show, you should arrive between 1½ hours and 15 minutes early to try for any leftover tickets—sometimes excellent seats can be had for as little as 10% of the original price. Of course, you can always get tickets by phone from **Fnac** (tel. 1/40–41–40–00) or **Virgin Megastore** (tel. 1/49–53–50–50), though availability may be limited and you'll pay a small service charge.

While not uniformly responsive, many Parisian theaters have been making a concerted effort to accommodate patrons in wheelchairs; call one month in advance for tickets and access information for all theaters. Most antiquated houses have clumsy, if serviceable, ramps and elevators, while the new or renovated theaters have tried to achieve barrier-free access. Some theaters also have begun to provide services for the hearing- and sight-impaired.

CLASSICAL MUSIC AND DANCE

CENTRE GEORGES POMPIDOU—IRCAM One of the four divisions within the Centre Georges Pompidou (*see* Major Museums, in Chapter 2), the IRCAM, or Institut de Recherche et Coordination de l'Acoustique et de la Musique, takes care of the "gestural" arts. Performances at the institute's multipurpose hall, under the place Igor Stravinsky, include contemporary music, computer-generated videos, dance, drama, lectures, philosophy seminars, and debates. *31 rue St-Merri, on pl. Igor Stravinsky, 4e, tel. 1/42–17–12–33. Métro: Rambuteau. Tickets sold at counter on ground floor. Open Mon.–Thurs. 9:30–1 and 2–6, Fri. 9:30–1 and 2–5. Wheelchair access.*

In 1994, French designer Christian de Portzamparc was awarded the Pritzker Prize, the world's most prestigious award for an architect. To evaluate his characteristic stacking of sinuous forms yourself, you can check out the Conservatoire National at the Cité de Musique or the Café Beaubourg across from the Centre Pompidou.

CONSERVATOIRE NATIONAL SUPERIEUR DE MUSIQUE ET DE DANSE Since its founding in 1784, the Conservatoire has featured concerts by its budding students; most are free and aren't planned far in advance—stop by and check the information desk for flyers and schedules. In early 1995, the Conservatoire's performance space in the Parc de la Villette's Cité de Musique will be more than doubled when the rest of the complex is inaugurated. Designed by Christian de Portzamparc, the complex has been one of the quieter successes of Mitterrand's Grands Travaux—not likely to make the tourist circuit, but the international community has taken notice. *209 av. Jean Jaurès, 19e, tel. 1/40–40–46–46. Métro: Porte de Pantin. Wheelchair access.*

EGLISE DE MADELEINE Though it's one of the gloomier churches in Paris (*see* Houses of Worship, in Chapter 2), the Madeleine is a spectacular concert hall; the position of organist here is one of the most coveted musical appointments in Paris. The expansive nave hosts several classical concerts every week; admission usually runs around 140F, 100F for students. *Pl. de la Madeleine, 8e, tel. 1/42–65–52–17. Métro: Madeleine.*

MAISON DE RADIO FRANCE The government's broadcasting center until the privatization of the airwaves, the vast complex is now the seat of little duchies set up by countless radio and TV stations. In addition to studios, meeting halls, and a small museum on itself (tours in French run 14F, 7F for students), the complex includes the smallish, modern Salle Olivier Messiaen, home to the **Orchestre National de France,** which also performs often at larger venues. The orchestra's 1995 Maison de Radio France schedule includes a retrospective of the Viennese musical tradition, a Wagner special including Margaret Price singing the "Prelude et Mort d'Isolde" (March 1995), and a series on contemporary composers. You might enjoy stopping by to catch a rehearsal—you're not really supposed to be here, but act like you are, and the guards just might not notice. Seats are available one month before a show, or turn your radio dial to 91.7 or 92.1 (France Musique) to hear the concert for free. *116 av. du Président Kennedy, 16e, tel. 1/42–30–15–16. Métro: Renelagh. RER: Maison de Radio France. Box office open Mon.–Sat. 11–6.*

The streets behind the Maison de Radio France serve as a kind of showcase for France's best art nouveau architect, Hector Guimard. Most of his interesting stuff is on rue La Fontaine, including No. 14, the beautifully detailed Castel Béranger (1894)—his best-known work—and Nos. 17, 19, 21, 60, and 65. Other examples include 11 rue François-Millet, 120 avenue Mozart, and 18 rue Henri-Heine, where Guimard himself lived.

OPERA BASTILLE In his quest to join the likes of Louis XIV and Napoléon III as one of the grand builders of Paris, President Mitterrand had the Opéra Bastille built on place de la Bastille to replace the renowned Opéra Garnier. Mitterrand's 3-billion-franc project was the city's second redefinition of the opera house and an ambitious attempt to become once again the center of European opera. A half-decade later, the media is declaring Paris's opera doomed because of poor direction, but it's a little early to be giving it last rites just yet.

Inaugurated on July 13, 1989, the Bastille, designed by Uruguayan-born Canadian architect Carlos Ott, received resoundingly negative criticism and was unflatteringly compared to a sports arena. (Ott retorted that he didn't want a modern version of the opulent Second Empire showpiece, the Opéra Garnier.) Though critics continue to sneer, and the checkerboard postmodern facade refuses to dominate the busy place de la Bastille, the Opéra Bastille has received Paris's highest mark of architectural acceptance: Students hang out to smoke and smooch on its black stone steps.

Those who have condemned the building's appearance nonetheless enthusiastically file in to experience the "perfect" acoustics and clear sight lines available to all 2,700 of the democratically designed theater's seats. Directors have taken advantage of the move from the cramped Garnier into their new, expansive digs with elaborate stagings and seemingly eternal seasons. Downstairs from the Grande Salle, the **Studio Bastille** challenges strict traditionalists by offering "Parallèles," an experimental, inexpensive program of recitals and films related to the operas; tickets cost around 25F.

Taking part in all the excitement and controversy requires minimal planning: Tickets go on sale at the box offices two weeks before any given show or a month ahead by phone. Schedules and tickets are available at either Bastille or Garnier. Seats range from 60F to 570F for most shows. Student and youth (under 25) rush tickets cost 100F just before a performance, though for the biggies there's often nothing left; get in line a couple hours in advance if you want any chance at a seat. *120 rue de Lyon, 12e, tel. 1/44–73–13–99 for information, 1/44–73–13–00 for reservations. Métro: Bastille. Box office open Mon.–Sat. 11–6:30. Wheelchair access.*

OPERA COMIQUE The seasons are shorter, the director is less flamboyant, and the late-19th-century building is less grandiose than the Opéra Bastille or Opéra Garnier; the Opéra Comique stages a dozen operas and concerts each season in a more intimate setting than the other major theaters can offer. Concerts by the **Orchestre Symphonique Français** cost only 50F for any seat in the house; other performances cost 40F–500F, with 50F rush tickets available 15 minutes before curtain time to students and those under 26. In 1995, look for Gounod's *Mireille* (Mar. 30–Apr. 18) and alternate performances in Italian and French of Puccini's *La*

Bohème (June 22–July 14). *5 rue Favart, 2e, tel. 1/42–29–12–20. Métro: Richelieu-Drouot. Box office open Fri.–Wed. 11–7, Thurs. 1 hr before curtain.*

OPERA GARNIER The most pompous of all Parisian buildings, the Opéra was built by Charles Garnier after he won an architectural competition in 1861. Unable to settle upon any one style, Garnier chose them all: a Renaissance-inspired detail here, a rococo frill there, Greek shields put up at random. The regal lobby, with grand stairways and a mirrored ballroom, is as big as the auditorium; together they cover over three acres. The hall itself is rich, velvety, and gaudy, with an extraordinary number of gilt statuettes and a ceiling repainted by Marc Chagall in 1964; if you're one of those who spend 30F for the *sans-visibilité* (without visibility) seats, at least you'll have images from Chagall's favorite operas and ballets to stare at.

At the end of the 19th century the Opéra Garnier became a center of Paris's artistic and social life—a place where the haute bourgeoisie could watch a little bit of opera and a lot of each other. It no longer serves either purpose, but it still sits in the middle of place de l'Opéra and provides a home for the **Paris Ballet.** Because of renovations (set to end in mid-1996), the ballet's 1995 season will play at the Bastille, but the building is still open to visitors. Those who spring for the 28F admission fee are allowed to climb the ornate stairway and check out the plush auditorium. A small museum features Degas's simple portrait of Wagner. Tickets (normally from 60F) go on sale a month in advance over the phone or two weeks in advance in person. Call or stop by the Opéra Bastille (*see above*) for ticket information during the 1995 season. *Pl. de l'Opéra, 9e, tel. 1/47–42–57–50. Métro: Opéra. Open daily 11–4:30.*

SAINTE-CHAPELLE While many stunning churches put on performances at night, the intimate size and utter exquisiteness of the building make seeing a concert at Sainte-Chapelle

A Scandal of Operatic Proportions

It's no secret that Parisians have always considered French works of art superior to all others, and nowhere is this more apparent than in their tastes in opera. Until recently, Paris audiences had largely disregarded operas outside the French and Italian traditions. Even Richard Wagner was not welcome here until the very end of his career; his early stays in Paris were marked by poverty and rejection. His racy, Venus-centered orgy of an overture to Tannhaüser caused such an uproar that he had to compose an alternate version for the prudish Parisians. With the 1989 opening of the new Opéra Bastille, though, the management tried to expand the types of opera performed in the city: The 1993–1994 season actually opened with Wagner's Der Holländer (1841) and went on to include Strauss's Salome and Shostakovich's Lady Macbeth. You'd think that such established operas would hardly make a ripple in Paris's opera scene . . . but you'd be wrong. The turnover of artistic and musical directors within the opera's first decade has been remarkably speedy, as very mixed reviews of the opera's performances pour in. Most recently, in September 1994, the newest musical director, South Korean Myung Whun Chung, was asked to renegotiate his contract almost immediately after being awarded it. He refused and was consequently physically blocked from entering the house for rehearsals. The court ordered his contract be honored and specified he was to be paid $9,260 for each day his access to rehearsals was blocked. Apparently, incoming opera director Hugues Gall wants utter artistic control and approves of neither Chung's six-year contract nor his power of artistic veto. Chung is back in the seat for now, but Gall vows he'll have the last word.

(*see* Houses of Worship, in Chapter 2) worth the cost and hassle of getting a ticket. Most seats start at 120F, and the concerts, mainly small classical ensembles, often sell out early. *4 blvd. du Palais, 1er, tel. 1/42–05–25–23. Métro: Cité.*

SALLE PLEYEL Another grand old hall, this one has the unique distinction of having hosted Chopin's last public performance. These days it's the main stomping ground of the **Orchestre de Paris,** which will give a concert version of Berlioz's *La Damnation de Faust* in May 1995. The hall also sees some dance and jazz, including regular stops by the **Golden Gate Quartet.** Tickets are sold on a looser schedule than at other theaters; call about specific shows. *252 rue du Faubourg-St-Honoré, 8e, tel. 1/45–63–07–40. Métro: Ternes. Box office open Mon.–Sat. 11–6.*

THEATRE DE LA VILLE The fraternal twin of the Beaux-Arts Chatelet across the place, the Théâtre de la Ville stages comtemporary dance and music in its starkly renovated theater. In 1899, Sarah Bernhardt bought the theater, named it after herself, and began performing regularly here. When the city took over, it naturally renamed the hall after itself, and now only the café next door and the fine print over the theater's entrance bear Sarah's name. Most shows have seats at 90F and 140F. *2 pl. du Châtelet, 4e, tel. 1/42–74–22–77. Métro: Châtelet. Box office open Mon. 9–6, Tues.–Sat. 9–8. Wheelchair access on Seine side of building.*

THEATRE DES CHAMPS-ELYSEES This large, fancy musical theater stages a bit of everything—operatic soloists, ballets, orchestras, marionette shows, and jazz acts. Tickets generally run 40F–700F; for students, all seats are half price 30 minutes before the show, except for Orchestre National de France (*see* Maison de Radio France, *above*) concerts, when all seats drop to the lowest price. *15 av. Montaigne, 8e, tel. 1/49–52–50–50. Métro: Franklin D. Roosevelt. Box office open Mon.–Sat. 11–7.*

THEATRE MUSICAL DE PARIS–CHATELET Ideally located on the place du Châtelet by the Seine, the Théâtre Musical is less self-important and less worried about catering to the crowds than its famous cousins, the Opéras Bastille and Garnier. The excellence of the theater's productions tends to draw a devoted crowd—nobody claps between arias. The hall is discreet by Parisian standards, though no late-19th-century theater could forgo frilly detailing and plush red velvet. The 1995 season includes operas like *La Petite Renarde rusée* and *Fidelio*; dance by the Frankfurt Ballet; and a 40-concert cycle of Ludwig van Beethoven's compositions, including the famous *Ninth Symphony* performed by the chorus and orchestra of the Berlin Staatsoper. Tickets cost 55F and up, with 50F rush tickets available 15 minutes before curtain time to students with ID or those under 20. The theater is also continuing its "Midis Musicaux" (Musical Noons) series, with concerts in the foyer on Monday, Wednesday, and Friday, starting at 12:45; seats cost 50F. *1 pl. du Châtelet, 1er, tel. 1/40–28–28–40. Métro: Châtelet. Box office open daily 11–7. Wheelchair entrance 17 bis av. Victoria.*

Kiosque Théâtre, on the place de la Madeleine and in the Châtelet RER station, sells half-price tickets for same-day shows in any theater in Paris. Both locations are open Tuesday through Saturday from 12:30 PM and accept Visa. Count on waiting in line.

THEATER

CHAILLOT Founded by Jean Vilar in post–World War II Paris as part of the movement to revive live theater, France's first *théâtre national* stages highly regarded theatrical and musical productions in its two halls under the terrace of the Trocadéro. The 1995 season includes a recital by soprano Ute Lemper and *Savannah Bay* by Marguerite Duras. Tickets run 80F–150F, depending on the show and your status; discounted student rush tickets are available on the day of the performance. *1 pl. du Trocadéro, 16e, tel. 1/47–27–81–15. Métro: Trocadéro. Box office open Mon.–Sat. 11–7, Sun. 11–5.*

COMEDIE-FRANCAISE–SALLE RICHELIEU The Comédie-Française traces its origins to 1680, when Louis XIV merged Molière's acting company with other troupes, establishing the first completely French theater. The group lost its lease in 1770, but Louis XV saved the Comédie-Française by ordering the construction of the Odéon; four years later the troupe was brought under even tighter royal control with the construction of the Théâtre Français (now called the Salle Richelieu) in the Palais Royal. Since then, this stage has been the permanent playground for the ghosts of Great French Theater.

The Comédie-Française has a reputation as a bastion of traditionalism; the fact that the lobby holds the chair in which Molière collapsed and died after a performance in 1673 only reinforces this myth. The company, however, doesn't always produce Racine and Molière; sometimes they branch out to Camus. Tickets run 45F–165F, with 65F rush tickets available 45 minutes before curtain time to students and those under 25. *2 rue de Richelieu, 1e, tel. 1/40–15–00–15. Métro: Palais Royal–Musée du Louvre. Box office open daily 11–6.*

COMEDIE-FRANCAISE/THEATRE DU VIEUX-COLOMBIER Founded in 1913 by Jacques Copeau, the Théâtre du Vieux-Colombier has traditionally staged the works of controversial playwrights, including Sartre, Federico García Lorca, and Arthur Miller. The company folded 60 years after its opening, but the state acquired the theater in 1986, putting it under the control of a Comédie-Française eager to have a venue for non-Racine-like productions. The theater was beautifully renovated in 1993 and now stages plays by Marivaux and Duras, among others. All seats are 130F; 60F rush tickets are available 45 minutes before curtain time to students and those under 25. *21 rue du Vieux-Colombier, 6e, tel. 1/44–39–87–00. Métro: St-Sulpice. Box office open Tues.–Sat. 11–7, Sun. 1–6. Wheelchair access.*

ODEON THEATRE DE L'EUROPE Under the direction of Lluís Pasqual, the Odéon has made pan-European theater the primary focus at its temple-like digs. The 1995 season will feature British productions, with *Hamlet* playing in late June. Tickets run 90F–170F, with half-price rush tickets available 50 minutes before curtain time. Student tickets are always 20F less. The basement holds the experimental **Petit Odéon,** where all seats cost 70F. *1 pl. Paul Claudel, 6e, tel. 1/44–41–36–36. Métro: Odéon. Box office open Mon.–Sat. 11–6:30.*

THEATRE DE LA HUCHETTE It was at La Huchette that Eugène Ionesco—whose death in 1994 saddened the literary and dramatic worlds—founded and developed a theatrical and philosophical style that came to be known as Theater of the Absurd. Parisians, while somewhat confused by Ionesco's surreal story lines, were so smitten by his words that his first produced

Theaters on the Fringe

As Paris becomes more and more self-consciously crowd-pleasing, the more innovative—and often more interesting—theaters seem to be pushed farther and farther out of the center. Here are a couple of theaters worth the trip:

- *Cartoucherie Théâtre du Soleil. A four-stage complex run by avant-garde director Ariane Mnouchkine hosts refreshing shows for 260F a seat, 220F for students. Rte. du Champ de Manoeuvre, 12e, tel. 1/43–74–24–08. Métro: Château de Vincennes (then free shuttle to theater).*

- *Centre Dramatique National–Théâtre Gennevilliers. Seats cost 130F, 110F for those under 25, for such productions as May 1995's Peer Gynt by Ibsen. 41 av. des Grésillons, Gennevilliers, tel. 1/47–93–26–30. Métro: Gabriel Péri.*

- *Maison de la Culture–Bobigny. The 1994–95 season includes Peter Sellars's version of The Merchant of Venice and a visit from St. Petersburg's Maly Theater. Tickets cost 130F, 95F for those under 25. 1 blvd. Lénine, Bobigny, tel. 1/48–31–11–45. Métro: Bobigny–Pablo Picasso.*

play, *La Cantatrice chauve,* has been performed every night in the city since its premiere in 1950. Both it and Ionesco's 1951 play *La Leçon* have played at La Huchette for years (exactly how many is a matter of dispute). *23 rue de la Huchette, 5e, tel. 1/43–26–38–99. Métro: St-Michel. Tickets: 100F, 70F students ages 25 and under except for Sat. performances. Box office open Mon.–Sat. 5–9:30. Wheelchair access.*

THEATRE NATIONAL DE LA COLLINE This glass-and-concrete mass of urban sophistication behind place Gambetta is a major part of the emerging *nouvelle culture* (new culture) of Belleville and produces large-scale, mildly controversial plays (a lot of Beckett and Lamas). All seats run 150F, 110F for students and those under 25. Classical concerts produced by Radio France (seats 100F) are given from time to time. There are no rush tickets, but students age 25 and under can get 60F seats for Saturday-afternoon performances in the Grande Salle or Wednesday shows in the Petite Salle. *15 rue Malte-Brun, 20e, tel. 1/44–62–52–52. Métro: Gambetta. Box office open Tues.–Sat. 11–9, Sun. and Mon. 11-6. Wheelchair access.*

SMALLER VENUES **Les Bouffes du Nord.** Founded by famed British theater man Peter Brook, whose influence ensures a continuing repertoire of out-of-the-ordinary productions, this theater is beautifully decrepit, lending an otherworldly feel to any performance. Tickets are cheap: 40F–130F. *37 bis blvd. de la Chapelle, 10e, tel. 1/46–07–34–50. Métro: La Chapelle.*

La Crypte St-Sulpice. In late 1993, a new venture sprang up underneath the Eglise St-Sulpice. So far, productions are few and amateurish, but the setting is fantastical, so check by to see how things are progressing. Seats (only 90 per show) cost 100F. *40 rue St-Sulpice, 6e, no phone.*

Théâtre de la Bastille. Trendy and experimental theater and dance productions appropriate to the neighborhood go on in this black-toned, minimalist hall. Tickets are almost always 100F, 70F for students. *76 rue de la Roquette, 11e, tel. 1/43–57–42–14. Métro: Bastille.*

CAFE-THEATRE This subgenre of Paris theater is devoted to low-budget, comedic or musical, and potentially subversive productions. Unless your French is pretty good, you'll have a hard time understanding, but it's still worth it—these little shows often present funny views and critiques of French society and culture. Despite the name, most café-théâtres do not sell refreshments. Some well-known and popular venues include **Au Bec Fin** (6 rue Thérèse, 1er, tel. 1/42–96–29–35), with fairly large-scale productions, and **Le Point Virgule** (7 rue Ste-Croix-de-la-Brétonnerie, 4e, tel. 1/42–78–67–03), which specializes in comedy.

Café d'Edgar. Tongue-in-cheek skits are the specialty at this small, red-benched café-theater in Montparnasse. Three shows are performed nightly except Sunday, and the price is 80F a show, 65F for students during the week, and 65F for everyone on Monday. *58 blvd. Edgar Quinet, 14e, tel. 1/42–79–97–97. Métro: Edgar Quinet.*

Café de la Gare. A happy crowd piles onto wooden benches to catch the comedies at this popular theater where the young Gérard Depardieu and Miou-Miou have played. On stage are two quality 1½-hour shows per night at 80F, 50F on Tuesday. *41 rue du Temple, 4e, tel. 1/42–78–52–51. Métro: Hôtel-de-Ville. Closed Sun.–Mon.*

ENGLISH-LANGUAGE THEATER A healthy number of Parisian theaters host occasional English-language productions. Paris-based English-language troupes to look out for (especially at the theaters listed below) include **Dear Conjunction,** the **Gare St-Lazare Players,** and the **On Stage Theater Company,** though larger troupes like the Royal Shakespeare Company also pass through the city.

Théâtre de la Main d'Or. The student-oriented company **ACT** is based here and performs both in this former garage and at schools throughout Paris. In 1995 the Main d'Or will see their productions of Arthur Miller's A *View from the Bridge* (April 3–15) and Sue Townshend's *The Secret Diary of Adrian Mole* (March 20–April 2). Tickets are 140F, 80F for students. *15 passage de la Main d'Or, 11e, tel. 1/48–05–67–89; ACT tel. 1/47–00–33–88. Métro: Ledru-Rollin. Wheelchair access.*

Théâtre Marie Stuart. The English-language Compagnie Robert Cordier is based here and puts on some of the most highly acclaimed small productions in Paris, many of them bilingual. Tickets run 75F and up, 55F and up for students. *4 rue Marie Stuart, 2e, tel. 1/45–08–17–80. Métro: Etienne Marcel.*

Performing Arts Schedules

The following are the dates and times of many of the performances scheduled during the 1994–1995 season at Paris's major concert halls and theaters. For schedules of events for the 1995–1996 season, which swings into full gear in September 1995, stop by the individual venues for brochures once the season begins.

CLASSICAL MUSIC AND DANCE

OPERA BASTILLE The Ballet de l'Opéra National de Paris is dancing here while the Opéra Garnier is being renovated.

➤ **OPERA** • Gaetano's Donizetti's *Lucia di Lammermoor.* February 1, 4, 8, 11, 14, and 17 and April 5, 8, 11, 14, and 20 at 7:30 PM; April 16 at 3 PM.

Hector Berlioz's *La Damnation de Faust.* Februrary 9, 15, 18, 20, 23, 25, and 28 at 7:30 PM; March 2 at 7:30 PM; March 5 at 3 PM.

Giuseppe Verdi's *Un Bal Masqué.* March 16, 20, 23, 29, and 31 and April 4 at 7:30 PM; March 26 at 3 PM.

Christoph Willibald Gluck's *Iphigénie en Tauride.* April 18, 21, 24, and 27 and May 4, 6, 9, and 12 at 7:30 PM.

Wolfgang Amadeus Mozart's *La Flûte Enchantée.* May 3, 5, 8, 10, 13, 16, and 20 at 7:30 PM.

Vincenzo Bellini's *Les Capulet et les Montaigu.* May 26 and 30 and June 3, 5, 9, and 12 at 7:30 PM.

➤ **BALLET** • *Magnificat.* Music by Johann Sebastian Bach, choreography by John Neumeier. March 6, 7, 8, 9, 10, 11, 15, 17, and 18 at 7:30 PM.

Nijinska/Nijinski. Including "Noces," music by Igor Stravinski, choreography by Bronislava Nijinska; "Till Eulenspiegel," music by Richard Strauss, choreography by Vaslav Nijinksi; and "La Sacre du Printemps," music by Igor Stravinsky, choreography by Vaslav Nijinski. June 7, 8, 10, 13, 14, 15, 16, and 17 at 7:30 PM.

Giselle. Music by Adolphe Adam, choreography by Jean Coralli, Jules Perrot, Patrice Bart, and Eugène Polyakov. June 20, 21, 22, 23, 24, 26, 27, 28, 29, and 30 at 7:30 PM.

Romeo et Juliette. Music by Sergey Prokofiev, choreography by Rudolf Nureyev. July 6, 7, 8, 10, 11, 12, 13, and 15 at 7:30 PM; free matinee on July 14 and 15.

OPERA COMIQUE As well as the major events listed below and some smaller productions, the Opéra Comique hosts **Pro Musicis,** an international contest for upcoming musicians. Concerts are given twice, once at normal rates and once free for those who rarely get to concerts (i.e., the elderly, the disabled). Shows are at 8 PM on January 30, February 13, April 3, May 22, and June 27. Call the Pro Musicis foundation (8 rue François Miron, 4e, tel. 1/42–77–95–30) for tickets. The **Orchestre Symphonique Français** will also be performing three different shows here on February 17 (8 PM), April 9 (4 PM), and June 15 (8 PM).

➤ **OPERA** • Leo Delibes's *Lakmé.* January 31 and February 2, 3, 4, 6, 8, 9, 10, 11, 14, 15, 16, and 18 at 7:30 PM; Februrary 12 at 4 PM.

Charles Gounod's *Mireille.* March 30 and 31 and April 1, 4, 5, 7, 8, 10, 11, and 13 at 7:30 PM; April 2 at 4 PM.

Gian Carlo Menotti's *Le Médium* and Marcel Landowski's *Les Adieux.* April 25, 26, 27, and 28 at 7:30 PM.

Giacomo Puccini's *La Bohème.* Shows in Italian June 22 and 28 and July 1, 5, 8, 11, and 14 at 7:30 PM; June 25 at 4 PM. Shows in French June 23, 26, and 29 and July 4, 7, 10, and 13 at 7:30 PM; July 2 at 4 PM.

➤ **DANCE** • *Requiem*. Music by by Wolfgang Amadeus Mozart, choreography by Alain Germain. Performed by La Compagnie Alain Germain. February 21, 22, 23, 24, and 25 at 8 PM.

Les caprices de Cupidon (music Jenz Lolle), *Daphnis et Chloé* (music Maurice Ravel), and *Mouvements* (music Sergey Prokofiev). Performed by Ecole du Ballet de l'Opéra National de Paris. March 17 and 18 at 8 PM; March 18 and 19 at 2:30 PM.

Extraits du répertoire du XXème siècle. Performed by Les Etoiles du Ballet de l'Opera National de Paris. May 10, 11, 12, 13, 15, 16, 17, and 18 at 7:30 PM.

SALLE PLEYEL Though the Salle Pleyel sees some jazz and other small ensembles, their main role is as home to the Orchestre de Paris. All shows start at 8:30 unless otherwise indicated.

February 1 and 3: Wagner's *Die Walküre* Act I, concert version. **Februrary 8 and 9:** Stravinsky's *Les Noces*; Shostakovich's Symphony no. 4 in C Minor. **February 15 and 16:** John Adams's Violin Concerto; Bruckner's Symphony no. 7 in E. **Februrary 22 and 23:** Prokofiev's Symphony no. 1 "Classical"; Schnittke's Viola Concerto; Stravinsky's *Rites of Spring*.

March 1 and 2: Honegger's Symphony no. 2; Saint-Saëns's Piano Concerto no. 2 in G Minor; Dvorak's Symphony no. 9 "New World." **March 8 and 9:** Debussy's *Music for King Lear, Martyre de St-Sébastien,* and symphonic fragments; Hollinger's *Trakl Lieder*; Berg's *Lulu*. **March 15 and 16:** Mendelssohn's *A Midsummer Night's Dream* Overture; Schumann's Piano Concerto in A Minor; Tchaikovsky's Symphony no. 6 "Pathétique." **March 22, 23, and 25** (4 PM): Schubert's Symphony no. 8 "Unfinished" and Mass no. 6 in E-flat.

April 5 and 6: Mahler's *Rückert Lieder* and Symphony no. 1. **April 12 and 13:** Schubert's Symphony no. 4 "Tragic"; Wagner's *Wesendonck Lieder*; Chausson's *Poème de l'amour et de la mer*; Saint-Saëns's *Le Rouet d'Omphale, Danse macabre.* **April 19 and 20:** Mendelssohn's Symphony no. 1; Mozart's Violin Concerto no. 5 in A (K. 219); Haydn's Symphony no. 100 "Military." **April 26 and 27:** Janáček's *Suite for string orchestra*; Mozart's Symphonic Concerto for Violin and Alto (K. 364); Brahms's Piano Concerto no. 1 in D-minor.

May 17, 18, and 20 (4 PM). Berlioz's *La Damnation de Faust.*

THEATRE MUSICAL DE PARIS-CHATELET In addition to the concerts, operas, and listed below, the **Ballett Frankfurt** will be in residence here in June and July. Their first program will be performed at 8:30 PM on June 19, 20, 21, 22, 23, and 24; the second program at 8:30 PM on June 28, 29, 30 and July 1 and 3; and at 3 PM on July 2. Beethoven fans can gorge themselves during the 40-concert Beethoven Cycle from October 1994 to June 1995; pick up the schedule for a complete list of performances, but potential highlights include Symphony no. 6 "Pastoral," op. 68 on April 1 at 8 PM; Symphony no. 9, op. 125 on April 21 at 8 PM; Symphony no. 3 "Eroica" op. 55 on June 7 at 8 PM; and the *Missa solemnis,* op. 123 on June 16 at 8 PM.

➤ **OPERA** • Henry Purcell's *King Arthur, or the British Worthy.* February 9, 10, 13, 14, 16, and 18 at 7:30; February 12 and 19 at 3.

Benjamin Britten's *Peter Grimes*. March 25, 28, and 30 and April 4 at 7:30; April 2 at 5 PM.

Ludwig van Beethoven's *Fidelio.* April 19, 22, 24, and 27 at 7:30; April 29 at 8:30.

Leoš Janáček's *La Petite Renard rusée,* May 29 and June 1, 6, and 8 at 7:30; June 11 at 5 PM.

➤ **CONCERTS** • Concerts are at 8 PM unless otherwise noted.

February 22: Philharmonia Orchestra performs Symphony no. 4, op. 98 and Symphony no. 2, op. 73 (Brahms). **February 23**: Philharmonia Orchestra performs Symphony no. 3, op. 90 and Symphony no. 1, op. 68 (Brahms).

May 10: *Morgenmusik* (Paul Hindemith); *The 1.X.1905,* (Leoš Janáček); *Legend* (Georges Enesco) *In memoriam György Zilcz* (György Kurtag); *Capriccio* (Leoš Janáček). **May 13**: Quartet for Piano and String Trio (Gustav Mahler); *Sonata* for violin and piano, *Presto* for cello and piano, *Fairytales* for cello and piano, and *Concertino* for piano and small ensemble (Leoš Janaček); *Serenade* for two violins and viola, op. 12 (Zoltan Kodaly). **May 16:** *Sonatine* for oboe, clarinet, and bassoon (Sandor Veress); *Sonata* for bassoon (Edison Denisov); *Ten Pieces* for wind quintet (György Ligeti); *Wind quintet,* op. 2 (György Kurtag); *Mládi* ("Youth") for wind sextet (Leoš Janaček).

June 10, 11 AM: *Projection,* from one of Leonard Bernstein's youth concerts. June 14, 3 PM: Extracts from *La Petite Renarde rusée* (Leoš Janaček). **June 15:** *Sequenza for bassoon* (Luciano Berio). **June 25,** 4 PM: *Turangalîla-Symphonie* (Olivier Messiaen).

THEATER

COMEDIE-FRANCAISE–SALLE RICHELIEU Because of theater renovations, only general information about the 1995 season was available at press time. Look for George Fédo's *Occupe-toi d'Amelie* and Molière's *Don Juan* (January and February), Schiller's *Intrigue et Amour* and Racine's *La thébaide* (March and April), and Hugo's *Mille francs de récompense* and Kleist's *Le Prince d'Homberg* (May and June).

COMEDIE-FRANCAISE–THEATRE DU VIEUX COLOMBIER In addition to the following productions, look for smaller Saturday-afternoon productions of the "Les Samedis du Vieux-Colombier" series.

Marivaux's *La Double Inconstance* (1723). February 1, 3, 4, 7, and 8 at 8:30 PM; February 2 and 9 at 7 PM; February 5 at 4 PM.

Marguerite Duras's *Le Square/Le Shaga* (1955). March 14, 15, 17, 18, 21, 22, 24, 25, 28, 29, and 31 and April 1, 4, and 5 at 8:30 PM; March 16, 23, and 30 and April 6 at 7 PM; March 19 and 26 and April 2 at 4 PM.

Racine's *Bajazet.* May 9, 10, 12, 13, 16, 17, 19, 20, 23, 24, 26, 27, 30, and 31 at 8:30 PM; May 11 and 18 and June 1 at 7 PM; and May 14, 21, and 28 at 4 PM.

ODEON–THEATRE DE L'EUROPE The following is the schedule of pieces that will be staged in the Grande Salle. Call for info about smaller experimental productions in the Petit Odéon.

Hated Nightfall, written and directed by Howard Barker. In English with French subtitles. February 1, 3, and 4 at 8:30 PM; February 2 at 7:30; and February 5 at 3 PM.

The Castle by Howard Barker, directed by Kenny Ireland. In English with French subtitles. February 7, 8, 10, and 11 at 8:30 PM; February 9 at 7:30.

Le Baladin du Monde Occidental by John Synge, directed by André Engel. In French. March 15, 17, 18, 21, 22, 24, 25, 28, 29, and 31 and April 1, 4, 5, 7, 8, 11, 12, 14, 15, 18, 19, 21, 22, 25, 26, 28, and 29 at 8:30; March 16, 23, and 30 and April 6, 13, 20, and 27 at 7:30 PM; March 19 and 26 and April 2, 9, 16, 23, and 30 at 3 PM.

Peines d'Amour Perdues by William Shakespeare, directed by Laurent Pelly. In French. May 16, 17, 19, 20, 23, 24, 26, 27, 30, and 31 and June 2, 3, 6, 7, 9, 10, 13, 14, 16, and 17 at 8:30 PM; May 18 and 25 and June 1, 8, and 15 at 7:30 PM; May 21 and 28 and June 4, 11, and 18 at 3 PM.

Hamlet by William Shakespeare, directed by Sam Mendes. In English, with French subtitles. June 27, 28, and 30 and July 1 at 8:30 PM; June 29 at at 7:30; July 2 at 3 PM.

SHOPPING 6

By Baty Landis

Stores in Paris take all forms: World-famous designers like Issey Miyake have their primary boutiques here; the *grands magasins* (department stores) flaunt the latest popular styles; chains like Pro-Mod and Kookai provide hipsters with stylish looks; and secondhand shops bring it all back at slashed prices. But if you thought you'd find some great fashion bargains here on haute couture's home turf, think again. That great suit you find in the boutique where the doorknobs are shaped like Chanel No. 5 crystal perfume stoppers just *might* be cheaper at home—if your home has any stores that sell Chanel, that is.

That's not to say you have to go home empty-handed. Flea markets, used-book stores, and vintage-clothing shops are great places to pick up goods that are at least French, if not necessarily chic. August and January are religiously observed as sale periods, so save most of your shopping for these months if you're able. But be aware that in France, shoppers' rights are less sacred than in the United States: Often you're not allowed to try on heavily discounted items before buying, and returns are virtually unheard of (though exchanges are usually okay). Most stores stay open until 6 or 7 PM and close on Sundays, and many take a lunch break some time between noon and 2 PM. All the grands magasins accept American Express, MasterCard, and Visa. You can also use a Visa or MasterCard at many specialty stores, though some of the smaller places take only cash.

Some shopping lingo: soldes—sale; braderie—clearance; occasion or brocante—secondhand; nouveautés—new arrivals; dépôts-ventes—last season's unsold clothes.

Grands Magasins

The grands magasins are among Paris's greatest contributions to modern consumerism. Started by upper-middle-class merchant families in the mid-19th century, these huge establishments attracted the curious and the wealthy who flocked to these stores to buy fabrics, furniture, and other items imported from France's all-too-vast empire. Au Bon Marché, whose huge, glamorous halls became the model for La Samaritaine, Galeries Lafayette, and a proliferation of department stores in New York and London, opened its doors in 1869. By the end of the century, the grands magasins had changed the nature of shopping in Paris, to the detriment of the city's small neighborhood stores.

Au Bon Marché. The world's oldest grand magasin, with a central structure designed by Mr. Eiffel himself, sells itself as a more down-to-earth establishment than its Right Bank counterparts. Well, maybe . . . it's a stretch. Certainly the clientele is a bit more mixed, but the clothes

Zola spent several months doing research at Au Bon Marché before writing "Au Bonheur des Dames" (The Ladies' Paradise), his examination of the symbolic, social, and economic significance of the grands magasins in late-19th-century Paris.

are basically the same. The music section offers 20% discounts on new releases, and the extensive art supplies department has a wide selection of prints. While you're here, don't miss the gourmet grocery store annex (*see* Non-French Foods, in Chapter 4). *rue de Sèvres and rue de Babylone, 7e, tel. 1/44–39–80–80. Métro: Sèvres-Babylone. Open Mon.–Sat. 9:30–5.*

Au Printemps. Behind the Opéra, Au Printemps competes for customers with Galeries Lafayette next door, making for easy price comparisons if you actually want to buy something. The building itself isn't very appealing—unless you climb all the way to the colorfully domed top-floor café—since modernization has marred most of the original 19th-century decor. The three-store complex displays housewares, furniture, and scads of clothing for men and women. Free fashion shows happen every Tuesday and Friday morning at 10; go to the information desk ahead of time to get an invitation. *64 blvd. Haussmann, 9e, tel. 1/42–82–50–00. Métro: Havre-Caumartin. Open Mon.–Sat. 9:30–7.*

BHV. The store's name stands for Bazar de l'Hôtel de Ville, referring to the original BHV location. This unglamorous grand magasin is slightly cheaper than the others, specializes in housewares, and has a huge basement hardware department. Its clothing selection is minimal. *52 rue de Rivoli, 4e, tel. 1/42–74–90–00. Métro: Hôtel-de-Ville. Open Mon.–Sat. 9:30–7, Wed. until 10.*

Galeries Lafayette. This successful store has branches throughout France. The main store's central gallery features counters of designer beauty products under a stained-glass dome. Wading through the trendy boutiques and stylish shoppers, climb up to one of the six interior wrought-iron balconies for a different perspective on the frenzy below. *40 blvd. Haussmann, 9e, tel. 1/42–82–36–40. Métro: Opéra or Havre-Caumartin. Open Mon.–Sat. 9:30–7, Thurs. until 9.*

La Samaritaine. This sprawling magasin dominates a whole section of rue de Rivoli east of the Louvre. It specializes in pricey household items, though the snacks sold in the basement food hall are usually a pretty good deal. Samaritaine also offers what locals generally consider the best view of Paris; follow the PANORAMIC signs to the rooftop terrace, where a café serves lunch until 3 PM. If you arrive later, you can order just a drink (coffee 10F, beer 15F) and gaze out the window. *19 rue de la Monnaie, 1er, tel. 1/40–41–20–20. Métro: Pont-Neuf. Open Mon.–Sat. 9:30–7, Thurs. until 10.*

Specialty Stores

ANTIQUES

The only cheap places to buy antiques are the flea markets (*see below*), but that doesn't mean you can't have fun poking around some of the shops. **Louvre des Antiquaires** (2 pl. du Palais-Royal, 1er, tel. 1/42–97–27–00) is a mall designed for and completely devoted to small dealers in antiques; here you can check out large collections of war medals, china, or antique weapons. **Village St-Paul,** between rues St-Paul and Charlemagne in the Marais, is a little "village" of shops open Thursday through Monday 11–7, selling small furniture and general junk (no offense, collectors of old water bottles). The **sixth arrondissement** is full of shops selling old-fashioned goods at too-modern prices.

ART SUPPLIES

Prices for art supplies in Paris are surprisingly reasonable—only slightly more expensive than in the States. The biggest concentration of stores is in **St-Germain-des-Prés** (thanks to the Ecole des Beaux-Arts), in Montparnasse, and in gallery districts like the **Bastille,** where shops tend to be less showy and more practical. For **photography** equipment, dozens of **Fnac Services** branches offer supplies, including Ilford papers and film, at pretty reasonable prices. The Fnac at 136 rue de Rennes in Montparnasse has by far the best selection. The staff there knows a lot about photography and is extremely helpful.

C.T.S. Individual- and industrial-size containers of paints, plasters, and other materials brewed from C.T.S.'s own recipes sit alongside more mainstream brands. A 20-ml tube of house extrafine oil paint starts at 17F. *26 passage Thiéré, 11e, tel. 1/43–55–60–44. Métro: Bastille. Open weekdays 9–1 and 2–6:30, Sat. 9–1.*

Graphigro. Parisian art students frequent this chain, which sells all types of paints, papers, and other materials. The two-story branch on rue de Rennes offers about the largest selection you'll find in any one spot. A 200-ml tube of Amsterdam oil paint costs 65F. *133 rue de Rennes, 6e, tel. 1/42–22–51–80. Métro: Rennes. Open Mon.–Sat. 10–7.*

Rennes 80. This store has links to the Ecole des Beaux-Arts and so carries many of the materials recommended for students there. The prices are comparable to elsewhere in the neighborhood, though the service is less friendly. *80 rue de Rennes, 6e, tel. 1/45–48–54–27. Métro: St-Sulpice. Open Tues.–Sat. 10–7, Mon. 3–7.*

BOOKSTORES

French people love their books. You'll see them reading on the Métro, in the park, and even while walking their dogs—quite a change if you come from a country where reading is regarded as only slightly less useful than, say, banging your head against the wall. **Fnac,** with four major locations in the city, and **Gibert Jeune** (pl. St-Michel, 6e, tel. 1/43–25–70–07) are the big mainstream bookstores. Don't miss the **bouquinistes,** small-time used-book sellers who also peddle old postcards, prints, and other knickknacks from stalls along the banks of the Seine. If you look hard, you might find some great antique books.

ENGLISH-LANGUAGE BOOKSTORES Paris has several English-language bookstores. **Brentano's** (37 av. de l'Opéra, 2e, tel. 1/42–61–52–50), **Galignani** (224 rue de Rivoli, 1er, tel. 1/42–60–76–07), and **W. H. Smith** (248 rue de Rivoli, 1er, tel. 1/44–77–88–99) carry a wide selection of big, shiny, expensive books in English—a single paperback volume can cost 75F or more. All three are closed Sunday. Before you forgo breakfast, lunch, and dinner to buy a

Parisian Passages

The early 19th century witnessed the creation of the passages, iron-and-glass structures covering the ruelles (tiny streets) of Paris's village-like neighborhoods. Quickly becoming a center of commercial and social life, the passages provided a well-lit, sheltered environment for residents to visit the shops, cafés, and bars lining the street. Though city planner Baron Haussmann wiped out most of these tiny passageways in favor of wide, open-air boulevards, several passages remain in the first, second, and ninth arrondissements. Galerie Vero Dodat (off rue J.-J. Rousseau, 1er), decorated with luxurious, dark wood paneling, houses specialty shops, galleries, and cafés. Passage Choiseul (rue des Petits-Champs and rue St-Augustin, 2e) has less picturesque but cheaper dress shops and toy stores; poet Paul Verlaine (1844–1896) had his first verses published at No. 23, the former workplace of editor Alphonse Lemerre. Galerie Colbert (off rue des Petits-Champs near pl. des Victoires, 2e) has been redone but is still a pleasant place to wander through galleries and boutiques and have a cup of tea. Passage Verdeau (off rue du Montmartre, 9e) is a bit run-down but lined with shops selling antique books and photographs, as well as a casual café and bar.

copy of John Grisham's latest, check out the city's numerous sources for used English-language books.

The Abbey. This two-story Franco-Canadian enterprise specializes in literature from Québec. Their fine French and English selection includes both new and used books. *29 rue de la Parcheminerie, 5e, tel. 1/46–33–16–24. Métro: St-Michel. Open Mon.–Sat. 11–8.*

Shakespeare and Company. This institution has long acted as a haven for expatriates, including Joyce and Hemingway, who hung out here when it was a literary salon. The original founder, Sylvia Beach, published Joyce's *Ulysses* in 1922 after it was deemed obscene and turned down by other publishers. Nowadays you can find new and used books for as little as 15F. Check out the bulletin board for apartment rentals, goods for sale, and French-English conversation exchanges. The store periodically hosts poetry readings and literary discussions. *37 rue de la Bûcherie, 5e, tel. 1/43–26–96–50. Métro: St-Michel. Open daily noon–midnight.*

Tea and Tattered Pages. This tiny, cluttered, and eminently comfortable little shop near Tour Montparnasse sells knickknacks and used English-language books, with a few German and Spanish works thrown in for good measure. The tearoom in back serves brownies, cheesecake, and muffins, and hosts occasional literary talks on French and English literature. There's even a basket of free books in front for the especially hard-up. *24 rue Mayet, 6e, tel. 1/40–65–94–35. Métro: Duroc. Open daily 11–7.*

FEMINIST BOOKSTORES **La Fourmi Ailée.** This bookshop has a large selection of literary works by women and a refined tearoom in back where you can enjoy a pot of tea (25F) and two scones (33F) while you read. *8 rue du Fouarre, 5e, tel. 1/43–29–40–99. Métro: St-Michel. Open Wed.–Mon. 12–7.*

La Librairie des Femmes. This feminist bookstore is strong on theoretical feminist texts and weaker on activist/radical/lesbian books. *74 rue de Seine, 6e, tel. 1/43–29–50–75. Métro: Mabillon. Open Mon.–Sat. 10–7.*

FOREIGN-LANGUAGE BOOKSTORES **Ediciones Hispano-Americanas.** This is a small but thorough collection of Spanish and Latin-American novels, political and cultural books, and critical studies, in Spanish only. *26 rue Monsieur-le-Prince, 6e, tel. 1/43–26–03–79. Métro: Odéon. Open Mon. 1–6:30, Tues.–Sat. 10–6:30.*

Editeurs Réunis. This large bookstore specializes in Russian books, with hundreds of original-language texts on every subject imaginable. A small section is devoted to French translations

---

Extra-Special Specialty Bookstores

- *Aux Films du Temps. Books on filmmaking and film history, as well as posters and magazines. 8 rue St-Martin, 4e, tel. 1/42–71–93–48. Métro: Châtelet.*

- *Cosmos 2000. For all you sci-fi and comic strip fans. 17 rue l'Arc de Triomphe, 17e, tel. 1/43–80–30–74. Métro: Charles de Gaulle–Etoile.*

- *L'Espace Bleu. All manner of spiritual texts and books on alternative medicine and yoga. 91 rue de Seine, 6e, tel. 1/43–54–99–00. Métro: Mabillon.*

- *Librairie Gourmande. Cookbooks and new and used literature on the art of cooking. 4 rue Dante, 5e, tel. 1/43–54–37–27. Métro: St-Michel.*

- *La Librairie Musicale de Paris. Music scores, books about music, metronomes, and other music accessories. 68 bis rue Réamur, 3e, tel. 1/42–72–30–72. Métro: Réaumur-Sébastopol.*

of major Russian works. *11 rue de la Montagne-Ste-Geneviève, 5e, tel. 1/43–54–74–46. Métro: Maubert-Mutualité. Open Tues.–Sat. 9:30–6:30.*

Librairie de l'Inde..The mostly French translations of Indian texts in this tiny shop are spiced with a few original-language works and English translations. *20 rue Descartes, 5e, tel. 1/43–25–83–38. Métro: Cardinal Lemoine. Open Tues.–Thurs. and Sat. 12:30–6:30.*

Librairie Tokyo. Selling scores of Japanese-language books, this shop also has a limited selection of Japanese paper supplies and some French-language books on Japan. *4 rue Ste-Anne, 1er, tel. 1/42–61–08–71. Métro: Pyramides. Open Mon.–Sat. 10–7.*

Nan-Hai Video and Audio. Primarily a Chinese video-rental shop featuring hundreds of films and TV shows, Nan-Hai also sells books on Chinese health and philosophy, as well as cassettes and CDs of Chinese music. Everything is in the original language. *90 av. de Choisy, 13e, tel. 1/45–82–11–06. Métro: Tolbiac.*

Présence Africaine. This is *the* place for African works in the French language. *25 bis rue des Ecoles, 5e, tel. 1/43–54–15–88. Métro: Maubert-Mutualité. Open Mon.–Sat. 10–7.*

GAY BOOKSTORES Les Mots à la Bouche. Paris's main gay bookstore features magazines, art, photography, novels, and poetry in French and English. It carries only a few things of interest to lesbians and very little political literature, but it's a good place to find out what's going on in town. *6 rue Ste-Croix-de-la-Brétonnerie, 4e, tel. 1/42–78–88–30. Métro: Hôtel-de-Ville. Open Mon.–Sat. 11–11.*

CULINARY SUPPLIES

Though the departure of the grand Les Halles food market has taken the wholesale edge off the neighborhood, **rue Etienne Marcel,** just north of Forum des Halles, has several stores with great deals on essential kitchen items like crêpe spatulas. Among these shops, **S.A.R.L. Horecol** (32 rue Etienne Marcel, 2e, tel. 1/42–36–15–15) has a fairly limited selection of utensils and appliances, but sells them at good prices.

A. Simon. There are a few cooking utensils and pots tucked within the crevices, but the house specializes in the tools of the bistro—carafes, café bowls, escargot baking dishes—that are hard to find outside France. The showroom is overflowing with china and flatware. *36 rue Etienne Marcel, 2e, tel. 1/42–33–71–65. Métro: Etienne Marcel. Open Mon.–Sat. 8–6:30.*

La Bovida. The top floor has bins of knives and other cooking tools, an extensive assortment of copper pots, and a wall of checkered pants—only certified chefs are allowed to don the black-and-white-trousers. Even more interesting is the mezzanine, where bologna and other lunch meats are sold in containers by the liter. *36 rue Montmartre, 1er, tel. 1/42–36–09–99. Métro: Etienne Marcel. Open weekdays 8–12:30 and 1:30–5:30, Sat. 8–noon.*

FLEA MARKETS

If you are excited by the prospect of shopping in Paris, imagine finding 20 acres of stuff you can *actually afford.* Parisian *marchés aux puces* (flea markets) sell old treasures, vintage clothing, handmade fashions, shoes, appliances, and (you will soon discover) a lot of junk. Keep a close eye on your wallet to avoid being an easy target in these crowded conditions.

Near the Porte de Clignancourt Métro in the 18th arrondissement, the enormous **Marché aux Puces Clignancourt** abuts another flea market, **St-Ouen,** which extends past the city's periphery. Be careful or you could spend days wandering aimlessly among Hello Kitty accessories and racks of acid-wash jeans. These markets are huge, touristy, junky (except for some high-class antique malls that have popped up in the middle of St-Ouen), and a lot of fun. They're open Saturday through Monday 9:30–dusk.

The **Marché aux Puces Montreuil** (20e, Métro: Porte de Montreuil) is smaller and funkier than Clignancourt. Alongside hordes of fashion slaves bargaining for their next outfit, shop for vintage clothing and stuff from Africa and Asia. This market is open on weekends until dusk and on Mondays until noon. For a cheap stolen stereo or car part, go to **Marché aux Puces Vanves** (14e, Métro: Porte de Vanves), open weekends 7–7.

Paris also has several specialized outdoor markets, including a **stamp market** at the corner of avenues Marigny and Gabriel on Thursdays, Saturdays, and Sundays. Three **flower markets** brighten the city streets Tuesday through Sunday from 8 AM until about 7; the main one, at place Lépine on the Ile de la Cité, turns into a bird and pet market on Sundays, while the markets at place de la Madeleine (8e) and place des Ternes (8e) stick to flowers and such.

MUSIC

Some branches of Fnac sell a wide variety of music as well as concert tickets in a sleek department store setting. Try **Fnac Musique Bastille** (4 pl. de la Bastille, 12e, tel. 1/43–42–04–04) or **Fnac Forum** (1–7 rue Pierre Lescot, in the Forum des Halles, 1er, 1/40–41–40–00), which has a good world music department. The **Virgin Megastore** (52 av. des Champs-Elysées, 8e, tel. 1/40–74–06–48) is just that—megahip, with a megaselection. The opening of the Bastille opera house has revived the music scene in the surrounding area, and **boulevard Beaumarchais** is a good place to look for musical scores or instruments.

Le Silence de la Rue (8 rue de la Fontaine-du-But, 18e, tel. 1/42–55–61–34) is a tiny shop that sells punk, garage, rare vinyl, picture disks, and music that would make your mom cringe. They also have listings for shows. **Paris Jazz Corner** (5 rue de Navarre, 5e, tel. 1/43–36–78–92) is staffed by people who know all about the jazz and blues they have on vinyl and CD, both new and used. For African music and salsa, try the specialty record stores **Afric' Music** (3 rue des Plantes, 14e, tel. 1/45–42–43–52) or **Anvers Musique** (35 blvd. de Rochechouart, 9e, tel. 1/42–80–18–56). For Arab music, go to **Le Disque Arabe** (116 blvd. de la Chapelle, 18e, tel. 1/42–54–95–71).

Copa Music. This store specializes in classic jazz and world music CDs and records, being careful not to skip over the groovy '70s. *14 rue des Prêcheurs, 1er, tel. 1/40–13–03–28. Métro: Les Halles. Open Mon.–Sat. 11:30–7:30.*

CrocoJazz. Come here not only for jazz and blues but for Cajun and gospel music as well. Used CDs start at 50F or 100F for three. *64 rue de la Montagne-Ste-Geneviève, 5e, tel. 1/46–34–78–38. Métro: Maubert-Mutualité. Open Tues.–Sat. 11–1 and 2–7.*

La Dame Blanche. If they haven't got it here, they'll find it—though maybe not for the 50F that most of the used CDs sell for. They stock lots o' vinyl from 5F and also sell biographies of musicians. *47 rue de la Montagne-Ste-Geneviève, 5e, tel. 1/43–54–54–45. Métro: Maubert-Mutualité. Open Mon.–Sat. 10:30–2 and 3–8.*

Gilda. This place has been around since the '60s and now sells used CDs for 60F and under. Many collectors do a lot of selling and buying here, so the selection is always fresh. *36 rue des Bourdonnais, 1er, tel. 1/42–33–60–00. Métro: Châtelet–Les Halles. Open Mon.–Sat. 10–7.*

SPIRITS

Caves des Abbesses. The owner really knows his grape juice; he follows a wine for years before buying it, often bottling it himself and then reselling it cheaply. Bottles start at 8F, though most run 10F–15F. *43 rue des Abbesses, 18e, tel. 1/42–52–81–54. Métro: Abbesses. Open Tues.–Sat. 9–1 and 2–8, Sun. 2–8.*

Grains Nobles. At this boutique at the foot of the Panthéon, you can take a three-session course in French wine tasting (1,200F, 1,000F students) or just buy a couple bottles at discount prices. *5 rue Laplace, 5e, tel. 1/43–54–93–54. Métro: Maubert-Mutualité. Closed weekends.*

Juveniles. This Brit-run cellar sells about 60 of the owner's favorite wines from around the world for 25F–175F a bottle; specialties include wines from the Rhône Valley, Australia, and Spain. At any given time, about 12 wines (12F–40F) and several sherries (30F–45F) are offered by the glass, so you can try before you buy. Grab one of the few tables to make a meal of it: Throughout the day, you can get a full meal or reasonable snacks (like 35F rabbit brochettes with chutney) to accompany your wine. Food is served Tuesday–Friday noon to 11, Monday and Saturday noon to 3 and 7 to 11. *47 rue de Richelieu, 1er, tel. 1/42–97–46–49. Métro: Palais Royal–Musée du Louvre. Open for drinks Mon.–Sat. 11 AM–midnight.*

Nectar France. This small corner shop sells a wide range of French and imported beers and liquors and a good selection of wine as well. Prices are what you'd find in a grocery store, only you'd have to visit about 43 grocery stores to compile this collection. Wine-sized bottles of corked *kriek* (cherry-flavored beer) go for 26F. *26 rue des Ecoles, 5e, tel. 1/43–26–99–43. Métro: Maubert-Mutualité. Open Mon.–Sat. 10–8.*

STATIONERY

If you find yourself wandering around the lower Marais on the south side of rue de Rivoli, check out **rue du Pont Louis-Philippe,** where you can buy some fancy paper supplies to impress your pen pals. **Papier Plus** (tel. 1/42–77–70–49) at No. 9 has good deals on writing paper by the gram. At Nos. 4–6 on the same street, **Calligrane** (tel. 1/48–04–09–00) transforms recycled paper into cool stationery. At No. 10, **Mélodie Graphique** (tel. 1/42–74–57–68) specializes in Italian paper, stationery sets, journals, and paper by the sheet. All three close on Sunday.

VINTAGE CLOTHING

If you're tired of window shopping at glitzy boutiques you can't afford, the Left Bank and Les Halles offer some good deals on used clothes, though the best place to seek ratty 10F jeans are the flea markets (*see above*). Not exactly vintage but definitely cheap, **Tati** is a Paris institution. This bargain-basement store is like a zoo, but if you're willing to forage through bins, you can find some very cheap stuff. There are four locations in Paris, but for the most complete experience, go to the main store at 4 boulevard de Rochechouart (18e, tel. 1/42–55–13–09), which takes up several blocks.

Eurofripe Mod. This store stocks lots of used shoes, jeans, and leather, with the cheapest items running 70F–80F. Also sold are creations handmade on the premises. *15 rue Daval, 11e, tel. 1/48–06–24–29. Métro: Bastille. Open Mon. noon–8, Tues.–Sat. 11–8.*

Jacqueline Jacquelin. Here you'll find a wonderland of mostly women's clothes from the '50s on, much of it shiny or fuzzy, from 80F an item. *9 rue Pierre Lescot, 1er, tel. 1/45–08–11–48. Métro: Les Halles. Open Mon.–Sat. 11–7.*

Magique. Racks and racks of leather and suede jackets and vests, most at 150F, make up the bulk of this indoor/outdoor collection dominating a corner in Les Halles. The rest of the inventory is cheap cotton items and handbags. *60 rue St-Denis, 1er, tel. 1/42–33–59–99. Métro: Châtelet–Les Halles. Open Tues.–Sat. 10:30–7:30.*

Orlando Curioso. You'll have to sift through tightly packed racks, but in the end you just may pull out the perfect leather vest for 120F, or a 100F dress for tonight's party. The focus is on women's clothing from the '40s, '50s, and '60s. *78 rue de Rennes, 6e, tel. 1/42–22–28–66. Métro: St-Placide. Open weekdays 11–6:30.*

Neighborhoods

EIGHTH ARRONDISSEMENT This wealthy area provides far and away the best window-shopping in Paris. Of course there's the Champs-Elysées, with its car dealerships, designer boutiques, and fast-food chains, but much more impressive are the streets and squares off it. **Rue du Faubourg St-Honoré** is notorious for its posh boutiques; if you're determined to buy something along the strip, pick up a small bag of Godiva chocolates at the corner of rue Castiglione; a few pieces go for 30F. Equally hopeless is **avenue Montaigne,** housing the workshops of designers like Chanel, Christian Dior, and Valentino. **Place de la Madeleine** and the surrounding streets also cater to the upper crust. While walking through the eighth, chant repeatedly "thousands of francs, thousands of francs," so you don't accidentally fall in love with anything.

LES HALLES In Les Halles, expect lots of OCCASION signs: Here you'll find secondhand CDs, secondhand hats, secondhand shirts, secondhand shoes, and probably even a secondhand car or two. **Place des Innocents** is completely uninteresting, devoted to the same chains you see everywhere—Kookai, ProMod, Burger King, and Pizza Pino. Meanwhile, though huge and claustrophobic, the underground **Forum des Halles** mall actually does have some good shops, which you might find if you attack the labyrinth with exceptional patience. Above ground off place des Innocents and north of the Forum are the dumpy little new and secondhand stores that are the real reason to shop here.

QUARTIER LATIN The Quartier Latin's shopping scene revolves around its student population: This is where you'll find the coolest and wackiest bookstores and some of the strongest coffee beans. Although boulevard St-Michel is schlocky and crowded, the area around **place Maubert** has fantastic specialty bookstores. The shopping strip of **rue Mouffetard** tries to be more offbeat than it actually is, but an open-air produce market brings the locals out among the tourists gazing at all the small jewelry and clothing stores. All 17 branches of **Au Vieux Campeur,** which carry everything you could possibly need for outdoor excursions, are in the Quartier Latin. The main store is at 48 rue des Ecoles (5e, tel. 1/46–34–02–04).

Rigodon (12 rue Racine, 6e, tel. 1/43–29–98–66) is a tiny shop in St-Germain selling wonderful, expensive puppets and marionettes. The shop's fragile, magical interior is set up as a cave to better showcase all the witches and gnomes hanging from the walls.

ST-GERMAIN-DES-PRES Boutiques are the name of the game here. Reasonable stores appear on and below boulevard St-Germain, but the serious shopping happens above the boulevard. **Rue de Rennes** is a major shopping hub, and little streets all along it harbor clothing, antiques, gifts, and art stores. Good shopping streets include **rue St-Placide,** home to the five-shop markdown bliss of **Mouton à Cinq Pattes** (8–18 rue St-Placide, 6e, tel. 1/45–48–86–26), where real and aspiring designers drop their damaged and outdated extras. Rue de Rennes itself has some vintage clothing stores, and **rue de Sèvres** boasts affordable chains and small names alongside the priceless untouchables.

ILE DE FRANCE 7

By Remy Garderet and Baty Landis

There are four reasons you might want to explore the Ile de France, the region surrounding Paris: (1) You're a real history buff and want to see where Louis XVI, Marie Antoinette, Joan of Arc, and Napoléon and Josephine hung out. (2) You're hoping to find artistic inspiration by exploring the haunts of Monet, Renoir, Rodin, and Hugo. (3) You want to hear what Donald Duck sounds like speaking French. (4) You're experiencing cultural overload in Paris and need to escape. If any or all of this sounds good, the Ile de France is definitely worth exploring.

While not exactly an *île* (island), the region is roughly cordoned off from the rest of France by three rivers: the Seine, Marne, and Oise. These and a large number of brooks and streams have long stood to defend the area and keep it lush, two factors that attracted royalty with a get-away-from-the-masses mindset. Forests full of animals were also a big draw, enticing a contingent of the rich and bloated who enjoyed nothing more than preying on easily catchable game.

Once used as weekend getaways and hunting lodges, the châteaux of the Ile de France stand as monuments to the wealth, power, and taste of the French monarchy. The enormity of Versailles and Fontainebleau makes it hard to believe that they were built as second homes for city dwellers. Today many Parisians follow in the footsteps of the kings and queens, making the forests and small towns of the Ile de France their weekend retreats.

You can almost feel a royal presence in the region, especially governing restaurant and hotel prices. The only way to eat without putting down serious cash is to picnic; luckily, that's also one of the best ways to enjoy the countryside, and markets are plentiful. Lodging is even easier, thanks to the youth hostels that have snuck in among the châteaux and cathedrals in some towns.

The Ile de France also has lots to offer hikers, bikers, and rock climbers. You could go to a Paris museum in the morning and enjoy rock-climbing in the Forest of Fontainebleau or biking in Compiègne (*see below*) in the afternoon. If you have a couple of extra days around Paris and a couple of extra francs to spend on transportation, it's worth getting out of the city into the playground of France's rich and famous.

Versailles

It's hard to tell which is larger at Versailles—the château that housed Louis XIV and 20,000 of his courtiers, or the mass of tour buses and visitors standing in front of it. Louis XIII originally built the château as his hunting lodge in 1631, but when Louis XIV, "the Sun King," converted

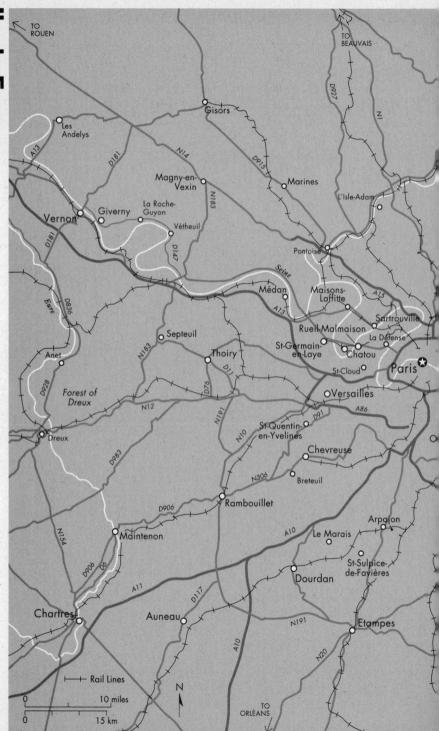

Ile de France

TO ROUEN

TO BEAUVAIS

Les Andelys

Gisors

Marines

L'Isle-Adam

Magny-en-Vexin

Vernon

Giverny

La Roche-Guyon

Vétheuil

Pontoise

Médan

Maisons-Laffitte

Sartrouville

La Défense

Rueil-Malmaison

St-Germain-en-Laye

Chatou

Septeuil

St-Cloud

Paris

Thoiry

Anet

Versailles

Forest of Dreux

St-Quentin-en-Yvelines

Dreux

Chevreuse

Breteuil

Rambouillet

Arpajon

Le Marais

St-Sulpice-de-Favières

Maintenon

Dourdan

Chartres

Auneau

Etampes

Rail Lines

N

0   10 miles

0   15 km

TO ORLÉANS

184

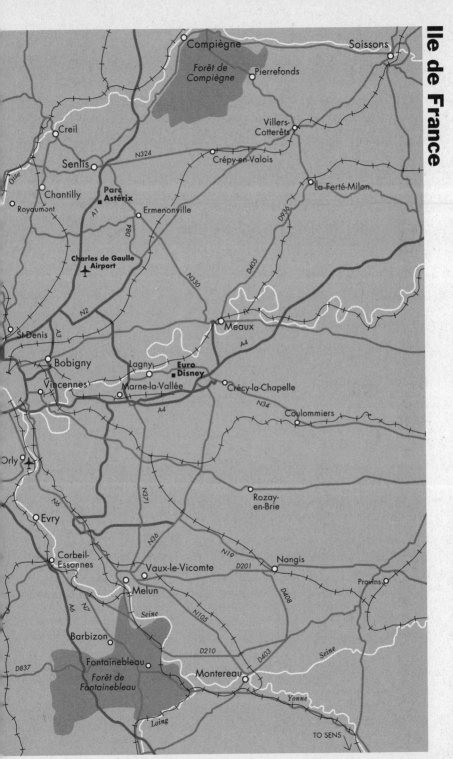

it from a weekend retreat to the headquarters of his government, he didn't cut any corners. Classical architect Louis Le Vau restored and added to the original lodge, while Charles Le Brun was responsible for the interior decoration. Jules Hardouin-Mansart later remodeled the whole thing, expanding on Le Vau's improvements. Together, during over a half-century of construction beginning in 1661, they designed everything his royal acquisitiveness could want, from a chapel to a throne room dedicated to Apollo, the king's mythological hero. Jacques-Ange Gabriel (another classicist) later added an opera house so Louis XV could be entertained at home without troubling himself to mingle with the populace. Reconstruction efforts aimed at bringing the entire estate back to how it looked when the Sun King lived here will continue for the next couple of decades; billboards provide updates on what's currently being worked on.

As you wander through this monument to splendidly wretched excess, try to imagine what life was like here during the two centuries that it served as the home of French royalty. Granted, you have to have a good imagination to look beyond the overflowing trash bins and cigarette-butt-littered cobblestones, but try to picture France's overdressed nobility promenading through the gardens plotting dangerous liaisons or fawning over the king and queen in the dazzling **Galerie des Glaces** (Hall of Mirrors) under Le Brun's painted homage to Louis XIV's reign. Imagine Louis XVI and Marie Antoinette entertaining in the **Grands Appartements,** decorated with sumptuous marble, gilded bronzes, and ceiling paintings of mythological figures. Now imagine the day in 1789 when a revolutionary mob marched the 15 miles from Paris to Versailles to protest the bread shortage, only to find Louis lounging in this pleasure palace. It's no wonder they forced the king to leave Versailles and set up camp at the Tuileries Palace in Paris, where they could keep an eye on him.

You may be able to avoid the hour-and-a-half wait for a tour if you arrive here at 9 AM sharp, when the château opens. The hard part is figuring out where you're supposed to go once you arrive: There are different lines depending on tour, physical ability, and group status. Frequent guided tours visit the private royal apartments. More detailed hour-long tours explore the opera house or Marie Antoinette's private parlors. You can also go through without a tour—by means of yet another line, of course. To figure out the system, pick up the brochure available at the information tent at the gates of the château, or consult the information desk in the ticket center. *Tel. 1/30–84–76–18. Admission: 40F, 26F under 26, under 18 free. Tours: additional 22F–44F. Open May–Sept., Tues.–Sun. 9–6:30; Oct.–Apr., Tues.–Sun. 9–5:30.*

If you don't feel like hassling with crowds and lines, or if you don't have any money left but still want to say that you've been to Versailles, head straight back behind the château to the **gardens.** This is where you'll find Versailles's hundreds of famous fountains. By the way, if you're wondering why the fountains don't work, they do—but you'll have to come on a Sunday and shell out 18F to see them in action. However, ongoing reconstruction means they may not oblige even then. For a real spectacle, come on one of several Saturdays during the summer for the **Fêtes de Nuit,** when the fountains come to life with music and lights. Ask at a tourist office for dates and ticket prices, which range from 90F to 185F. Move farther away from the château

Upstaging the King

Versailles's evolution from weekend hunting lodge to permanent royal residence/small city actually began within the halls of another French château, Vaux-le-Vicomte. Nicolas Fouquet, Louis XIV's finance minister, had this lavish palace built in just five years and then threw an outrageous party to show it off. Not a smart move, since the guest of honor was well aware that his employee could only have funded a place and a bash like this with embezzled francs. Embezzlement is one thing, but upstaging the king is another; Fouquet was imprisoned for life, while his designers—including landscape architect André Le Nôtre—were transferred to Versailles and ordered to create a palace like Fouquet's, only much bigger.

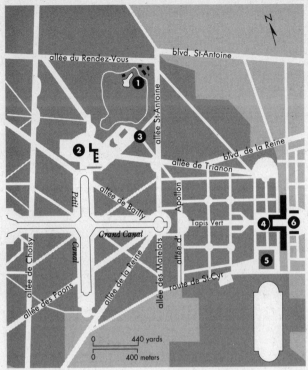

to discover 250 acres of gardens and lose the less adventurous tourists huddling around the fountains in the safety of the château's shadow. The tourist brochures request that you don't picnic on the lawns, but they don't say anything about the grottoes, groves, and grassy areas scattered throughout the woods. *Open daily 7–sunset, weather permitting.*

A guide written by Louis XIV himself, *Manière de montrer les jardins de Versailles* (The Manner of Showing the Versailles Gardens), is being consulted as the gardens are returned to their Sun King days. Formally laid out, with walkways, pools, viewpoints, woods, velvet lawns, a **Colonnade** of 24 marble columns, and an **Orangery,** Le Nôtre's gardens are brimming with statuary (Le Brun commissioned over 100 pieces for the gardens), including an equestrian figure of Louis XIV by Bernini. Perhaps most impressive are sculpture groupings emerging from two pools: the **Neptune Basin**'s sea god with dragons and cherubs and the **Apollo Basin**'s sun god in his chariot emerging from the sea amid sea monsters to bring light to the world. Beyond the Apollo Basin is the **Grand Canal,** which Louis XIV equipped with brightly colored gondolas operated by gondoliers. Today you can pay about 25F for a boat ride down the canal, though tours may be interrupted by renovations of the area.

In the northwest corner of the gardens are the smaller châteaux, the **Grand Trianon** and the **Petit Trianon,** used as guest houses for everyone from Napoléon I to Richard Nixon. Although you can go inside, there's not much here, and the visit is particularly anticlimactic if you've just toured the big château. Behind the Petit Trianon is the **Hameau de la Reine** (Ham-

The best investment you make at Versailles might be at the bike rental stand in Petite Venise, at the head of the Grand Canal, directly behind the château. For 30F an hour you can rent a groovy bike with a bell and everything. Ride out to the farthest end of the canal to see locals jogging, walking their dogs, and picnicking in grand fashion, as only the French know how.

let of the Queen), a collection of cottages where Marie Antoinette came to get away from her getaway and play peasant among the real-life versions who were recruited to fill her wonderland. You can reach this corner of the gardens on a tram (29F) that leaves every 35 minutes from the north side of the château, but walking is the easiest way to go. *Admission: Grand Trianon, 20F, 13F under 26, under 18 free; Petit Trianon, 12F, 8F under 26, under 18 free. Both open May–Sept., daily 10–6:30; Oct.–Apr., Tues.–Fri. 9–12:30 and 2–5:30, weekends 10–5:30.*

VISITOR INFORMATION There are three **Office de Tourisme** locations in Versailles. The office opposite the Gare Rive Gauche train station in the shopping mall Les Manèges (tel. 1/39–53–31–63) is closed on Mondays. Just north of the château, next to the auto entrance at 7 rue des Réservoirs (tel. 1/39–50–36–22), is another office, which closes on Sundays. May through September, a constantly crowded office sets up at the main gate of the château every day but Monday. All locations have loads of brochures and helpful English-speaking employees, and each is open until around 6 PM.

COMING AND GOING The cheapest way to get to Versailles from Paris is to take the **yellow RER line C** to Versailles–Rive Gauche (13F50), which deposits you a few well-marked blocks from the château in about 35–45 minutes. Otherwise, trains from Paris's Gare Montparnasse stop at Gare des Chantiers (rue des Etats Généraux), south of the château, while trains from Gare St-Lazare arrive at the Gare Rive Droite behind place du Marché de Notre-Dame. Both Versailles train stations are within walking distance of the château.

FOOD Picnicking is by far the cheapest and easiest way to eat here. If you don't bring your own food, be prepared to work up an appetite walking to the grocery store. You'll find a **Monoprix** on avenue Général de Gaulle, five minutes to your right as you leave the Gare Rive Gauche. If you're not hot on the picnic idea, try one of the small restaurants behind place du Marché de Notre-Dame, or one of the brasseries on avenue de Paris, the main street that runs smack dab into the château's gates. The farther you get from the château, the better luck you'll have finding something that isn't priced for tourists with a capital *T*. If you have the time, walk down to **Traiteur Philippe Joly Charcutière** (62 rue d'Anjou, tel. 1/39–50–28–46) and stand in line with the locals to get a freshly made sandwich for 10F–20F.

Chartres

Travelers who make their way to Chartres to see the **Notre-Dame de Chartres** cathedral are following in the footsteps of religious pilgrims who began coming to the city over 1,000 years ago: In the late 9th century, King Charles the Bald presented Chartres with the *sacra camisia* (sacred tunic) of the Virgin Mary, turning the city into a hot spot for the Christian faithful. The magnificent Gothic cathedral was built in the 12th and 13th centuries, replacing a church that burned to the ground in 1194, leaving Mary's tunic miraculously unsinged.

The mismatched towers of Chartres cathedral are a result of lightning striking the north tower in the 16th century, decapitating its spire.

The cathedral has survived seven centuries of wars. If that doesn't impress you, consider the fact that it features over 2,000 square meters (21,500 square feet) of glass, including 12-meter- (38-foot-) high stained-glass windows, some of which date back to 1210. The oldest window, and perhaps the most interesting, is *Notre Dame de la Belle Verrière* (literally, Our Lady of the Beautiful Window), in the south choir. Don't spend all your time looking up, though; the black-and-white pattern on the floor of the nave is the only one of its kind to have survived from the Middle Ages. The faithful were expected to travel along its entire length (about 300 meters) on their knees. Malcolm Miller, who looks like he stepped right out of an *Addams Family* episode, gives fabulous tours in English daily at noon and 2:45, providing information on the narrative stained glass and his own travels for 20F. For an additional 18F that might be better spent elsewhere, you can climb the northern tower for a view of the city and of people on the terrace below looking at the same view for free. Organ recitals are given on Sundays from July through October at 4:45 PM free of charge, though definitely not free of tourists. Show up early to stake out a seat.

If you venture outside the cathedral, you'll discover that the city around it is schizophrenic. One part is beautifully designed and historic, the other side bland, awkward, and modern. To see the historic side, follow the **route touristique,** which starts behind the cathedral. Clearly marked with shiny gold signs, the route winds through old Chartres on narrow streets. If you stray from the tourist route, though, you're slapped into reality by boring modern houses and tasteless apartment buildings. It's kind of like going behind the scenes at Disneyland—the magic disappears.

The **Musée des Beaux-Arts,** behind the cathedral, sits in the former bishop's palace. The collection of drawings, tapestries, and archaeological finds will be interesting only to those who have a real fascination with Chartres's history. If anything interesting is unearthed during the excavation of the medieval convent in front of the cathedral, the museum may get a needed infusion of artifacts. Check the sign in front of the museum to see if the changing contemporary exhibit is worth 20F (students 10F) to you. *29 cloître Notre-Dame, tel. 37–36–41–39. Open Apr.–Oct., Wed.–Mon. 10–1 and 2–6; Nov.–Mar., Wed.–Mon. 10–noon and 2–5, Sun. 2–5.*

The **Centre International du Vitrail** (5 rue du Cardinal-Pie, tel. 37–21–65–72) displays temporary exhibits of stained-glass works from the Middle Ages to the present. The exhibition shop in the same complex has beautiful pictures and gift items of old and new glass works. Admission is free, but you might be tempted to blow a bundle. Beneath the shop is a huge, vacant underground hall with vaulted ceilings. The center is open daily 9:30–12:30 and 1:30–6.

VISITOR INFORMATION The **Office de Tourisme** is well stocked with information about the cathedral, the town, and special events in the region (including a 10F guide to town and cathedral). The comfy reading nook here is the perfect place to take a break if you don't have any money for a café. *Pl. de la Cathédrale, tel. 37–21–50–00. Open Mon.–Sat. 9:30–6, Sun. 10–12:30 and (Apr.–Sept. only) 2:30–5:30.*

COMING AND GOING Hourly trains make the 50-minute, 66F trip from Paris's Gare Montparnasse to Chartres's **train station** (pl. Pierre Sémard, tel. 37–28–50–50), which puts you within walking distance of the cathedral. A nifty map in the station shows you exactly where to go. You can check your bags from 8 AM to 7:30 PM for an extortionate 20F. From the terminal next door, buses run to Orléans (three daily Monday through Saturday, only one on Sunday) for 73F; for other destinations, check inside or call 37–18–59–00.

WHERE TO SLEEP The **Auberge de Jeunesse** is the only affordable place to crash in Chartres. Its ugly exterior doesn't reflect the whole; inside, it is clean, comfortable, and quiet. Many visitors to Paris who have rail passes stay out here and make the daily commute just to escape the chaos of city living. Each room has two to eight beds, a sink, and plenty of storage space. The large stomach attached to a head walking around belongs to the hostel director, who'll shoot the breeze if he's having a good day. The hostel is toward the bottom of the old town, across the river from the cathedral, a well-marked 20-minute walk from the train station or five-minute trip on Bus 3. Beds are 60F with a hostel card, 75F without. Breakfast is included; sheets are an extra 16F. *23 av. Neigre, tel. 37–34–27–64. 16 rooms. Reception open noon–10, but you can usually check in earlier. Closed Dec.–Feb.*

FOOD Chartres has not made much (okay, any) name for itself in the culinary world, but you can do just fine if you avoid the cathedral area and stick to the old town, especially rue Noël Ballay, rue du Cygne, and rue du Bois-Merrain Marceau. There are a few grocery stores around for basic fuel, but to put a smile on your face, check out **La Napolitaine** (27 rue de Porte Morard, tel. 37–34–30–26), where a student lunch special features pizza, ice cream, and a drink for 49F.

Giverny

In 1883, Claude Monet settled in the small town of Giverny, about 60 kilometers (40 miles) outside Paris on the river Seine. During the almost half-century he lived in Giverny, Monet painted some of his most famous works in and of his gardens. Of course, he didn't just choose a spot, set up camp, and pick up his paintbrush—the gardens themselves are a work of art that

Monet spent several years perfecting before he began re-creating them on canvas. He planted colorful checkerboard gardens, installed a waterlily pond, put up a Japanese bridge, and finally decorated the interior of his house to match it all. Finally, he began to paint series of the same scene in different seasons and weather conditions and at various times of day, innovating techniques for capturing light, water, and reflections on canvas.

The 126F round-trip train ride may sound extravagant for a day trip, but it's worth it if you're a fan of impressionism. Don't limit yourself to the gardens, though; inside, the bright house is decorated with Monet's beloved Japanese prints, and you'll be glad you invested the extra francs to get in. For the full effect, come midweek in the morning to avoid the crush. The colors radiate best on sunny days, especially in late spring. *Tel. 32–51–28–21. Admission: gardens 25F; gardens and house 35F, 25F students. Open Apr.–Oct., Tues.–Sun. 10–6.*

VISITOR INFORMATION The **Office de Tourisme** has brochures on Monet's stay at Giverny and trail maps for hiking and biking in the surrounding forest. *36 rue Carnot, tel. 32–51–39–60. Open Tues.–Sat. 9:30–12:30 and 2:30–6:30, Sun. and Mon. 2:30–6:30.*

COMING AND GOING Trains leave every couple of hours from Paris's Gare St-Lazare for the 50-minute, 63F ride to Vernon; buses meet the trains and whisk you away to Giverny for 7F more. If you have the time and energy, the 6-kilometer (4-mile) walk from Vernon to Giverny along the Seine is worthwhile, and not just because you'll save 7F. From the train station, walk through town to the river, cross the bridge, and hang a right on the road to Giverny.

WHERE TO SLEEP **Auberge de Jeunesse.** If you decide that Giverny deserves more than a day trip, the youth hostel in nearby Vernon is clean and spacious. The sprightly man who runs the place advises you on how best to spend your time in Giverny. Beds are 43F a night; sheets are 16F. The big garden doesn't quite rival Monet's, but it connects the hostel to a great 20-site campground with kitchen and laundry facilities and hot showers, all for 23F a night. *28 av. de l'Ile de France, tel. 32–51–66–48. 2 km (1¼ mi) from train station on road marked* PARIS. *16 beds. Family rooms, breakfast 17F. Reception open 8–10 AM and 6:30–10:30 PM. Reservations advised.*

OUTDOOR ACTIVITIES The hills and forests surrounding Vernon and Giverny are loaded with trails ideal for hiking and biking. About 20 trails climb up hills or run alongside the shady river; to find the best of them, pick up the hiking guide from the tourist office before you go. If you want a regular bike for the ride to Giverny and around town, rent one at the train station in Vernon for 55F a day (plus a 1,000F or credit-card deposit); bikes must be back by 9 PM. If you plan to bike the rougher trails, you'll need a VTT (mountain bike). In Giverny, **Martin Cycles** (84 rue Carnôt, tel. 32–21–24–08) rents them for 100F a day, 150F for the entire weekend; a 4,000F or credit-card deposit is required.

Beauvais

Two quality museums and one stunning cathedral are all that's left to recommend this drab town 100 kilometers (62 miles) north of Paris; some 2,000 buildings were destroyed during World War I, sparing only a few scattered medieval streets and leaving the rest to unimaginative rebuilders. The **Cathédral St-Pierre,** though, is impressive from the outside and positively dizzying from within—the Gothic arches reach so high you nearly keel over craning your neck back. The original designers set out in 1225 to create the biggest cathedral in Europe, and they would have succeeded if it hadn't kept falling apart or getting knocked down. What remains is a fascinating panorama of stained glass and one of the most richly colored church interiors anywhere—some original pieces remain from as far back as the 13th century, but most were replaced after World War II by artists who weren't afraid to show their century.

The **astronomical clock** inside the cathedral was built in 1865 and restored in 1929 to its original Roman-Byzantine, gold-embellished self. It tells the hour, season, inclination of the sun, saint of the day, and times of sunrise and sunset, as well as who is going to win the French Open next year. At 10:40, 2:40, 3:40, and 4:40, the clock's 90,000 pieces animate Christ's Final Judgment (which doesn't seem so final when it happens four times a day). The nearby **musical clock** is a simpler timepiece with its own claim to fame: It's one of the oldest working clocks in existence. This one would put even Timex out of business—it's been ticking since 1302.

If you think of tapestries as stuffy château decor, the snazzy **Galerie Nationale de la Tapisserie** (22 rue St-Pierre, tel. 44–05–14–28), next to the cathedral, might change your mind. Its tapestries range from the beginning of the art form to last year's works. The museum closes during lunch and on Mondays. Just on the other side of the cathedral, the collection of the **Musée Départemental de l'Oise** (1 rue du Musée, tel. 44–06–37–37), closed Tuesdays, is housed in an old episcopal palace and includes furniture by art nouveau bigwig Henri Bellery-Desfontaines.

VISITOR INFORMATION *1 rue Beauregard, tel. 44–45–08–18. Open Tues.–Sat. 9:30–7, Sun. and Mon. 10–1 and 2–6.*

COMING AND GOING Trains (1¼ hrs, 60F) arrive from Paris several times a day and, thank God, leave just as often. The town centers on the sprawling **place Jeanne Hachette,** which is bordered on one side by the Hôtel de Ville and on the other sides by cafés and stores. The pedestrian zone branches off behind the square, away from the Hôtel de Ville and toward the cathedral.

WHERE TO SLEEP AND EAT One of Beauvais's rare medieval blocks is along **rue 4 juin,** home to plenty of half-timbered houses and half-baked brasseries. The popular bar **Rustic** (68 rue Gambetta, tel. 44–45–10–43) also rents cheap, dingy rooms for 100F a single, 120F a double (200F with shower). A considerable step up is the central **Hôtel du Palais** (9 rue St-Nicolas, tel. 44–45–12–58), whose truly nice singles with shower start at 145F, doubles at 170F. The eating scene is the pits—choose the best-looking brasserie in the pedestrian zone, or stick to grocery shopping at **Nouvelles Galeries** (pl. Jeanne Hachette).

Chantilly

The château came first and the stables and racetrack later, but older isn't always better—even in France. The spectacular **Grandes Ecuries** (Grand Stables), which hold the **Musée Vivant du Cheval** (Living Museum of the Horse), house an elite cadre of racehorses in luxury. No fancy tapestries here, but high arched, intricately molded ceilings make the stables pretty posh for horse digs. Surprisingly, the stables aren't just for show; the horses in them are actual racehorses. In the rooms around the training courtyard is a huge, well-done collection of jockey uniforms, harnesses, bits, biological diagrams—everything imaginable to do with horses. The museum visit includes a casual show-off session for the horses. On Sunday afternoons at 3:15 and 4:45 the show goes upscale with costumes, music, and special tricks; admission, however, doubles. *Tel. 44–57–13–13. Admission: 45F, 40F students. Open Apr. and Sept.–Oct., Wed.–Mon. 10:30–5:30; May–June, daily 10:30–5:30; July–Aug., Wed.–Mon. 10:30–5:30, Tues. 2–5:30; Nov.–Mar., Wed.–Mon. 2–4:30, weekends and holidays until 5:30; closed Dec. 1–15.*

The only official races are held in June, with the major international ones on the first and second Sundays and smaller ones on various weekdays. You can enter the stands on the far side of the racing oval for 40F (students 20F) and bet the rest of your cash on a sure thing. Call the

Festival Jeanne Hachette

The Festival Jeanne Hachette, celebrating the woman who led Beauvais's female citizens to victory over Charles the Horrible in 1472, is a candidate for longest-running annual festival in France—it has been going on for 512 years. On the last weekend in June, locals and visitors fill Beauvais's streets decked out in medieval garb to watch or participate in reenactments of Jeanne's victory.

S.E.C.F., which organizes the international races, in Paris (tel. 1/49–10–20–39) for race information and schedules.

The **château** behind the stables is the icing on the cake. It makes the stables more elegant, and the stables make the château more realistic—they work together in conjuring up images of leisurely picnics with stout-bellied men and women in large, flowery hats. Totally surrounded by water, the château houses a so-so collection of furniture, paintings, and clothes, including Napoléon's hat. The **Musée Condé,** displaying mostly mediocre paintings and sculpture, claims to be one of the "most beautiful museums in France." I wouldn't go that far, but judge for yourself, since admission is included with château entrance. *Tel. 44–54–04–02. Admission: 37F, 27F students. Open Mar.–Oct., Wed.–Mon. 10–6; Nov.–Feb., Wed.–Mon. 10:30–12:45 and 2–5.*

Versailles landscape architect André Le Nôtre also created Chantilly's château **gardens.** Beyond the grandiose fountains by the castle, they stretch to either side encompassing bridge-linked canals, lily ponds, and clearings in manicured woods. Each section of the garden represents a period of history from the 17th to 19th centuries: **Le Jardin Français** (the French Garden), laid out in the 1600s, is the most formal and full of flowers; **Le Petit Parc** (the Little Park) and **Le Hameau** (the Hamlet), which inspired the one Marie-Antoinette frolicked in at Versailles (*see* Versailles, *above*), are from the 18th; and **Le Jardin Anglais** (the English Garden) is from the 19th. If you're feeling active, toss a Frisbee around; otherwise, lie back with a book and relax— as the original owners once did. *Admission: 17F, free with château visit. Open 10 AM–dusk on days the château is open.*

The town of Chantilly doesn't have much to offer besides a tree-lined main boulevard and a smattering of cafés. You'll be rested and ready to leave by evening, which is a good thing, since there's no cheap place to sleep.

VISITOR INFORMATION The **Office de Tourisme** has brochures on horse races and **hot-air-balloon rides** (tel. 44–57–35–35), which cost 60F and up. It also has the most confusing hours in all of France. *23 av. Maréchal Joffre, tel. 44–57–08–58. Open May–Sept., Mon. and Wed.–Sat. 9–12:30 and 2:15–7, Tues. 10–noon, Sun. 9–noon; Oct.–Apr., Mon. and Wed.–Fri. 9–12:30 and 2:15–6:15, Tues. 10–noon, Sat. 9–12:30 and 2:15–5:15.*

COMING AND GOING You can get to Chantilly from Paris's Gare du Nord on RER line B (30F) or on the regular train (38F); both take 40 minutes. From Chantilly's train station, head straight down rue des Otages and hang a left when it ends; a beautiful 15-minute walk across a field brings you to the stables. If you want to bus it, hop on any city bus passing in front of the station, but you'll miss a great first view of the stables if you don't walk.

FOOD The **Felix Potin** (55 rue du Connetable, tel. 44–57–01–47) grocery store has all you need for snacks on the lawns. Surprisingly, the snack carts at the entrance of the château won't completely rip you off. Restaurants around town tend to be pricey and not terribly exciting (serving your basic 90F menu or 40F salad), though **La Calèche** (3 av. du Maréchal Joffre, tel. 44–57–02–55), near many of the fancier restaurants, has a tasty lunch menu for 49F. Most town eateries offer a ton of expensive desserts topped with mounds of *chantilly*—the French word for whipped cream.

Chantilly's Culinary Contribution

The Château of Chantilly had an excellent reputation for fine cuisine during its 17th-century heyday and today remains the eponym for fresh cream beaten to mousselike consistency, then sweetened to go with all kinds of desserts. Anything you order à la chantilly will come with a glob of the stuff, which is lighter, creamier, and less sugary than the plasticky, super-sweet Cool Whip popular in the United States. One of the stranger French recipes to include chantilly has to be poularde à la chantilly—chicken coated with a whipped cream sauce.

Amusement Parks

EURO DISNEY

It's controversial, it's expensive, and it's a hell of a lot of fun. Though the park's chances of survival have become a popular topic for debate among politicians, intellectuals, and ordinary citizens—particularly after losing almost $1 billion in 1993—way too much has gone into this venture for Disney to roll up the carpet just yet. The most serious problem, it seems, has not been attendance but length of stay (not enough folks in those hotels) and the few francs spent within the park—after the hefty admission fee, that is. What was designed as a weekend resort is too easy to cover in a day, and the "no outside food or drink" rule hasn't quite been taken to heart. Frequent cold, damp weather has not helped attract crowds, either. Discounting those of us who snicker at Disney's financial woes, the rest of the Mickey-smitten world might want to throw away a month's pay on the spotless grounds, good rides, and long lines that characterize this meticulously conceived fantasy world. Basically, Euro Disney has taken the best attractions of the American Disney parks and rolled them into a very condensed version. "Star Tours," "Captain Eo," "Big Thunder Railroad," "It's a Small World," "Peter Pan" . . . they're all here, and more state-of-the-art than ever. New stuff includes "Indiana Jones and the Temple of Peril," with Disney's first-ever roller-coaster loop, and "Alice's Curious Labyrinth," a trippy maze of hedges and Wonderland characters. Best of all, though, is seeing how Europeans react to this big dose of American culture on their own turf—and seeing them try to figure out what a drinking fountain is. Although Adventureland's Middle Eastern Grand Bazaar and Fantasyland's Alsatian village give the park a bit of international flair, it's definitely more "Disney" than "Euro." The American Old West theme seems to find its way into everything, and the Roaring Twenties are bigger here than they ever were in the States.

Unless you want to significantly help Disney pay off its debts, time your visit carefully. Confusingly enough, rates do not simply rise with the temperature; they fluctuate based on school and national holidays, weekends, and tourist season. During most of June, for example, entrance costs 175F, while during February or March (ski season) it jumps back up to 250F. Call ahead to verify prices for specific dates—going a day later could make a big difference. Lines within the park are usually ridiculous on weekends, but apparently everyone rushes to get here first thing in the morning, then poops out by early afternoon. Signs at the beginning of each substantial line tell you about how long you'll wait. As always, Disney is careful about wheelchair accessibility, though for most of the good rides you must have an attendant to help you leave the chair. Pick up the pamphlet "Guest Special Services Guide" for specific accessibility info. *Tel. 1/64–74–30–00. Take RER line A to Marne-la-Vallée/Chessy (35F). Admission: 175F–250F. Open daily 9–7, until 11 in summer.*

All Disneys Are Not Created Equal

The following are some Euro Disney quirks that would never fly at its American counterparts:

- **Wine served in the park (they changed their no-alcohol policy in 1993).**

- **Tombstone inscriptions at "Phantom Manor": "Jasper Jones, loyal manservant, kept the master happy. Anna Jones, faithful chambermaid, kept the master happier."**

- **No Mickey walking around—he was too mobbed by kiddies, so he stays in one spot, and you have to line up to see him.**

- **No good ice cream.**

- **Cast members who look like they need a cigarette.**

WHERE TO SLEEP AND EAT One result of the park's money problems is the possibility of a relatively cheap night's stay. The least expensive hotels within the resort, the **Hotel Santa Fe** and **Hotel Cheyenne**, offer rooms for up to four people at 300F–650F, and April through September the **Davy Crockett Ranch** offers cabins for up to six people from 500F. Hotel/park admission packages can make a night here even more attractive. Call 1/49–41–49–10 (from the United States call 407/W–DISNEY; from the United Kingdom call 0171/753–2900) for all reservations.

Though most budget visitors just smuggle food into the park, a few restaurants inside actually have menus that won't break your bank, including the **Café Hyperion** (inside Videopolis in Discoveryland), with a menu from 40F; the **Pizzerria Bella Notte** (Fantasyland), with a menu from 50F; and the **Cowboy Cookout Barbeque** (Frontierland), also with a menu from 40F. The restaurants serve mostly American-style food.

PARC ASTERIX

All French kids know comic book hero Astérix and his loyal sidekick, Obélix. They're the short, fat Gauls living in the year 50 BC who beat up invading Romans trying to attack their village in Brittany—a magic potion makes the heroes invincible in battle. Read one of their adventure books before laying down a hefty sum of cash to experience this cartoon world.

If you think you know amusement parks, this French-style one could be a real eye-opener. You learn about French history on your way from one attraction to the next, from a Gaul village with print makers and potters, to a little Roman village, to a miniaturized version of Paris complete with a Dixieland band (Dixieland in Paris?). In the Gladiator Arena you can watch an action-packed comedy of errors starring gladiators and some guy who looks like Julius Caesar—the story is easy to follow whether or not you understand French. A Dolphinarium, though strangely out of place, is currently all the rage, as is the new Ancient Greek Village, complete with a replica of the Eiffel Tower that winks at Big Ben. Unfortunately, many of the ride lines are undeservedly long for what waits at the end. Most are glorified versions of carnival rides, spinning and twirling you around until your lunch makes an encore appearance. There are some fun ones, though, like the ultra-loopy "Goudurix" roller coaster and "Grand Splatch," which will get you soaked.

If you decide to make the Parc Astérix investment, come on a weekend when it's nice and crowded. When it's empty, it's really empty, and there's nothing more depressing than a lonely amusement park. Also, some attractions close on weekdays, and when you spend this much money, you want to make the last centime count. *Tel. 44–62–34–34. Admission: 150F, 105F under 12. Open mid-Apr.–mid-Oct., weekends 10–6, until 7 PM on peak days; also open weekdays July–Aug.; for other weekdays, call ahead.*

COMING AND GOING From Paris, take RER line B3 to the Charles de Gaulle/Roissy terminus (30F), where you can catch a special 15F shuttle (20 minutes) that runs to the park (9:30–1:30) and back (4:30 to park closing) every half-hour.

Compiègne

It's possible to do Compiègne in one day, but you'll have to be selective or move damn fast to see the château, the forest, and nearby Pierrefonds all in one swoop. If you can deal with the tricky lodging, though, you may end up staying longer than expected, exploring the Oise Valley and drinking with the students of the Université de Technologie de Compiègne (UTC).

Compiègne is a mix of shaggy half-timbered houses and modern stucco buildings that went up after World War I flattened parts of the town. In fact, the armistice ending the war was signed in a railway car just 6 kilometers (4 miles) away from the then wiped-out town. If you rent a bike (*see* Outdoor Activities, *below*), you can visit the railcar, called the **Clarière de l'Armistice,** and pay 7F to look through the windows at memorabilia of the event. (No buses go there.)

Louis XV built the **château** of Compiègne in the 18th century. It saw some war action of its own, losing all of its furniture during the Revolution. Never one for beanbags and milk crates,

Napoléon re-did the whole thing in marble, gold, and silk, but all that's left is some old furniture and flaking gold paint. You can see everything during a drab one-hour guided visit. From the looks of the park and gardens behind the château, Compiègne's royalty must have spent most of their time in the backyard. The colorful English garden and wide expanse of grass and trees make one of the nicest hang-out spots in France. Admission to the château also gets you into two museums. At the **Musée de la Voiture** (Car Museum) in the north wing, follow the animated tour guide to get the lowdown on the cars. One used for picnics looks like an early rendition of the Batmobile, but the others just look like ornate chariots. Old-fashioned bicycles sneak their way in, too. The ho-hum **Museum of the Second Empire** is a mishmash of furniture, clothes, and art set up in stark rooms. *Tel. 44–38–47–00. Admission: 31F, 20F ages 18–25. Open Wed.–Mon. 9:15–5:30.*

Though it doesn't sound particularly exciting, the **Museum of Historical Figurines** in the passage next to the tourist office has a collection of superbly detailed dolls, fully decked out in costumes. *Tel. 44–40–72–55. Admission: 12F, 6F students. Open Tues.–Sat. 9–noon and 2–6, Sun. and Mon. 2–6; Nov.–Feb., closes at 5.*

Locals and tourists focus as much attention on Compiègne's surrounding **forest** as on the town itself. It's fine for hiking, but you might as well rent a bike (*see* Outdoor Activities, *below*), which will get you to the Clarière de l'Armistice (*see above*) painlessly and to Pierrefonds (*see* Near Compiègne, *below*) without dealing with infrequent buses. Once you enter the maze of trails, you're guaranteed to get lost if you don't have a map—pick up a free one when you rent a bike, or buy the 15F *Circuits Pédestres* (Walking Tours) booklet at the tourist office.

VISITOR INFORMATION The bustling **Office de Tourisme** next to the Hôtel de Ville is jam-packed with leaflets and brochures on all the sights of Compiègne, the forest, and the castle at Pierrefonds. *Pl. de l'Hôtel de Ville, tel. 44–40–01–00. Open Mon.–Sat. 9:30–noon and 2–7, Sun. 9:30–noon and 2:30–5; Nov.–Easter, closed Sun. afternoon.*

COMING AND GOING Trains leave hourly from Paris's Gare du Nord for the 66F, one-hour trip to Compiègne. The train and bus station is across the river from the center of town—a five-minute walk, max. Just cross the bridge in front of the station and walk straight on through to place de l'Hôtel de Ville. City Buses 1, 2, and 5 are free and run from the station into the center of town (except on Sunday). Continue through the place onto rue Magenta; the château is down any street to your left, and the cobblestone pedestrian zone is to your right on rue des Lombards.

WHERE TO SLEEP Finding lodging can be tricky, so call ahead if you plan to stay beyond the last train back (check at the station to find out when that is). Cheap options are few and far between. Two of the best choices are the **Hôtel du Lion d'Or** (4 rue Général Leclerc, tel. 44–23–32–17), with cute, small singles for 115F, doubles for 145F; and the **Hôtel St-Antoine** (17 rue de Paris, tel. 44–86–17–18), with doubles from 90F to 120F.

➤ **HOSTELS AND STUDENT HOUSING** • Monsieur Taguchi, who owns the laundromat next to **Pizzeria Anaïs**, rents out rooms to UTC students during the year, but sometimes has openings for travelers in July and August. Call at least a day ahead to check the availability of his 12 clean rooms, costing from 80F to 100F. You share the kitchenette, bathrooms, and showers with other guests. *Cnr of rue Notre-Dame de Bon-Secours and rue du Port à Bateaux, tel. 44–20–16–91.*

Auberge de Jeunesse. The only real budget accommodation in town, this conveniently located hostel offers bunk-filled rooms for 27F a night, plus 13F for sheets. The showers are hot and the rooms are clean, but the hostel has one big drawback: The woman who runs it would rather let you sleep in the streets than break her precious 10 PM curfew. *6 rue Pasteur, tel. 44–40–72–64. Reception open 7–10 AM and 5–10 PM. HI card required. Closed mid-Sept.–Mar.*

FOOD Brasseries abound around the place Hôtel de Ville and in the pedestrian area, but they're not cheap. Try **Le Songeons** (40 rue Solférino, tel. 44–40–23–98), one block down toward the river from the center, for a decent 50F lunch menu. **Stromboli's Pizzeria** (2 rue des Lombards, in passage la Potene, tel. 44–40–06–21), closed Sundays, is a local favorite. You may have to wait a while to be seated, but the crispy-crusted pizzas (35F) and pungent pastas (40F) are worth it. Pass the time with a glass of wine in the friendly, close quarters.

For picnic packers, the open-air **Marché Place du Change** behind the pedestrian zone, open until 12:30 on Wednesdays and Saturdays, will ready you for the road. Otherwise, **Djerba Market** (cours Guynemer, tel. 44–40–01–36), open Tuesday to Sunday 8–8, has everything from trail mix to fresh Sicilian olives, homemade couscous, and good old baguettes.

AFTER DARK Au Bureau (17 pl. de l'Hôtel de Ville, tel. 44–40–10–11) makes a good starting point for an evening out. In booths surrounded by English-pub paraphernalia, you can enjoy a 45F pizza as you down your first cold one. Once you're ready, ease over to the bar to choose from over 100 beers from 20-odd countries—order a "meter" of beer if you're up to it. For a cozier, more student-oriented scene, try the **Sweet Home Pub** (cnr of rues St-Corneille and d'Austerlitz), where things get wild later in the evening.

OUTDOOR ACTIVITIES Endless trails—paved, unpaved, and downright sloshy—wind through shady groves of birch and oak in the **Forêt de Compiègne.** There are only a couple of steep trails, but plenty of opportunities for exploration and discovery. The man at **Picardie Forêts Vertes** (4 rue de la Gare, tel. 44–90–05–05) is terrific: Just call the day before you want a bike and he'll have it waiting for you at the station. Tell him what you want to explore and how steep a ride you want, and he'll also give you a map with your own personalized route. On weekends you can usually find him at the Carrefour Royal by the campground, where trails into the forest start. All of this pampering has a price, of course—100F per day.

NEAR COMPIEGNE

PIERREFONDS Tucked away in the Forêt de Compiègne, the 12th-century **Château de Pierrefonds** looks like what a kindergartner would come up with if asked to draw a castle: round towers with pointy tops, cannon notches in the walls, a moat—everything a proper château should have. It was the first château built by Louis d'Orléans—not bad for a first try. Between the château and a lake, half-timbered houses and teardrop spires rise out of Pierrefond's tiny village. Inside the château, medieval memorabilia rules the day. *Tel. 44–42–80–77. Admission: 26F, 17F students. Open Apr.–Sept., daily 10–6; Oct.–Mar., daily 10–5.*

➢ **COMING AND GOING** • Getting here from Compiègne is easy by bike (*see* Outdoor Activities in Compiègne, *above*). The bike ride is a flat 14 kilometers (9 miles) through lush green forest, and the initial view of the château as you round the final curve is worth the effort. Buses from Compiègne only run three times daily (except Sunday) from the station and charge 8F.

➢ **WHERE TO SLEEP** • The **Château de Jonval** (2 rue Séverine, tel. 44–42–80–97) has been converted into a hostel with rooms for two to eight people. If you've ever wondered what it would be like to open the window of your own castle bedroom and gaze across a tiny valley at a majestic medieval castle glistening in the morning light, here's your chance to find out. For 70F, you get a simple bed and breakfast, but the superb setting is what makes it worthwhile.

Fontainebleau

The sentimental might be turned off by the fact that François I built the château at Fontainebleau as a royal hunting lodge so he could track down and kill furry forest creatures. But in 1528, the king had license to kill just about anything he wanted, so no one complained when he commissioned this upscale hunting lodge—and we're talking *way* upscale.

The château was used as both a hunting lodge and an official residence for nearly eight centuries by more than 30 sovereigns. Each king who lived here left his mark—a tower here, a staircase there—with additions that reflect the style of his period. Because of these hundreds of years of architectural influences, Napoléon I called Fontainebleau "La Maison des Siècles" (The House of Centuries).

One 32F ticket (21F students) lets you into the **Grands Appartements** and the **Salles Renaissances,** the fully furnished living quarters of François I, Napoléon III, and all the royalty in between. The same ticket admits you to the **Musée Napoléon I,** 15 rooms filled with arms, guns, hats, uniforms, and other relics of Napoléon's life. An extra 12F (students 8F) allows you into the **Musée Chinois,** which holds the Empress Eugénie's private collection of Chinese goodies, and into the kings' private rooms, the **Petits Appartements.** If you really have your heart set on seeing these smaller rooms, call ahead (tel. 1/60–71–50–70) to find out if tours are running that day. The château and the museums are open Wednesday through Monday 9:30–5, but from November to February they close between 11:45 and 2.

The **gardens** of Fontainebleau, like the château, reflect a mix of styles. Designed in part by Versailles's landscape architect extraordinaire, André Le Nôtre, they don't quite achieve the same magnificence. The nice thing about these gardens and Fontainebleau in general is that they are relatively untainted by tourists. Locals fish for salmon and carp in the Grand Canal and walk their dogs along Le Prairie, the grassy expanse on the edge of the sculptured gardens.

The gardens back right onto 17,000 hectares (42,000 acres) of the **Forêt de Fontainebleau,** one of the biggest national forests in France. If Le Nôtre's regimented gardens seem overly controlling, or trees sound more appealing than humans, head out into the thick forest (see Outdoor Activities, below).

If you have a burning desire to know more about Napoléon or French military history, walk up to the **Napoléonic Museum of Military History** (88 rue St-Honoré, north of rue de France), which claims to be the third-biggest military museum in France. It's open Tuesday through Saturday 2–5.

VISITOR INFORMATION If you're going to stick to the château, you can pick up everything you need at the main entrance. If the forest is calling, however, the **Office de Tourisme** has some crucial items, including a very detailed forest map (35F) and the schedules of irregular local buses. The hard part is finding the office. Hint: Look behind the carousel on the place du Napoléon Bonaparte. *31 pl. du Napoléon Bonaparte, tel. 1/64–22–25–68. Open Mon.–Sat. 9:30–6:30, Sun. 9:30 AM–12:30 PM; Oct.–May, closed Sun.*

COMING AND GOING Trains leave every hour from Paris's Gare de Lyon and cost 37F for the 40-minute trip. The 3-kilometer (2-mile) walk from the train station to the château takes about 30 uninteresting minutes along avenue Franklin Roosevelt. Or take Bus A (every 15 minutes) from the station until you see the château. The bus doesn't cost a thing if you slip on without a ticket like most visitors, or costs around 8F if you do it the legal way and buy a ticket before boarding.

FOOD It's unusual, but not unheard of, to get good food near an Ile de France château. At **Au Délice Impérial** (1 rue Grande, near the tourist office, tel. 1/64–22–20–70), "Une Big Salade," which truly lives up to its name, will set you back only 36F.

OUTDOOR ACTIVITIES If you want to play in the woods, don't come on a Monday, when most of the rental-equipment facilities are closed. The tourist office sells a 35F topo guide called *Guide des Sentiers de Promenades dans le Massif Forestier de Fontainebleau,* which covers paths throughout the forest. For a good view of the whole beech-, birch-, and pine-covered expanse, head up to the **Tour Denecourt,** about 5 kilometers (3 miles) northeast of the château.

➤ **BIKING** • The trails here are a dream—endless and totally unrestricted. The tourist office has trail maps and guides, but you can easily explore the former hunting grounds on your own. **La Petite Reine** (14 rue de la Paroisse, tel. 1/64–22–72–41) rents bikes for 80F per weekday, 100F per weekend day. **Mountain Bike Follies** (246 Grande Rue, tel. 1/64–23–43–07) is another rental option but charges 120F a day. Most of the steeper trails are west of town, but ask the bike store people to point out the best places to ride on your map.

➤ **CLIMBING** • Rock clusters and small gorges abound, but getting the gear and then both the gear and yourself to them is tricky. **Top Loisirs** (73 bis av. de Fontainebleau, tel. 1/60–70–10–88) in Veneux-les-Sablons rents gear but is 8 kilometers (5 mi) away; if you're relying on buses to get here, the day will be over before you touch rock. Your best bet is to rent in Paris, then arrive in town early enough to stop at the tourist office to book one of the many guides. Once you've done that, you can check the bus schedules, or walk the 5–8 kilometers (3–5 mi) to your climbing spot.

Elsewhere near Paris

PROVINS If you've never seen a fortified medieval town, visiting Provins is a must. Built mostly in the 12th and 13th centuries, the **ville haute** (upper village) is entirely surrounded by stone ramparts and has all kinds of medieval stuff to explore. See the tower where they used to keep criminals; an enormous church with imposing wooden doors and a big, black dome; an executioner's house; subterranean passages running under the whole town; and, of more recent origin, a beer garden where locals come to hear live music. From the train station, walk across the bridge, through the commercial center, and up the hill, following the signs that say ITINÉRAIRE PIÉTONNES (pedestrian route).

The ramparts and medieval building are courtesy of the Count of Champagne, who brought money, people, and ideas to Provins in the early 13th century, turning it into a major commercial center. People came to buy, sell, and trade their goods, paying taxes to the count, who, in turn, offered them protection. Apparently the system worked; the count made enough money to build the town and the convent in the neighboring forest. Everything was running smoothly until river transportation became all the rage in Europe, and Provins found itself high and dry. Eight centuries later, without its superpower status, it's just a great day trip from Paris.

➤ **COMING AND GOING** • The 45 minute train trip will set you back 51F, but it's definitely worth it. Take one of the three morning trains from Paris's Gare de l'Est; the only afternoon train is at 4 PM and won't leave you enough time to get back to the city. And, if you do miss the last train back to Paris, the only lodging option is a three-star hotel that will cost you as much as a small horse.

ST-GERMAIN-EN-LAYE Scale down Versailles, take away 95% of its tourists, plop it down on a terrace overlooking the Seine, and you have the **château** of St-Germain-en-Laye. The original château here, the first palace built by French royalty outside Paris, was started by Louis VI, known as Le Gros (the Fat), in the early 12th century as a defensive stronghold. François I and his successors transformed St-Germain from a fortress to a royal residence. Louis XIV then called in Hardouin-Mansart and Le Nôtre to make additions and improvements. Never satisfied, he finally abandoned the château entirely and built Versailles.

St-Germain is where Alexandre Dumas wrote his magnum opus, The Three Musketeers, in 1844. His home here was named Monte Cristo after his other very famous work, The Count of Monte Cristo.

The château now houses the **Musée des Antiquités Nationales**, an archaeological collection from paleolithic times to the Middle Ages. If that's not your thing, you can enjoy an unobstructed view of the Seine below and the distant Paris skyline from the **Grande Terrasse** in front of the château. The gardens are free and always open. They stretch into the endless Forêt de St-Germain, which is ideal for long peaceful walks. All this serenity is just a 20-minute RER ride from Paris. Take the red line A1 from La Défense for 8F50. *Museum admission: 21F, 14F students. Open Wed.–Mon. 9–5:15.*

Index

199

Notes

Notes

Escape to ancient cities and exotic

islands  *with CNN Travel Guide, a*

wealth of valuable advice. Host Valerie Voss will take you

to all of your favorite destinations,

including those off the beaten path.

Tune into your passport to the world.

CNN TRAVEL GUIDE
SATURDAY 10:00 PMpt   SUNDAY 8:30 AMet

THE BERKELEY GUIDES
1995 "Big Bucks and a Backpack" Contest

Four lucky winners will receive $2,000* cash and a Jansport® World Tour backpack to use on the trek of a lifetime!

HOW TO ENTER:

Complete the official entry form on the opposite page, or print your name, complete address, and telephone number on a 3" x 5" piece of paper and mail it, to be received by 1/15/96, to: "Big Bucks and a Backpack" Contest, PMI Station, P.O. Box 3562, Southbury, CT 06488-3562, USA. Entrants from the United Kingdom and the Republic of Ireland may mail their entries to: Berkeley Guides Backpack Contest, Random House Group, P.O. Box 1375, London SW1V 2SL, England.

You may enter as many times as you wish, but mail each entry separately.

* One Grand Prize — £1,000 and a Jansport® World Tour backpack — will also be awarded to entrants from the United Kingdom and the Republic of Ireland.

Prizes: On or about 2/1/96, Promotions Mechanics, Inc., an independent judging organization, will conduct a random drawing from among all eligible entries received, to award the following prizes:

(4) Grand Prizes—$2,000 cash and a Jansport® World Tour backpack, approximate retail value $2,180, will be awarded to entrants from the United States and Canada (except Quebec).

(1) One Grand Prize — £1,000 and a Jansport® World Tour backpack, approximate retail value £1,090, will be awarded to entrants from the United Kingdom and the Republic of Ireland.

Winners will be notified by mail. Due to Canadian contest laws, Canadian residents, in order to win, must first correctly answer a mathematical skill testing question administered by mail. Odds of winning will be determined from the number of entries received. Prize winners may request a statement showing how the odds of winning were determined and how winners were selected.

To receive a copy of these complete official rules, send a self-addressed, stamped envelope to be received by 12/15/95 to: "Big Bucks and a Backpack" Rules, PMI Station, P.O. Box 3569, Southbury, CT 06488-3569, USA.

Eligibility: No purchase necessary to enter or claim prize. Open to legal residents of the United States, Canada (except Quebec), the United Kingdom, and the Republic of Ireland who are 18 years of age or older. Employees of The Random House, Inc. Group, its subsidiaries, agencies, affiliates, participating retailers, and distributors and members of their families living in the same household are not eligible to enter. Void where prohibited.

General: Taxes on prizes are the sole responsibility of winners. By participating, entrants agree to these rules and to the decisions of judges, which shall be final in all respects. Winners must complete an Affidavit of Eligibility and Liability/Publicity Release, which must be returned within 15 days or prize may be forfeited. Each winner agrees to the use of his/her name and/or photograph for advertising and publicity purposes without additional compensation (except where prohibited by law). Sponsor is not responsible for late, lost, stolen, or misdirected mail. No prize transfer or substitution except by sponsor due to unavailability. All entries become the property of the sponsor. One prize per household.

Winners List: For a list of winners, send a self-addressed, stamped envelope to be received by 1/15/96 to: "Big Bucks and a Backpack" Winners, PMI Station, P.O. Box 750, Southbury, CT 06488-0750 ,USA.

Random House, Inc., 201 East 50th Street, New York, NY 10022

Complete this form and mail to:
"Big Bucks and a Backpack" Contest, PMI Station, P.O. Box 3562, Southbury, CT 06488-3562.
Entrants from the United Kingdom and the Republic of Ireland, mail to: Berkeley Guides Backpack Contest, Random House Group, P.O. Box 1375, London SW1V 2SL, England.

Mail coupon to be received by 1/15/96.

NAME

ADDRESS

COUNTRY   **TELEPHONE**

WHERE I BOUGHT THIS BOOK

A T-SHIRT FOR YOUR THOUGHTS . . .

After your trip, drop us a line and let us know how
things went. People whose comments help us most
improve future editions will receive our eternal
thanks as well as a Berkeley Guides T-shirt. Just
print your name and address clearly and send the completed survey to:
The Berkeley Guides, 515 Eshleman Hall, U.C. Berkeley, Berkeley, CA 94720.

Your Name _____

Address _____

_____ Zip _____

Where did you buy this book? City _____ State _____

How long before your trip did you buy this book? _____

Which Berkeley Guide(s) did you buy? _____

Which other guides, if any, did you purchase for this trip? _____

Which other guides, if any, have you used before? (Please circle)
Fodor's   Let's Go   Real Guide   Frommer's   Birnbaum   Lonely Planet
Other _____

Why did you choose Berkeley? (Please circle as many as apply)
Budget information   More maps   Emphasis on outdoors/off-the-beaten-track
Design   Attitude   Other _____

_____

If you're employed: Occupation _____

If you're a student: Name of school _____ City & state _____

Age _____ Male _____ Female _____

How many weeks was your trip? (Please circle) 1 2 3 4 5 6 7 8 More than 8 weeks

After you arrived on your trip, how did you get around? (Please circle one or more)
Rental car   Personal car   Plane   Bus   Train   Hiking   Biking   Hitching
Other _____

When did you travel? _____

Where did you travel? _____

_____

The features/sections I used most were (please circle as many as apply):
Basics   Where to Sleep   Food   Coming and Going   Worth Seeing   Other

The information was (circle one):
Usually accurate   Sometimes accurate   Seldom accurate

I would _____ would not _____ buy another Berkeley Guide.

These books are brand new, and we'd really appreciate some feedback on how
to improve them. Please also tell us about your latest find, a new scam, a budget deal, whatever—we want to hear about it.

For your comments:

_____

_____